CAMERON

PRACTICALLY A CONSERVATIVE

FRANCIS ELLIOTT & JAMES HANNING

FOURTH ESTATE • *London*

Fourth Estate
An imprint of HarperCollins*Publishers*
77–85 Fulham Palace Road,
Hammersmith, London W6 8JB

This Fourth Estate edition published 2012
1

First published in Great Britain as *Cameron: The Rise of the New Conservative*
by Fourth Estate in 2007 and in paperback by Harper Perennial, 2009

Copyright © Francis Elliott and James Hanning 2007, 2009 and 2012

Francis Elliott and James Hanning assert the moral
right to be identified as the authors of this work

A catalogue record for this book is available from the British Library

ISBN 978-0-00-743642-2

Set in Minion and Akzidenz Grotesk

Printed and bound in Great Britain by
Clays Ltd, St Ives plc

LIST OF ILLUSTRATIONS

Mary Mount at the Coronation Ball, Sandhurst. (**Illustrated London News Picture Library**)

Annabel Astor. (**Alun Callender**)

Cameron with team-mates from a Heatherdown cricket XI. (**Private Collection**)

Cameron at Heatherdown. (**Private Collection**)

Cameron with his sister, Clare. (**Private Collection**)

Cameron at a Home Counties cricket match. (**Private Collection**)

Cameron on the Kenyan coast in 1986. (**Private Collection**)

Cameron at a party in Oxford. (**Private Collection**)

Cameron on safari, 1986. (**Private Collection**)

Cameron poses with the Bullingdon Club. (**Private Collection**)

Cameron with Tim Collins by the Berlin Wall. (**Private Collection**)

Cameron at a Treasury meeting. (**Private Collection**)

Cameron with the Chancellor, Norman Lamont. (**Mirrorpix**)

Michael Green, Cameron's boss at Carlton. (**Reuters**)

David and Samantha Cameron on their wedding day in June 1996. (**Private Collection**)

Cameron in a shooting party at Glenarm Castle. (**Private Collection**)

Cameron with a fire brigade at Glenarm Castle. (**Private Collection**)

Cameron on holiday in Siena, Italy. (**Private Collection**)

Cameron in County Antrim. (**Private Collection**)

Andy Coulson, Cameron's head of press. (**Martin Argles/Guardian News & Media Ltd. 2008**)

George Osborne and Cameron riding to Westminster in May 2006. (**Rex Features**)

Cameron on his bicycle. (**Peter Macdiarmid/Getty Images**)

Cameron and Boris Johnson celebrate winning the London mayoral election. (**Stefan Rousseau/PA Photos**)

Steve Hilton. (**Andrew Parsons/PA/EMPICS**)

Cameron with his family on Portobello Road, London. (**Andrew Parsons/PA/EMPICS**)

Cameron with his family at the wedding of Samantha's jeweller half-sister, Flora. (**Private Collection**)

Cameron and Nick Clegg at the coalition's first press conference. (**AFP/Getty Images**)

Cameron and Rebekah Brooks. (**Dafydd Jones**)

PEASEMORE
A Berkshire boyhood 1966–1973

'So let a message go out from this conference.' David Cameron paused, letting his audience know that he was building towards a dramatic conclusion. 'A modern compassionate Conservatism is right for our times, right for our party – and right for our country. If we go for it, if we seize it, if we fight for it with every ounce of passion, vigour and energy from now until the next election, nothing and no one can stop us.'

For a moment the Empress Ballroom in Blackpool's Winter Gardens seemed bleached out by the photographers' xenon flashes rippling round the hall as if synchronised with the sudden roar of approval. The applause intensified when the candidate was joined on stage by his wife Samantha, then pregnant with the couple's third child. Her pregnancy gave the photographers a powerful image to illustrate his message that the time had arrived for a 'new generation of Conservatives'. The cheering delegates may not have known that that line owed a good deal to John F. Kennedy. But they believed that the Tories had found their own young saviour.

Cameron's speech to the Conservative Party conference on 4 October 2005 launched him into public consciousness and set him on course for victory in the party's leadership election. Its success took almost everyone by surprise. Even his most senior allies had not realised until a few days before how charismatic he could be. Indeed there had been some discussion about whether he should pull out of the race and declare his support for David Davis, who was then the firm favourite. But Cameron wanted a chance to perform on what was, at that point, the biggest stage of his career. He was confident that he could deliver a powerful speech. The newspaper headlines on 5 October confirmed that he was right. It turned out to be a speech of such momentum-creating power as to carry him over the finishing line a winner.

Reflecting on his sudden burst from the rear of the leadership field to its front, a former colleague said: 'Like all political overnight sensations, it was twenty years in the making.' This is the story of the making of David Cameron – of how, as one of his friends put it, Cameron climbed 'floor by floor' to the top of the Conservative Party and became Prime Minister despite failing to win an overall majority in the general election five years later. It was an ascent achieved by hard work and intelligence, but it also benefited from luck and the efforts of others. This is the story, too, of a childhood spent in an England that barely exists any more. Cameron's was a world first of nannies and matrons, then of beaks and boys' maids. But his privilege is peculiar not so much for its material as for its emotional wealth. He likes to say that he is an optimist, and the man whom he credits with instilling in him that quality is his father.

David Cameron's great-great-grandfather Ewen left Scotland early in Queen Victoria's reign and started his business career, in the mid-nineteenth century, in the Far East, working for the Hong Kong Shanghai Bank. Having become a director, he eventually returned to London to manage the bank, and was knighted for his services. His son, David Cameron's great-grandfather, was Ewen Alan Cameron, who rose to become senior partner of stockbrokers Panmure Gordon. He lived partly at Blairmore Castle, near Huntly in Aberdeenshire (originally a family home of his wife, Rachel Geddes) and partly in London. They had four children, one of whom was Donald Cameron, born in 1906. At the age of twenty-six, Donald – who followed his father in becoming a partner of Panmure Gordon – married Enid Agnes Maud Levita. Two years later, on 12 October 1932, when they were living at 25 Chesham Street, SW1, their only son Ian was born.

The bald facts of Ian Cameron's early life might not be expected to encourage the development of a positive outlook. In the language of the day he was born a cripple, his legs severely deformed from the knees downwards. A bout of German measles during his mother's confinement was blamed, incorrectly, at the time, but the cause remains obscure. Its effect was to shorten his legs below the knee and twist his feet, one of which had three toes, the other four. He had a series of operations in very early infancy to provide some relief to the problem – although after the age of three he was never particularly in pain – and straighten his legs, but while the rest of him suggests a man of about six foot two, he was actually about a foot shorter than that.

The young Ian was sent away to boarding school, wearing specially adapted shoes. He went first to Betteshanger School in Kent, where, because of his disability, he was made to have an extra hour's rest every day. At home, in London during the holidays, his mother treated him with a great deal of affection but also with some firmness. She believed that the effect of his disability had to be minimised, that he had to do as much as possible for himself. Friends say it was from her that he acquired much of his tough-mindedness and independence. All his life he felt in her debt for pushing him beyond what, at the time, he thought he was physically capable of doing.

By the time Ian Cameron was preparing to go to Eton he suffered another blow – his father left his mother and married an aristocratic Austrian. Marielen von Meiss-Teuffen had been born in 1918 in Attersee near Linz, Austria, and was sent, while still a teenager, first to France and then to Britain. When she met Donald Cameron in wartime London, she was working as an announcer for the BBC having already divorced her first husband Reginald Critchley, with whom she had had a daughter, Verena. Now in her late eighties and living in a nursing home in Vienna, Marielen says that at first Enid Cameron was friendly and 'didn't mind me being around'. When the exact nature of her husband's relationship with her was revealed it was clearly a painful shock. 'You can imagine what the woman must have felt to realise her husband was in love with another woman.' While Donald Cameron and his new wife set up home in Clareville Grove, Kensington, his son was left to support his mother. It was a lonely, difficult and formative time for Ian Cameron.

The failure of Enid Levita's marriage may have prompted her to reflect on the shame of her grandmother, Lady Agnes Duff, who was shunned in society following two elopements and a divorce. Agnes, David Cameron's forebear, eventually took refuge in nursing. It was there that she met and married Dr Alfred Cooper, a specialist in sexual ailments. (Cooper used to claim that between them he and his wife were acquainted with the private parts of all the peers in London.) Agnes's parents were the 5th Earl of Fife and Lady Agnes Hay, but her most noteworthy relative from the more recent past was one of her four children, Duff Cooper, who became Sir Winston Churchill's Minister of Information during the Second World War and whose beautiful wife Diana aroused such admiration. The philandering Duff Cooper was thus Ian Cameron's great-uncle (although they never met). He was also, like Ian Cameron, a chairman of White's, the men-only club in St James's. David Cameron has expressed relief that he has not inherited Duff Cooper's remarkable appetite for wine and women.

Donald Cameron did not cope well with having a disabled son, and it has been said he did not encourage Ian to believe that he would be joining him at Panmure Gordon, where he was a senior partner. Had the father seen more of his son at Eton he might have revised his opinion. Ian Cameron did not shine academically at school, but his peers learned not to underestimate his determination. A lifelong friend Ben Glazebrook remembers playing a rumbustious game of indoor football in a corridor at Eton. 'I had the ball at my feet … and I said "Oh yes, this is Ian, I can get past him." Suddenly my wrists were seized in an iron grip by Ian, because all the strength of his legs had gone into his arms and wrists. I virtually needed a course of physiotherapy after that. He had this amazing strength, and he was always incredibly resilient, courageous and outgoing. He'd never been shy, and he was always very open. He said, "I can do everything except ski," which I think he regretted.' He also enjoyed cricket and tennis, and at Eton, when he took part in the Field Game, the school's own soccer–rugby hybrid, he played in a position comparable to scrum-half, where, on occasions, a low centre of gravity can be an advantage.

Leaving school in 1951, Ian Cameron made a decision he later came to regret. Perhaps conscious of the need for a remunerative career, instead of going to university he decided to train as an accountant. While professionally useful, he found it less than entertaining (and was to forbid his children to enter the profession). Having qualified, he spent two years as a banker at Robert Fleming before joining Panmure Gordon, where he worked exceptionally hard to overcome the stigma that some had attached to his physique, and in 1957 emulated his father and grandfather in becoming a partner. He was, he admitted privately, a 'nepotistic heir'. Socially Ian Cameron was no less determined to triumph over his disability. He moved out of his mother's house in Lowndes Square, near Harrods, into a flat of his own round the corner in Basil Street. 'Ian was always incredibly social,' remembers Glazebrook, who lived near by. 'He used to have endless parties with the most beautiful girls.'

In 1958 Donald Cameron died, leaving an estate valued at £57,408 (worth £928,000 today) and an inheritance that enabled his son to consider marriage. When the charming Mr Cameron set out to woo her, Mary Mount saw not deformity in him but spirit. He threw himself around the dance floor with the same gusto with which he had played football. The couple married on 20 October 1962, two days before Mary's twenty-eighth birthday. It might have surprised his father that Ian Cameron married so well, into a family that has belonged to the British Establishment since long before that phrase was coined. Tall, stately and sure of herself, Mary is a typical Mount. From the beginning she had two qualities that her friends and family most admire in her now – compassion and common sense – and she is typical too for having served as a magistrate for over thirty years, as her mother and grandmother did before her.

The patrician spirit of the Mounts is neatly captured in a story about David Cameron's great-great-great-grandfather William Mount, an MP (then unpaid) for an Isle of Wight seat and a man of some wealth. He employed a young boy – whose father had died – as a bird-scarer in his fields, and presented the boy with a book ('the first book I had ever owned'). The boy remembered the gesture and in later life wrote gratefully to Mount's son, William George Mount: 'You will always be a means of doing good and exerting influence in quarters as unexpected as in my case.'

'W.G.', as he was known, was a barrister, 'gentleman and landed proprietor' (of Wasing Place, Berkshire), and became MP for Newbury. Perhaps the most formidable of the Mount ancestors, like most MPs at the time he had little truck with godlessness. In 1851 the family invited Samuel Wilberforce, the Bishop of Oxford, to stay. He, famously, was a vigorous opponent of Darwin's theories of evolution and was later to cross swords with T. H. Huxley at a meeting of the British Association when he provocatively asked his opponent whether it was from his grandmother or his grandfather that he claimed descent from a monkey. In the 1880s, W.G.'s eldest daughter Elizabeth, every bit as devout as her father, took a weekly Bible class, which was attended by the groom's boy, the schoolroom maid, the upper laundry maid, the laundry maid and the house, kitchen and scullery maids, as well as the butler, doorman and members of the

Mount family. Staff were obliged to attend, and were excused only when beaters were needed for a shoot.

According to the 1880 census, W.G., by then running the Wasing estate, employed thirty-two men to look after his 500 acres and a further fifteen servants to staff the house and attend to his six young children. One of these children was William Arthur Mount (educated at Eton and New College, Oxford, and also a barrister), who in 1900 succeeded his ailing father, unopposed, as Conservative MP for Newbury, before losing it to the Liberal candidate six years later. 'Billy' worked diligently and regained the seat in 1910, frequently speaking out against Home Rule for Ireland, until he stood down twelve years later. He continued in public life as chairman of Berkshire County Council and as chairman of the South Berkshire Hunt. He was made a baronet in June 1921 and died in 1930 at the age of sixty-four. He had three sons, the eldest of whom, William Malcolm Mount (the second baronet, known as Bill), succeeded to the title at the age of twenty-six.

'W.M.' was David Cameron's grandfather. He too was educated at Eton and New College, Oxford, where he played cricket with Alec Douglas-Home, later to become Prime Minister. He was a keen fisherman and horseman and became joint master of the South Berks hounds and chairman of Newbury Conservative Association. He had three daughters, the middle of whom, Mary, was born in 1934. As a lieutenant colonel he fought impressively in the war with the 61st Reconnaissance Regiment (Royal Armoured Corps), but was invalided out, having been shot in the thigh the day after D Day. His wife Lady Nancy was also active, taking a leading organisational and welfare role in the Women's Land Army, a loosely structured band of 200,000 women who worked ploughing, dung-spreading and threshing. During the war, the young Mary, her two sisters and mother moved out of the big house at Wasing, which was to be used by evacuees from London, to a neighbouring farm. In February 1945,

Wasing Place was virtually burned to the ground and many works of art were lost. Two years later, possibly in part to help pay for the restoration, W.M. placed over a thousand acres of family land at Thatcham on the market. Mary's mother Nancy took a prominent role in the rebuilding of Wasing Place, and eventually she and her husband returned to the house that the Mount family had owned for nearly 200 years.

In 1947, William Mount served as Sheriff of Berkshire, the fourth Mount in 170 years to hold the title. He was also president of the Newbury Show, a governor of the Royal Agricultural College at Cirencester and served on the Council of the County Landowners Association, which enabled him to sustain his interest in timber. He was also appointed Berkshire County Scout president and originated the Berkshire Supporters of Scouting, which raised money for Scout troops, as well as opening up the Wasing estate for use by Scout camps. In 1952, in a comparable act of public-spiritedness, 'Lieutenant Colonel Sir' William Mount took command of the 3rd South Berkshire Home Guard, which aimed to afford some protection to the civilian population in the event of a nuclear attack. The proximity of Aldermaston, the home of Britain's nuclear weapons, and the political protests that accompanied its setting up in 1950, may have had a good deal to do with that.

Mary's cousin Ferdinand Mount, a journalist and former adviser to the Thatcher government (who inherited but does not use the title), confirms the impression offered by the family history: 'The Mounts are very old fashioned, slightly stiff, you might say … They had a very comfortable upbringing. They were churchgoing, I don't think any of them have ever been divorced. They are straitlaced and full of a sense of duty.' But let those who are suspicious of parvenu politicians be further reassured. W. G. Mount's mother was a Talbot, as was the first Earl of Shrewsbury, John Talbot, who, in his late seventies, died with his two sons in the final battle of the Hundred Years War. The admiring French called him the 'the English Achilles'. The journalist William Rees-Mogg, no less, calls the Talbots 'one of the great families' of English history, like the Cecils or the Churchills, only much older. Among the later Talbots were one of Sir Robert Walpole's Lord Chancellors, a Bishop of Durham, a Roman Catholic Archbishop of Dublin, another medieval Archbishop of Dublin, the great building heiress Bess of Hardwick, and William Fox-Talbot, inventor of photography.

There was even a Talbot who became Prime Minister, or the equivalent (before the title was coined). Charles Talbot, the 12th Earl and the first and only Duke of Shrewsbury, born in 1660, did several stints as First Minister, first under William III in 1689, after the Glorious Revolution, and again under Queen Anne and yet again under George I. How did he do it? According to Rees-Mogg's researches, by charm and moderation. Dean Swift called Shrewsbury 'the finest gentleman we have', while Bishop Burnet wrote that he had 'a sweetness of temper that charmed all who knew him'. Women loved him. A political moderate, he was decisive when the revolutionary situation required it, but was one of those politicians who stand above parties and are seen as relatively non-partisan.

David Cameron was born on 9 October 1966. In a typically Mountian display of honour towards their forebears, the parents gave the newborn the names of their fathers, William and Donald. He was Ian and Mary's third child. Their first, Alexander, had been born the year after their marriage (and had been given the Christian names of Ian's uncle), with their second, Tania, arriving nineteen months later. The latest Cameron was christened at Wasing, attended by his godparents Tim Rathbone and Ben Glazebrook, Ian's friends from Eton, and Fiona Aird, a former flatmate of Mary. Also present was John Sumner, with his wife Heather, also old friends of Mary. With three children under the age of four, Mary had her hands full, but she had help, and of a singularly old-fashioned and British kind.

Gwen Hoare is a key figure in the life of both Mary and David Cameron. Born just west of Swindon, the daughter of a market gardener, she had been 'in service' with the Mount family all her adult life, had never married, and had looked after Mary – thirteen years her junior – as she was growing up. For nearly twenty years after the war, she lived in a variety of houses at Wasing. Then, in her early forties, she moved to join the family in Phillimore Place, Kensington, to help look after Alexander.

When, in 1969, the family moved to Peasemore, a village in Berkshire, Gwen Hoare moved with them. The move required Ian Cameron to make the daily train trek from Didcot Parkway to the City of London, where he added a directorship of the estate agency firm John D. Wood to his work for Panmure Gordon. It meant leaving the house before seven in the morning, and not returning until after seven in the evening. Mary Cameron meanwhile was often out, sitting as JP in Newbury, or doing other good works locally. It was, therefore, David Cameron's nanny who oversaw much of his early upbringing. 'Gwen pretty much brought them up,' says a family friend. 'She was always a hugely important figure in that house,' says another. 'She was much more than an old-fashioned nanny. She was a real rock in that family, as if there weren't enough already.' Five years after the birth of David, Mary was delivered of her fourth child, Clare, and Gwen Hoare had another charge. By this stage the second son had followed his brother in attending Greenwood pre-preparatory school near Newbury, and was driven there every day by a rota of local mothers.

Lying six miles north of Newbury, there can be no more quintessentially English country village than Peasemore. At its centre is the church of St Barnabas, built in the eighteenth century and embellished a hundred years later. And the Cameron family are central to the life of the church – Ian Cameron used to be a church warden, and Mary remains on the flower-arranging and cleaning rotas. Little wonder that David, who was brought up in the splendid Queen Anne rectory close by, has said, 'When I think of home, I think of church.' Home was decidedly old-fashioned if not notably bookish ('They are very county,' explains one friend). Dinner was served upon the return of Ian Cameron promptly at 7.45 p.m. His children, once old enough to graduate from tea with their nanny, were expected to display immaculate manners. It was a house, recalls a guest, that still played parlour games. After dinner parties 'the ladies' would withdraw to another room. But the Old Rectory was also hospitable, its swimming pool – the result of a big win on the horses – and tennis court always at the disposal of the children's friends (if not of other villagers, a cause of resentment among some).

From the youngest age, David Cameron lacked bashfulness. 'He was very articulate,' says a friend. 'I remember him liking a good argument. He was quite precocious from a very young age. He certainly knew what he thought.' A family member recalls that on holidays he was always 'argumentative and interesting, holding court the whole time'. After school, he, Alex and Tania would run around in the fields or feed Mary's bantams. As they got older, they would go further afield, encouraging one of their Jack Russells to hunt down rabbit holes. Airguns would be in evidence too, but despite a profusion of rooks, rabbits and pigeons around the Old Rectory, shooting was carried out – or was meant to be – in a controlled environment. As the boys grew up, they would accompany their father on shoots, often at Wooley Park, the estate of Phillip Wroughton, later Lord Lieutenant of Berkshire.

Early on the boys developed an interest in tennis, playing frequently and with some élan. David showed a greater determination, or at least aptitude, tending to beat his brother, and it was at Peasemore that the seeds of competitiveness were first sown. 'He doesn't like not to win,' says a lifelong witness of David Cameron the tennis player. 'He gets very cross with himself. He's very gracious in defeat because he is very old fashioned, but then he'll secretly go and get his racket restrung.'

The annual cricket games, played between two teams captained by the brothers and played either at Wasing or on the Peasemore village pitch, would be equally hard fought, and provided David with the opportunity to exhibit a lusty death-or-glory batting style and medium-paced left-arm bowling. In later years the game, though still hard fought, took second place to the feverish competition in the preceding weeks to recruit capable ringers. Not that either of them had difficulty finding players. Those who played have idyllic recollections of the games.

The brothers, who shared a room, always got on well, teasing one another and fighting playfully enough. Their sister Tania, sandwiched in between, had to be something of a tomboy if she was to join in the fun, or else she played with Clare, six years her junior. An exception to this was horse riding, which Alex and Tania took to with enthusiasm, but which David, at that stage at least, didn't enjoy to the same degree. The prevailing mood seems to have been one of contentment, rarely broken by parental displeasure. The boys went away to school from the age of seven, where a more explicit discipline would be taught, and the school holidays were something of a refuge from the pettiness of school. In any event, growing up with a large garden in a secluded part of Berkshire ensured that parental strictures would be minimal.

Yet there was always a keenness not to disappoint. Those close to the family remember few occasions when either parent was moved to anger. Both of them exerted an implicit but benign authority, an enviable degree of control, which meant that the children always knew where they stood. If standards had not been met, a quiet 'I see' and a knowing glance would be sufficient. Indeed, this seems to have been enough to instil a strong desire to succeed, to win parental approval. 'In some homes, where there are bright children, they can get the better of the father, but Ian was definitely the boss – he ruled the roost,' says a friend. It was, says Susan Rathbone, the widow of David Cameron's godfather, 'quite a tight household ... you wouldn't get away with just lounging on the sofa. No beer cans on the carpet. It was a lovely, comfortable, delicious home, but there was no slacking.'

This was true of school reports too, when the formality of the process alone would imply a certain seriousness. The children would be called in to see their father, who would read out the report before they had a chance to see it. Disapproval did not have to be obvious to be effective. It was clearly spelt out, though, on at least one occasion when, a family friend remembers, Ian had been informed of a misdemeanour at Eton. David Cameron was firmly told that his father was not paying the hefty school fees in order for him to break school rules.

While all families go through friction and periods of stress – and the Camerons have had their share of crosses to bear – their friends speak uniformly of their readiness to support one another. Neither parent took a dominant role, and David Cameron appeared to be equally respectful towards both. Ian and Mary Cameron 'had a good, healthy relationship, thoroughly solid and practical', says Susan Rathbone, speaking in 2006. 'It's a great image of marriage he has grown up with. They're just very good at dealing with life.' A former girlfriend of David agrees: 'His parents are very cool, settled in themselves, very calm and sure of themselves. There are no psychological issues there. There's something very wholesome, but not in a boring way.' For Giles Andreae, whose mother had been a debutante with the young Mary Mount and who is one of David's lifelong friends, there is something almost intimidating about the Camerons' partnership: 'That couple, they're both so self-assured and magnanimous. They have so many friends. It's almost quite scary if you're not very confident yourself.'

While the parents wanted their children to be aware of how privileged they were, it must have been difficult for a playful, popular little boy to imagine how different 'real life' was for the majority of the population. In this Eden of cricket matches and gambolling through fields, it would have been understandable if the Cameron children had taken it for granted that the world is a pretty happy place. 'It is a very natural age,' says Giles Andreae, now a writer of children's books. 'Obviously you are aware that some people have big houses and some people have small houses, and that not everyone spends their time swimming and playing tennis. Privilege in itself is not a bad thing, it is how you deal with it that matters.'

The house of David Cameron's childhood is now owned by his elder brother Alex, who lives there with his wife and children. Gwen Hoare, for whom the family built a flat in the Old Rectory's stables (she had her eighty-sixth birthday in February 2007), is thus seeing a third generation of the family grow up. Mary Cameron lives in a smaller house abutting its grounds. The influence of both parents on their now famous son is clear. 'Mary is one of the most compassionate people I know,' says Susan Rathbone. 'She's level headed, not remotely impressed by froth and completely no nonsense.'

In the early 1990s Ian Cameron had to have one of his legs amputated and replaced by a prosthetic one, and in early 2006 he had the other one amputated, but as ever he minimised the inconvenience. In the latter year, he got an infection in one eye following an operation and lost the use of it. With two prosthetic legs and a walking stick, Ian Cameron had to succumb, to a degree at least, to being disabled. Speaking in 2006, Giles Andreae said, 'Ian is one of the most confident and self-assured people I have ever met. I don't remember his disability ever being an issue. It wasn't that it was not discussed out of good manners, it just wasn't an issue. He's a breezy, sociable, outgoing, affable man. Those are the qualities that would have had more effect on David.' Yet the influence of Ian's disability was enormous, if unstated. For a start, the children had a constant reminder that the petty everyday complaints of childhood were minor indeed. 'Whingeing wasn't on the menu,' says one family member. Cameron himself has said he had a very strong relationship with his father. 'He was an amazing man.' 'Great optimist. Always believed the best about people and thought things would turn out OK.' It may be that Ian Cameron, while seeking to impart certain values, was anxious to protect his sons from the pressures – emotional and financial – that he had felt when growing up. '[David's] parents were fantastic,' says Pete Czernin, an Eton friend. 'They were never pushy with their children; they gave them all implicit confidence without cockiness.'

Yet, for all the lack of witting parental pressure to succeed, Ian's unstated determination made him a hard man to live up to. Without wishing it, he set a high bar. Susan Rathbone agrees that, tacitly, a standard was set. There may be, she says, 'a subconscious drive that Dave has got from Ian's incredible example. Ian had vast enthusiasm – which Dave inherited – and a sort of unstoppableness which I'm sure is very inspirational to live with.' When he was thirteen, Cameron is said to have told a friend: 'He is my role model. Dad has never let his disability hold him back. He has proved you can do anything you want in life.'

HEATHERDOWN
Prep school 1974–1979

At the age of seven David Cameron was sent to Heatherdown Preparatory School near Ascot in Berkshire. With just under a hundred pupils, Heatherdown was small but smart, with one former master claiming that it was 'the most select school in the country'.

Its business was to take impressionable young boys from comfortably-off families and unapologetically mould them into little gentlemen of the old school. Prince Andrew and Prince Edward were both educated at Heatherdown. Their cousin Marina Mowatt has said: 'I'll never forget the smell of the place – pencil sharpenings, sausages and boys.' David Cameron's manners, confidence and sense of duty were all enhanced at Heatherdown. It may also have helped develop his mental and emotional resilience, and it certainly fixed him in the highest social milieu.

Today very few children are sent to boarding school so young, and in the mid-1970s it was beginning to fall out of fashion even among the rich. (Heatherdown itself closed while Cameron was still at Eton.) He says that it was an 'absurdly young' age to be required to leave home. It was some comfort to him that his elder brother Alex was already a pupil. And, like generations of other prep school boarders before him, Cameron seems to have adjusted to his new life, helped in his first few weeks by being just one of a group of seven-year-old boys a long way from home. He spent his first term in a pleasant adjunct to the main school called Heatherlea, where the boys could be gently acclimatised to life in a boarding school. 'We were mollycoddled a good deal at Heatherlea,' says an old boy. 'Mostly what I remember is the endless pillow-fights and non-stop ragging in the dorm.' After a term or two at Heatherlea, boys were confronted with a more forbidding and traditional dormitory of about a dozen boys in the main school. On arrival, new occupants were allowed to bring their own rug – to cover the Spartan wooden floorboards – and their own teddy. But Christine Carder, the school matron, said Heatherlea was no easy place to start. 'The pupils only had thin blankets, the ceilings were full height with lino on the floors. The huge sash windows had icicles on the inside in the depths of winter … I must admit looking back now it was an unbearably young age for them to start.'

As he progressed, curriculum classes began. But before the conventional teaching began, there were two rituals to be observed, both of which seem to have left a mark on those who carried out or observed them. One was 'Rep', the parrot-fashion learning of Latin verbs, kings and queens of England, the world's rivers and so on. The other, performed simultaneously, was the post-breakfast visit to the lavatory. Boys' names would be listed on cubicle doors, and each child, while reciting, say, the names of the Tudor monarchs, would do his business, tick his name off and call out that of the boy next on the list. It was scarcely a routine designed to inculcate originality of thought, one might conclude. The education was determinedly traditional. Even by the mid-1970s, Heatherdown saw little advantage in following what it would have seen as fashionable new methods. The teachers themselves were mostly products of English public schools and the war. The much respected Maths and Geography teacher, Monty Withers, had been at Harrow, the Science teacher, Frank Wilson, had been at Sedbergh, the headmaster was a Radleian and Christopher Bromley-Martin, the French master, an Old Etonian. These were the core staff around whom the school revolved, and to whom a succession of younger, short-staying visiting teachers (some very young and ill-qualified) deferred, to varying degrees. What had served that senior echelon well would do the trick for the new generation.

The school's head was a remote, forbidding figure who, with his wife Barbara ('Bar'), a devoted gardener, ran a conservative regime. Edwards would insist – at an early stage – that boys learn to recite the Kings and Queens of England and their dates on the throne. The same went for the names of all the books of the Old and New Testament. R. V. Watson's *La Langue des français* and Ritchie's *First Steps in Latin* were considered unimprovable introductions to their subjects, and there was little truck with 'the new Latin' or 'the new Maths', which other comparable schools were beginning to investigate. After lunch (liver on Thursdays, fish on Fridays) boys were expected to rest on their bed with a book, a break rich with opportunities for insubordination and mischief, followed by games – cricket in the summer, soccer from September and rugby in the Lent term. Tea, as might be expected in so resoundingly comfortable an institution, was a meal of some importance. Boys would take it in turns to sit next to matron, who would wearily insist on faultless table manners.

The academic day ended as it had begun with another ten-minute chapel service, except on Sundays when the service was rather longer. The last meal, a light supper, could be light indeed. On Thursdays it consisted of a single brick of Weetabix. At one point a looming revolt by parents was bought off by the introduction of chocolate and biscuits to fill the gap between the early supper and bedtime. Nevertheless, David Cameron, who admits that he was 'rather tubby' as a boy, says he 'lost a stone every term because the helpings were so small'.

He seems otherwise to have been happy, however. His easy affability, which has since helped smooth his path, was early in evidence. A contemporary remembers him as 'bright, bushy-tailed and good fun. He had a good ability to get on with people.' 'My memory is of someone who was always smiling, very social and chatty,' says Rhidian Llewellyn, who, as an eighteen-year-old doing his gap year, taught Cameron briefly (having been a boy at Heatherdown himself) and went on to teach at Arnold House, the Dragon and Papplewick. 'Both he and Alex had a lot of charm, although David was the noisier of the two. He was quick-witted, full of jokes, a natural boarding school boy. They were terribly easy to get on with, and I imagine very easy for their parents to bring up. He was a bright boy, but at the time no brighter than many of his contemporaries. Among all those titled children, Cameron was one of the most normal. He was just a middle-class boy from a nice family.'

'The parents all knew each other, of course,' says Daniel Wiggin, a former pupil, and a good number of the boys saw one another during the school holidays for cricket games, for example. 'It was quite smart,' says Wiggin, 'very much one of the grandest. The Kleinworts, the Hambros, the royals, the St Andrews. But they weren't there to be smart. They were there because a lot of the fathers had been there themselves.' When Prince Andrew was sent to Heatherdown, it was partly on the recommendation of Lord Porchester, the Queen's racing manager, whose two sons had flourished there. Evidently satisfied, the Queen sent Edward there as well. David Cameron was two and a half years younger than Edward, but the prince and Alex Cameron were contemporaries and friends. The Queen could occasionally be seen driving a green station-wagon, dropping her sons off at the end of a weekend at home or at the beginning of term, sometimes stopping by for a cup of tea with the headmaster. More often, though, the royal presence was indicated by the series of low-key royal detectives.

'I think it is fair to say that the headmaster used to choose according to the stable rather than the colt,' says Llewellyn. 'If you were of the right sort of background, it wouldn't have been terribly difficult to get in. You didn't have to be brilliantly clever. Certainly there was no formal exam. Its business was to get boys into Eton, which was via the

Common Entrance exam.' Among the eighty or so sets of parents of David's contemporaries, there were eight honourables, four sirs, two captains, two doctors, two majors, two princesses, two marchionesses, one viscount, one brigadier, one commodore, one earl, one lord (unspecified) and one queen (*the* Queen). One former pupil, the son of a mere MP, said, with only some exaggeration, that the place was so full of titled people that he was one of the few boys there whose name didn't change – as he inherited some title – during his time there. At the school's annual sports day, two or three helicopters bearing smartly dressed parents would land on the playing fields. Instead of the customary signs for Ladies and Gents, Heatherdown had a third category: Ladies, Gentlemen and Chauffeurs. 'It was deadly serious – the drivers were not supposed to mix with the other guests,' says a former teacher. Another alumnus of the school recalls that Cameron may have been particularly conscious of these social gradations. 'He was the most terrible snob at the age of seven, I remember, always deriding others' use of words like "toilet",' he recalls.

The school attached great importance to good manners. One Wednesday in the mid-1970s, the headmaster James Edwards decided that standards were slipping, so after games, instead of giving the boys their customary free time, he stood in the middle of the rugby pitch and made the boys walk around doffing their caps to the corner flags and saying 'Good afternoon, Sir.' The importance attached to courtesy sprang from deeper values that the school was trying to instil. 'It was about the ability to get on with people of all backgrounds. The notion of *noblesse oblige* was very strong, both for the school and David Cameron at home, I think,' says Rhidian Llewellyn. Alexander Bathurst, who later became a consultant on leadership, agrees: 'It was very much small-"c" conservative, with good principles – honesty, enthusiasm, upholding the honour of school, family and friends.' Dan Wiggin says the school sought to cultivate 'a sense of duty, Christian moral responsibility and awareness of people around you and how to behave properly'. The relative lack of academic pressure allowed the inculcation of such values to be something of a priority.

Nor was Edwards squeamish about the use of corporal punishment in fostering those values. Carrots, as well as sticks, were deployed. A boy who did a good deed or commendable work, or who behaved particularly nicely, would be given what was called an 'Alpha'. If he won three Alphas, he was given a Plus and a reward. If, though, he misbehaved, he would get an 'Omega'. Too many of those meant a certain beating – with a clothes brush on the trousers. This would be administered by Edwards, pipe clenched between his teeth. The punishment was followed by a manly handshake as if to wipe the slate clean. 'It stung a bit,' remembers Llewellyn, 'but James Edwards wouldn't have been unusual in that respect at the time.' Some crimes carried a beating without question. One Cameron classmate, Rupert Stevenson, remembers that that was his punishment for talking in chapel.

But to speak to the school's old boys is to gain the impression that they thrived on defying authority. There was no stigma, physical or otherwise, to being beaten – rather the opposite. Alexander Bathurst says that he and his contemporaries used to 'see how many petty rules we could break. We weren't supposed to read comics after lights out, for example, so you could be quite sure that is exactly what we would try to do. But it is still fair to say that you did rather live in awe of the senior masters and matrons.' One former boy remembers that there was a regular opportunity for misbehaviour, charmingly mild though it was. Early on Sunday evenings, when only one teacher was on duty, boys would tune in to Radio 1 to listen to Alan Freeman's *Pick of the Pops*, dancing on desks and chairs, playing air guitar. The Boomtown Rats' 'I Don't Like Mondays', which topped the UK singles chart in Cameron's last term at Heatherdown, was a particular favourite.

Half a century earlier the actor David Niven had been expelled following a misdemeanour with a marrow. In the 1970s the principal target was strawberries – or more particularly the strawberries grown by Bar Edwards. Determined groups of small boys, David Cameron prominent among them, repeatedly mounted midnight raids on her kitchen garden, with a view to devouring her produce back in the dorm. This classically jolly jape ensured hours of hilarity spiced with the fear of discovery. Deep into the night, formidable matrons with torches would patrol the sleeping quarters in the knowledge that those whose beds were empty would most likely be found whispering among the soft fruit. Cameron more than once felt the sting of the clothes brush. Simon Andreae recalls similar escapades: 'Dave and I used to creep out of our dormitory windows to go midnight swimming in the school pool, which was freezing. Or we would have trysts with girls from nearby Heathfield School, in the graveyard which lay in between the two.'

Because it was a small school, all the pupils knew one another, giving an air of intimacy that some more soulless establishments of this type might have lacked. Former Heatherdown boys remember with fondness the woods and the lake. Here, dressed in distinctive green boiler-suits, pupils would make dens, arrange mock fights and generally play. In many respects, it seems to have been idyllic and carefree. 'It was a very happy place, a great school,' says Alexander Bathurst. 'One or two might not have been well suited to it, but the majority would have certainly enjoyed it.'

The Cameron boys played their parts in school plays, although it was the older brother – as David was to admit subsequently – who showed the truer talent for the stage. At the age of eight, David played the part of Harold Rabbit in *Toad of Toad Hall*, while Alex caught the eye with his performance of Ratty. Prince Edward played Mole. Chris Black, a former teacher at Heatherdown, said much later that 'although he was somewhat overshadowed by his brother, the young Cameron Minor's determination and ambition was already much in evidence'.

Both Cameron boys played for the school's cricket First XI, Alex with marginally greater accomplishment. David was a stylish, medium-pace bowler with a good eye. 'He was the sort of person who just knew how to throw a ball,' said a friend later of the way sports came easily to him. Cricket was his strongest team sport, with rugby his weak spot. 'He didn't have the physique of a great sportsman, but he didn't hang back. He was quite a brave little boy; he wasn't windy at all,' recalls one who knew him well.

Rhidian Llewellyn was dutifully raking a long-jump sandpit on the school's sports day in 1978 when he was approached by Mrs Gordon Getty. She was making plans for her son Peter (grandson of the oil billionaire John Paul Getty) to invite four classmates to the USA, and would he like to accompany the boys, by way of looking after them? As the young teacher was barely out of school himself and had never flown, he jumped at the opportunity. The trip turned out to be even more lavish than he can have dreamed. One of the lucky four friends of Getty was David Cameron, and such a dizzying glimpse of the high life may have contributed to his perception of wealth. Years later, answering claims that his was a life of privilege, he said he wasn't rich because he didn't 'own a private jet and I have no friends with a private jet'.

At lunchtime on 21 July 1978, two days after the end of term, Getty, Cameron, Simon Andreae (brother of Giles), Peter Romilly and Fergus Wylie, accompanied by their eighteen-year-old minder Rhidian Llewellyn, boarded BOAC Flight 579 (Concorde, as it happened) at Heathrow to fly to Washington DC. As the excited boys tucked into their caviar, salmon and beef bordelaise, Llewellyn turned round to check that all was well and that his charges were more or less behaving themselves. He was met with the sight, a few rows behind, of David Cameron, eleven years old, cheerily raising a glass of Dom Pérignon '69 and exclaiming 'Good health, Sir!' 'Sir', only seven years older than Cameron, was so disbelieving of his own good fortune that he felt it would be churlish to challenge Cameron's cheek. This willingness to nudge jovially at the barriers of authority (rather than to throw stones at them, for example) came from Ian Cameron, and generally seems to have been carried off disarmingly. 'There were times when you needed to tell him to shut up,' says Llewellyn. 'Like any ten-year-old, he would get a bit out of line and need a bit of a metaphorical cuffing, but I was never irritated by him and often amused by him.'

Washington was going through a heatwave that summer, but no matter. For four days the excited boys from the UK were conveyed to all the capital's most celebrated sights in an air-conditioned Lincoln Convertible. It also took them to a French restaurant where they enjoyed the spectacle of roller-skating waiters. From Washington they went on to a further three days of sight-seeing in New York, where they were based at the Hotel Pierre. The itinerary included the Empire State Building and the World Trade Center. They then flew on to Disneyworld in Florida, roller-coasters and all, and, to celebrate Peter Getty's twelfth birthday, to the Kennedy Space Center at Cape Canaveral. Next it was Las Vegas, where the temperatures reached 120°F, which somewhat curtailed the sight-seeing, restricting them to hanging round the MGM Grand Hotel's pool and investigating the hotel's gaming devices. The tour was rounded off with three days at the Grand Canyon, including a helicopter flight, followed by a trip to Hollywood. They regained their bearings with a week based at Pacific Heights, the Getty home overlooking San Francisco's Golden Gates and Alcatraz.

At Heatherdown there wasn't a great push, as there is at many schools nowadays, to get children into a certain public school. It seemed part of the natural order of things that it would go on doggedly churning out boys who got into Eton (and less often Harrow), and it saw no reason to change. The only scholastic pressure that most boys felt came in the last year, when the exam was nearly upon them. But this began to change in the late 1970s. Eton started making greater demands of its pupils and upping its standards. Heatherdown was shaken when one or two boys started to fail the Common Entrance exam (often being taken away to a crammers to retake it, generally with success). David Cameron was fortunate that only at the end of his spell at the school was Common Entrance beginning to be a problem. In any event, he applied himself to the task with what has become his customary efficiency and in the summer of 1979, he was accepted at Eton.

ETON
Public school 1979–1984

Asked in 2004 whether he thought his schooling would hold him back politically, David Cameron sighed heavily. 'I don't know. You can try and be logical about it and say the upside is a terrific education, the downside is the label that gets attached and mentioned in every article. Or you can just think to yourself: I am what I am. That is what I had, I am very grateful for it.' Cameron, by his own confession a late developer, has good reason to be grateful. Eton unearthed rich talents in a boy who at first seemed remarkable only for being thoroughly average.

To any boy on the threshold of his teens, arriving at Eton is a daunting experience – even for prep school boarders like Cameron, used to being away from home from the age of seven. Six and a half centuries of history crowd around new arrivals. Cameron, short for his age and a little overweight, could at least take refuge in a room of his own, his first private space either at home or at school. This was in John Faulkner's house, JF, situated near the end of Eton's Common Lane, one of twenty-five houses of around fifty boys each that make up the school. Each one is its own universe, a more intimate home from the buffetings of the wider school. The refuge of having one's own room is not unassailable, but an Eton boy can generally shut out as much of the rest of the world as he wants. To a newcomer, this can be invaluable, a quiet place to learn the school's arcane names, rules and acronyms and for coming to terms with wearing a tailcoat every school day for five years.

One of the distinctive features of Eton is 'private business', when a handful of boys meet a master – known, in the first three years, as their Classical Tutor – allocated to them for a weekly meeting to discuss a range of extra-curricular topics. For new boys at Eton, this can be one of the best ways of talking informally with a master and getting one's bearings. As was the practice in several houses, John Faulkner himself played the role of Classical Tutor to the new boys in his house. This was in part to provide a forum in which to get to know the boys in his charge, something not always easily achieved in the hectic day-to-day life of running a house.

When Cameron arrived at Faulkner's house in late 1979, he once again had the implicit protection of his brother Alex, three years above him. A friend describes the older Cameron as a 'glamorous, popular and arty' presence at the school, which would have gone some way towards smoothing the younger boy's path. In his first terms Cameron was 'precocious and naturally self-confident and clearly enjoyed having a popular and well-known brother in the school', says a friend. Alex's presence would have offered a sense of belonging to the 'new bug'. This protection was not without its downside, though. David was intensely aware of the swathe his elder brother had cut through the school, something which might have cast a pall on a less assured sibling. Nonetheless the extent to which David and Alex might 'by being in the same house, tread on one another's toes', as one family member puts it, was a slight concern. Cameron himself has said he worried that he might never escape his brother's shadow. Cameron was spared 'fagging'. By the time of his arrival the practice of serving older boys had been all but phased out. Only the vestigial obligation for younger pupils to deliver the occasional message for their older housemates remained.

Alex might have afforded protection but he had also set an academic standard that David could not at first match. Cameron minor, although described by some close to him as having a good brain, scarcely set the school on fire academically. New boys go into F year, and for each subject are graded, with the brightest boys going into F1 and the least promising into, say, F7. For most subjects Cameron was around halfway down his year. At that stage, he hardly made an impression on his French teacher, Tom Lyttelton ('he wasn't at the top of the class and wasn't at the bottom'), although their paths were to cross higher up the school. Bob Baird, who taught Cameron Maths in that first year, says that of all the boys he taught who went on to become famous, Cameron was the only one he couldn't recall.

By Lent term 1980, Cameron had in effect moved up slightly, having survived Trials, the end-of-term exams which determine progress in the next term and which arouse much fear in boys of lesser ability or lesser application. When Cameron moved into E block, in his second year, an English teacher, Jeff Branch, became his Classical Tutor in place of John Faulkner. Branch's preference was for a smaller group, so Cameron joined just four other boys for the weekly sessions. The emphasis was on drawing out boys in artistic areas they might not have experienced elsewhere, to discuss issues of relevance to the school and the wider community. Branch remembers them as being 'a pretty accomplished group, urbane and bright', in which the articulate Cameron was well able to hold his own. 'He showed a lively interest in literature, music and art, and was generally forthcoming and perky. I had few worries about him. He seemed to be heading for a place at a decent university. At that stage there was no special sign of an interest in politics' (unlike, he says, an earlier pupil of his, Oliver Letwin).

Academically, a boy's first three years at the school required a level of proficiency in a wide range of subjects. Before he could embark on his A-levels he would be required to pass five O-levels, and this represented quite a hurdle for some. Although from his prep school days Cameron had been regarded as bright, that intelligence had been more evident in person than in his academic work. Around this time he told a friend of his concern that he might not make the grade.

Notwithstanding the size of the school, in Cameron's first term a quick familiarity would have been achieved among those he encountered. It might not have been apparent at the time, but many of these boys were to become friends for decades (quite a few he knew already, from Heatherdown and elsewhere). In F year in Faulkner's house, for example, there were just nine other boys, at least half of whom can call themselves good friends of Cameron to this day. The names James Learmond, Simon Andreae, Roland Watson, Tom Goff and 'Toppo' Todhunter crop up throughout Cameron's life, as does that of Pete Czernin, in the same house but the year above.

In those early weeks, the sense of sharing an ordeal binds young boys together. They would exchange notes about Eton's curious rituals, which parts of the town are out of bounds, the agony of starched collars and the impenetrability of Eton argot. These and other topics would be kicked around in a 'mess', a ritual of considerable seriousness – for the youngest at least – in which boys form groups of three or four and meet every afternoon in the room of one of them for comforting quantities of tea and toast.

Friends who remember Cameron from that time say he adapted well to his new school. He was good company, placid, with a ready wit, invaluable for keeping bullies at bay – just as he had done at Heatherdown. He had made the step up from being a big fish at his prep school to being a minnow at Eton with no obvious difficulty, reticence or homesickness. One master recalls: 'He wasn't a shy or retiring person, even in F, just a pleasant personality, a very natural, basically happy person.' Another new boy, pointing out how everyone treads on eggshells in their first term, remembers Cameron coming up to him and asking 'What's your name?' The boy nervously gave his surname, to which Cameron replied, 'No, I mean your Christian name. I'm David.' 'He was just being friendly. It struck me as being incredibly personable and human and level headed of him,' says the boy in question. 'He clearly wasn't fazed by the place at all.'

But, with the onset of adolescence, some began to find his natural buoyancy verging on the bumptious. Someone who met him one school holiday around that time said he was 'a typical Etonian, rather full of himself, and nothing like as funny as he thought himself'. The mother of an associate of his reports that she was told by the rather over-assured young man that 'women have the intellectual span of a gnat'. By his early teens, he was inclined to have the odd furtive cigarette with his friends, and they would nip behind the cricket pavilion for an excited swig of beer or wine. He told friends then that he preferred to be called Dave, presumably because it sounded cooler. Although an early girlfriend, Caroline Graham, now the *Mail on Sunday*'s Los Angeles correspondent, says he was shy, she remembers Cameron as an 'expert kisser' at the age of thirteen. Cameron has no recollection of this, and wonders if she was thinking of his brother.

He showed artistic leanings in his early years at Eton, and spent a good deal of time at the Art Schools. The master in charge was John Booth, described by a widely experienced figure at the school as 'unquestionably the finest art teacher I've dealt with in my career'. Cameron had some etchings displayed at the school's open day, the Fourth of June. He dabbled a bit in painting, and allowed his foot to be made into a plaster cast, for the art show of his talented sculptor friend Crispin Gibbs (with the toe as a spout), but – while studying for around five hours a week – principally enjoyed the relaxed ambience of creativity and exchange of ideas that Booth encouraged. 'It was a really nice community of people, slightly apart from the school,' remembers Booth, who inspired a marked increase in the number of boys taking O-level Art.

'The facilities were superb, and John Booth ran a really beneficial regime,' says one regular there. 'He encouraged us to paint big, to have ambitious ideas. The building was new, with big plate-glass windows looking out, and he didn't just want staid public schoolboys' art, he wanted to encourage young investigative artists to try out new things.'

It was characteristic that Booth encouraged one boy to paint a forty-foot-high crucifix. His alumni in the early 1980s included Jay Jopling, who went on to create the White Cube Gallery, Max Wigram, who now runs a contemporary art gallery in central London, Nick Fiddian-Green, a sculptor, Dominic Ramos, a watercolourist, and John Martin, another gallery owner in central London. BritArt had many fathers, but John Booth could reasonably claim to have been at least an uncle.

Cameron played sports – one contemporary described him as the rock of an unglamorous house team – but not to a high enough standard to represent the school. His best sport was tennis, which he had played extensively on the court at home. He was a stylish and forceful player, and came close to getting into the school's second team. Lyttelton, who had briefly taught him French and tennis, remembers Cameron, above all, as an extremely social creature. 'It is no effort at all to remember him. Some boys tend to hide, but he was the sort who would say, "Do you remember, Sir, you taught me French in F," not in a pushy way, but simply out of natural friendliness.' He says that teachers often have a certain trepidation about whether a group they are in charge of will 'gel'. 'Sometimes,' he says, 'the reason it does can be ascribed to one particular individual. I remember David Cameron (with gratitude) as one of these: no group, in schoolroom or on tennis court, of which he was a member failed to gel in the happiest possible way.' Michael Kidson, who taught him History, agrees. 'I recall an easy, civil, courteous, intelligent and vigilant young man,' but not 'conspicuously a high-flyer'.

By the start of 1982 Cameron was studying for his O-levels that summer, the grades of which would determine whether he would be allowed to stay at the school. He had not yet shone academically, so the threat of his Eton career ending in failure was not a remote one. But just six weeks before the exams Cameron came close to being expelled before he could even sit them.

Towards the end of May a number of pupils were found to be both using and distributing cannabis. The affair made the national newspapers, in part because, unusually, the police were involved. Eton generally told the local drugs squad of any illegality the school had uncovered and the drugs squad in turn was content to leave the school to sort it out. On this occasion the police oversaw an investigation by the school, apparently determined, at least at first, to root out all drug-users. The initial culprits were called upon to reveal to whom they had sold drugs, an offence that ensured automatic expulsion. On the first day seven were summarily thrown out and the investigation began to snowball.

'They called in more the next day, and the day after, but after that everyone just clammed up,' says one former pupil who left that term. 'A couple of the guys were going to Slough to buy the stuff, but it wasn't as if there was real dealing going on in the school.' He added: 'We were heavily leaned on to give names. There were a lot of people involved. They tried to accuse me of dealing in it, which was nonsense. I told the headmaster, "If you kick me out, you'll have to kick an awful lot of people out." I didn't like the way it was handled. We weren't told our rights or anything, and apart from a few confessions from people, they had very little evidence.' A senior member of staff at the time admits that a 'nice teacher, nasty teacher' technique was used, and says: 'I have no doubt that we wouldn't be allowed to handle it in the same way nowadays – we would be involved with human rights legislation and so on.' Estimates vary of how many were questioned, but the school was anxious to send a strong signal, including to those on the fringes who had experimented but otherwise knew little of the drugs world. The school authorities, evidently, were taken aback by what they found. 'They realised the numbers were much greater than they thought,' claimed one former pupil. 'They couldn't rusticate [temporarily expel] everybody.' While, in theory at least, the 'hard nuts' were thrown out, others received milder punishments.

JF was on the edge of Eton, with views out over the countryside and towards the railway arches, both domains offering handy cover for illicit smoking and drinking. From the house, it was possible on occasion to witness the surreal scene of groups of two or three teenagers in tailcoats trudging back towards the school, their purported interest in the botany of east Berkshire temporarily sated. Cameron's house was a stone's throw from the Art Schools, and the drugs purge took a disproportionate toll on those who attended them. (Much later, the headmaster gently pointed out to John Booth that three-quarters of the boys who were expelled did Art; Booth replied jovially that all of them did Divinity, but that proved nothing.) 'It was a group of pretty naughty characters and they tended to get into trouble,' said another regular visitor to the railway arches who was expelled. He remembers the drugs clean-up as being 'like a military operation' and still resents what he sees as its draconian enforcement and the suspicion (about who gave names to the headmaster) it created.

In the inquisition of May 1982, an acquaintance of David Cameron named him as having smoked cannabis. He was called before the headmaster and confessed. Because he had only smoked and not sold the drugs he was not thrown out. Instead he was fined, gated (refused all leave) and given a Georgic (a classic Eton punishment requiring the offender to copy out 500 lines of Latin). To acute personal embarrassment, he was barred from attending the Fourth of June celebrations. He was also invited to reveal the names of other boys involved but did not do so. Eric Anderson (now Sir Eric, and provost of Eton), who did not become one of Eton's most popular former headmasters by smallmindedly remembering every misdemeanour he has been called upon to punish, says he does not recall Cameron's involvement, but makes a general point. 'There are those who get in on the fringes. It is a matter of excitement and experimentation. We would have said, "Let's get the ringleaders," and if there were others involved, we would have scared them off from doing it again. We're dealing with young boys, and young boys sometimes do silly things. But I would very much resist the idea that we "put the lid back" on anything.'

The incident was all but forgotten when twenty-three years later Cameron stood on the brink of the Tory leadership. A discussion took place about whether to allow a friendly journalist to break the story so that it wouldn't fester and fall into hostile hands to be revealed at an embarrassing moment, but Cameron decided against answering any questions about his drugs use. It was a decision that has brought enduring innuendo about alleged cocaine use but one that has ensured that, while he may have inhaled cannabis, no 'drugs lies' have left his lips.

Typically, he did not allow the drugs episode to get him down. Happy, well adjusted, social but academically average (although he surprised himself by passing twelve O-levels, with moderate grades), Cameron's Eton career appeared to be drifting into an agreeable obscurity in the summer of 1982, the height of his youthful rebellion behind him. His tastes were not untypical. He had a poster of the American model Cheryl Tiegs on the wall of his room and enjoyed the Jam (whose 'Eton Rifles' had come out in his first term), Stiff Little Fingers and XTC and developed an interest in the drums. Like so many schoolchildren with excess energy to burn off, he would tap rhythmically on his desk before classes began. A friend at the time remembers him having a coltish obsession with the distinctive drum break in the middle of Phil Collins's 1981 single 'Something in the Air Tonight', and decided that playing air drums to it was not enough. With characteristic gusto, he went so far as to take lessons. His drum teacher Steve Lees has no recollection of his having formed or joined a band, though.

Despite this amiable pottering, something remarkable was to happen over the next two years that propelled him out of the ranks towards the front. He told an interviewer later 'when I was sixteen I was definitely going off the track a bit, losing interest in school and study and doing things wrong ... And living in the shadow of an elder brother. I remember thinking, "Hold on a minute, if you carry on like this you're not going to get any decent grades, you're not going to make much of your life."' An awakening interest in politics, a steely ambition and an academic facility flowered in him, seemingly simultaneously, just in time for his A-levels. Not for the last time in his life, he suddenly burst from the pack when the prize was in view.

From C block, which he reached in September 1982, onwards, boys are known as 'specialists'. Becoming a specialist is akin to reaching adulthood, and it marks the point when boys are permitted to drink, in moderation, at Tap, the school pub; they are also allowed more weekends away from the school. By this time Cameron's brother had gone on to Bristol University, but he would go back to Peasemore, often seeing his sisters Tania – then heading for A-levels at St Mary's, Calne, in Berkshire – and Clare – who was still at the Manor prep school in Abingdon – as well as his parents. Cameron, as he says himself, didn't really 'get going academically' until he started doing A-levels. He was now beyond the reach of those set subjects required by the Eton curriculum and he could follow his own interests more closely. He chose as his three A-levels History of Art, History and Economics with Politics. It is at this stage, perhaps, that the benefits of Eton come to the fore. Cameron was fortunate to be taught History of Art by William Franklin, undoubtedly one of the school's stars, and Bill Winter, the convivial organiser of the Political Society. He was taught History by Giles St Aubyn and Michael Kidson, a kindly and scholarly man whose faux pomposity endeared him to generations of Etonians. But it was his enthusiasm for Economics (and Politics) that really fed his academic appetite.

As a specialist, a boy is free to choose the Tutor who will see him through to A-levels, with whom he would share twice-weekly informal private business sessions. As before, these sessions, often just 'talking things through', as one master puts it, were not oriented towards exams but were designed to give boys a taste for off-curriculum culture at its broadest. John Clark, who taught Cameron for his last four terms, sees private business as one of the keys to what might be called 'the Eton experience'. 'The school is remarkably informal,' he says, 'despite the exterior that the outside world sees. It gives tremendous opportunities to talk and discuss and be taken seriously by adults, and private business is a case in point.'

Cameron chose as his Tutor Tim Young, an Etonian himself, who ran the school's First XI soccer team. Paradoxically, although Young himself had been a scholar (remarkably, the fourth in what is now a family line of five to win a King's scholarship), his reputation among the boys was as much for gregariousness as for academic excellence. 'Tim Young is very nice,' says one gifted contemporary. 'It shows Cameron wasn't at that stage very academically ambitious. Of all the choices you make at that age, it's one of the more revealing ones about who you are. I imagine he chose him as much because he was a good bloke as anything else.'

Yet Tim Young remembers Cameron on the launchpad: 'What I saw was the start of a developing of the considerable academic motor that took him on to Oxford. Physically and mentally he took off in the sixth form. He was beginning to discover that he had a potential which people had never identified.' John Clark agrees: 'He was very much a late developer academically, one who came good once he did a series of subjects that suited him. He didn't make a great splash at Eton, but of all the people I taught he was one of the most impressive. What is striking is that his subject choices, History, History of Art and Economics, might have been thought as relatively light by some universities. But they didn't stop him doing very well.'

In the spring of 1983, two masters took a party of twenty-six boys to Rome to help them with their Art History studies. When such a group is let loose on a foreign jaunt, good behaviour is not a priority. For much of the trip, while most of the boys saw the sights, David Cameron was immobile, having sprained his ankle dancing over-enthusiastic reels to the bagpipe-playing of his friend Ben Weatherall.

'[He] was busking at the top of the Spanish Steps,' Cameron explained, 'trying to raise some money so we could go and have a drink. I got slightly exuberant and turned my ankle over.' Cameron thought the leg was fine, so his friends left him. It turned out it was quite badly twisted and he had to crawl all the way down the Spanish Steps on his hands and knees. As a result he had to miss a good many of the sights, but as a contemporary at the time said euphemistically, he 'made up for it well in other departments'. Quite what this means must remain a mystery, although, as one of Cameron's close friends remarked, Dave, while no prude, was always 'measured'.

For the first time in his life, he was enjoying real academic achievement. In the summer of 1983, at the end of the first year of his A-level course, he won the Trials Prize for Politics, which gave him a distinction, an excellent augury for the following summer. The following term, at the start of his second A-level year, his Option was the Spanish Civil War, drawing largely on Hugh Thomas's celebrated history of the conflict, taught by Timothy Wilson Smith. For his work on that topic he won another award, though this was a marginally less impressive achievement – there was only one other candidate in his year.

Sustaining his interest in politics, in the following (Lent) term he chose a subject taught by Dr Andrew Gailey, who was later to be housemaster to Princes William and Harry. The area he chose was 'Northern Ireland: A Study in Conflict', which suggests an awakening interest in the Conservative and Unionist Party. Gailey, himself from Northern Ireland, took the boys through issues such as how the state deals with terrorism, why there are great literary outpourings at times of stress and so on. It was a more serious and demanding course than many boys chose. Although little homework accompanied the course, Gailey said, 'it never struck me that he was someone who went for the soft option'.

Gailey got to know Cameron well, becoming his Tutor for the second of his two years as a specialist when Tim Young took a sabbatical. He also taught him History of Art, during which Cameron had to choose a topic for a dissertation as part of his A-level course work. Gailey recalls his wife, an art historian, inviting Cameron to hold his arms out straight in front of him and piling ever more books on top of them. 'I remember thinking, "Has he got time to read all this?"' says Gailey. But, suddenly, he got to grips with it. As has happened many times since, he summed up what was required and did the necessary. 'He just took the books, worked out his brief, wrote a very good thesis and got a decent mark. It was an impressive piece of work. He has the front of being quite jovial, laid-back, not very serious in a way, but if you told him, "You've got to get this done," he could turn it on. I was quite surprised at his capacity to devour books.'

Eton and the Conservative Party go together. This was more true than ever in the early 1980s. Thatcherism was getting into its stride and with the Falklands reconquered and Michael Foot's Labour Party humiliated at the polls, to back anyone but the Tories was to back the losers. But there were dissenters. James Wood, now a well-known literary critic and a contemporary of Cameron at Eton, was editor of the school magazine. He challenged the right-wing orthodoxy and wrote a philippic against Thatcherism which caused a fuss in the national press. Ian Cameron, having read about it in the *Express*, called David to lament the fact that the school was now evidently full of 'Reds', a complaint Cameron teasingly passed on to Wood (whose nickname, incidentally, was 'Red' Wood). Wood, though, says now, 'I don't recall [Cameron] being involved in any political activity at Eton.'

Had Cameron in fact decided on a career in politics from an early age? He has claimed that he hadn't. In defending himself against the charge of having had a wild time at Oxford, he told the BBC that he didn't know at the time that he was going to be a politician. He chose Augustus Pugin for his History of Art dissertation topic. But it was

Pugin's work on Chirk Castle, Wales (to which, handily, Cameron had access, through a relation) that was the subject of the dissertation, not the architect's more famous decorations at the Houses of Parliament. John Clark says, 'I'm pretty sure I viewed him as politically ambitious even then. He was articulate and politically motivated and interested. He was interested in the business of politics, in politics as a profession, even at that stage. I don't think he'd planned it out in the way [Michael] Heseltine is supposed to have done. He found politics stimulating, in a good pragmatic Conservative way. He was intrigued by politics as an art, as a way of resolving problems.'

One acquaintance, asked when Cameron decided on politics as a career, faltered before answering and went off the record: 'He decided at Eton, I think, that politics was the career for him.' Another Eton contemporary says that he didn't know Cameron well at school, but that he was referred to by a mutual acquaintance as 'the guy who wants to be Prime Minister'. Another friend recalls Cameron, relaxing at Peasemore in his late teens, saying he wanted to be leader of the Conservative Party. (Sir Eric Anderson, Eton's headmaster, cautions against reading too much into any such pronouncements. 'When I was fourteen I told people I wanted to play rugby for Scotland: that doesn't mean there was the faintest prospect of it happening,' he says.)

Cameron's attitude to Eton was a healthily forward-looking one. 'I always got the impression that Eton was a preparation, not an end, which is as it should be,' says Andrew Gailey. 'It was all about the future. I'm not sure what he wanted to be but I'm not surprised he's in politics. It's the interest plus the way he operates which means you're not going to want to dig too deeply into philosophy but you're going to want to make things happen.' James Wood says: 'I would say he didn't seem someone who would certainly be in politics; what he seemed was someone who would be successful. His charm and decency – almost a kind of sweetness, actually – marked him out for a kind of general success in whatever he did. But politics did not look likely.' Cameron's friend James Fergusson remembers a conversation in which he discussed which boys in his year might emulate some previous Etonians and go on to become Prime Minister. One boy, and Fergusson believes it was Tom Goff, Cameron's old friend from prep school, said he thought that, if anyone might, it would be Cameron. Asked about the exchange, Goff says: 'James may well be right but I'm afraid I have no recollection of it.' Another close friend, in Cameron's house, says he remembers a conversation between him and Cameron as they looked at the statues of past Etonian prime ministers. 'We were convinced there would never be an Etonian prime minister again. I certainly didn't think Dave would have a go at it. His only acting roles at school were as a serving-man and as a girl. He was never outrageously extrovert – just quietly popular.'

Cameron's political persona as a teenager is hard to pin down. It is neatly illustrated by his choice of extra-curricular activity. Boys usually faced a choice between being a member of the Corps, the school's junior army, or undertaking good works in the local community. Cameron did both. He would also go to Windsor, sometimes with a friend, to visit an old lady, a Mrs Creek, and provide her with some company over a cup of tea. The next day he would shoulder his Eton rifle.

Although Cameron was always going to be a Conservative, he once put on a slide show for a morning assembly about poverty and unemployment, to the backing of UB40. Some took this to be as much a reflection of a teenage desire to acquire credibility from association with a fashionable band as an expression of concern about the nation's mounting unemployment figures. But his associates recall that his real passion was reserved for railing against the iniquities of the 'Common Market'. Brussels, it seems, has been a Cameron target from the moment he started taking politics seriously. 'It wasn't brilliantly original but it was generally fairly soundly argued,' says one who knew him well at the time.

Trade unions were another favoured mark. His appearance as a writer in the *Chronicle*, the school magazine, is limited to a solid but unremarkable review of a talk by former Labour minister Eric Heffer.

Eric Heffer, chairman of the Labour Party, gave us an interesting and informative talk about the relationship between the trade union movement and the Labour party. He emphasised the historical connection between the two and the basic principle of putting working class men into the house of Commons and then went on to explain that Tory trade union legislation, past and present, was tantamount to class legislation. Many of the questions were directly in response to what he had spoken about, but others ranged into the areas of Labour party leadership, Grenada [the tiny Commonwealth country recently invaded by the US] and the abolition of public schools. In an effective analogy, Mr Heffer then compared the trade union movement to a guards regiment, saying that if attacked they would 'go down fighting with their backs to the wall'. It was a fascinating if slightly depressing forecast.

Tony Benn was another unlikely stimulus. Cameron has said that reading Benn's book *Arguments for Democracy* helped pique his interest in politics. 'Lots of it I disagree with, but I loved reading it. I like being stimulated by things I disagree with, almost rather than reading something and saying: "Yes, that is my creed."'

But – in a pattern to be repeated at university – Cameron preferred to keep at one remove from the junior political practitioners. He attended the Political Society, which invited distinguished speakers from outside to address it. In his time Lords Home and Carrington, Len Murray, William Waldegrave, Frank Field and Grey Gowrie came to speak. But he was never on its committee (which would have offered the chance to meet and dine with the speakers), unlike, say, Boris Johnson, a year his senior and later to become a Tory MP and mayor of London. 'It just wasn't his style,' says John Clark. 'He didn't draw attention to himself. He wasn't effusive or loud. He certainly didn't dominate in private business. You'd have to remind me of the others from that tutorial, although there was something about him that made him very memorable.'

But there was something more. There was an episode in private business when the Tutor asked each boy to put in words what they thought of other members of the group. Whether this was a test of diplomacy, of honesty or of human perceptiveness is unimportant. It was to reveal something not readily apparent in David Cameron, who was generally regarded as an affable, emollient, easy-going character. 'I expected people to dance around the edge,' says the Tutor in question, Tim Young. But the participants were brought up short when one of their number, John Crossley, perhaps displaying the candour of his Yorkshire heritage, pointed across the room at David Cameron and said, '*You* are tough as nails, you are, and no one realises it.' The group fell silent. Tim Young recalls how struck he was by Crossley's comment: 'We didn't do much in the session after that, everyone was so startled by what had been said.' But, according to Young, Crossley – who died in a skiing accident some years later – was right. 'I do remember him being very pleasant, yes, but there was also a steely determination which has been revealed since. I think he has quite a core to him, and it was a side of David that I hadn't noticed.'

Others were coming to see the drive, though. Among them was Ferdie Mount, then working for Mrs Thatcher in Downing Street. Mount had received a call from his cousin Mary (Cameron's mother), asking if David could come to his office to do an interview for the school magazine. Mount explained that he was tremendously busy and in any event tied by the Official Secrets Act but that he would think about it. This was never likely to fob off the young Cameron, who rang Mount's office, fixed an appointment and simply turned up. He looked, says Mount, 'pink and perky' (he didn't shave daily till after he left Eton), and 'abounding in self-confidence'. 'He instantly put me at my ease and his genial chutzpah dissolved my ill-humour in a trice. It would not have taken extra-sensory powers to see that he would go far, though not perhaps with the miraculous speed that he did.' Cameron worked extremely hard and thrived in the freedom that being a specialist allowed. John Clark says, 'I did rate him very highly. I knew he was an ambitious, bright, intellectually curious guy. He was really quite sharp, able to pick up ideas quickly, to communicate them well.' Another Old Etonian friend, although not of Cameron's vintage, ascribes his emotional toughness to his schooling. Rupert Dilnott-Cooper, who was to work with him at Carlton Television, said: 'I think that – albeit as a generalisation and I am not suggesting it applies to David – some Etonians can be emotionally "distant" sometimes about things. I think there can be a degree of dispassionate ruthlessness that comes down to saying, "Thanks very much. Next?" And whether that's being at a boys' boarding school at the age of thirteen, I don't know. I have no idea if David is like that, but, in any event, I'm confident that he would be capable of being as ruthless as he needs to be.'

In an early newspaper profile, 'a lifelong Conservative who has known Cameron since Eton' said: 'I don't like David. He's hugely arrogant. But everyone from my background is so enthralled about the idea of having a prime minister from among their ranks that to say anything against him would be seen as disloyal.' Another school contemporary who finds the Cameron charm resistible says he has always had a calculating talent for impressing those who matter ('If you weren't socially interesting, one of the in-crowd, he would be very dismissive'), while yet another says, 'He always struck me as a bit of a greaser.' Cameron is also blessed with what some see as a very Etonian sense of entitlement, a feeling that there's no reason he shouldn't be a beneficiary of whatever might be in the offing.

Both facets of his character are evident in his choice of 'Option', an unexamined subject, like a hobby, often of a cultural or possibly professional nature. Cameron's cultural tastes, his exasperated friends will confirm, have never been highbrow. Yet he chose 'The Rise of the English Novel', taught by the headmaster. For most Etonians the prospect of being taught by 'the Head Man', even one as popular and respected as Eric Anderson, would fill them with dread. The majority would prefer to keep their head down. That Cameron should choose to be taught by Anderson, just three months after nearly being expelled for taking drugs, says a good deal for his insouciance. This was not a boy to shrivel away into the corner.

People tend to assume that Cameron must have been in Pop, the (then) self-electing society of prefects, chosen for their popularity and illustriousness. He was, after all, well liked, he was good at tennis and he was head of house. Indeed, some contemporaries now have trouble believing that he wasn't in Pop, so well does he fit the bill. Maybe his comparatively low-profile house worked against him, in that it can help a boy to get into Pop if another boy in his house can promote his cause. Yet notwithstanding the house's middling ranking, it managed to get no fewer than three boys in Cameron's year into Pop, James Learmond, Roland Watson and Pete Davis. Conceivably, it was thought that there were already too many boys from JF in Pop. One member speculates – because he cannot remember – that Cameron might have been 'slightly too polished for his own good. There might have been a feeling that he was socially a bit pleased with himself.' A former master as the school says Cameron didn't get in 'because he so wanted to get in'.

John Clark is unsurprised at Cameron not getting into Pop. A cerebral Etonian contemporary says: 'Everybody who was close to getting into Pop would have cared very much about not doing so, possibly very, very much. He would have found it very hard to deal with, especially as his brother was in Pop. He wasn't cool and he was square and not particularly nice – not a good combination. He was bombastic and would put people down and tease them mercilessly in order to make himself look good. He was overbearing and overconfident. From that time he developed a desire to sit in at the heart of the Establishment, he wanted to be at the middle of things.'

He might have made a good member of Pop, though. When he replaced his friend Roland Watson as Captain of his house (Watson stood down to concentrate on his cricket, at which he excelled), Cameron seems to have taken to his new position of responsibility comparatively well, and at a difficult time. Eric Anderson recalls that John Faulkner was going through a period of illness and was not therefore able to fire on all cylinders. 'I remember hearing that John relied a good deal on David, as his head of house, to hold things together at that time, and that John found him good at making sure that the junior boys were properly treated.' Mark Dineley, who, as a junior boy, overlapped with him by just one term, confirms this: 'I do recall him being unusually approachable and affable. He never had his head in the clouds. You could always talk to him.' Tom Rodwell, a year older, says that unlike most senior boys, who tended to seem 'godlike' for their imperiousness and authority, Cameron was 'always someone you could have a talk to on the stairs. He was a friendly and fair person. I remember having a not very serious bet with him about whether Wales would beat England at rugger. I bet that they would, and they did. He still owes me a fiver for that!'

On one occasion, Cameron intervened to protect a boy, now evidently a senior figure with a financial firm in the City who wishes to remain nameless, who was being bullied about his Jewishness. 'Cameron was very mature,' says the man in question. 'He didn't get angry with them, or punish them, because then they would have taken it out on me. I'd have been fucked. Dave said, "It's beneath you both to behave like this." He was giving half the blame to me, you see, which I now understand was quite brilliant.'

Cameron's development at Eton might be held up as an advertisement for what the place can offer those whose qualities need to be unearthed. 'I think down at the bottom of the school there were lots of people who were identified as natural leaders of other pupils at the age of thirteen and fourteen,' says Tim Young. 'They might have been head of their prep school, but often these are the people who end up at the peak of their life being secretary of the golf club. They never again achieve the great heights that they achieve in their teens. The great thing about David is that he wasn't pigeonholed like that and developed his obvious potential in the sixth form. He did so in his own way, unmarked by the sort of expectation which surrounds, say, the captain of the under-fourteen rugby team.'

Andrew Gailey says there is a discernible trend in boys whose academic talents flower late. 'People who do that,' he says, 'although they grow in confidence more and more, they are never as confident as those who have started at the top. And there's a sense in which he has always wanted to push himself and test himself more, not waste his time. He was able and ambitious, in a proper sense, but he was not one of those who was academically self-confident. There was a sense of him wanting to prove himself *to himself.*'

Unusually among Etonians, Cameron waited till he was eighteen before being confirmed. He wanted to make sure it was what he believed, he told an interviewer. 'I was a good, sceptical questioning Christian when I was younger. I liked to think it through, thinking am I really sure about this? But I don't feel I have a direct line [to God].'

Is David Cameron a 'typical Etonian'? Can there be such a thing in a school which supposedly encourages individuality? He does seem to have some of the characteristics that are associated with Eton. Jane Austen has a term, 'happy manners', which certainly seems to apply. Tom Lyttelton says: 'I wouldn't use the word charm, which can be pejorative. But a facility for putting people at their ease. That, I would have thought, Cameron had in spades.' Confidence, too, he says, which 'is helped by spending your teenage years in a rather beautiful place, having your own room, being in an essentially happy environment with some very good characters around you, older and younger'. John Clark says Cameron certainly appreciated what Eton offered him: 'If you come from a well-to-do background, you're surrounded by able people, you do well academically, you've got a lot of advantages, you feel fairly strong about that. Apart from private business, the range of social contacts that operate within a house, for example, mean you are mixing with the house master, the Dame [matron], a whole series of teachers and so on. I think these encourage a sense of social ease, and not one uniquely associated with your own group but one which moves beyond that. This explains something of the charm of Eton.'

But social (as opposed to academic) confidence is not as evident in many Etonians as it is in David Cameron. For all those who display that celebrated sense of entitlement, there are also others more inclined to question it, to be squeamish about such privilege. Why me? Is this really right? Do I want to be on the conveyor belt my parents put me on? James Wood says that Cameron was 'confident, entitled, gracious, secure ... exactly the kind of "natural Etonian" I was not'. There is little outward sign of David Cameron having kicked against what he had. Instead he accepted his parental assumption that 'It's okay as long as you put something back.' 'In every walk of life people try to find their own identity in relation to their parents, but David Cameron doesn't seem to have done that,' says one thoughtful Etonian outside his immediate circle. 'He's a strange product of my generation. He just seems to have a mind-boggling level of self-belief. He seems to represent a continuation or perhaps regression to that *noblesse oblige* Toryism. Do we want to be ruled by the Arthurian knights again?' As another puts it, 'He's a bit too "to the manor born" for my liking.'

Yet others, more admiring of Cameron, say Eton's role should not be overstated. Tom Lyttelton says Cameron's groundedness and contentment may well predate his attending the school: 'One really wonders whether someone so standing-on-your-own-two-feet can ascribe that much to Eton, or whether he would be doing so well whatever school he had been at.'

Certainly Cameron took full advantage of the academic excellence that Eton offered. The boy who one contemporary described as 'a bit of a nonentity at school' got three As in his A-levels, then an even better result than it would be today. Another contemporary, who regarded Cameron's success as a student of Politics – a subject which attracted few boys – as a misleading measure of his abilities, said at the time: 'It is a scandal and a complete travesty that someone as mediocre as Dave Cameron can get a distinction.' Cameron also sat the Scholarship Level exam in Economics and Politics and received a 1 grade. (He failed to turn up for another S-level exam in History, and so earned himself an X, for no score.) Having not been a likely Oxbridge candidate at all, he was now a strong one. Politics had become his forte, and his tutors were well placed to advise him on which college he should aim for. Tim Card and John Clark at Eton had connections with Brasenose College and encouraged Cameron to apply to read Politics, Philosophy and Economics. 'We wanted him to do well and it was a very good place to do PPE,' remembers John Clark, citing the presence of its politics tutor, the prolific Vernon Bogdanor, who, in addition to enjoying a good reputation in academic circles as a scholar, had something of a name in the wider world.

Cameron sat the entrance exam at the end of the Michaelmas term 1984. This so-called 'seventh-term' option was later forbidden as it was deemed to give too much of an advantage to pupils of private schools. He was accepted for an interview, which in hindsight may seem like a formality, but he was caught bluffing about how much philosophy he had read. It did not hold him back. He was awarded an exhibition to the college of his choice, Brasenose.

Having left school a fortnight before Christmas 1984, Cameron now had nine months in which to enjoy himself. James Learmond went to Nepal. Roland Watson went to Latin America. But few of his friends can remember what Cameron did in his gap year. 'Whatever it was, it didn't change him,' said one. But while it is true that his travels were not as exotic as those of his peers Cameron *did* undergo a life-changing experience between school and university. In January 1985 he took up a temporary post as a researcher for Tim Rathbone, his godfather and the Conservative MP for Lewes.

If his mother's family, the Mounts, represent the patrician element of Cameron's political heritage, the late Tim Rathbone stands for a more radical, liberal tradition. Indeed Rathbone's father John became Liberal MP for Bodmin from 1935 until, as a fighter pilot in the Battle of Britain, he was lost in action in 1940. His great-aunt Eleanor Rathbone was a suffragette and was later elected an independent MP for the Combined English Universities in 1929. She campaigned for women's rights and against poverty and was among the first to spot the dangers of National Socialism in Germany in the 1930s. It is said that she once tried to hire a ship to rescue Spanish Republicans from reprisals during the Spanish Civil War.

Her great-nephew chose the Conservative Party, however, when after Eton and Oxford (he, too, read PPE) and a spell as an advertising executive in New York he was recruited to Central Office in 1966 – the year of Cameron's birth. He became an MP in 1974, but by the time David Cameron turned up in his office in the Commons had found himself hopelessly out of step with the Thatcher government. Pro-European (he was later expelled from the party by William Hague for advocating support for the breakaway Pro-Euro Conservatives in 1997) and a vigorous opponent of apartheid in South Africa, he had also just rebelled against the abolition of the Greater London Council when his godson showed up for the first leg of a work-experience package that might have been designed to help him choose between politics and business.

Rathbone set him to work on two favourite themes, the lack of adequate nursery education and the manifold failures of his government's drugs policy. (The latter prefigured Cameron's own efforts as an MP in this area sixteen years later.) Inspired, Cameron started attending debates in the chamber of the House of Commons. He was present when Enoch Powell, speaking in an embryo-research debate, was interrupted by protesters throwing rape alarms from the public gallery.

But commerce as well as politics flows in his veins, and three months after arriving in the Commons he left it, heading for Hong Kong. Ian Cameron, through his employers Panmure Gordon, was stockbroker to the Keswick family. Henry Keswick was Chairman of Jardine Matheson, the Hong Kong-based conglomerate. Through that connection, Cameron was given the opportunity to work for the company in Hong Kong for three months. 'His father Ian is a good friend of my father and uncle and of mine,' explains Keswick. 'We get friends of the firm, some of whose children want to go and get some experience of living abroad, under our mantle. We take a lot of interns before they go to Oxford or Cambridge and we take them for three months.' Cameron – as his brother Alex had done three years earlier – worked for the Jardine Matheson shipping agency as what is known as a 'ship jumper'. When a ship – for which Jardine is the agent – arrives in Hong Kong, a ship jumper would go out with a pilot in a launch, meet the captain, tell him which buoy to go to and check that all the documents were in order. The job was administrative, requiring no great talent, but it did need someone presentable and personable.

Cameron lived in one of Jardine's company flats, sharing with other employees, and being generally well looked after, if modestly paid. He lived a largely expat life, mixing mostly with business people and enjoying the penultimate decade of Britain's imperial control of the colony. It was an agreeably safe way of seeing the exotic East, a risk-free brush with the orient, interesting enough to feed the mind, but scarcely worthy of Indiana Jones. One day some acquaintances, anxious to explore a more vernacular Hong Kong beyond the bland, globally ubiquitous office blocks, said they wanted to go out in search of a small market or local restaurant of the sort where 'real' Hong Kong residents would go, and asked if Cameron might care to join them. In the event he was busy, but he couldn't resist observing that the Hong Kong of big business was every bit as representative of 'the real Hong Kong' as any back-street enterprise of the sort they were talking about.

His journey back from the colony was rather more adventurous. In early June, he sailed (via a few days in Japan) to Nakhodka in what was then still the Soviet Union, before moving on to Khabarovsk, where he joined the Trans Siberian Railway and travelled to Moscow to meet a schoolfriend, Anthony Griffith. Although the reforming Mikhail Gorbachev had just become the Soviet leader, the country was still gripped by Stalinist illiberalism. For two young men to venture there without a guide was unusual. The pair travelled to what is now called St Petersburg, from where they flew down to Yalta on the Black Sea, scene of Winston Churchill's famous 1945 encounter with Stalin and Franklin D. Roosevelt.

While there, lying blamelessly on an Intourist (state-sanctioned tourist) beach, they encountered two men, rather older than them. One spoke perfect English, the other perfect French. They were normally dressed, extremely friendly and evidently well off. Cameron and Griffith were not going to look this gift horse in the mouth and gratefully accepted their invitation to dinner. They were treated to vast amounts of caviar, sturgeon and so on, while being asked lots of questions about life in the UK. They sensed they were being encouraged to make disobliging remarks about Britain, but, patriotic even in the face of a caviar bribe, they resisted. The Russians were not to be put off. At the end of the meal they suggested meeting again the following night, to which the Old Etonians agreed. In the event, the Brits, by now a bit concerned and wondering whether their new friends' motive was political, or possibly homosexual, failed to turn up at the chosen restaurant. Back in England, Cameron told friends this story, idly wondering if this was possibly a KGB attempt to recruit them, and – James Bond fan that he is – is tempted to believe it was. Had things gone differently, he and Griffith might have become the Burgess and Maclean *de nos jours*. As it turned out, their flit was westwards. From Yalta they headed for Kiev and thence, by now armed with Interrail passes, on to Romania, Hungary and western Europe, where Cameron dropped in to see his step-grandmother Marielen Schlumberger at her lakeside family home on Attersee, in Austria.

Cameron's gap year gave him a taste of the two worlds to which he was attracted. Commerce would have been happy enough to have him. 'We did say to David', remembers Keswick, 'that if he'd like to come back and work for us, he should apply to us after university.' But politics – and the influence of Tim Rathbone – won. Today as he tries to steer his party leftwards towards the political centre, Cameron knows that his late godfather, the man who helped inspire him to become a Tory MP in the first place, would have approved whole-heartedly.

OXFORD
University 1985–1988

It was both a hostage to class warriors and a stroke of some brilliance – whether spontaneous or planned – when Cameron claimed in October 2005 that he had had 'a normal university experience'. Regularly child-minding a Rastafarian's infant son while the father cooks goat curry is most decidedly not a standard 'university experience'. Punting with Jade Jagger is not normal. And dressing up in tailcoats and drinking dangerous quantities of vintage claret is normal only for a very small number of people. Cameron made his claim in deflecting a question about whether he had taken drugs at university. 'If you go to university and don't go to parties there is something wrong,' he continued at a conference fringe event the day after his leadership election-winning speech. Had he answered the question directly and honestly the answer would almost certainly have been yes. But his consumption of cannabis – at most infrequent and moderate – during his three years at Oxford University is one of the less interesting features of his 'normal' residence at that great seat of learning.

David Cameron arrived at Brasenose College in Michaelmas term 1985 to read Politics, Philosophy and Economics. By the mid-1980s Oxford colleges were coming under pressure to admit more candidates educated at state schools, but the intake of Brasenose in 1985 suggests that that college's tutors, at least, were not minded to submit. In lining up for his matriculation photograph Cameron found himself in familiar company. Five other Old Etonians had won places that year out of around a hundred freshers. Cameron was only the second Etonian in twenty-seven years to read PPE at the college. It was an unusually large intake from the school, especially for Brasenose, not one of Oxford's grander colleges. While Christ Church and Balliol tend to attract the cream of the public school clientele, Brasenose is more modest, smaller and more intimate than most. It is located at the heart of the university on Radcliffe Square but is proud of its insularity; new members are not generally anxious about making a big impact on the wider Oxford stage.

Toby Young, a satirist, who overlapped with Cameron for a year at Brasenose, has drawn a caricature of its social ecology at the time. Its students, he has written, divided between 'stains' and 'socialites'. The former anorak-wearing products of suburban state-education are contrasted with the more physically attractive scions of the elite. 'Stains' tried to get on in life, both academically and socially, and were despised as they did so by their rugby-playing, hard-drinking, privately educated peers. Young records how Cameron's 'unusually large number of Etonians' threatened to disturb this scene when they arrived on the battleground in 1985. 'Loud, hearty and unpretentious', they joined forces with the 'stain'-baiters eventually. 'Initially the "sound" college men were a little suspicious of these young bloods, imagining that their apparent sympathy was merely a sophisticated form of taking the piss. However after the Old Etonians had proved themselves to be solid drinkers and didn't complain when the hearties parked tigers [that is, vomited] all over their Persian rugs they were accepted into the fold.'

It would be unfair and wrong to suggest that Cameron did not mix socially at Brasenose, or that he was an unthinking member of the 'socialite' set. He picked his way carefully through the various camps, siding with the humorous against the earnest, but all the while keeping his eye on the goal he had set himself. One friend at the time remarked that Cameron had been motivated to get into Oxford partly to trump his elder brother. In truth, the pair had always got on well and – says someone who knows them both extremely well – were genuinely pleased at one another's success. Whatever the spur, there was no doubt of Cameron's next ambition: to get a first-class degree.

Some Etonians feel that after five years in charmed surroundings, they are ready for a dose of something a bit different. David Cameron was not one of these. At Eton, a boy's timetable is finely calibrated to pack as much as possible into a day. On leaving, some boys breathe a sigh of relief at escaping the regimentation. But Cameron, showing a trait also evident in his father, managed his time as a student with the sort of ruthless efficiency that most people never manage in their careers. His relaxed manner belied a remarkable degree of self-discipline. By the end of his first year he had managed so to arrange his affairs that he reckoned he could complete his work in half the week and spend the rest of his time on other pursuits.

It helped, of course, that his new educational establishment was so like his old. Having developed a verbal fluency in tutorials at Eton, Cameron was always an impressive performer in similar arenas at Oxford. Brasenose's PPE students were, in the words of one tutor, 'quite a chatty lot' and would readily confer with one another to thrash out problems with which they had been confronted. 'David was an outstanding student,' says one of his economics tutors, Peter Sinclair, who often taught in classes of a dozen or more. 'He was very, very good at economics and his academic record was really unblemished. He was very endearing, and would be very supportive of the others.' Sinclair points to a technique – perhaps Cameron would call it good manners – which has become something of a hallmark of his style in later life. 'When he disagreed with something he'd really worked hard on and thought about a lot, he'd say, "Well, I don't know much about this, but don't you have a feeling that so-and-so," when in fact he'd been researching quite carefully and knew so-and-so was probably right. He wouldn't parade his knowledge arrogantly. His contributions in classes would be thought out and charmingly delivered, often to make a joke or make light of it.'

While in the abstract this might sound condescending – the public school boy playing the didact with his social inferiors – those who were there deny this. For one thing, there was little question that he was one of the cleverest. Vernon Bogdanor says he was among the brightest 5 per cent of students he has ever taught, and believes that Cameron's influence was such that his presence in tutorials improved the grades of some of his contemporaries. 'He was liked by his tutors since he was both courteous and stimulating to teach. He enjoyed an argument. It was clear from the moment he arrived that he was likely to secure a very good degree. I would have been surprised if he had not achieved a First. He is one of the ablest and nicest students whom I have taught,' recalls Bogdanor today.

Outside tutorials he was popular with most – if not all – of his fellow students. 'He was clearly an Etonian,' says a Brasenose contemporary Steve Rathbone (no relation of Tim), who came from North Yorkshire and was state-school educated, 'but he wasn't swaggering around in a braying Sloaney way. Equally, he wasn't trying to be something he wasn't. He never tried to adopt an estuary accent, as many students do from major public schools, or wear right-on trendy clothes. He was a good mate of people from very different backgrounds.' It must have helped, too, that he rarely forgot the little courtesies. Unusually, he would say 'thank you' to his tutor at the end of every tutorial.

He studied hard. 'I do remember being impressed and slightly alarmed by how focused he was,' says James Fergusson, an Eton and Brasenose contemporary who read English. 'I was keen on my subject, but nothing like as keen as he was. He knew exactly what he wanted, which was to be the top-dog student and to get a First. That was it without a doubt. He loved it, he was passionate about it. At Brasenose a lot of life went on in the back quad, and you would see the PPE lot were having a good time. Dave would hold court in a classic Oxford way, quoting Locke and Hume. He loved it.'

His tutors, in recognition of his application and intelligence, upgraded his exhibition to a full scholarship. Cameron chose to continue with all three elements of his PPE course after the first year, rather than drop one and sit additional specialist papers in the remaining two as he was entitled to do. It is a testament to his self-confidence that he chose what Bogdanor insists was the harder path. 'The tripartite option was the more difficult option, since it was harder to achieve an alpha standard in three such disparate subjects as Philosophy, Politics and Economics than in just two. During the time David was an undergraduate, fewer of those taking the tripartite option secured First than those taking the bipartite option.'

While university can be a time for experimentation and exploration, much of Cameron's Oxford experience seems to have served to validate what had gone before. Peasemore remained close to him in more than simply a geographical sense. Some of his friends from Eton found his incurious side, his undeviating closeness to his cultural roots, a little stifling. While they were stepping gauchely out of the parental mould and exploring fresh fields, Cameron knew what and whom he liked and saw little reason to stray. He would invite his friends over to Peasemore to stay. Often there would be a lavish dinner, where his father – with characteristic generosity of spirit – would happily offer up excellent bottles of wine and port from his cellar.

One frequent guest at these occasions was James Fergusson, who admits he would be a strong candidate for the title of closest but most argumentative friend of Cameron. One afternoon, having recently returned from a mind-expanding stint backpacking, Fergusson remembers launching into Cameron: 'I had just come back and was full of a left-wing vision of Latin America and I said very pompously to Dave, "The trouble with you is, you're complacent." It sort of bothered him, and I think he knew what I meant. The façade dropped. He said, "What do you mean? What do you mean?" I wouldn't say he was blinkered, but he was quite safe, just utterly confident that the way he lived was the right way to live. He just didn't see that it might be a bit narrow.'

If psychologically he was anchored to his upbringing, intellectually he was more challenging. Vernon Bogdanor has called him a classic Tory pragmatist, and it has often been said that his politics, first really in evidence in his studies at Oxford, is non-ideological. But James Fergusson says the guiding light is clear. 'He thinks exactly like the philosopher David Hume,' he says. 'He's a complete sceptic … it's all about throwing out dogma and starting again from scratch. The revolutionary side of the early philosophers is precisely what turned him on.'

His fellow students tended to be left of centre, but not radically so. The SDP was well represented among his contemporaries, but there was never any doubt of Cameron's allegiance to Margaret Thatcher. At a time when the country was polarised and a great many people despised the Tories, Cameron might well have become a remote or even hated figure. 'After David Hume, he loved the free market and Thatcher,' remembers Fergusson. 'There was a strand of loving Thatcher in a tongue-in-cheek way. "Marvellous," he would say, as if he was imitating an old buffer. He was always funny enough and clever enough so you couldn't lampoon him for it, but at heart he believed it.' Personal likeability seems to have done much to make his politics more acceptable to non-Tories.

Fergusson's room in their first year at Brasenose was on Staircase 15, four doors down the corridor from Cameron's, and they spent a great deal of time together. Fergusson was learning the guitar, not with unqualified success, and would pick away at Pink Floyd's 'Wish You Were Here' and the Who's 'Won't Get Fooled Again' while waiting for Cameron to finish an essay and go for a drink with him. 'He partied too, but he was incredibly organised about it,' says Fergusson. The Brasenose of Cameron's era has been written about almost as if it was Dorothy Parker's Algonquin, not least by those with an interest in it being so. It was, though, a small pond where Cameron thrived, developing his interest in repartee and wordplay with Din Cellan-Jones, James Fergusson, Toby Young, Tim Harrison, Will McDonald and Mark Mitchell. 'There was a core of quite intelligent people who did a lot of heavy drinking and had a lot of fun,' says one. While Cameron was well entrenched within his own set at Brasenose, some outside it objected to what they saw as his Etonian arrogance and resented him drifting in and out in his tailcoat for smart dinners. To some of those with a proprietorial sense of loyalty towards the college, he seemed to be having it both ways. There was something else about his social polish that some contemporaries found offputting. They claim that if Cameron found someone 'socially interesting' he would turn on the charm. For those not in favour, however, he had little time. This was nothing to do with class, assert his detractors, more a feline disposition to insinuate himself with the current in-crowd.

In his second year he joined the Ball Committee, tasked with organising the college's May Ball. The committee's chairman was Andrew Feldman, with whom he became friends. Cameron won a certain credit by persuading Dr Feelgood to play, despite the college's scant resources (to save money, Feldman arranged for Brasenose to use the flagging flowers from Worcester College's ball the night before).

Cameron's membership of the Bullingdon Club has attracted much attention. It is an elitist dining club characterised by vast, boozy dinners and subsequent debauchery. Evelyn Waugh satirised it in *Decline and Fall*, calling it the Bollinger Club. 'It numbers reigning kings among its past members,' wrote Waugh. 'At the last meeting, three years ago, a fox had been brought in in a cage and stoned with champagne bottles.' Its defenders would say it represented merely youthful letting off of steam, a harmless juvenile excess. But members of 'the Buller' saw themselves as being in a class of their own and were inclined to glory in the antagonism they provoked in others (who would be accused of envy, bourgeois small-mindedness, priggishness and so on). If their over-exuberance was hard to swallow at the best of times, during the Thatcher years their snobbish and youthful self-regard would have shown them at their very worst.

When at the end of his first year Cameron was invited to join this socially prestigious, if rowdy, company he was flattered. 'If you're young and good looking you want to put your toe in all the waters,' says Susan Rathbone, whose husband Tim had been a Bullingdon member a generation earlier. 'Tim, who David admired and liked, would certainly have said to Dave, as he said it to his own children, "Make the most of it and don't work too hard." You can miss so much if you are totally studious at Oxford, although the Cameron family would not have liked the hooray side of it.'

With the approbation bestowed by the club came a price (even if his tailcoat was borrowed). One night, David Cameron returned to his room in college to find it had been ransacked. His furniture had been removed and considerable damage done. Cameron was called to see the Dean, a move of some seriousness. It was explained that this sort of thing was not welcomed, least of all at a college like Brasenose, and that the culprits needed to be identified. Cameron, obliged by the Buller's code of *omertà*, refused and bore the punishment alone.

By general consent, Cameron was not a typical Bullingdon member. As one of his more thoughtful and deft Etonian friends puts it, with some understatement, 'Dave is a cautious man, someone who would think twice before throwing a bottle at a policeman.' Some say the control he applied to his excesses shows him as being rather more calculating than a carefree teenager ought to be. When policemen's helmets were being removed, shotguns being loosed off from the back of cars or waitresses insulted, McCavity wasn't there.

Giles Andreae and Dominic Loehnis (a school and university contemporary who became very friendly with Cameron in the early 1990s) both say they have never seen Cameron 'out of control' drunk. 'He would have got off his face at the Bullingdon,' says a close friend, 'but all that vomiting and so on would not have been him at all.' Another friend, no stranger to disciplinary procedures, says: 'All that stuff with people being sick over each other just wasn't his thing. He was a responsible sort of person. Without being square, what flicked his switch was wit and repartee. He just wasn't the sort to get roaring drunk and destroy the fittings – he wasn't nearly wild enough. If he was in company when people were doing that sort of thing, he'd worry and say, "Oh, don't do that."'

Why, then, did he agree to join the Bullingdon? One longstanding friend said he was 'amazed' that he accepted, as it didn't seem his cup of tea at all. According to his own account, it was because 'Friends did. You do things at university.' He was, though, a popular figure, had been to Eton and could afford it. 'Because he was confident and sociable and easy in his skin, people liked him,' said a friend. Wanting to enjoy Oxford to the full, he was disinclined to say no. As Susan Rathbone said in another context, 'He's a great one for giving something a go.' And, as James Fergusson says, Bullingdon dinners 'did at least start off sober'. A bit like the man who buys *Playboy* magazine for the interviews, Cameron seems to have gone along to the Bullingdon for the conversation.

Those less well disposed to Cameron see a need for vindication, going back to his snub by Pop at Eton, behind his Bullingdon membership. 'That Eton requirement to make you compete,' says someone familiar with both institutions, 'creates an edginess, so that you either succeed and feel you have made it and do your own thing or you don't, which makes you want to "belong" more than anything. So having not got into Pop, people challenge all the harder to get in. That's what he achieved in his own mind by joining the

Bullingdon.' It is a view endorsed by an unnamed former Eton master.

Even for the sensible Mr Cameron, being a member of the Bullingdon was not a risk-free business and he had some close escapes. One evening, after the statutory drunken dinner, a handful of Bullingdon members took against a pot plant growing outside an unpretentious restaurant in central Oxford, presumably because it infringed the members' exquisite notion of good taste. So they threw it through the window of the restaurant, causing mayhem and distress. The police were called and arrests were made. At this point 'the Etonians' (as one present described them) saw no point in getting themselves needlessly into trouble with the law – and ran for it. One who witnessed the event remembers the innocent making hasty excuses: 'Boris Johnson turned out to be remarkably nippy for a cruiserweight, his bulky torso seen disappearing over Magdalen Bridge on a pair of skinny legs.' A passing taxi-driver saw two weary revellers and called out, 'Hop in, they've just arrested your mates over there,' and they drove off into the night. Cameron ('tired and in need of rest' according to one eyewitness) had gone to bed before the incident – aware that trouble was brewing.

At the start of his second year, Cameron joined the Octagon Club, a lower-key affair but one which required members to dress up in yellow-lapelled tailcoats. He was not proposed for Brasenose's slightly smarter Phoenix Club, one of Oxford's oldest dining clubs and the successor to the celebrated Hellfire Club. His exclusion from membership of Brasenose's pre-eminent dining club was on the grounds of insufficient sporting prowess, explained a contemporary. The resentment aroused among those educated at more minor public schools by Cameron's ease with all members of the college is probably nearer the mark.

Did he take drugs at Oxford? A heavy-lidded public school friend says: 'It was never his thing. It was all booze, mostly beer then. I was into smoking dope. He just wasn't. If he'd wanted it he could have asked me. He was a social boozer, in a perfectly civilised sort of way.' Giles Andreae says: 'I couldn't swear on my life that he never smoked a joint at Oxford, but I saw a lot of him and would be very surprised.' The ethos of Brasenose indulgence was very much focused on alcohol, a long way from, say, that of Christ Church, where Olivia Channon, the Cabinet minister's daughter, died at a party in 1986. Cameron's interest in narcotics seems to have been minimal. As his friend back at Eton had said, he was always 'measured'. A close friend says that while some of his contemporaries were trying speed, for example, he wasn't interested. The most he had indulged in was 'occasionally a joint or something'.

Cameron's good looks and unforced charm meant he was rarely short of female attention. He had had lots of girlfriends in his teens and, as one friend put it, 'he went out with some absolute crackers'. At Oxford, he would go to old-fashioned sherry parties to meet girls. He also went to the Playpen nightclub, which was run by friends and was a popular haunt for those anxious to find likemindedly uninhibited souls. There Cameron would set to work on the opposite sex for what he would call, a little crudely perhaps, an evening's 'wooding'. Purely as a precaution, he once felt the need to visit a sexual diseases clinic (this was not, as has been suggested, for an HIV test). On other occasions, he would simply stand at the back, puffing on a Marlboro Lite and chatting with his male friends. Women were attracted, specifically, by his intelligence, his sweetness of nature and his emotional security. Many of his friends speak of how candid, how unEnglish, he is about his emotions. Frequently he will be in tears at the end of a play or film, and be quite open and willing to talk about it. This is no wheeze: he is confident enough not to regard it as a sign of weakness.

In his first term he dated a girl called Catherine Snow, who was at St Edmund Hall. Snow was notably strong-willed. 'Dave didn't have to do much decision-making while he was going out with her,' says a friend. The most serious of his Oxford girlfriends was Francesca ('Fran', as she was known then) Ferguson, a statuesque, artistic and forthright half-German History student. Cameron was, according to a friend, 'mad about Fran'. She arrived at Oxford having had no serious boyfriend and became a thoroughly worldly and lively character. They started going out shortly before Christmas in their first term and it quickly became a pretty serious affair. The daughter of a peripatetic diplomat, she was very conscious of not being from the same settled Home Counties milieu as Cameron, but they seemed a good pair. 'I didn't go skiing with everyone else, or stay in the same house in France as they all did, so I didn't really feel a part of his very English world,' she says. 'I was bored senseless with that party scene in England. He managed to be always comfortable in it but his life had more content. He would read more, think more. He wasn't one of that bland lot.'

She invited him to stay with her parents in Kenya in the summer of 1986, prompting him to take a temporary job shifting crates near Newbury to help earn enough money. Both enjoyed the holiday hugely, spending time away on 'a real safari, with trucks', and Cameron, having missed his plane home and delayed returning by a week, enjoyed the celebrated (from *White Mischief* days) Muthaiga Country Club and playing golf with Francesca's father, John. He impressed her parents with his charm, but there was an initial sticky moment involving her German mother Monika. He brought a present for his hosts of a Monty Python record, presumably thinking it would be something of an ice-breaker, should that be necessary. What he did not recall until the record was playing on the first evening was the North Minehead By-election sketch, which includes a scene of highly dubious taste featuring a 'Mr Hilter'. Monika Ferguson still remembers with amusement the look of embarrassment on Cameron's face. Nonetheless, so impressed was she by Cameron's easy manner and intelligence that she told her daughter one evening, 'That chap is going to be Prime Minister one day.' On leaving he won further good-will by discreetly leaving a tip and a thank-you note for Alice, the Kenyan woman who had cleaned his room.

Francesca and Cameron went out for nearly eighteen months. She wanted to experiment, but her boyfriend didn't feel the same. 'I was too much for him,' remembers Ferguson, who now runs an archi-tectural practice in Basel, Switzerland. 'I was too demanding of his time. I wanted to have arguments and be distracted, but when someone is very ambitious and wants to get a First they don't want someone demanding too much of them, and I think I probably did that. Also, I was quite jealous and would provoke him to try to shake him out of his self-assuredness.' When Cameron ended the relation-ship, she was very upset and asked a friend to speak to him on her behalf. The friend remembers he was unshakeable. The relationship was to end. She was also struck by how much he seemed genuinely concerned that Francesca should not feel too hurt.

Generally he is good at keeping up with old girlfriends, but his relationship with Lisa De Savary, a retiring, sweet-natured girl and daughter of the flamboyant property developer Peter De Savary, did not end well. She fell for Cameron in a big way, but, as a friend puts it, 'Dave kind of dumped her and she was very cross about it. It all left rather a nasty taste.' He also went out with Alice Rayman, a student at Wadham, who marked a reversion to type. She became an entertain-ment lawyer and married the son of Tory politician Tom King.

Oxford offered plenty of opportunities for Cameron to play sport. He captained the college tennis team, and played cricket ('badly', says a staff member), also for the college. He also made the occasional (restful) sortie on to the river. One Saturday towards the end of his second year at Oxford, Cameron invited his sister Clare, then aged fifteen, to visit. She was preparing for exams and Dave thought it would be a good opportunity to show her his new surroundings. She brought along a friend, Jade Jagger, daughter of Rolling Stone Mick

Jagger, a fellow pupil at St Mary's, Calne, whose budding beauty did not pass unnoticed among Dave's friends. Dave decided to take his little sister and her friend out in a punt in time-honoured fashion. He asked James Fergusson to join them, and he helped contribute to an idyllically innocent afternoon on the river by taking turns with the punt pole and chatting idly. At tea later in the Christ Church room of James Delingpole, now a journalist, Fergusson played an imperfect version of 'Satisfaction' on the guitar, whereupon Jade piped up proudly, 'My dad wrote that!' The following Monday, Cameron's mother Mary received a call at home. It was Mick Jagger, not pleased. 'What's all this my daughter's been getting up to with your son?' he demanded. 'You know I don't approve of bloodsports.' Mary, dipping lightly into her reserves of breeding and politesse, explained gently that *punt*ing is what one does in a punt, and that his daughter had enjoyed an entirely peaceful afternoon *punt*ing on the river. Cameron, who adores retelling the story, later muttered a little impatiently that 'it shows how much these people have to learn'.

Having spent his second year living in college, with a big, panelled sitting room and tiny, cold bedroom, Cameron's third and final year was spent living at 69 Cowley Road, sharing with Giles Andreae, his friend from earliest times, Sarah Hamilton (a product of St Paul's Girls School, who was studying law) and David Granger, a popular sportsman, now in television. While the pressure was on for the keen student anxious to get a First, Cameron continued to enjoy himself. The house had a laid-back flavour, and benefited from his enthusiastic efforts in the kitchen, often to cook the odd Peasemore pheasant for an informal dinner party. 'He would always be very concerned that you were enjoying yourself, and then if you were he would be full of self-mocking praise for himself,' remembers a friend.

'There was a fair amount of beer and wine about,' says Giles Andreae, 'but it certainly wasn't a house full of ravers.' They would use the local kebab van a good deal, as well as the Hi-Lo, a cheap Jamaican restaurant directly opposite their house patronised by generations of undergraduates. There Cameron, Andreae and their friends would go once or twice a week – sometimes late at night – for goat curries, funky chicken and Red Stripe lager, served up by the Rastafarian chef–owner Hugh Anderson, who is also remembered for his over-proof rum. 'He was a happy, easy-going character, quite pleasant,' remembers Andy, as the Rastafarian is known to everyone. 'He was very modest and very orderly, not a wild guy at all.' So orderly were Cameron and Andreae that Andy would hand over his one-year-old son Daniel to the two undergraduates to look after. The little boy was known, a little distantly perhaps, as 'boy child'. Cameron and Andreae would bounce him on their knees as they watched daytime television when Andy was busy in the kitchen over the road. Cameron, for one, made a point of never missing *Going for Gold*, a programme presented by Henry Kelly, which he may have omitted to mention in some of his subsequent job interviews.

One Lent term, he was chosen, as a guinea pig, to spend five weeks at Stanford University. Friends say it was five of the most enjoyable weeks of his life. He shared a room with two Americans and was required to do pretty well no work. He told an interviewer much later that he won a karaoke contest ('I don't think it's something you want to do in your own country', a view he was to amend subsequently) in Portland, singing Chrissie Hynde and UB40's 'I Got You Babe'. Camilla Cavendish, now a journalist with *The Times*, who followed in his footsteps a year later, says that the Americans had all adored Cameron, not least for his accent. 'I got the impression I was a big let-down after Dave,' she says.

It is said that Cameron is notably loyal to his friends – one says his dependability is the best of his many assets – but in a milieu as privileged as his, where the going was pretty well always good, there might not be a great many opportunities to show it. Yet Giles Andreae was a beneficiary of his – and his parents' – steadfastness. During their last year at Oxford, he was found – after several wrong diagnoses – to have Hodgkin's disease. The delay in the diagnosing of the cancer required him to have intensive chemotherapy, sedatives and steroids, as well as a variety of experimental drugs. For each bout of chemotherapy, he had to undergo a general anaesthetic and was left debilitated and low.

Andreae's survival was a matter of touch and go for some months. To help him recover his strength after the treatment, Cameron would drive his friend to his parents' house at Peasemore in a battered Volvo he owned as a student. 'Dave used to take me down in his car, tuck me up in bed and give me some videos,' says Andreae, who would then stay for two or three days until he was strong enough to go back to Oxford. 'Dave, despite it being the middle of finals, would pop by to say hello, and managed to find some humour in a pretty grim situation. He was a very supportive friend, but it was typical of his family to do that.'

On the night of 11 June 1987 Cameron held a party in his college room to celebrate Margaret Thatcher's third successive election victory. It was a rare political act at university. While future Tory stars like Michael Gove, Boris Johnson, Mark Field, Ed Llewellyn and Ed Vaizey threw themselves into student politics, either at the Oxford Union or in the Oxford University Conservative Association, Cameron stayed on the sidelines, rather as he had at Eton. He would go along to hear a big-name speaker, but he took little part, seemingly sharing John F. Kennedy's view of undergraduate precocity ('show me the student politicians of today and I'll show you the student politicians of tomorrow'). Some took this detachment as disdain. 'If I had to name the most snobbish, elitist and condescending person in my year at Oxford, it would be him by a mile,' said a contemporary with no evident axe to grind. And his non-participation irks some fellow Tories. One contemporary, who remains active in politics, said: 'You might think it a little strange that at the time – the height of

Thatcherism, when just a year before there had been bus-loads of left-wing students going to the miners' strike – he wasn't galvanised.' Cameron, as an implicit, deeply tribal Tory, felt little need to prove he was a Conservative. Another student politician contemporary says that Cameron was 'too cool for school'. Steve Rathbone says he and Cameron shared a distaste for serious political discourse, particularly with opponents. 'The trouble with some of the lefties was not that they were left wing – that was fine – but that they were earnest and humourless. They were too po-faced and didn't know when to park their ideology outside. Dave and I did use to bait them a bit about that.'

That Cameron was not active in student politics is not to say that he did not have a definite view. 'Dave's politics were very much centrist Tory,' says Rathbone. 'He was very mistrustful of the Monday Club types who were always banging on about how Mandela [then still in prison] was a terrorist.' Later Rathbone, as the elected president of Brasenose Junior Common Room (JCR), had to escort John Carlisle of the Monday Club into the college. 'Neither of us had any sympathy with Carlisle's views and I didn't like the guy, but there was a student demo about it, with a tangible level of hatred against him, spit flying and everything. It was really unpleasant, much worse than the standard sort of student demo. Dave was flat against that sort of thing.'

While David Cameron supported the right of Carlisle to speak – against the opposition of his friend Andrew Feldman – he was at least consistent in his libertarianism. In March 1987 he caused some unhappiness among those who felt he was not pulling his weight ideologically when, during one of his generally passive encounters with the Union, he supported the decision to allow Sinn Fein leader Gerry Adams to speak there. Cameron's view was that he should be allowed to have his say and that his audience should be able to make an informed judgement, in favour or against. He tried this line on his tutor Vernon Bogdanor, who disagreed, saying that Sinn Fein's relationship with the IRA was unhealthily close and that the normal democratic rules should not apply. Having heard Adams speak, Cameron told a friend that he felt 'grubby' about listening to the Northern Irishman, and that Bogdanor had been right.

Academically, Vernon Bogdanor would have been an ideal person to stimulate Cameron's learning. He was among a number of Oxford academics who, disenchanted with what they saw as a damaging leftward move by the Labour Party, had joined the newly formed centrist Social Democratic Party. Bogdanor, who in some ways had helped provide some of the intellectual underpinning of the new party, was ideally placed to challenge his star pupil's assumptions. Further, he preferred to be challenged by his students, so Cameron had every opportunity to fight his corner on, say, the rights and wrongs of the electoral system. Bogdanor has spoken of Cameron's old-fashioned, highly pragmatic approach to politics. While he had leanings towards Euroscepticism, he tended to approach problems on a 'whatever works' basis.

His Economics tutor, Peter Sinclair, remembers: 'Typically when David was debating he would take a more pro-market view than a number of them.' Sinclair would encourage his students to take the pure 'market' position as a point of reference and 'pep it up with very recent, interesting, controversial stuff, typically from American academics, stuff about to be published, or really good working papers, which they would have read, and try to avoid clichés. Don't just come up with slogans, really think. And he was exceptionally good at that.' Again, the Cameron manner seems to have made his message more palatable. 'I can remember some of his interventions,' says Sinclair. 'He'd say, "Hang on, you can't really say that – look at the stats." He'd always put it very nicely. He was rather keener than the others on the logic of what the market would lead to and slightly less concerned with the wrinkles that could justify a different view. He was quite free-thinking and would not tend to take a standard view. His views were on the whole a bit more to the right than most of the others.'

John Foster, his Philosophy don, said he was very clever, but showed little inclination towards being an academic. 'He focused on what was required. He didn't lose sleep over philosophical problems, about the ultimate nature of things, but he was extraordinarily competent.' It is with reference to this philosophically incurious, pragmatist facet of David Cameron's nature that his non-engagement in student politics should be seen.

'The Union was lots of people trying to project themselves into a world of politics where they had to prove themselves rhetorically,' says Francesca Ferguson, 'but he'd never had any trouble with winning an argument. Loads of people at Oxford were redefining themselves but he didn't need to redefine himself. He was part of that whole part of society which is heading for running the country. It's as simple as that. He didn't feel he had anything to prove. Actually maybe he was just a lot more adult than a lot of people at Oxford.'

Coming from a family line of Tories, via Eton, to Oxford did not encourage him to advertise his political colours in formal surroundings. While he was as happy as anyone to thrash out arguments about the role of the state, personal freedoms and so on in small informal groups, he disappointed his more zealous Tory contemporaries by not joining in with the further humiliation of the Labour Party. It could be that attitudes at Brasenose compounded the numbing of his political ambition at that time. 'People would just sit around and drink coffee, chatting and just loving it, and that was their life,' says Peter Sinclair. 'It was a contented, cheerful, unstressed place. When he arrived, people in the year above would have said, "Don't bother with the Union, they're horrible hacks, knifing each other, publicity-seeking creeps." That's the line he would have heard from everybody in Brasenose, so he might have thought, "Right, that sounds good advice."'

For some students getting to Oxford is enough, but for Cameron it was a staging post. Some, like Francesca Ferguson, say his privileged background helped him deal with an experience that some can find overwhelming. 'You have to be really attuned to that level of privilege to actually make something of it without having an issue with it or being so overwhelmed that you don't actually achieve,' as Francesca Ferguson puts it. 'David totally took it in his stride. He always knew what he wanted, was hugely disciplined and did a lot of work. He never felt he had to prove anything to anyone except to his professors in his exams.'

By now acquisitive for achievement, he did just that. In the summer of his third year, as predicted by Vernon Bogdanor, he acquired a First. He celebrated by going to the pub with his friend David Granger (who was to learn later that he had got a Third). Years later, he conceded to an interviewer that it may be naff to be proud of your degree, but that he was proud nonetheless. It was vindication of his talents. Now he had to put them to some use.

SMITH SQUARE
Conservative Research Department
1988–1992

David Cameron's political career began with a 'judicious prodding' from the Royal Household. Although he had applied for a number of management consultancy and banking jobs while at Oxford (but before he had taken his Finals), none of these came to fruition. With a first-class degree in PPE, previous experience as a Conservative MP's researcher and impeccable Tory pedigree, he had every chance of success. But evidently it was decided that nothing should be left to chance when, in due course, he was invited to attend interviews at Conservative Central Office (CCO), the party's London headquarters, then in Smith Square, Westminster. Applicants were seen first by the Research Department's deputy director, Alistair Cooke, and then, if judged suitable, by its director, Robin Harris.

Lord Cooke (enoblement came in Cameron's first Honours list as Prime Minister) recalls a curious episode on 15 June 1988, the day Cameron's appointment fell due. 'Shortly before David Cameron's interview, the telephone rang. The voice announced that it was calling from Buckingham Palace. Its tone was distinctly grand. The person on the other end of the line said, "I understand that you are to see David Cameron. I've tried everything I can to dissuade him from wasting his time on politics, but I have failed. I am ringing to tell you that you are about to meet a truly remarkable young man." ' He adds, 'I thought, "Why is this unknown person giving me this unsolicited testimonial?" if that is what it was: there was no attempt to persuade me either way, to take him or not to take him.'

A call like that is bound to lodge in the mind. Indeed Cooke says he dined out on it endlessly, long before Cameron became well known. The story first surfaced publicly shortly after Cameron became leader when Harris was thought by some (erroneously, says Harris) to have suggested that the new Conservative leader owed his first position in politics, in part, to string-pulling. In any event, Cooke disagrees. He says he told Robin Harris about it at the time, and that it had no bearing on the outcome. 'Clearly David was quite outstanding – one of the very best of all the young people I interviewed over the years – and needed no help from anyone to impress the people at Central Office. But that does not alter the fact that what the voice from the Palace told me was absolutely true.'

So who was the mystery caller? It might be fair to assume that it was Captain Sir Alastair Aird, then Comptroller and later equerry to the Queen Mother and husband of Fiona Aird, Cameron's godmother. That, indeed, was David Cameron's own belief when the story first surfaced. But the suggestion is vehemently denied by the Airds. Lady Aird, having repudiated the suggestion, consulted her husband for confirmation and said: 'Alastair has never ever made that sort of call. He was incredibly careful about being thought to have used his position or anything. It could not possibly have been Alastair. They're hugely proscribed from doing anything political. I just know that it could not have been Alastair.'

When this was put to David Cameron's office, they suggested that perhaps the caller had been Sir Brian McGrath, a Peasemore neighbour and friend of Cameron's parents who then worked as private secretary to Prince Philip. But he, too, though named as a referee for the job, denies it. 'It wasn't me,' he says. 'I don't think they even called me, to ask me to vouch for his character and so on. I certainly didn't initiate anything. He's quite capable of standing on his own two feet without any help from me. One thing I'm certain of is that I didn't ring Central Office.' Frustratingly, the phantom string-puller has yet to be unmasked.

Assuming the call wasn't a hoax, the story illustrates, as if that were needed, how well connected Cameron is. But, tantalisingly, it fails to answer the question of how committed he was to going into politics when he left university. The mystery caller had said he was determined to enter politics, despite attempts to persuade him against it, yet in fact he had already applied for other jobs. At what point had this determination struck? Was it when prospective employers failed to detect an aptitude for knuckling down to a City career? He was also interviewed by the *Economist* but was turned down – mercifully, he says, as he is not by nature a journalist. He has said that he applied for CRD when he came across a brochure from the Oxford careers department in his pigeonhole. Some say he simply fell into the Conservative Party because, having applied to all the blue-chip merchant banks and management consultants (William Hague's McKinsey's among them), he had failed to find a job elsewhere.

Robin Harris has no recollection of Cameron's interview but thinks he would have asked him two standard questions. One, 'Why do you think you are a Conservative?' to assess ideological commitment, and the other, 'What do you think of the Medium-Term Financial Strategy?' to apply a little intellectual pressure. Even for those familiar with the rigours of one-to-one tutorials with Oxbridge dons, CRD interviews could be an intimidating experience. But Cameron, despite – rather than because of – the royal intervention, did well enough to be offered a position.

When he first reported for duty at Smith Square on 26 September 1988 he was stepping on to an established fast-track to high political office. The list of former CRD staffers who have gone on to greatness is a long one. When Cameron was there, Michael Portillo was the most recent of its graduates to have made it into the Cabinet. Portillo's biographer, Michael Gove, describes CRD as a 'nursery of Tory talent'.

'The CRD is part of the party machine but subtly superior to the rest of it – in much the same way as the Guards are to the rest of the Army. It is primarily a secretariat to the party when in government, an alternative civil service when in opposition, a supplier of ammunition in elections, and an intelligence-gatherer and disseminator at all times. But its status and influence extends beyond the sum of its functions.'

Cameron joined at a crucial juncture in the history of the Conservative Party. Just eighteen months earlier, Margaret Thatcher had won a third successive election victory – a feat that hadn't been achieved for more than a century – but her power was beginning to ebb away. Michael Heseltine had already dealt the first blow by resigning over the Westland affair in 1986 while Cameron was in his first year at Oxford. Tensions over Europe, the direction of economic policy and the political consequences of the poll tax ground away at Thatcher's waning power base during her third term. With Heseltine a standard around which rebels on the backbenches rallied, Thatcher thought she could at least rely on the total, unswerving loyalty of the Research Department.

Her speech on 20 September 1988 in Bruges, Belgium, setting her face against a European Union 'super state', might have infuriated some parliamentary colleagues. But nowhere would it have been more rapturously received than on the fourth floor of Conservative Central Office, home of the CRD. One of those already there describes a 'hyper right-wing Zeitgeist' infecting the young zealots working under Harris and Cooke. Cameron, says his former colleague, quickly fitted in. He showed few signs of disavowing this Zeitgeist, which entailed Thatcher herself being universally and reverentially referred to in private conversation as 'Mother'.

The young PPE graduate was handed the Trade and Industry, Energy and Privatisation brief, a respectable if rather dry subject area. He shared an office, 512, with another researcher under the direction of Ian Stewart, head of the Economic Section. The office was one of a number arranged down a long corridor with Harris and Cooke at one end; next in superiority was Guy Black, head of the Political Section, and thereafter offices corresponded roughly to the great Whitehall departments. Thus Cameron, aged twenty two, was nominally in charge of Conservative Party research into trade and industry policy.

The formality and hierarchy of the office accommodation reflected the ethos of the CRD, which was run much like a school. A call to see the director or his deputy could be a prelude to a bruising encounter for young men and women more accustomed to being told how clever they were. Set exacting standards, Cameron learned quickly to prepare accurate, succinct papers to order. His facility for writing clear and powerful briefs was honed in CRD, although one of his managers said he showed natural ability from the start. But while the department's professionalism would stand him in excellent stead, what was really invaluable were his new colleagues.

It is a remarkable feature of the backroom staff and kitchen cabinet that have surrounded Cameron since he won the leadership that so many worked with him at CRD in the run up to the 1992 election or shortly afterwards. Just as in the private sphere, where his circle of friends has not greatly widened from those that he made at Eton, so politically he has fashioned a Praetorian guard from early allies and friends. His stint in Smith Square holds many keys to his choices a decade and a half later.

This 'gathering of the gang' is worthy of some scrutiny. The first important contact Cameron made was another Old Etonian graduate of Oxford. Ed Llewellyn, a year older, had been a distant figure at both school and university (where he, unlike the current Tory leader, was active in student politics). Even now that they were colleagues – Llewellyn was handed the tricky European Community brief – his relative seniority put him, initially at least, above the new arrival's station.

The next to arrive was another Oxford graduate named Ed with a reputation as a hack. The name Ed Vaizey had become a fixture in *Cherwell* during his time at Oxford as the student newspaper detailed the exuberant antics of the right-wing son of Lord Vaizey, the eminent economist ennobled by Harold Wilson in his infamous 'lavender list' of 1976 (allegedly for advising Marcia Falkender on her sons' education), and Marina Vaizey, the art critic. Both Vaizey and Llewellyn had already done some voluntary work for the CRD before going up to Oxford and so had an 'in' with Cooke and Harris that Cameron did not. But on arrival at CRD in early 1989 Vaizey found himself junior to Cameron just as Cameron was junior to Llewellyn by dint of length of service. Not himself the retiring sort, the young Vaizey was immediately struck by how at ease Cameron already appeared around even very senior politicians.

Although Vaizey was to become a friend and ally, the next two figures on the scene are the most important for Cameron's political development. In ideological terms – as well as in any other – Rachel Whetstone is a thoroughbred. Her grandfather was Sir Antony Fisher, an Eton-educated former RAF officer who made millions from the introduction of intensive chicken farming to Britain from the US and used part of the proceeds to fund right-wing think-tanks. Organisations like the Institute of Economic Affairs, which he founded and chaired, helped inject the ideas of Frederick Hayek and Milton Friedman into the political mainstream across the world. Sir Antony died just before his granddaughter started working at CRD but his daughter, Rachel's mother Linda Whetstone, remains an influential figure on the libertarian right. Rachel's father, Francis Whetstone, is a Conservative councillor in East Sussex. Their daughter was raised in the couple's manor house near Wealden, and was edu-cated first at Benenden and then at Bristol University. Socially, as well as politically, Cameron and Whetstone were cut from the same cloth and it was not surprising that the two became friends soon after she joined the CRD in early 1989.

A far more unlikely addition to the set arrived three months later. Small, cocky, shaven-headed and foreign-born, Steve Hilton blew through the doors of the Conservative Party on the back of a hurricane. The young undergraduate was processing claims from the Great Storm in early 1988 in a Brighton insurance firm. It was tedious work for an intelligent man and he happened to see a party political broadcast in which Peter Brooke, then Tory Party chairman, invited any viewers who wanted to help the Conservative Party to dial 01 222 9000. He dialled the number and some months later found himself working as a volunteer in the CRD's library – an early and personal lesson, perhaps, in the power of political advertising.

Something about Hilton impressed Harris that summer. Perhaps he was taken with the fact that he had made a conscious choice to join the Tories, rather than being born into the party. Hilton's mother and father had moved from Hungary to Britain in the mid-1960s not, as has been reported, to flee the Soviet repression of 1956 but to further their education. Nor did the surname come from the first hotel they stayed in on arrival: Hilton thinks his father chose it because it was a close approximation of his real name, Hircsak. His parents' relationship did not withstand the move and his father moved back to his homeland. At the age of twelve, upset that letters to his father were no longer being answered, Hilton set out to visit him during a holiday to see his mother's family in Hungary. Having caught the train to Budapest alone, he went to his father's last known address and discovered the sad truth. His father had died, and nobody had told him. Hilton's upbringing in Brighton was modest – his stepfather, also Hungarian, was a builder and his mother a former student – but he won first a scholarship to Christ's Hospital School and then a place at New College, Oxford to study PPE. (He and Cameron did not meet at university.) His Labour friends say it is his family experience of, and subsequent hatred for, communism that informs his politics, rather than any instinctive love of the Conservative Party. 'Were it not for what the Soviets did to his parents, Steve would be one of us,' claims a member of Tony Blair's inner circle. Unfortunately for Labour, however, Harris offered the young Hilton a job at CRD.

Other members of Cameron's current inner circle to have worked at CRD include Catherine Fall, his gate-keeper, Peter Campbell, who helps him prepare for Prime Minister's Questions, George Bridges, his former political director, and George Osborne, his shadow Chancellor. The latter two arrived after Cameron had left and are not members of his original 'gang'.

While long-term prospects at CRD may have been good, short-term finances were poor. Cameron's pay would have been between £10,000 and £12,000 a year when he started and probably not much more when he left after the election of April 1992. The contrast with the incomes of friends who had gleefully signed on with big City firms could hardly have been greater. After university he shared a flat with Pete Czernin, his friend from Eton. The address, 46 Harrington Gardens, was in South Kensington, a red-brick block of the sort favoured by foreign City employees on secondment to London. It was a pad for bachelors of the most eligible sort. As the only son of Mary Czernin, matriarch of the Howard de Walden dynasty, Cameron's former flatmate can expect a sizeable portion of his family's £1.5 billion fortune. Czernin, now a film producer, has said suggestions that affluence bought excess are wide of the mark, however. 'You're never going to get Dave in a Six-in-a-Bed Supermodel Drug Orgy. Sorry, that's just not Dave.' Indeed a guest at a poker party attended by Cameron at around this time remembers him being the only guest to refuse a cannabis joint passed around the card table. His ostentatious refusal was, even then, marked down to political ambition.

What Cameron really enjoyed was a good argument. He had liked 'sounding off' in Oxford, and now, in London and working for the governing party, he was mixing with people even better qualified to match him in debate. He would hone his rhetorical skills in social settings. Several of his friends testify to how much he enjoyed jousting across a dinner table, and sometimes with a degree of antagonism and competitiveness that suggests he was practising with a higher forum in mind. 'He is infuriating to argue with,' says his friend James Fergusson, a regular late-night sparring partner. 'It's extremely stimulating, but you never win. I know every trick of his. He'll change the subject. He'll overwhelm you with statistics. If that doesn't work, he'll make a joke or play to the gallery. If he's losing he'll never let it remain as one on one, he'll get other people to giggle on the sidelines. That's the way it works. It's infuriating but it's a very effective political trick.'

The budding politician was given a major opportunity to experience life at the campaigning coalface when he was appointed to be the Central Office researcher to Michael Keegan, the Tory candidate in a by-election in the Labour-held seat of Vauxhall, just across the river from Westminster. The seat, though conveniently close to home geographically, was in the borough of Lambeth, home of the 'Loony Leftism' and factional strife among progressive forces. It was scarcely winnable for the Tories, but the new man from Central Office was anxious to make his mark. While, ten years into the Thatcher administration, there were some easy targets for extremism-bashing (mooted black sections, Militant at large), it was anything but restful. The local Tory party office on Kennington Road had a lit (but easily extinguished) petrol bomb put through its front door, and Keegan was the subject of a death threat and police protection.

Cameron's role was to brief Keegan, then a Lambeth councillor with the young John Bercow, of what had been in the press, 'lines to take' and warn him of upcoming hazards, a job Keegan says he did with customary polish. They would meet at 7.00 a.m. every day and prepare for a 9.30 press conference, then spend the morning together before Cameron disappeared shortly before lunch, presumably back to Central Office. 'What I very quickly learnt was that he was very professional, very considered and meticulous in detail. He had a real feel for what to say ... what was the best way of presenting the argument to wrong-foot the local Labour government.'

The young Cameron showed Keegan a self-assurance seeming now to verge on didacticism. 'I remember one expression that he used to prepare me,' said Keegan, 'was he said: "Remember that the job of the press is to sort of prise you apart from the government candidate or from the government minister sitting next to you and then basically toss you around the room like a pack of hounds would some raw meat. So what their job is to separate you out from their party. And kick you out the room. So what you've got to do is show them you're master of the facts and keep to the line that we're taking so they can't do that."'

Despite the mayhem around him, Cameron showed a belief in retaining the moral high ground. One veteran of the by-election recollects a 'jolly brave' Mr Cameron reprimanding a far more senior Tory for blurting out racist jokes as they drove through Lambeth. 'You can't say that,' Mr Cameron had shot back.

The count was marked by a degree of violence and ill will, although Michael Keegan says he doesn't remember Cameron being there. The Conservatives were never going to unseat Labour's Kate Hoey, but came a respectable second and were felt to have fought an honourable and smooth campaign.

He was conscientious at work. Even when it came to Central Office's drinking culture, Cameron was not one of those who would take boozy lunches or, as one or two did, drink wine at their desks. 'He was clearly very ambitious,' recalls a former colleague who joined the CRD some time after Cameron. 'We all worked hard, but David would really burn the midnight oil.' It was not long before this serious, good-looking, intelligent man started attracting admiring glances. 'He was very young, boyish looks, clearly very bright,' recalls Angie Bray, then the Tories' head of broadcasting and now a Tory MP.

Caroline Muir, a secretary at the time, remembers: 'He seemed to be the only human being in the Research Department and he had superb manners.' Another former Smith Square secretary says: 'All the girls fancied him – he talked to people. He was always bobbing in and out of his office, willing to pitch in.'

One colleague who took a shine to him was Laura Adshead, whom Cameron had known slightly at Oxford. In common with a number of Cameron's former girlfriends or close female friends, she is from a diplomatic family. She had been educated at Cheltenham Ladies' College and Christ Church, Oxford before arriving at CCO around the same time as Cameron. The romance began in the spring of 1990 and lasted until summer 1991, although it does not seem to have ended very tidily. 'I seem to recall the young lady had to be given a period of compassionate leave to recover,' says one of the couple's managers at the time. (After her relationship with Cameron, Adshead, a close friend of Whetstone, dated the historian Andrew Roberts. Later she moved to New York, where she underwent a spell as a nun, tending goats and immersing herself in Catholicism, the faith of her birth. She subsequently became a management consultant before returning to London.)

When he had been in Smith Square for several months, an outstanding opportunity presented itself, but one which in later life he may have come to regret. How would Cameron like an all-expenses-paid eight-day trip to South Africa taking in the sights of Durban, Cape Town and Johannesburg? Perhaps with happy memories of his holiday to Kenya, in mind the young adviser, rising fast through the ranks at CRD, said he would like it very much. But South Africa, unlike Kenya, was still under the control of an apartheid regime, pursuing overtly racist policies in defiance of international opinion. At the time Cameron was climbing the ladder in Smith Square, Nelson Mandela had been imprisoned for more than a quarter of a century, and a worldwide campaign (opposed by Margaret Thatcher) to impose economic sanctions on South Africa had become bitterly controversial.

Nonetheless, the trip had been offered to him by his Research Department boss Alistair Cooke and it seemed too good an opportunity to turn down. The fact that Cameron's godfather, Tim Rathbone, was a passionate opponent of the apartheid regime but was himself opposed to sanctions may also have played a role in sweeping away any qualms Cameron might have had. The trip had been offered to the Research Department by Derek Laud, who fifteen years later was to become known to a wider public as a contestant on *Big Brother*. But in 1989 he was best known as a fixture on the scene of the Tory far right. That he was both black and gay made him unusual enough, that he was an enthusiastic member of the Monday Club, the anti-immigration group, and liked to ride to hounds ensured that few in Conservative politics were unaware of this flamboyant libertarian.

Laud had started in politics as a research assistant to Michael Brown, at the time the Tory MP for Scunthorpe. Through Brown, Laud had met Cameron's future father-in-law Sir Reggie Sheffield, a grandee of his local party, with whom he became friends. Other contacts included Michael Colvin and Neil Hamilton, two Tory MPs who were later to become embroiled in the cash-for-questions scandal, partly through their association with Laud. Laud was working as a lobbyist and was employed by Strategy Network International, which had been set up in 1985 specifically to lobby against the imposition of sanctions on South Africa and as a propagandist for Unita, the Angolan opposition group, and for the so-called 'transitional government' of Namibia set up in defiance of a UN resolution. Rival lobbyists accused SNI of being controlled by Pretoria. Laud recommended Colvin and Hamilton, who were both recruited as consultants – something they failed to enter properly in the House of Commons register of members' interests, which came back to haunt them when the cash-for-questions scandal broke in 1994.

According to a contemporary report, one of Colvin's jobs was:

to identify sympathetic MPs who might be interested in what came to be called the 'Bop run' – trips, generally all expenses paid, for hand-picked Tory MPs to the unrecognised Bophuthatswana 'homeland', one of the dumping grounds for the three million black people evicted from their homes in the former South African government's 'whitening the cities' offensive … Appearing before the Select Committee on Members' Interests in 1989, Ian Findlay, who ran Bophuthatswana's London office, was asked: 'Are you satisfied that your government is getting good value for money from visits by British MPs?' He replied: 'Yes, very much so.'

There is no suggestion that the trips were not declared in the register, but allegations of a 'gravy train', paid for by the apartheid regime, abounded. To the annoyance of the homeland authorities, the form would sometimes be a one-day stop in Bophuthatswana before MPs escaped to a beach holiday in Natal or Cape Town. The usual practice was to offer first-class travel, with the alternative of cashing in a single ticket for two club class seats, enabling MPs to take spouses. A number chose the second option.

Findlay's full evidence to the committee provides an illustration of the sort of largesse pro-apartheid groups were prepared to dish out to sympathetic Tories. Trips, sometimes led by Colvin himself, would typically last ten days and cost SNI around £2,000 a head in flights, hotels and meals for the fact-finding Tories and their wives, he said.

But it wasn't just MPs who attracted the attention of the pro-apartheid lobbyists. Laud, who also picked likely targets on behalf of SNI's clients (they included big mining concerns and other multi-nationals like Anglo American, Bear Stearns and the South African Chamber of Mines), was delighted to be able to accommodate one of the Tory Party's bright young things. He invited Cameron to South Africa to 'see for himself' what effect sanctions would be likely to have on those who were employed in the mines and elsewhere. That the imports of cheap South African coal had helped the Thatcher administration win the miners' strike would have been an additional attraction for Cameron, who had worked in the CRD's economic section before being promoted. Alistair Cooke decided that Cameron was a suitable recipient of what he looks back on as 'simply a jolly'. 'It was all terribly relaxed, just a little treat, a perk of the job,' says Cooke. 'The Botha regime was attempting to make itself look less horrible, but I don't regard it as having been of the faintest political consequence.'

A senior bureaucrat recalls that the civil service advice about such trips was 'not to touch them with a barge-pole'. It was also felt inadvisable for special advisers, who were unconstrained by the demands of political neutrality, to accept such deals. But David Cameron, neither a civil servant nor a special adviser, evidently saw no reason to look this gift-horse in the mouth, and spent eight days with Derek Laud, being treated lavishly, visiting mines and factories in Durban, Johannesburg and Cape Town. Perhaps inevitably, the prospect of Laud and Cameron spending a week travelling together (a third person was supposed to have gone on the trip with them, but dropped out at the last minute) provoked a degree of tittering in Central Office. Someone remarked that if, after a trip down a mine, Laud suggested having a shower, Cameron was not obliged to accept.

Nelson Mandela was released from prison in February 1990 and was later president for five years, honoured all over the world for his championing of reconciliation. David Cameron visited South Africa for the first time as Tory leader in August 2006 in order to meet him. Amid a great fanfare, he announced a major break with Margaret Thatcher's foreign policy, while keeping noticeably quiet about his own. He advertised himself as being on the side of Mandela and said: 'The mistakes my party made in the past with respect to relations with the ANC [African National Congress] and sanctions on South Africa make it all the more important to listen now.' Such talk cannot but be seen, at the very least, as an insurance policy against his earlier visit becoming public knowledge.

Cameron was only in his early twenties when he made the trip. He may defend it now as fact-finding, but it was hardly the act of a vigorous and typical anti-apartheid campaigner. Nor does the list of fellow Tories who made the trip sit well with the new-found liberalism of the modern Conservatives. As Lord Hughes of Woodside, then a central player in the anti-apartheid movement, says, 'It is almost impossible now to find anyone who wasn't against apartheid; I wish there were as many opposed to it then as say they were now.'

As might be expected given its school-like atmosphere, the Cameron-era CRD seems to have seen its fair share of shifting allegiances, slammed doors and tearful scenes. As he had done before, Cameron thrived on being 'one of the gang'. Among those of his peers he admired and could see were going places, he was charming and fun. Those outside the circle did not often see his best side. Some thought him bumptious, others bullying. 'He had personality, intelligence, ambition and good judgement, but he could be a little sharp-tempered and wasn't charitably disposed to people who thought differently from him.' Another colleague was more vehement: 'He saw it as a way of making himself look good to make other people look stupid. He was a bombastic bully dismissive of those who didn't agree with him.'

Rupert Morris, author of a book about the Tories, says Cameron 'had a certain golden-boy aura about him. He was sleek and tanned, wore an expensive suit, and his eyes moved impatiently – as if he was unlikely to waste time chatting to anyone unimportant.' Perhaps as a result of the fall-out from his affair with Adshead, Cameron thereafter dated women outside politics. Bray remembers him arriving at the party's social functions with 'various young lovelies' unknown to the Smith Square set. She recalls Cameron emerging as the pre-eminent figure of their group at this time. A senior figure describes Whetstone as being 'taut and nervy', Hilton as an 'oddball' (he used to wear a voluminous poncho to work) and Vaizey as 'idle'. They were all outshone by the self-assured, cool, intelligent and hard-working Cameron.

Michael McCrum, a former headmaster of Eton, has said that Etonians have 'the priceless art of putting adults at their ease'. But Cameron had something else. Guy Black, director of the CRD's most important arm, the Political Section, saw in him not only intelligence but a rare political ability – an instinctive feel for opponents' weak spots and a ruthlessness in exploiting them. Black liked his tactical nous as well as his arrogance. He had quickly moved Cameron out of CRD's Economic Section to work under him at the Political Section. When, in 1989, Black left to become a special adviser to John Wakeham, the then Energy Secretary, he recommended that Cameron become his successor as its director. Cameron was to have his hands full. A widespread perception that the Thatcher government was 'out of touch', open Cabinet warfare over Europe and spiralling interest rates were putting the Prime Minister under real pressure. She had won three elections, had defeated the most powerful unions including the National Union of Mineworkers and had opened up much of the state sector to market forces, but she had made a grave political mistake in introducing the poll tax. The magnitude of that error was brought violently home on 31 March 1990 when a protest by 200,000 people in Trafalgar Square turned into a riot. Electoral defeat for the Tories at the next general election looked a near certainty after a disastrous showing in local polls shortly afterwards.

At a launch party for a book about the Research Department in 1989, Cameron revealed while working there he had conducted espionage on Labour extremism, adopting a pseudonym of Robin North to join Militant tendency and Red Wedge. The news aroused some media interest, but few who were with him recall any subterfuge, and those who do say it was limited to acquiring a false name in order to enlist with other parties and receive their literature.

In early 1990, soon after becoming head of the Political Section, Cameron was invited to a secret conference of the party's top strategists at Hever Castle, in Kent, to discuss the worsening political climate. There, Cameron became much better acquainted with Andrew Lansley, who was the new director of CRD. Lansley had been a civil servant before entering politics via the British Board of Commerce. But as Norman Tebbit's private secretary he had proved himself perfectly in tune with his master's ideology and, when Harris went to Number 10, Lansley was recommended to succeed him.

Lansley was not impressed by what he found on his first day. 'The Research Department had been gathered together,' he remembers, 'almost entirely men, just one woman. I walked into the room and they all stood up. I felt like I had walked into the officers' mess, it was just bizarre. Clearly this thing worked on a completely different basis.' He set about modernising the outfit and ordered a fundamental shift in strategy: the CRD began to behave as if the Tories were in opposition, rather than in power. By attacking Neil Kinnock, the leader of the Opposition, reasoned Lansley, the Tories would deflect attention from their own difficulties while knocking the gloss off Labour. 'I know history moved on but we moved from 20 [percentage] points behind [in the opinion polls] and by September we were in single figures. We had a really good summer being beastly to Labour. And actually through that summer we established a proposition which was very important in the subsequent year, that even though we were eleven years on from Labour 1979, the public still believed in their negative views of Labour, they did not believe that they had changed,' says Lansley. With Labour nowadays campaigning as if it is in opposition, anxious to prove that its opponents are still extremists, Cameron – as a leading member of Lansley's CRD – can reasonably claim that he helped write the book on how to 'attack from office'.

John Major, then Chancellor of the Exchequer, and Kenneth Baker, who had succeeded Brooke as Conservative Party Chairman, launched the offensive in May 1990 with the Tories in one poll trailing Labour by 15 percentage points. Labour's policies on the economy, trade unions' rights, defence and education, and its plans to replace the poll tax with a 'roof tax', were all to come under attack. With Cameron right at the heart of the new propaganda factory pumping out negative stories on Labour, he appeared more mature than his peers. 'I remember when he became head of the political desk he suddenly grew up a lot. He suddenly seemed older than me. He was grown up. The political desk was right at the edge of the battle,' says Bray. Another colleague recalls Cameron watching television some months earlier when news came in of Nigel Lawson's resignation as Chancellor. 'I remember him just coolly observing, "I think Margaret's done for. I think there will be a stalking horse now" (as there was). David was always more patrician than some of the others. As that remark suggests, he was always a bit detached from the rah-rah stuff.'

Although the summer offensive demonstrated that voters were still suspicious of Labour, it could do little to stop the festering rebellion among Tory MPs, an increasing number of whom were determined to rid themselves of their leader. Change was in the air and Heseltine, the dashing 'king over the water' who had garnered credit with every government difficulty, was the pundits' bet to succeed Thatcher at Number 10. Here it seems Cameron may himself have played a dangerous game. For although the CRD was generally regarded as an ultra-loyal Thatcherite outpost, he was not above pushing Heseltine's cause on occasion. Bray recalls that when she was stuck for a front-bencher to put up for BBC1's *Question Time*, the head of the Political Section casually suggested she ask Heseltine to step in. 'I said, "Well I'm sure they [*Question Time*] would love it but officially we're not supposed to be fielding Michael Heseltine." But Dave said Michael did these things very well. Funnily enough Dave was always a great fan.'

Bray said that she was impressed that Cameron was 'thinking outside the box'.

His defiance of orthodoxy was less favourably received in an embattled Number 10 where his insouciant recommendation of 'Tarzan' marked him out – to some at least – as a Heseltine supporter. It seemed that he had borne out a suspicion harboured among some of Thatcher's most loyal aides that he was not 'one of us'. Such apparent disloyalty could have cost the aspiring politician dear had the events of November 1990 fallen differently. Shortly after 9.30 a.m. on 22 November a messenger wordlessly placed a piece of paper on every desk in the CRD. On it was the Press Association 'snap' report that Margaret Thatcher had told the Cabinet she was resigning. Cameron watched the unfolding drama of her departure from the press office. Lansley sent a message of condolence from the Research Department (and remarkably received a handwritten note in reply that afternoon).

Cameron has said that he was 'very sad' that day. But what are we to make of his relations with the Tories' greatest leader since Winston Churchill? Their meetings have been fleeting and mostly embarrassing. His first encounter with her was at Central Office and might have ended his political career. 'I was the Trade researcher and she asked me what the trade deficit was. I didn't know,' he said. On the second occasion, at a lunch, she commiserated with him for the fact that Labour had stolen Tory language, but said that they would never understand the importance of individual liberty under the law. 'It's an old tune but a good one,' Cameron wrote later. So that Lady Thatcher could give some sort of benediction to young Cameron after he became leader, a 'casual' meeting at a party was arranged between the two in early 2006. Cameron, dressed in a jacket and crisp white open-necked shirt, was duly brought before Baroness Thatcher, by now in her eighties and no longer at her physical and mental peak. The young man displayed appropriate deference and thoughtfulness, impressing the elderly former PM and prompting her to inquire for which seat this youthful political aspirant was hoping to stand at the next election. Lady Thatcher, when gently informed of her mistake, is said to have remarked that she could not believe that anyone not wearing a tie could possibly be a Conservative leader. Cameron's office lost little time in briefing a rather more positive version of the meeting. Lady Thatcher, his press officer said, had told the new leader to make sure he got enough sleep.

Although it may appear trivial, Cameron's relations with Thatcher go to the heart of the dilemma he faces in positioning at the political centre of a modernised party. He recognises that for many former Tory voters she represents almost all that they grew to dislike about the Conservatives. Yet he was, as university friends confirm, a dyed-in-the-wool Thatcherite himself, and his own parents, especially his father, idolised her. He dare not disown her completely for fear of enraging those that remain her admirers. Her good opinion – and that of those who speak for her – still matters more than Cameron and his supporters like to admit.

Michael Keegan recalls little ambiguity at the time. 'Without a shadow of a doubt he was a convinced Thatcherite then,' he says. 'To be honest with you, we all were. Anyone who was young, Tory and wanted a political career was; she was our leader. He never in any way struck me as being anything else. In those days, the divide was between 'wets' and 'dries', that was how the Conservative Party used to speak about itself. He was absolutely one of the dries. I'm sure, because I was. I connected with him, not on a friendship level, but on a political level, we were on the same wavelength. He didn't come across as a Michael Heseltine or anyone else from the left wing of the Tory party. There was no way he was on that side of the political fence. He was a Thatcherite, pure and simple. Or that's how he came across to me. All I can say is that on the Vauxhall by-election, he presented himself as on-message.'

In the winter of 1990 it was her successor John Major's good opinion that mattered most, however. Just as it was important to make a good impression on the new regime, Cameron earned his first press notice – for an embarrassing blunder that earned a rebuke from the Speaker himself. In truth the matter was a minor administrative cock-up. Cameron had gone to sit in on a Commons debate on Labour policy one day in January 1991. But instead of taking his place in the seats set aside for party officials in an upper gallery, he had sat in the chamber itself in a box reserved for civil servants. Labour members, spotting the error, let out a howl of indignation and wrote to the then Speaker alleging a 'potential breach of security' and demanding that he investigate. A short article in the *Guardian*, Cameron's first mention in a national newspaper, records that Speaker Weatherill said: 'I have received a letter of apology from the Chancellor of the Duchy [of Lancaster, Chris Patten's job-title in the Cabinet], who accepts personal responsibility that an official of the Conservative party was on the list for the civil servants' box and was admitted to that box.' There was no breach of security and the matter was closed.

At first Major left the CRD as it was. It had proved itself effective over the summer. But Cameron must have felt a little vulnerable when Kenneth Baker – with whom he got on very well – was moved to make way for a new party Chairman, Chris Patten. Patten liked Cameron well enough, however. He certainly shared his and Lansley's analysis that Labour was weak on the issue of trust. It had already been decided as early as the summer of 1990 (nearly two years before the poll as it turned out) that the next election would be fought on the proposition that, if the voters were asked whether they could really place their faith in Labour, sufficient numbers would balk to allow the Tories back in. But when to put it to the test? When should a new PM go to the polls? Immediately on succession, riding a wave of goodwill in order to secure his own mandate? Or after a steadying period of calm in which the new premier has demonstrated his fitness for office?

Unsurprisingly Major wanted both options, long and short, kept open, so Central Office was secretly set to work preparing for the possibility of an election that autumn. For Cameron this meant the daunting task of preparing the official 'campaign guide' – a vast document that laid out every Tory policy in clear and simple language, as well as explaining 'attack lines' against each Labour and Liberal Democrat alternative.

It was at this point that Cameron and Hilton began to forge their working partnership as message-crafters. The Tories had rehired Saatchi & Saatchi as their advertising agency, but Lansley says the admen struggled to understand the nuances of Smith Square's new messages. The solution was to second Hilton to the agency to provide a link that chained the admen to the politicians. Cameron was to be the second such link. Cameron and Hilton worked on the political messages emanating from Smith Square and then communicated them to the Saatchi brothers and their lieutenants, carrying their resulting ideas back to Central Office. The two had also become personally close, spending a summer holiday that year together in Italy, the first of a number of shared vacations in the years to come. It was a process that consolidated Cameron's power, according to his friend Angie Bray. 'Where Dave really came into his own was taking on the whole Labour threat in the build-up to the 1992 election campaign. That was really when Dave was at his most powerful at Central Office.'

And then in early summer the call came from Number 10. Could Mr Cameron please help the Prime Minister prepare for Prime Minister's Questions (PMQs)? This was to be his first close-up insight into how government works. PMQs – then a twice-weekly affair – became the highlights of his working week. Every Tuesday and Thursday the twenty-five-year-old would get up very early to read all the newspapers in Number 10. Also present was a new-intake backbencher, David Davis, who was given the task of distributing to loyal

MPs friendly questions that give the PM some respite from the Question Time onslaught.

At 9 a.m. Cameron (but not Davis) was called up to the room directly beneath the Number 10 flat for the key meeting with Major. Here the Prime Minister would decide which issues he would attack on and which he needed to be prepared to defend. Not only did those meetings educate Cameron about Major's view of the full range of subjects, domestic and international, he also witnessed key decisions being taken – often in anticipation of a Labour attack. After the meeting Cameron would write up Major's 'script' at a little desk reserved for him in the office of Judith Chaplin, Major's political assistant. The young aide was then invited to a second, lunchtime meeting with the Prime Minister where Major would rehearse his lines over tea and sandwiches.

Cameron himself has described this period of his early career in the sort of military metaphor politicians love. 'I spent several months in the 1990s combing the newspapers for opposition party quotes which could be made into bullets for Mr Major to fire at Prime Minister's Questions.' Gratifyingly for Cameron his source material appreciated his efforts in the armaments factory. 'John Major's Commons performances have become sharper of late,' noted the 'Atticus' political diary in the *Sunday Times* on 30 June 1991. 'Major had Neil Kinnock squirming on Thursday when he brandished a dreadful piece of doublespeak from Tony Blair, Labour's employment spokesman, about the impact a minimum wage would have on unemployment. Where did such timely anti-Labour ammunition come from? Step forward David Cameron, of Conservative Central Office, who has been drafted to the prime minister's question time team with evident effect.' Cameron had Major quote from a letter Blair had sent on his position on the minimum wage. 'I have not accepted that the minimum wage will cost jobs. I have simply accepted that the econometric models indicate a potential jobs impact.' Major scored a hit when he shouted across the despatch box that 'those words would make a weasel blush'.

It is Cameron who must blush, but with satisfaction, to read his notices after the passage of more than fifteen years, particularly given the inclusion of Blair in the Cameron-crafted fusillade. In fact so gushing is the prose that those of a cynical cast of mind might wonder whether diarists were puffing Cameron in the hope of some useful information from him at a later date. Certainly the young staffer was already attracting a loyal collection of journalists. It is likely that Bruce Anderson, a journalist and John Major's biographer, had recommended Cameron to the Prime Minister. Anderson had spotted Cameron's potential and had cultivated his friendship.

And the young staffer was not above telling journalistic friends of the many good stories to which he had access. This boastfulness cost him dear when he bumped into another Old Etonian, Dom Loehnis, at a party around this time. Loehnis, then a reporter at the *Sunday Telegraph*, recalls how Cameron told him that he was 'in charge of stories' at Smith Square, disclosing one about a new Tory education policy that he was about to give to the *Independent*. Understandably Loehnis took this information, together with its source, back to his newspaper which promptly scooped its rival, thereby landing Cameron in deep trouble. (Surprisingly, perhaps, the incident heralded the start, rather than the end of a relationship. Loehnis marks from this moment the beginning of their friendship.)

There was more puffing copy later in the summer – this time tipping Cameron for stellar promotion right into Major's kitchen cabinet. *The Times* reported that there was dissatisfaction that Chaplin was spending too much time fighting the seat of Newbury, incidentally a constituency that includes Peasemore. The newspaper quoted 'insiders' saying that she needed help. 'There is increased speculation about the role of David Cameron, head of the political section at Tory Central Office research department, who is credited with improving Major's performance at prime minister's question time. With Chaplin inevitably spending even more time in Newbury as the election draws closer, Cameron is being tipped as the man to watch.' In the event this was to prove the first of a number of false dawns, and those months briefing John Major in 1991 and 1992 for a long time represented the closest he came to working in Downing Street.

David Cameron's two and a half years at the Conservative Research Department equipped him with important political skills, inculcated institutional memory and provided him with his most important political allies. The very high standards set by Cooke and Harris remain a benchmark against which Cameron and Hilton judge the quality of briefing material they are given today. When he succeeded Black as head of the Political Section, Cameron received formal recognition for his tactical nous. His involvement in the 'Summer Heat on Labour' campaign further consolidated his reputation for exploiting opponents' weaknesses. He was considered excellent at preparing Cabinet ministers for media appearances and by 1992 had his own circle of journalistic admirers. In surviving three party chairmen and two leaders, Cameron also showed himself adept at managing internal change. It is likely that he had foreseen the fall of Thatcher and to some extent had prepared for it. Most importantly, however, in Llewellyn, Vaizey, Whetstone and Hilton he had four friends and allies, all of whom were going to play their parts in clearing his way to the top.

GAYFERE STREET
General election campaign 1992

It was well before dawn when David Cameron slipped into Tory headquarters in Smith Square on 3 March 1992. Assembled before him at 5 a.m. were a team of Tory staffers, many wondering why they had been asked to come to work so early that day. Cameron told them that this was a 'dry run' for the election campaign to be announced by John Major the following week. They had about two hours to gut that day's newspapers, monitor every television and radio bulletin and prepare a brief for the Prime Minister on any topic he might face at a press conference at 8.30 a.m. In addition, said Cameron, the staffers were to prepare the launch of a new policy on education, that day's theme. The exercise, to be conducted under conditions of extreme secrecy, would determine whether they – and Cameron himself – could be trusted in the heat of the looming battle.

The morning went well and Cameron was duly handed the critical campaign role of briefing John Major before each morning's press conference. Chris Patten recalls: 'I approved that appointment. It was a job I had at one time done myself. He was intelligent and hard-working.' Others who had held the position include Michael Portillo in 1983 and David Willetts in 1987. Cameron has described his role as a 'pretty hairy job'. By now he was being routinely termed 'high-flying', but his latest job carried a different order of responsibility.

In fact the Conservatives' successful election campaign of 1992 strengthened his self-belief as well as his most important political bond. During the campaign Cameron and Hilton shared lodgings in Gayfere Street, a smart Westminster road leading directly on to Smith Square. The house belonged to Alan Duncan, who had made millions in the oil industry before becoming an MP. It had already served as the campaign headquarters for Major's leadership campaign two years previously. Now it was the 'bunker' to which Cameron and Hilton retired for a few hours' sleep when they could.

It was a frenetic existence, as one of Cameron's colleagues recalls. Maurice Fraser worked in the Foreign Office and moved on the eve of the election to take on a role briefing the Tory leader. 'At 4.30 David and I would get into Central Office and pick out the stories that were likely to come up at that morning's press conference. We'd provide a one-side briefing note with a "line to take" on twenty to thirty subjects. David managed the exercise and did all the domestic issues, I did foreign. His briefing notes and mine would then go to the PM or whoever was doing the presser.' At 7.30 a.m., Cameron briefed Major himself at Central Office, preparing him for the daily press conference, at a meeting that included Tim Collins and Shaun Woodward, two more youthful Tory aides. Once on the road, Major was kept informed about events back at base by Ed Llewellyn, who travelled with him. The youth of Major's backroom staff did not go unnoticed at the time. The press dubbed them the 'brat pack' – noting that Hilton was too young to have voted in a previous election.

To be re-elected the Tories had to discredit the alternative administration being offered by Neil Kinnock. The party knew from the previous campaign, 'Summer Heat on Labour', that sufficient numbers of voters had serious doubts about Labour to give them a chance. Cameron, who had worked on this embryonic campaign, had also helped decide twelve months previously to make 'trust' the key issue. The tactic was clear: run a negative pre-campaign undermining confidence in a future Labour government before playing on Major's reputation for decency during a far more positive 'short' campaign, the period from the formal election announcement to polling day.

The initial battery had to be fast, it had to be slick and it had to be accurate – or at least not provably inaccurate. Above all it had to be capable of adapting to Labour's counter-attacks and the news of the day. 'We were quite literally working late into the evening and we would deliver a text to Saatchis at midnight,' says Andrew Lansley, then Cameron's boss as director of the Conservative Research Department. Waiting for the text at the ad agency was Hilton and his team, who then produced effective, punchy documents overnight. 'They would have printed and bound copies for the press conference at 11a.m.' Cameron's skill then in exploiting Labour's weak spots – CND membership or union influence, for example – reminds Lansley of his remarkable success as Tory leader in finding the 'right' issue. 'What I noticed then that reminds me of David now is how he fashions things that are lucky, things that work. That feeling of balls rolling downhill rather than having to push them up. They worked. There was quite a lot of that in '91 and '92.'

The trump card and the theme of the offensive's launch was tax. If there is one image that captures the essence of the 1992 election campaign it is the 'Labour's tax bombshell' poster. It was the culmination of months of painstaking work by the CRD working with figures like Andrew Tyrie, special adviser to Norman Lamont at the Treasury. Using Labour's own spending commitments and tax proposals, the Tories compiled a worst-case scenario for how much an average family would have to pay in increased tax. Eventually they settled on a global bill for Labour's programme of £35 billion and an individual cost per family of £1,250. Hilton's team illustrated 'Labour's tax bombshell' with the stark outline of a Second World War-era finned bomb, an image that the advertising experts thought would be instantly recognisable.

When it was launched on 6 January 1992 the 'bombshell' poster was one of the most successful in British political history; from then on

Labour's poll rating dipped every time the Tories pressed on the issue of tax. Its success made Labour's decision to launch a 'shadow budget' on the eve of the election all the more of a gift for the Tories. The intention of the event on 17 March had been to reassure: the effect was the opposite. Cameron was part of a small team of backroom staff assembled to comb through John Smith's figures. With him were two future colleagues: Bill Robinson, a special adviser to Norman Lamont, and Patrick Rock, then Patten's adviser, later to work for Michael Howard. As they watched Smith's pre-election 'budget' on Sky TV they could hardly believe their luck. It was supposed to neutralise Tory claims about Labour's spending commitments – instead it gave them boxes of fresh ammunition. 'I just think [it was] the sheer weight of stories and of material – if anything we were grinding Labour down,' says Lansley. Again the Tories were 'turning government into opposition'. 'Labour were having to justify themselves as if they were already in government and of course they couldn't.'

But the Conservative campaign wasn't without its own tensions. On arrival in Number 10 Major had purged Central Office of a number of Thatcher loyalists. It was Major's man – Patten – who had encouraged the promotion of many of the 'brat pack' and now, when the heat was truly on, senior Tories wondered whether they could cope. In particular there were doubts about the Tories' new director of communications Shaun Woodward, a thirty-three-year-old former *That's Life* and *Newsnight* producer brought in by Patten to replace the far more experienced Brendan Bruce. Much of what is now said by Conservatives about Woodward must be seen in the context of his subsequent defection to Labour in 2000. Although Cameron shared in the behind-the-hand mockery of Woodward (he called him 'the nodding prawn') he was on good terms with the new director of communications. But privately Patten was getting cold feet, confiding to a colleague on the eve of the election that he had made a mistake in appointing Woodward. One day in January 1992 he pulled Lansley to one side and said that Woodward was 'not up to it' and asked him and the rest of the Research Department to cover for him. It is not known whether Cameron was aware of these conversations.

Patten's nervousness may have been made worse by the knowledge that he would have to leave Central Office every day to fight his own highly marginal seat in Bath when the 'short' campaign was finally launched. Minding the shop in his absence from around 10 a.m. to 6 p.m. would be John Wakeham, the Energy Secretary, and Richard Ryder, the Chief Whip. The arrangement was fraught with potential conflict, made all the more combustible by the predominance in the lower ranks of very youthful staffers. Lord Wakeham today says that Patten ran Central Office 'more like an Oxford college'. He, by contrast, wasn't minded to be collegiate in the midst of an election campaign and demanded prompt action from the youngsters. When Patten left to travel by helicopter to Bath clutching a portable fax and television, his team came under the command of Wakeham and Ryder. And when he returned in the late evening Cameron and Hilton were waiting to brief him on the day's events and evening broadcast bulletins and to prepare him for the next twenty-four hours. It made for a very long day: 'We are expected to work anything from a twelve- to a twenty-hour day. As the campaign progresses it will probably get worse,' a newspaper quoted one female party worker as saying in mid-March. 'Small wonder that the "brats" have been spotted taking mid-afternoon naps at their desks,' noted the paper.

It was in this pressured, overwrought atmosphere that Cameron made a casual misjudgement, a mistake that had it come to light might have changed the course of the election. If tax was the Tories' trump card, then the health service was supposed to be Labour's, and everyone knew that at some point in the campaign they would play it. That day arrived with the broadcast of a powerful film about a little deaf girl forced by the Tories' NHS cuts to wait for at least six months for a simple operation that would restore her hearing. Journalists attending the screening of Labour's party election broadcast were told that the case study was based on a real person but – for reasons of patient confidentiality – the girl was to remain anonymous. What happened over the next seventy-two hours was to blunt Labour's most potent attack in a welter of claim and counter claim.

First the girl's identity emerged, prompting a row about who had leaked the information to whom. Then the facts of the case were disputed as it became clear that Jennifer Bennett's parents differed sharply over what had caused the delay to her operation. Finally, and most damagingly for Labour, Jennifer's GP, whose letter to her father had been the basis of the whole party political broadcast, recanted and said he should not have blamed a lack of resources for the waiting time. Collectively the media firestorm that raged across three days became known as 'The War of Jennifer's Ear', an obscure pun on the 1739 War of Jenkins' Ear between Britain and Spain.

Cameron's own role in this 'war' has until now remained hidden. But a former colleague in Smith Square has revealed that at the height of the controversy the man who is now Tory leader attempted to edit quotes given by Jennifer's mother and GP to make them more 'helpful' to the Conservative cause. On the morning of 25 March Central Office was under suspicion for leaking Jennifer's name to the press. In fact a junior staffer *had* passed Jennifer's name to the *Daily Express*, albeit without authorisation. Her name had been given to the party in a letter from her grandfather, infuriated by what he saw as political disinformation. Cameron and Patrick Rock knew that that day's afternoon press conference was going to be very difficult, not least because it was due to be hosted by the mild-mannered and donnish William Waldegrave, who knew next to nothing about the fast-moving story. Rock recalls how in the minutes before the conference was about to start, he and Cameron sought to warn the minister about what lay in wait for him. They were too late, however, and watched, unable to help, as journalists peppered Waldegrave with questions he could not answer.

Ten years later Cameron himself described what happened in the immediate aftermath of the press conference: 'I vividly remember being pinned to the wall and screamed at by Alastair Campbell, then political editor of the *Daily Mirror*.' 'Campbell was bawling, "What about the *Express*? What about the *Express*?"'recalls Rock. Before fleeing upstairs the two Tory staffers could only point out that Jennifer's name had also appeared in the *Independent*.

Wakeham was confident that the Tories could get back on the front foot in the row, especially since Labour's version of the case was being disputed by members of the family and by the girl's own GP. 'I took the view that the public was more likely to believe the word of a doctor, so we wanted to get the doctor's story written down, to ensure that the story didn't change. I asked Barney Hayhoe to go down to see him. I thought he was ideal, as a former health minister, and he agreed with the doctor what was said,' recalls Wakeham today. 'The draft [press release] was left lying around in Central Office and David saw it in the outer office. He felt he could improve it, and maybe he would have done. He was very good at that sort of thing.' But the document was an agreed text from an independent witness. Had Cameron's rejigged version been issued as a press release it might well have been disowned by the GP – handing Labour a clear victory in the 'war'.

Wakeham only discovered Cameron working on the document because he entered his office looking for something to drink after a hard day's campaigning. 'The blunt truth is that I walked in looking for a bottle of champagne – I was dying for a drink.' When he saw what Cameron was doing he became furious and laid into him in front of his colleagues, according to a witness. 'He exploded. Just went absolutely mad, attacking Cameron for what he had done.' Although the peer does not deny that he was angry, he exonerates Cameron from wilful deceit. 'He didn't change the quotes from the doctor, he was just reorganising it and moving paragraphs around. He wasn't to know what had been agreed. When it was explained to him, he fully accepted what the position was and what I was saying.' Fellow veterans of the '92 campaign say that the incident marked a distinct downturn in Cameron's stock within Central Office.

Poor opinion polls as March ended made a queasy contrast with the glowing tributes to the brilliance of the Tory young guns that had appeared in a number of newspapers. It wasn't long before the media smelled a backlash. Michael White, writing in the *Guardian*, predicted a 'discreet redistribution of power at Tory HQ, which will tilt authority away from the team of Chris Patten, the party chairman, towards the Thatcherite old guard around John Wakeham'. At the same time Michael Heseltine and Michael Portillo were reported to be insisting that the 'brats' be downgraded.

Suddenly it seemed that, if the Tories were to lose the election, the fall guys would be Woodward, Cameron, Hilton and Collins. By the end of March Cameron was so fed up he told a reporter that he was going to leave politics after the election 'to pursue a career in national journalism'. Cameron had another reason to feel disenchanted with a life in politics. He had hoped that John Major would choose him to be one of two political secretaries – the highest level of adviser in government. It was a characteristically ambitious aspiration for someone with only three years' experience of front-line politics. To Cameron's evident annoyance, Major decided to have just one political secretary, and it wasn't him. Instead he chose Jonathan Hill, whom he had brought in from the private sector to work in the Downing Street policy unit.

Major had once lost his temper with the young, smooth Etonian handing out his lines every morning. Cameron pointed out that Major could expect to get a few hostile questions over a Conservative election broadcast that had accused Labour of 'running down Britain'. When Major demanded to know what he was supposed to say to defend this propaganda, Cameron, for once, was stumped for words –

leading, according to one who was present, to a 'moment of temper loss' by the Prime Minister.

But it seems more likely that Major simply didn't see him as suitable material for Downing Street. The man who briefed him alongside Cameron had a different view. 'It sounds very corny to say this, but I assure you it's not hindsight. I was totally convinced this guy was going to be Conservative Party leader one day,' says Maurice Fraser. 'He had the keen intelligence, clearly the ambition, though I have to say worn lightly. And his social skills – which generally come to people later on – were extraordinarily keenly honed in someone of twenty-five. A lot of people were clever, others were perfectly solid but more pedestrian, but he had judgement – he was political to his fingertips – he always knew what you could say and what you couldn't.' Fraser adds, 'In drafting or advising on the key point to take, it would just trip off his tongue, the right thing to say in a given context. We were already into soundbite culture [and] he was able to recommend lines to take that were politically spot-on and in a very limpid style, but they were the right thing to say in the context. There was a lot of emotional intelligence there.'

Cameron may today profess to have been surprised by the result, but Andrew Lansley claims that at no time during the campaign did he or other senior Smith Square figures seriously believe that the Conservatives would lose. The issues of trust and tax had combined with lethal effect to undermine the Labour challenge – something that was clear to the political professionals with access to full polling data as early as January. But the blunting of Labour's attack on Conservative stewardship of the NHS in the confusion over Jennifer Bennett's grommet, as well as the miscalculated triumphalism of Neil Kinnock's Sheffield rally just a few days before the poll, helped nudge Major over the finishing line a winner.

The majority was just twenty-one seats, but given that the election had been held in the teeth of a serious economic recession it was an impressive victory. The only black spot was the defeat of Chris Patten, who lost his seat in Bath and agreed only with great reluctance to appear in celebration photographs. As the results came in, Cameron and his friends opened the champagne. After several bottles he led a posse of 'brats', including Hilton, across Smith Square to Transport House, the union headquarters used by Labour during the campaign, to chant and jeer at the defeated enemy. Later they headed off to Maurice Saatchi's house for more drunken revels long into the morning.

The following day Cameron could not resist a dig at his internal detractors, telling Andrew Pierce of *The Times*: 'The brat pack hits back.' During the campaign Lansley had forbidden Cameron to talk to the press – but now he was determined to put the record straight. 'Whatever people say about us, we got the campaign right,' he went on. 'Not being battle-hardened veterans, we had to learn to take the flak on the chin. But after the first two weeks we just got our heads down and decided to listen to what we were being told by our workers on the ground rather than the opinion pollsters, and especially newspaper reporters.' Cameron also said that Hilton, no longer an electoral virgin, had phoned him from his polling booth, excitedly telling him, 'I have done it. I have finally voted. They can't write that about me any more.' Presciently Pierce finished his despatch by saying that although the 'young guns' had made enemies among the old guard, they 'could be calling the shots for a long time to come'.

The election of 1992 plays a key part in understanding Cameron's political development. Although his behaviour during the 'War of Jennifer's Ear' reduced him in the eyes of some of his peers (one said he regarded his editing of the doctor's statement as being 'at best cavalier with, at worst contemptuous of, the truth'), Cameron had been tested in the heat of the battle and had emerged victorious. Veterans believed the Tories overhauled Labour because of their greater professionalism and their relentless focus on the issue of tax. The experience of taking part in a victorious campaign set both Cameron and Hilton apart from figures like George Osborne who joined the party after 1992 and whose overwhelming experience as a Conservative aide was one of defeat. This may help explain why it took Cameron and Hilton a little longer than some of their younger colleagues to grasp a key tenet of the early modernisers' message that tax is not always an election-winning bombshell.

11 DOWNING STREET
Treasury 1992–1993

After his office at Tory Party headquarters, David Cameron's suite in the Treasury made a welcome change. On one side of his large antique desk was a conference table set ready for his first meeting, with six chairs for officials. The window offered a commanding view of the Treasury's central courtyard, a hub of power occupied by only the highest echelon of this elite department. Through a side door a secretary was at hand to assist in a room that also housed the safe in which all documents were to be locked overnight, such was their secrecy and importance.

John Major had failed to pick him out to join him in Downing Street before the election victory. Since it was not to be Number 10, Number 11 was the next best thing. Cameron's appointment as Norman Lamont's special adviser had not been entirely straightforward, however. The job is an often fraught hybrid of policy, presentational and political duties. Success depends on the adviser's relationship not just with his boss but with civil servants who are often envious of his influence and – jealous of their own power – quick to assert their formal impartiality. Lamont was initially worried that Cameron was simply too inexperienced to negotiate the perils of the Treasury. His name had been put forward by advisers to Number 10, when the previous incumbent, Warwick Lightfoot, decided to quit after the election. But Lamont told one political ally he believed him 'too young'. The Chancellor may also have been offended by the advice offered by colleagues that he needed to take steps to improve his image. His hurt reply, 'My presentational skills are one of my strengths,' only reaffirmed the general view that the opposite was the case.

In truth, the Chancellor was not in a strong position to resist Number 10 at this time. It was not inconceivable that Major would sack him after the election, and a former aide recalls that the Chancellor was tense the day following the poll. Although an architect of Major's leadership campaign two years earlier, his star had waned with Britain's struggling economy. The UK's membership of the European Exchange Rate Mechanism required high interest rates. But the anti-inflationary discipline it imposed was viewed by many as unduly masochistic. And when the Chancellor was found to have unwittingly let his Notting Hill flat to a prostitute trading as Miss Whiplash he handed satirists an easy target. Lamont was also judged to have blundered badly with premature claims that he could see the 'green shoots' of recovery.

By contrast Cameron's media-handling skills were already getting rave notices among Cabinet ministers briefed by him ahead of appearances on showcase programmes like BBC1's *Question Time*. Having cut his teeth at the Conservative Research Department, by 1992 he was well used to telling senior politicians what line to take on any given subject – as well as plugging the more gaping holes in their knowledge of popular culture. Shaun Woodward recalls that some ministers began asking for Cameron by name when a date with the media loomed. When Lamont met him, though, he was won over. He was to be appointed his special adviser (and Rachel Whetstone was to take over from him as head of the Political Section in CRD). Given what was to occur just six months later, Cameron might have preferred it had he been passed over. If there was one event that a Tory politician would have not wanted to be associated with, it was Black Wednesday, the greatest political catastrophe to have befallen the Tories in modern times.

David Cameron was given security clearance to start work at Number 11 on 14 May 1992. A month before he had been introduced to his colleague, Dr Bill Robinson. Robinson, a respected economist in his own right and Lamont's principal policy adviser, recorded his first impressions in the diary he kept at the time. 'David Cameron is coming from Central Office. He is extraordinarily smooth and able but very young. An Old Etonian of 24 [in fact Cameron was twenty-five]. Fresh faced and extremely cool. Used to briefing ministers – including the PM – for Question Time (in the House of Commons or on TV). Good speech writer. Will be an asset. But how will the officials react to him? He made a bad impression on Brian Fox [an official], who was disappointing, as Brian put it, his expectations on salary.'

Cameron had made a 'bad impression', too, on Lord McAlpine, a former Tory Treasurer and close friend of Lady Thatcher. The grandee had taken grave exception to Cameron's remarks the day after the election victory about the 'brats hitting back'. 'I do not know Mr Cameron and from what I hear of him I have no desire to,' he wrote in the 14 April edition of *Countryweek*. 'It is tempting to put these appalling creatures out of one's mind,' he opined, but added that Cameron's 'obvious arrogance' required investigation. 'There must be an inquest and the activities of these young men put under the closest scrutiny.'

Fresh-faced and feeling underpaid – and no doubt a little exposed – Cameron was also sandwiched between two powerful neighbours. To one side was Alan Budd, the government's Chief Economic Adviser and right-hand man to Terry Burns, the mighty Permanent Secretary. And on his left was Andrew Turnbull, then head of public expenditure, later to become Tony Blair's Cabinet Secretary, the head of the civil service. Down the corridor was Jeremy Heywood, Lamont's private secretary, who was – in time – to do the same job for Tony Blair and later as Chief of Staff in Gordon Brown's Number 10. It was an intellectually stimulating environment, and he was encouraged to play a full part.

Michael Portillo had been appointed Lamont's new Chief Secretary (an appointment also imposed on the Chancellor by Number 10) and soon took to hosting special private seminars addressed by leading lights in the fields of arts and science. Only the Treasury's finest would be invited to these events – and that included David Cameron.

On 28 May Portillo invited Cameron to lunch at Le Gavroche, a Michelin-starred restaurant in London's Mayfair, and asked him – with Robinson – to contribute to a pamphlet on *The Economics of John Smith*. Also at the lunch was Frank Sharratt, who had helped secure a job for Portillo at Kerr McGee, an oil firm. This had been Portillo's experience of the 'real world' between being a special adviser and becoming an MP. Sharratt has been described by Portillo's biographer Michael Gove as 'a bloody-red-beef Tory' of 'robust views'. Sharratt, Portillo and Cameron were to dine together on at least two further occasions that year.

Portillo was impressed with this new special adviser. 'He had a bright, highly confident manner. From the earliest he had this really extraordinary appreciation of politics and ability to find exactly the right phrase. Very self-confident well beyond his years: he had a manner that made that self-confidence acceptable – most people don't,' recalls the former Cabinet minister. But, says Portillo, not everyone was so enamoured of the Old Etonian. 'I have heard that he is not, sometimes, as nice in private as you might think, which is also something that you hear about Blair. It was said by people beneath him. Sometimes when I sang his praises to people below him they would say he's not as nice as he seems. I heard that three or four times. Not that I think that it is a bad thing to be authoritative, tough, maybe even a bit abrupt.'

Despite his nerveless self-assurance and occasional arrogance, there was, recall colleagues of that time, something winning about the way Cameron obviously enjoyed his life. They recount how he would return from a weekend full of the joys of an Oxfordshire shooting party. Heavier than today's cycle-toned version, the young Cameron smoked heavily and enjoyed eating and drinking well. His dress sense did little to challenge any stereotypes: by the late 1980s, he had developed a taste for bright red braces.

In 1992 he bought a one-bedroom flat at 26 Lansdowne Crescent in Notting Hill, for £130,000. The flat was small but not so small that he could not take his turn at hosting the Sunday-evening bridge school initiated by Dom Loehnis. Loehnis had started the card school as a ruse to get his friends to share at least one night of the unsociably postponed weekends that are the lot of the Sunday-newspaper journalist. In time, however, Cameron persuaded his friend to leave the *Sunday Telegraph* and take a job as Peter Brooke's special adviser in the Department for National Heritage. The pair would travel to work together in Cameron's battered white BMW, Loehnis travelling to the world of art galleries and libraries, Cameron to the rather higher politics of the Treasury.

Cameron's new boss liked him well enough and respected his evident intelligence. Lamont says today that although Cameron's job was primarily 'political and presentational', he had an open invitation to attend any policy meetings he wished to. 'David's responsibility ... was primarily to do with Parliament and writing speeches. But he was also very bright – I always said that he could go to any meetings he wanted to and that if he had something to say he should say it.'

Now that he was no longer dating Laura Adshead, other eligible Tory women moved in and out of the frame. Petronella Wyatt, daughter of the Lamonts' close friend Woodrow Wyatt, a newspaper columnist, found herself sitting next to Cameron at a succession of dinner parties, at least once because Rosemary Lamont, who thought the two well matched, had so arranged it. Wyatt herself has described a close encounter at the Chancellor's fiftieth birthday party in Number 11. On accepting his proposal to dance she says she was amazed when Cameron 'touched the floor with the grace of Astaire and the manliness of Gene Kelly'. On the same night he squired Carla Powell around the floor with such practised ease that his colleague Bill Robinson mistook the wife of Charles Powell, who had been Margaret Thatcher's private secretary and continued in that role under Major, for Cameron's girlfriend. Robinson's mistake was a compliment both to him and to a woman who was at least two decades his senior.

Barely five months after Major's unexpected election victory the Tories' reputation for economic competence (and with it any realistic expectations of electoral survival) was destroyed in a single day. Like the 'winter of discontent' of 1978–9, 'Black Wednesday' is a term that resonated for more than a decade after the events themselves. Labour politicians still think it worth while to remind voters that Cameron was an adviser at the Treasury the day it was broken by rampant currency speculation. But what was Cameron's role in the disaster? And what did he, privately, think of the policy he worked so hard to defend? Some have tried to turn his association with it to his advantage. Lamont will have none of this: 'I once read ... that this showed he had great grace under pressure and courage under fire but basically he had nothing to do with it.' And yet Cameron *did* have something to do with Black Wednesday even if he was absent from and largely ignorant of the key meetings on the day.

Major, as Margaret Thatcher's last Chancellor, had taken Britain into the ERM in late 1990. He had been convinced – and had convinced her – that it was the only way to cure Britain of high inflation. It was Lamont who had to bear the consequences of the policy when he succeeded Major at the Treasury. Recession, negative equity, failing businesses, house repossessions – bad news spewed out in the official figures quarter after quarter. The straitjacket of the ERM, which pinned the pound within a range of other European currency values, meant that the Treasury could not cut interest rates to stimulate the economy as previous Chancellors had done during downturns. The newly appointed shadow Chancellor, Gordon Brown, was among the enthusiastic supporters of the anti-inflationary effects of the ERM. But Tory backbenchers were growing increasingly voluble about the political consequences of such anti-inflationary zeal. There was an ideological, as well as practical, dimension to the grumbling. The ERM was the vanguard for the single currency and as such a tangible expression of the 'ever closer political union' envisaged by European federalists.

In his memoirs, *In Office*, Lamont says he spoke of his own scepticism to his 'political advisers'. Today he draws a distinction between his view that Britain should suspend its membership of the ERM with more general doubts over how the European Union was developing. The first he says he shared only with his most senior civil servant and the Prime Minister as the crisis approached. In respect of the latter, however, he concedes that Cameron was a 'confidant'. 'It was very important that I maintained the credibility of the policy. I am certain that I never told David [that I wanted to suspend membership of the ERM] because it was too sensitive to tell anybody. Where David very much was a confidant was about the European Union and Maastricht and my unhappiness about the negotiations that we were conducting.' Lamont says he believes that his aide shared his views on the European Union, which the two 'debated endlessly'. In his Euroscepticism, at least, Cameron has always been a loyal Thatcherite. One Treasury colleague of Cameron's says: 'He was a twenty-five-year old natural Tory who had come to help the Conservatives – but to help the Tory Party that Margaret Thatcher had built.' Another recalls: 'His parents were very great admirers of Margaret Thatcher. Sometimes I thought David thought his function in life was to convince his father – whom he called "the Dad" – that John Major was, in fact, "sound".'

On 3 June 1992, British Eurosceptics celebrated the result of a referendum in Denmark on the proposed Maastricht treaty that, among other things, paved the way for a single currency. In his diary Robinson records Lamont's 'grin a mile wide' at the news. Later that day Cameron lectured his senior colleague on the iniquities of Brussels. 'He explains to me the so-called negative assent procedure, whereby Europe has some kind of veto over UK legislation if it is deemed to be unEuropean. I'm keen on the Single Market but do I want that? Perhaps Norman is quite right on Europe after all,' mused Robinson. Lamont thought that the Danish decision would spell the end of attempts to create a single currency and free Britain from the ERM. He was dismayed the next day, however, to find that Major and Douglas Hurd, the Foreign Secretary, had already decided to press ahead with the Maastricht negotiations. The effect was to turn back-bench unease into open revolt.

The news that the French, too, would be holding a referendum on Maastricht caused the markets to begin to take fright. The basic assumption, that exchange rates would remain stable as the European project progressed, was defunct. That belief, shaken by the Danish referendum, was now rocked by the prospect of a French 'non'. Huge amounts of money were leaving the more peripheral, risky currencies of the ERM, initially the lira and peseta, and piling into the far safer bet, the German Deutschmark. Since Germany had higher interest rates than its neighbours (and, significantly, than the US), it was an altogether more attractive currency for the world's savers. What was to be so telling for Britain was that, under the ERM, there was an obligation on members to shore up the value of their currencies against those inside the mechanism when they hit the 'floor' of their agreed range. A test of wills was therefore looming. The financial markets believed the ERM was bound to unravel, while the national governments were determined to press ahead with it.

The problem would intensify if the members of the currency club fell out among themselves. Just such a falling out happened at this crucial juncture between Germany and countries like Italy, Spain and, increasingly, Britain, who found they were spending billions of dollars shoring up their currencies to remain within the allowed range of parity with the DM. Far from agreeing to cut its rate – and therefore make its currency less attractive – the German central bank, the Bundesbank, hiked rates further on 17 July 1992.

Although sufficiently worried to consider cancelling his summer holiday, Lamont was still confident that the crisis could be weathered. Britain had only to hang on until 20 September, the date of the French referendum. If France voted 'oui' the pressure on the ERM would automatically ease as the single currency was put back on track; if 'non' the ERM was doomed and Britain could, in Lamont's view at least, escape with its reputation intact reasonably soon afterwards. The Bank of England was also confident that aggressive and concerted intervention – buying its own currency – could keep the pound within its allowed range of values.

With the advent of the summer recess the Chancellor set off first to Burgundy. For the first time, he reluctantly agreed to carry three mobile phones so that he could keep in touch with events back in London and the rest of the world's financial centres. Cameron, meanwhile, sought to forget about the currency worries in Spain, where he holidayed in a rented villa with his old friend and Smith Square colleague Angie Bray and Bruce Anderson, the journalist, who had become a friend and occasional drinking partner. Bray remembers a happy holiday entertained one evening by the sight of a well-refreshed Anderson stroking a hedge in the mistaken belief that it was a cat.

By 4 August, Cameron was back in London. He found nothing particularly sinister in his in-tray. After some desultory work preparing for Lamont's party conference speech to be delivered that October, the aide and his former girlfriend Laura Adshead went to a dinner organised by Sharratt to celebrate the publication of Portillo's pamphlet. At the Waterside Inn at Bray, a famous Roux brothers restaurant, Cameron and Adshead enjoyed a 'gorgeous evening'. Meanwhile Lamont and his wife Rosemary had moved to Porto Ercole, where they were guests at a villa rented by Woodrow Wyatt.

The Chancellor soon learned to avoid swimming in the pool, however, overlooked as it was by the long lenses of Fleet Street. As he dodged the cameras, a run on sterling grew ever more serious. By 14 August it was close to the floor. A week later a massive co-ordinated effort by eighteen central banks to prop up the dollar ended in failure. The crisis could be avoided no longer. Lamont returned to London the next day – far earlier than he had planned (although this was not appreciated at the time) – to face the music.

Even though the situation was bad, few if any in the Treasury or elsewhere in the government had any forebodings of what lay less than three weeks in the future. What to do in the event of a French 'non' was, instead, the hot political question of the moment. Lamont, in possession of more knowledge than almost anyone else about the state of currency markets, has admitted that it was a 'fateful decision' not to force the issue of ERM membership at this point. Mass central bank interventions were failing to persuade speculators that the mechanism could survive the tensions that were driving its member currencies apart. Even if the French voted 'oui', Treasury experts believed it would require a 2 per cent hike in British rates to protect the pound. This would have been a major blow to an already struggling economy, but few anticipated that it would not, in some sense, do the trick. Speculators were sensing a certain bet – whichever way the vote went, the pound was likely to go down. And if they could drive it below the ERM's floor, the Bank of England was committed to buying pounds at that level – and they had a licence to print money.

For all his deep misgivings, the only action Lamont took was to ask for one meeting with John Major. But when it took place and Lamont sought to discuss one of the most important economic issues facing Britain for decades, Major waved him away, saying: 'Oh no, I don't want to discuss that at all.' By early September it was clear that mass interventions by central banks weren't working. The Italian lira had plummeted out of its agreed zone and the pound looked like following. Some say Lamont should not have implemented a policy he did not believe in, and should have taken on the Prime Minister more vigorously at a point when, arguably, a debacle could have been avoided.

Cameron certainly knew of Lamont's feelings and shared his doubts about the political direction of European integration. As his political adviser, should he have done more to press the Chancellor to force the issue of the ERM? In a different context, Cameron's supporter Michael Gove has said: 'He's not rabidly ideological. He is the kind of poker player who waits and reads the other players and bets when he knows the alignment is in his favour.' On this occasion the odds did not look good. The Prime Minister – wanting to make a success of the policy he had sold to Margaret Thatcher, and bolstered by the presence in his Cabinet of three comparative Euro-enthusiasts in the shape of Ken Clarke, Douglas Hurd and Michael Heseltine – was showing no sign of wanting to pull out of the ERM. It would have been a brave senior adviser, let alone a recent graduate, who said to the Chancellor: 'Tell the PM he's got it all wrong.'

The one action we know that Cameron did take in those weeks leading up to Black Wednesday is a rather curious one. 'Just before Black Wednesday he bought me a cigar a foot long,' says Lamont. 'He said, "By the time you have smoked all of this, all your troubles will be over."' This is an emblematically Cameronian gesture, showing the adviser not only to be confident in his dealings with the senior man, but so much so as to advertise to the Chancellor his insouciance about the scenery collapsing around him. Lamont, evidently, regarded the gift presumably as it was intended, as a stylish display of moral support, a call to nervelessness. In the event, though, Lamont never smoked it.

A more prosaic defence of Cameron's low-key role is that he was on holiday with his parents in Italy the second week in September when the storm clouds were gathering. He returned on Monday 14

September to be briefed by Robinson on the largely unsuccessful diplomatic efforts to realign the mechanism.

The end, when it came, was savage. The same day that Cameron returned, the Germans finally cut their interest rates. But the cut was small and only in response to a revaluation of the lira, then the sickliest currency in the pack. With the lira gone, the pound was now the hindmost; and the devil – in the form of speculators like George Soros – was preparing for the kill. The final straw came in an interview conducted on 15 September with the head of the Bundesbank, Helmut Schlesinger, who seemed to imply that it would have been better if Britain too had taken the plunge and formally realigned along with Italy. Lamont's aides were in a 'markets meeting' with officials from the Bank of England late in the evening when rumours of the contents of the Schlesinger interview came through. The German bank chief, contacted by his furious British opposite number, agreed to 'vet' the transcript and the Treasury meeting broke up. Lamont recalls that he went to bed that night knowing that the morning – when the markets could react to Schlesinger's words – would bring a 'difficult day'. But neither he nor his advisers had an inkling that it would go down in history as the day the government spent £3.4 billion unsuccessfully propping up the pound.

Robinson's diary entry for Wednesday 16 September begins: 'I wake up to hear on the *Today* programme that everyone is talking about Schlesinger's reputed remarks. When I get in, a meeting is already under way. It is now obvious that we are in major crisis territory.' Lamont's huge office – big enough, he says, in which to practise putting – was a dark one, with forbidding Dutch paintings apparently nailed to the walls. It must have appeared particularly gloomy as Lamont sat with his officials and fretted about what to do. The Chancellor was reluctant to raise rates at first but was persuaded to agree to a 2 per cent hike if it became necessary. There was no 'if' about it: the Bank, 'overwhelmed by a wave of selling' (in Robinson's phrase), announced the rise as soon as it could. Lamont, watching the Reuters screen in his office, saw the pound flat-line in the minutes after the announcement at 11 a.m. 'I felt like a TV surgeon in *Casualty* watching a heart monitor,' Lamont said later, 'and realising that the patient was dead.'

There have been claims that Major suffered a sort of nervous break-down on Black Wednesday – and certainly he seems to have made himself unavailable for several hours when Lamont was desperate to pull the plug and quit the ERM. Major for his part suggests that it was Lamont who was 'overwhelmed by the morning's events'. When Lamont eventually managed to arrange a meeting that afternoon with Major, he found that the PM had invited the Cabinet's leading pro-Europeans, Douglas Hurd and Ken Clarke, who both successfully argued that one more massive rate rise – to 15 per cent, to take effect the following day – might just hold the speculators at bay. 'At 2pm the 15 per cent interest rate announcement is made. We watch the screens with bated breath,' Robinson wrote that night. 'Now we hope it won't work, so we can suspend [Britain's ERM membership]. There is no bounce-back on the rate.' But Major was still reluctant to announce suspension without another meeting of the Cabinet.

As the arguments raged, Cameron turned his attention to what his boss was going to say to the nation about the disaster. Robinson wrote: 'Jeremy [Heywood] and David now start to wonder aloud about what [Lamont] will say on TV in the evening. I ask if he has to say anything. It is agreed that he must – you can't put interest rates up to 15 per cent in the middle of a recession without saying something.' So it fell to Cameron to inject what dignity he could into one of the most humili-ating statements a British politician has made since the Second World War.

Lamont says he has no memory of Cameron on that day, but it is a fact that as he stood in the central courtyard of the Treasury, which had never before been used for such an event, he read words crafted by the current Tory leader. 'Today has been an extremely difficult and turbulent day,' began the Chancellor. With Cameron standing in the background, Lamont said that Britain had suspended its ERM membership and would rescind the interest rate rise to 15 per cent. He concluded: 'I will be reporting to Cabinet and discussing the situation with colleagues tomorrow and may make further statements then. Until then, I have nothing further to say. Thank you very much.'

The aftermath of Black Wednesday threatened to bring down the Major administration. Lamont, at least, would have to resign, or so the consensus seemed to demand. Mindful perhaps of the damage a sacked Chancellor could do on the backbenches, as well as of his continued value to the PM as a 'lightning conductor', Lamont was not pressured to resign by Number 10. On the contrary, Major told Lamont that he had an obligation to stay, to help see off calls for the PM's own resignation. The press wanted the Chancellor's blood, but Cameron helped set up back-to-back media interviews for his boss in the days after the event in which he repeated again and again that he had no intention of quitting. The exposure helped him weather the initial storm. In a sense, exit from the ERM suited the Chancellor very well – at last he had the scope for the interest rate cuts that were desperately needed to jump-start Britain out of its seemingly endless recession. He was not unhopeful, therefore, when he flew by Concorde to Washington for an IMF meeting on the Friday. It was, however, unwise to tell a journalist the next day – just four days after Black Wednesday – that he had been heard by his wife 'singing in my bath that morning'.

Back in London, David Cameron, whose job hung on the same thread as Lamont's, must have winced. As soon as Lamont returned, Cameron took him to one side and told him that the knives were out. Today he tells the story of how he phoned up Lamont to break the news to him that his face was on the front page of the *Sun*. 'That's the good news – the bad news is that it's in the middle of a dartboard.' Although Cameron plays the line for laughs, it must have felt far from funny at the time. His first job in government was turning into a disaster. His political career could be over before his twenty-sixth birthday that October.

With the scent of Lamont's blood in the water, Kenneth Clarke and Michael Howard began to circle. Both had been conducting a conspicuous number of interviews on the subject of the economy. Lamont waved warnings to one side, but took the precaution of warning Howard in particular off his turf. Lamont and his team knew that he was far from out of the woods – for a start he had the unappetising prospect of an emergency debate in a specially recalled Commons. Gordon Brown, the new shadow Chancellor, was anxious to land an early blow. 'The Chancellor has no shame, makes no apology and gives no hint of remorse for damaging the stability of people's lives,' Brown thundered, to a roar of Labour approval. To everyone's surprise, however, Lamont did well defending himself. He sat down to resounding cheers from his own side, far louder than those for the Prime Minister in the same debate. Cameron, watching in the box reserved for officials (the right one this time), thought his boss had done enough to survive. The next day he told a colleague that Lamont was 'becoming a cult figure' among Tory backbenchers who were beginning to recognise that the Chancellor was a Eurosceptic brake on the Major government.

The mood in Number 10, meanwhile, was darkening as a depressed Prime Minister wrestled with the question whether he should resign. Lamont, after featuring as a dartboard, had resolved simply to stop reading the newspapers that were daily calling for his head. Both men knew, however, that neither could escape the looming appointment with their party at its annual conference, to be held that year in Brighton. Another good speech at the party conference and Lamont could begin to relax. But it wasn't a good speech. It was a resounding failure – and one that David Cameron learned much from.

In fact Lamont's performance at Brighton was a tale of two speeches, both of which led to serious clashes with Number 10 as the already roiling tensions over Europe erupted at the conference. The exit from the ERM had left a deep bitterness towards Germany within the Treasury, and compounded Tory Eurosceptics' hostility to Brussels. Lamont could not resist a naked appeal to the right.

In a lecture to the Conservative Political Centre (CPC) on the eve of his main conference speech, Lamont made his pitch. Brilliantly crafted by Cameron to observe the pieties of the government's position on Maastricht, it left no one in any doubt about Lamont's true feelings. Near the climax of a speech that was given a standing ovation, Cameron had his boss say, 'No one would die for Europe.' It was a line that Major had wanted removed, but Lamont, urged on by Cameron, stuck to his guns. In his memoirs Lamont acknowledges that his young adviser had given him 'a lot of invaluable help' in its preparation, but Robinson's diary entry for 7 October provides an insight into just how difficult a boss he could be at this time of extreme stress. The Chancellor and his private secretary, Jeremy Heywood, were allocated rooms in Brighton's Grand Hotel for the party conference while his special advisers made do with inferior accommodation elsewhere. During the day Cameron shuttled between Lamont's and Heywood's rooms working on the two main speeches.

I ring Jeremy and go to his room – tiny – where he and David are working on the speech. We are summoned up to [Lamont]. He has a splendid room in one of the turrets, lots of windows, unusual shape. But the mood is vile. Too late to bed, too much to drink, bed too small and hard. Rosemary [Lamont's wife] is looking pretty pinched and strained as well and [Lamont] has a plaster on his neck where I had noticed an incipient boil. He glares at us [and] asks David if he has cleared the CPC speech with Charles Powell, mutters something about not being able to work with these people. David goes off to do a press release.

If Number 10 were nervous about the CPC speech, they were appalled at the first draft of the main speech. For a start, it repeatedly praised Margaret Thatcher's economic record, in direct contradiction of the project overseen by Sarah Hogg, the head of Major's policy unit, to distance her boss as far as possible from his predecessor. Then there was its failure to parrot Major's fatuous slogan of the day, 'going for growth', a phrase that, for instinctive free-marketeers like Lamont and Cameron, smacked of big-government interventionism. Finally, Major objected to Cameron's use of a Winston Churchill quotation about the need to curb public spending. 'If we do not face reality, reality will face us,' Lamont was supposed to intone gravely. Major made him take out a line he thought 'too bleak'.

It was, therefore, a neutered text that Lamont took to the rostrum, but it wasn't just the words that let him down that afternoon. Two bright lights shining directly on to the teleprompters in front of him meant that he struggled to read the speech at all. 'It was a nightmare,' he recalls. 'I could hardly read the words we had spent days drafting. Eventually I got the knack of it, but it completely destroyed the delivery.' The next day's headlines, predictably, were dire. It was a lesson the young Cameron never forgot. And when it came to making the party conference speech of his life, the speech that catapulted him from back-marker to frontrunner in the 2005 Conservative leadership race, he spoke without notes – the only candidate to do so.

As Cameron sought to exploit the political differences between Blair and Brown in 2006, he was working an institutional fault line between the Treasury and Number 10 he knew from the inside. For the remainder of that autumn and into 1993, relations between Lamont and Major continued to deteriorate. The Chancellor was exasperated by the PM's failure to provide leadership. Major meanwhile sought increasingly to bypass his Chancellor by handing key decisions to fixers like Lord Wakeham. Lamont says he kept from his political aide the full force of his opinion about Major but admits that Cameron must have 'picked up' what was happening. 'I had to be careful. I had to maintain that my relations with the Prime Minister were excellent. You know, everything leaks in government. It was more than my life was worth to let it be known that there was any problem.' He adds, 'I have no recollection about saying anything to David about Major. I suppose that there would be moments when I came back from meetings in Downing Street pretty fed up and angry. My relations with Major were not good, that is true, but in a way that is an inevitable situation between Prime Ministers and Chancellors. David would have picked that up, but it would be more on specific issues rather than my saying, "The PM can't make a decision," which was one of my specific complaints.'

In a Mansion House speech that November, Lamont defied Major by making an upbeat speech, suggesting that the post-Black Wednesday gloom had been overdone. A week later the Chancellor called in Cameron to rewrite his speech for the autumn 'mini-budget'. The aide had to cancel a trip to the opera to oblige his boss but, not being a great fan of the art form, probably regarded the cancellation as a bonus.

A more compelling drama unfolded ten days later as Cameron was given a masterclass in how the press can inflate a trivial incident to the point where it starts to inflict serious damage. Cameron learned that it didn't matter that Lamont had not, in fact, bought a bottle of cheap champagne and two packets of Raffles cigarettes from a branch of Threshers in Paddington, a false claim supported by the inaccurate testimony of one of the shop's workers. Once the tabloids had established that the Chancellor had exceeded his credit card limit, such delicious embellishments quickly attained the status of fact. It was Cameron who dealt with the journalists throughout 'Threshergate'.

So when the *Sun*'s much admired Trevor Kavanagh claimed at one point that he had documentary evidence of the disputed purchase, it was Cameron who took the call.

Behind the spin there were also some deep and important issues at play at this time, issues that resonate to this day. One was Bank of England independence, an idea which New Labour was to make its own at the 1997 election but which had been secretly supported by Lamont five years earlier. Another 'live' policy area was the issue of taxing fuel. When David Cameron became, in December 2005, the new leader of the Conservatives, he chose the environment as his first political battleground, a decision intended to demonstrate a radical departure from the party's past. But the decision also surprises his former colleagues who remember, as he must, the political pain caused the party by its imposition of VAT on fuel. This measure was prompted in large part by the government's need to reduce emission targets, the precursor to targets that Cameron has recently pledged to make statutory. In his desire to establish his green credentials, the new Tory leader has chosen to ignore how Labour was handed one of the most potent political weapons in the budget of March 1993. The VAT on fuel, something that disproportionately hurt poorer pensioners, allowed Labour to paint the Tories as malicious. The party also signalled three years of tax rises – increasing the overall burden by more than £10 billion by 1995 – scarcely a year after Major and Lamont had insisted they had no such plans. That budget was, in any case, always destined to be very difficult. The Treasury team of which Cameron was a part had simultaneously to plug a yawning deficit, nurse a fledgling recovery and restore credibility after Black Wednesday.

It was a tall order, and one made yet taller by relentless negative briefing from Lamont's Cabinet critics. Cameron, as the Chancellor's main political adviser, could hardly pick up a Sunday newspaper in early 1993 without finding some unnamed 'Tory source' attacking his boss. One of Mrs Thatcher's most loyal lieutenants, Norman Tebbit, had delivered a savage attack on John Major, reminding him that Lamont had been carrying out the Prime Minister's own policy. Some months earlier, at the party conference, Tebbit had privately offered Lamont blunt advice. 'I'd find an issue on which to resign if I were you. The two-faced bastard will push you in the end, when he feels safer and it is more convenient for him.' Now, with the public firmly blaming Lamont for the tax rises, Major's 'convenient' moment to dispense with his Chancellor was fast approaching. Lamont had attained the status of sitting duck, and Major needed a sacrifice to fend off the mob. The PM's task was made easier after one last Lamont gaffe – and one, this time, which has been blamed on David Cameron.

The call to help with the Newbury by-election of early May 1993 was all the more welcome since it enabled Cameron to drop in on his childhood home in Peasemore. His parents, Ian and Mary, made lunch for Lamont and their son in the Old Rectory before a spot of light canvassing. Even here, however, Lamont could not escape press attention and, cornered by the BBC's John Pienaar, he was asked: 'Chancellor, which do you regret most, seeing green shoots or singing in the bath?' Lamont blames only himself for his reply, but others have claimed that Cameron suggested it. In any case, quoting Edith Piaf's 'Je ne regrette rien', must go down as one of the most ill-considered quips in modern British politics.

Media hostility reached new depths following the Conservatives' rout on 6 May and much of the blame was laid at Lamont's door for his 'gross insensitivity'. Helping to marshal defenders proved an almost impossible task for Cameron. Woodrow Wyatt, a supportive friend but given to moments of eccentricity, was pressed into service to take up arms on behalf of the Chancellor on BBC's *Newsnight* but must have proved a grave disappointment for the young spin doctor when, in paying tribute to Lamont's accomplishments, he began to enthuse vividly about the Chancellor's gift for imitating a Scops owl.

A week later, at the party's Scottish conference, Cameron again warned Lamont that there was serious manoeuvring against him. While Major praised his Chancellor's 'determination, skill and guts' from the rostrum, Cameron overheard Conservative Central Office officials brief journalists that the new party boss, Norman Fowler, believed Lamont should be moved – an alarming piece of intelligence he passed straight to the Chancellor.

Two weeks later, as Lamont was helping to celebrate Michael Portillo's fortieth birthday, Cameron asked for a quiet word. He told his boss that there was definitely going to be a reshuffle the next day. Lamont seemed unfazed, but Cameron's political radar was accurate. The following morning, on Thursday 27 May, Lamont was summoned to see John Major, was offered another, lowlier job as Environment Secretary and – when he refused it – was sacked, just as Norman Tebbit had warned he would be. Among the first people he saw afterwards was Cameron, who, with William Hague, was waiting for him in his office at the Treasury. Hague, who had become an MP in a by-election in 1989, had been made Lamont's parliamentary aide the following year. Lamont has praised Cameron's 'wit', and Hague's humorous gifts are well known. If ever there was a moment for gallows humour, this was it. Lamont says the three 'mulled over' his sacking for a while, checking the markets' reaction to the news, and then headed out to Toto's, an expensive Italian restaurant in Knightsbridge, for a good lunch. That afternoon, the sacked Chancellor summoned his staff to his office, served them white wine, and then left office for the last time.

It was just over a year since David Cameron had arrived. Now he, too, was out on his ear. That he is forever associated with Britain's humiliating exit from the ERM and one of the biggest tax-raising budgets of recent times is at best embarrassing. But Cameron can at least claim to have been tested in government in the most difficult circumstances. He saw how in stormy times Number 11 can be made to deflect damage from its neighbour. But he saw also how useful the issue of Europe can be if one is prepared to flirt with the Eurosceptics. He witnessed also the arrival of Gordon Brown at the summit of his party, seeing both that man's formidable talents – and his vulnerabilities.

Cameron did well at the Treasury in difficult circumstances. He won round older and vastly more experienced colleagues who resented, as one put it, 'being told what to do by kids'. Lamont says that Cameron has told him he enjoyed the 'rigorous analysis and open discussion' that is the 'Treasury ethos'. The former Chancellor speculates that he may have helped shape Cameron's 'mild Euroscepticism'. He also says that their time together would have shown Cameron the downsides to power. 'He would have seen that politics can be a rough business, and that's no bad thing for a young man.' Eloquent testimony to Cameron's professionalism comes in Robinson's diary entry for one of the last days they spent together as colleagues, 10 March 1993. Cameron, the junior adviser, had asked him to help prepare a brief for backbenchers, a task he had previously regarded as a 'boring and useless chore to be delegated'. 'But I agree willingly, because David does so much and so well.' It wasn't enough.

TUSCANY
Romance 1992

In late 1992, Norman Lamont's precocious adviser was enjoying a quiet Sunday morning in his sunny Lansdowne Crescent flat with his new girlfriend. They had been going out for just a couple of months. At last, at the end of a busy week, she in Bristol, he at the Treasury, they were able to spend some time together. Then came an unwelcome intrusion. The phone rang. From the bed, Samantha, just twenty-one, called out: 'If that's Norman Lamont, tell him to fuck off!'

David Cameron, just turned twenty-six, has never been in any doubt what sort of woman he was getting involved with, and this story, while not typical, shows that she is more than willing to stand her ground. Some of his friends thought her a little too far removed from the mould of his usual girlfriends to be a long-term proposition, but he had seen something in his sister Clare's best friend. Samantha was the woman for him.

She was quite shy of her friend's brother, fully five years older than her. Neither had shown much interest in the other beyond mere courtesies in the past. Samantha Sheffield and Clare Cameron had known one another for years, but had not become close until their teens. They shared a mischievous sense of humour and a teenage taste for adventure. Samantha, in particular, seems to have gone to some lengths to avoid being typecast by her background. While socially smart, it was also fairly racy. Her mother was born Annabel Jones, daughter of Timothy Jones and Pandora Clifford. Timothy, an Eton scholar, was the son of Sir Roderick Jones, a self-made man who rose to become chairman of Reuters, and of playwright Enid Bagnold, author of *Chalk Garden* and *National Velvet*. Timmy, who lost a leg in the Second World War after stepping on a landmine, went on to Oxford. Good-looking, witty, wise and charming, he embarked on an affair with Pandora, one of the daughters of Sir Bede Clifford, a former Governor of Trinidad and Tobago. She was also the Duke of Windsor's goddaughter.

Pandora was a renowned beauty. It is said of her that she turned the head of every man who saw her. Certainly Jones was smitten, and would go to remarkable and romantic lengths to prove it. On one occasion, when she was still a schoolgirl, he followed her when she went on a family holiday to Antibes in the South of France. There, ignoring his disability, he swam across a bay every evening for secret meetings with her. The fact that, in late 1947, Pandora, of strong Catholic upbringing and just seventeen years old, was seeing a man six years older than her might itself have caused a stir. That she fell pregnant by him threatened a full-blown scandal. Jones 'did the decent thing', as a friend put it later. One curiosity, revealing of how the war had taken its toll, is that the three Clifford daughters were to marry men with only three legs between them. Anne married the able-bodied John Julius Norwich, but Atalanta married Richard Fairey, of a celebrated aeroplane and boat-building family, who had lost both legs when his ship was torpedoed during the war.

Pandora's wedding, on a dark January day at St Aloysius' Catholic Church in Oxford, was a hurriedly arranged and poorly attended affair. The bride's parents, strongly opposed, stayed away and refused to speak to their daughter. (The day before, Jones bumped into a college friend and asked what he was doing the following day. 'Nothing. Why?' asked the friend. 'In that case, why don't you come to my wedding?') One of the guests was Marmaduke Hussey, who later became chairman of the BBC, also on crutches, having lost a leg at

Anzio. The bride, two months pregnant with Annabel, wore black, and the festivities after-wards were minimal. If Pandora's parents disapproved of the match, Timothy's mother Enid Bagnold – herself a frustrated romantic – was thrilled by the headiness of the romance and happily provided emo-tional help and childcare for the besotted couple. In her eyes her son could do little wrong, and she was keen to help the couple all she could, although she offered a more cold-blooded explanation to a friend ('it gives us more hold on the whole thing', she said).

By the standards of Annabel's class, money was tight. 'Neither of my parents had a penny,' Annabel has said, which meant her mother had to live, not completely happily, with the in-laws in Rottingdean. (Diana Cooper, a friend of the Jones family and, as we have seen, distantly related by marriage to Ian Cameron, reported to a friend that Enid's painstaking and idiosyncratic cooking was not always a success, and that she might be offered cows' udders in marmalade.) When in London, Annabel remembered, her parents 'went endlessly to parties I can see my mother dressing up now – she had no money so she would make beautiful dresses, sewing away all day.'

The couple added a son seven years later but were to divorce when Annabel was twelve. The adjective that most often crops up today when friends talk of Annabel Astor is 'formidable'. It seems likely that that toughness was forged in childhood. In 1961 her mother – who had a talent for entertaining and interior design – remarried, this time to Michael Astor, son of the 2nd Viscount Astor. He had a large house in the country, Bruern Abbey in Oxfordshire, where writers, painters and politicians (Stephen Spender, Roy Jenkins, Woodrow Wyatt and Patrick Leigh Fermor among them) would be invited for lavish din-ners – 'never for fewer than twenty' – in surroundings sumptuously decorated by Pandora. During his seven-year marriage to Pandora, Michael Astor was a loving but firm stepfather to Annabel and instilled in her exemplary manners and a love of reading.

A friend says he has never seen Annabel do a business deal without coming off best. In the 1960s she was one of the original 'It' girls, and has been described as looking 'part society pin-up, part rock chick'. Her drive and talent were evident from the earliest time. When she was twenty, Quentin Crewe's brother Colin put down £25,000 for her to sell – and, soon afterwards, design – jewellery. She set up Annabel Jones jewellers (a favourite with Princess Diana) in Beauchamp Place. As designer Theo Fennell says: 'She was considered an unlikely person to be in the jewellery business, but her great skill was to tap into the Zeitgeist. There was nothing around for southwest London mums at that time and she created it.'

At just twenty-one she married Sir Reginald Sheffield, the eighth baronet two years older than her, whose family lineage can be traced to the crusades. He owned the 300-acre estate of Normanby Hall, outside Scunthorpe – by then largely leased to the council – which has been in the possession of the Sheffield family since 1590. The first baronet was the illegitimate son of the 1st Duke of Buckingham and Normanby. The third baronet, Sir John Astley, married Eleanor Corbett, grand-daughter of the 8th Duke of St Albans. The 1st Duke of St Albans was one of two illegitimate sons of Nell Gwynne and Charles II. This means that when Annabel and Reggie's first child Samantha arrived in 1971, she was, according to Cracroft's Peerage, the great-great-great-great-great-great-great-great-granddaughter of Nell Gwynne. The Sheffield family also owns Sutton Park, built in 1730 and set in 1,000 acres, eight miles north of York. It had been bought by Reggie's father in 1963 and he inherited it in the late 1990s. The Etonian Sheffield, a former chairman of Scunthorpe Football Club, but more at ease in White's Club or out with a shotgun, is an eccentric and colourful figure and a good deal shrewder, and more shy, than he admits. He likes to tell people, in his booming voice, and in defiance of his stammer, that: 'I live off unearned income, g-g-g-garnished by the occasional planning consent.' Among the residences that his family has sold off – admittedly nearly 300 years ago – was Buckingham House, since rebuilt as Buckingham Palace.

When Samantha was two, her sister Emily was born, but for their mother marriage to Reggie was not all plain sailing. He started having an affair with Annabel's friend Victoria and divorce followed. However, their relationship remained comparatively friendly – as did relations between Victoria and Annabel. Friends have spoken admiringly of how Annabel never held a grudge against Reggie, but then infidelity was far from being an unknown concept to the Jones family. When Annabel's grandmother Enid, something of a snob, confided in Diana Cooper that she was upset by her husband's philandering, Diana – who had put up with a good deal of cuckolding herself – told her not to be upset. 'Darling, it's so *common* to mind,' said Cooper. Within a decade or so of the divorce, all the dramatis personae were spending Christmases together.

Annabel would take her daughters up to see Reggie at Normanby, where he still had living accommodation. On one occasion in the mid-1970s when Annabel was visiting, she arrived at the council-run golf course's restaurant and asked if they would be open that Sunday, for lunch. She was told they would be. In that case, she said with her customary poise, could she possibly book a table for four and a table for one. Of course, she was told, although if she wanted a table for five, that would be fine too. No, no, she said, thank you very much, four plus one was what she wanted. As Sunday lunchtime approached, staff had to be discouraged from laying a table for five. Annabel, Reggie's mother, Samantha and Emily made up the table for four. The table for one was taken by their chauffeur.

In the mid-1970s, Annabel's stepbrother David Astor invited her down for the weekend. Her stepfather Michael, who lived next door, happened to have asked his nephew William to stay. They teamed up and two months later decided to get married. 'I think we both knew instantly that it was right,' she has said. 'For me, it helped that I'd grown up with the Astor family.'

Samantha Sheffield went to the Manor School and then, at eleven, to St Helen's (now St Helen's and St Katharine's), both in Abingdon, near Oxford. She later recalled that her mother 'wasn't the kind of mum who tidied your room and packed your tuckbox, but we never wanted her to be. We thought she was more glamorous than anyone else's mother; the working was part of that.' The Sheffield girls used to help, gift-wrapping and so on, at their mother's Knightsbridge shop in the school holidays. 'That is where my retail instincts were honed,' said Samantha recently.

She continued to see a certain amount of her friend Clare Cameron, who was at St Mary's, Calne, a school which encouraged girls to follow their own interests as much as any curriculum. It catered for the individual, making few concessions to orthodoxy. Among their friends, as we have seen, was Jade Jagger, daughter of the Rolling Stone Mick. Jade was expelled from St Mary's at sixteen, accused of sneaking out with a boy. 'It was a stupid thing,' she said at the time. 'No one even caught me red-handed. I was in bed and they said, "You're expelled." I said, "Fine, when do I pack?"' The boy in question was Josh Astor, who, as it happens, was a close relation of Samantha and had been in David Cameron's year at Eton until he was thrown out for smoking cannabis in the purge of 1982. (He was later imprisoned for cocaine use.)

On one occasion Clare held a party at home at Peasemore. It was then, according to David Cameron's recollection at any rate, that the couple first met. Recalling it later, in Samantha's company, Cameron was heard to say 'You were a sulky sixteen-year-old who thought, "Who's this crashing bore who is your friend's older brother?"' Evidently the encounter left little mark on 'the sulky sixteen-year-old'. When asked later when they had first met, she said she had 'probably' met him when she was at primary school, but had no clear recollection of him. It is her belief that they didn't meet until she was eighteen.

In September 1987 Samantha switched to Marlborough College, joining B3 house, with an art scholarship. She was one of a hundred girls among just over 200 boys. She had wanted to follow her mother into doing something commercial, like fashion design, but was talked out of it in favour of painting. She made sure she enjoyed Marlborough to the full, often dressing as a Goth, and left her sister Emily with something to live up to. (Emily succeeded: she was expelled from Marlborough when drugs were found in her dormitory.) On leaving Marlborough, Sam took an art foundation course at Camberwell College of Art in London, and then did a degree in Fine Art at Bristol Polytechnic, now the University of the West of England.

A contemporary says she was always slightly remote, at least from some of those on her course, and spent most of her time with her fellow student Katy Jacobs. Socially, she seems to have immersed herself in some of the wilder shores of Bristol life. According to rap star Tricky, she was, for example, a regular at the Montpelier pub, where they would play pool together. It was, Tricky (born Adrian Thaws) told the *Mail on Sunday*, a place where 'bikers mixed with drug dealers, hippies, students and guys from the ghetto. It was a cool pub but ... there were always fights. Samantha was an art student and she'd come in with friends. We'd all hang out, drink some beers and play pool. You could smoke weed in there without being hassled, smoke hashish, take psychedelic mushrooms. It was cool. I can't remember her smoking anything, though.'

Tricky and Sam (she was known to some as 'Snowy') were 'unlikely mates', he agrees. 'I was robbing houses, robbing stores, selling weed by the time I was 15. But I was a good pool player and so we often played together. I'd show her a few tips and tricks, how to hit a few shots. Sometimes it could get violent. I've seen girls knocked out in there.

Students would get robbed. Groups of ghetto kids might mug them as they left the pub. I'd watch out for her. From The Montpelier we'd walk across the road to The Cadbury, another pub. Samantha was safe with me ...'

Tricky knew nothing about her upbringing. She 'never mentioned that she was a baronet's daughter. I'd never have known. If she had told me that I would have assumed that, because of her privileged background, she was a bit of a bitch. But I guess you can be a baronet's daughter and still want to have street credibility. She was mousy blonde with a cute face and a good little body, though her eyes always looked a little sleepy. She was quiet, polite, humble. She wasn't innocent but she was sweet.' Someone who knew them both at the time has been quoted as saying: 'She belonged to a crowd we liked to call the trustafarians. Rich types who liked to slum it a little. But she was all right. She stood out somehow. There were rumours about them, of course. A nice posh girl mixed up with a bloke like him. But I don't think they ever got together. I bet he'd have liked to though.'

If her days and nights at Bristol were decidedly bohemian, her holidays were rather more in keeping with her upbringing – for the most part. Travelling to Bali with Clare Cameron she had a dolphin tattooed on her ankle 'on a whim'. But her eye was already on the world of retail. Her mother was socially friendly with the Menzies family, which owned the newsagents of the same name, as well as Smythsons, an upmarket stationer in Bond Street, central London. As a result, Annabel had been taken on as a design consultant. It seemed a natural match for Samantha, who was showing her mother's interest in business, to do the odd bit of holiday work there too.

Then, in the middle of 1992, Clare asked Sam if she would like to go on holiday with her family for the last week of August and the first of September. It was to be a special occasion. Clare's parents were marking their thirtieth wedding anniversary – and Ian's sixtieth birthday – and they planned to celebrate in style, block-booking a large part of a resort in southern Tuscany. The Cameron parents invited six couples of their own generation, and the children were also allowed to ask two or three friends each. Alex Cameron was unable to make the trip, but Tania invited Pete Czernin, David Cameron's friend from school, and Carl Brookes, a cardiologist whom she later married. Clare invited Samantha and two male friends. Cameron himself asked Dom Loehnis, Serena Elwes and Anastasia Cooke, on whom he was quite keen. Anastasia, though, was seeing James Baker, son of the former BBC news reader Richard Baker, who came to Tuscany to pick her up and drive her home at the end of the holiday.

But it was not long into the holiday before Cameron had set his sights on Samantha Sheffield. Clare Cameron is outgoing, and her brother had always been intrigued by her amusing but cool and reserved friend, the 'straight man' to his effusive sister. Five years older than Samantha, he was determined to make her laugh, conscious that to the twenty-year-old he might have seemed 'a serious, scary, slightly earnest older bloke', as a friend put it. 'When he's relaxed, Dave can be very, very funny,' he added. It helped that the fortnight was free-wheeling. Lochnis spent much of the day sitting in the bar complimenting Giovanni on the excellence of his cocktails, while others pursued similarly undemanding activities. With increasing frequency Cameron and Samantha found themselves poolside at the same time.

When the pair took to the tennis court it was clear that a romance was under way, for Cameron, a good and competitive player, very much dislikes playing with those who aren't. And Samantha, who has little aptitude for sport generally, is particularly bad at tennis. It is fair to say that their matches were more a milestone to be passed than the cornerstone of their romance. She struggled heroically and he took pains not to humiliate her. But it was clear they were never going to take on the world at mixed doubles. For Cameron that Tuscan holiday delivered a *coup de foudre*. His wife, never keen to discuss such matters in public, muttered 'kind of' when asked by an interviewer if it had been love at first sight. Cameron later described the coupling of a 'cool art student' and a 'stiff' special adviser as 'weird', but that he (peaceably) 'beat her into submission ... I wore her down.'

Back in London, they went on their first date at Kensington Place restaurant before the art student headed back to her earthier existence in Bristol. Sometimes she would come for weekends in London, at other times he would go down to her flat in one of the rougher parts of Bristol. If she had difficulty with this bifurcated lifestyle, he must have found it even harder, not least when having to jam coins into the student digs payphone when speaking to the Chancellor. He was regarded in Westminster as some-one with a really top-rank career ahead of him. His weeks were spent in the highest quarters of government. But in Bristol he was a nobody, or even less (although he was the first of Samantha's boyfriends to have a car, an elderly BMW, or even to invite her out to dinner). 'Sam's friends were unimpressed by the Tory Boy,' says Loehnis. 'There were lots of Tories saying, "Ooh look, a rising star," but Sam's friends just didn't think what he did was very cool. Some of us gave him a hard time about politics, but he just hadn't had that exposure to attack from people who thought it absurd to be a Tory.' On one occasion Cameron went out in the car and got lost trying to find his way back to Samantha's flat. He wound down his window to ask directions. 'It was a prostitute,' he recalled later, a little abashed.

Cameron, the Home Counties boy, was overjoyed by his catch. Although a product of Eton and Oxford, he would have been very conscious of how much further up the social scale his girlfriend was, particularly when he visited the Sheffields on home soil. The first time Cameron was invited to stay at Sutton Park, the magnificent 1730s home of the Sheffield family, he wore a three-piece tweed suit, which to the lofty Sheffields looked a little like trying too hard. His host was the formidable Nancie Sheffield, mother of Reggie, who wanted to know what the young pretender to Samantha's hand was like.

Predictably, despite Nancie's slightly intimidating air, Cameron pushed all the right buttons and impressed his girlfriend's grandmother with his easy manner and intelligence. Nonetheless, he and Samantha had to sleep apart, and at opposite ends of the vast house. To young lovers at the height of their passion, this presented something of a challenge, but one Cameron was disinclined to shirk. After everyone had gone to bed, he slipped out of his bedroom, tiptoed along a series of long and creaking corridors and eventually reached the room of his inamorata. Some time later, he returned to his room, mission accomplished, in plenty of time to present himself, rested and insouciant, at breakfast. The success of the trip was only a little undermined by Cameron receiving in the post, some days later, a package from Sutton Park, Yorkshire. It contained a neatly pressed pair of spotless underpants and an equally crisp message from Nancie: 'You left these behind, and not in your own room.'

After leaving university, David Cameron had shared a flat in South Kensington with the heir to the de Walden millions. Four years on, he was back spending half his weekends in student digs. But did they want the same things? Cameron always made it clear that he wanted to go into politics. Samantha has told an interviewer: 'When we started going out seriously he was very up front and said "I want to be an MP. If you think you would hate it, you have to say so." It certainly wasn't my natural inclination.' 'She wasn't in the mould of his girlfriends at all,' says James Fergusson. 'She was an art student, "hey man" type, but he saw the toughness in her very quickly. She is terrific, and was not a natural politician's wife, but she has has adapted to it so much', to the extent of defying the sneers from some in her family who, finding him earnest, referred to him as 'Boring Dave'.

'At the outset she didn't challenge him at all,' says another friend. 'At the start, she was only twenty and he was "my best friend's elder brother" and he would have seemed a lot older. She was young and giggly but matured very quickly. He was already being challenged plenty and she hardwired it into his private life.' Dom Loehnis agrees: 'By being prepared to stand up to him and always challenging him and saying, "You're being pompous" even when he wasn't, she managed to make sure that if he ever had a tendency that way, it wasn't going to get very far.'

One friend calls Samantha 'a hippy at heart', but she is very much her mother's daughter, according to the designer Jane Churchill: 'You can see Annabel in Samantha. They come from a long line of strong women who were in the right place when the right genes were handed out. They both have that rare mix of being extremely good at business but without being like those aggressive, killer women who try to get on by elbowing everyone aside. They both have discipline and are extremely practical; they do things themselves and just get on with it.'

QUEEN ANNE'S GATE
Home Office 1993-1994

Ken Clarke was very sorry, but he wanted his own advisers: David Cameron's first job in the government machine had come to a juddering halt with the dismissal of his boss, Norman Lamont, at the end of May 1993. Senior Treasury officials urged the new Chancellor to renew Cameron's employment in the wake of Lamont's sacking, and Ken Clarke expressed a wish to keep him. But Clarke also wanted Tessa Keswick, wife of the wealthy businessman Henry Keswick (of Hong Kong fame), who had been with him since his days as Health Secretary and had followed him to the Home Office. Keswick was less keen on Cameron and insisted that David Ruffley, Clarke's other political adviser, be given the job. Michael Portillo, who remained as Chief Secretary, Clarke's number two, asked the new Chancellor if *he* could have Cameron, but the request was refused. At the time the sacked aide's friends blamed Keswick. They claimed she had persuaded Clarke that to give Cameron to Portillo would create 'two poles' in Number 11.

That he was considered such a potential threat might have seemed a sort of backhanded compliment, but in fact Cameron was deeply wounded by Clarke's rejection. He was heading out of Whitehall and, it seemed, out of politics. There was talk of a position at the P&O shipping company, an early sign that he wanted a spell in the City. Clarke, feeling a twinge of conscience perhaps, began to ring around other Cabinet ministers offering them the redundant aide. One of those Clarke called was the man he had just beaten in the battle to succeed Lamont: his old friend and rival Michael Howard, who had been made Home Secretary. 'Ken phoned me up … and said, "I'm putting my own advisers in and there's this chap David Cameron – do you know of anyone who would take him?" And I said I would like a shot,' recalls Howard. Cameron had impressed Howard when, as head of the CRD's Political Section before the 1992 election, he had briefed the then Employment Secretary before television appearances.

So, as Keswick made herself at home in the stately office he had occupied overlooking the Treasury's central courtyard, Cameron trudged in the opposite direction, towards the building she had lately occupied, the Home Office's ugly HQ in Queen Anne's Gate. Howard was himself bewildered at the outcome of the reshuffle. His biographer, Michael Crick, quotes a 'close adviser' as saying that he had a moment of 'crisis' on being given the job. 'He said privately he never wanted to go there.' Howard confirms his surprise. 'It's certainly true that I wasn't expecting to go to the Home Office. I thought that there was a possibility that I might succeed Norman [Lamont]. I thought that if Ken moved from the Home Office, Norman Fowler would be Home Secretary. So it never crossed my mind. I had never spoken on any Home Office issue all the time I was in parliament or in my ministerial experience. So I hadn't focused on the Home Office, hadn't expected to come to the Home Office.'

For Cameron this was a chance to serve in 'one of the great offices of state', says Howard, who fails to banish entirely the suspicion that his new aide was lukewarm. 'I daresay he would have preferred to stay at the Treasury, but if he was leaving the Treasury I don't think there was any lack of desire to come to the Home Office.' In fact Cameron wasn't even Howard's adviser – that job was taken by Patrick Rock, with whom Cameron had worked in Central Office. Officially, he was special adviser to the Home Office's more junior ministers and had an office on their floor, one above the centre of power located around the Home Secretary's suite, where Rock worked.

Cameron confided in his new colleague that he didn't expect to stay long, saying that he thought most politicians 'only have two good law and order speeches in them'. In the event he stayed with Howard for only fifteen months. But they were fifteen months that afforded him a ringside view of a pivotal moment in British politics. Just as he was a witness in 1992 to Black Wednesday and the destruction of the Tories' reputation for economic competence, he was perfectly placed the next year to see Tony Blair steal law and order for Labour.

By the time Howard moved to the Home Office, Blair had spent four months pile-driving into public consciousness the slogan for which he is perhaps best known. It was Gordon Brown who coined 'tough on crime, tough on the causes of crime' but Blair who communicated it brilliantly. Borrowing heavily from the successful Bill Clinton campaign in the US, Blair and Brown had begun articulating a new sort of communitarian politics that stressed the importance of individual responsibility. Crime was no longer to be excused by reference to unemployment, poor housing, bad healthcare or any other social evil. Thus liberated, Blair soon served notice that he was going after territory that the Conservatives had grown used to thinking their own. Suddenly it was going to be a lot more difficult to paint the shadow Home Secretary as the mugger's defender or the burglar's best friend. Clarke, preoccupied with increasingly rancorous disputes with the police and judges over proposed reforms, had failed to spot or neutralise the growing threat and now it fell to Howard to stop Blair in his tracks.

Before Howard had a chance to get after Blair, Cameron's previous boss did his best to derail the whole Major government. In sacking Lamont, his erstwhile friend and campaign manager, Major knew he risked an attack from the backbenches similar to that unleashed on Thatcher by Geoffrey Howe, who had grievously wounded the former Prime Minister with a resignation statement less than three years before. It seems that Cameron and David Mellor were both discreetly deployed to assess the likelihood of such a move – and, if necessary, to dissuade him. Mellor, who had been forced to resign from the Cabinet the previous year but remained a staunch ally of Major, took the sacked Chancellor for a meal at La Tante Claire restaurant in Chelsea. After pâté de foie gras, duck and a bottle of champagne, Mellor believed that he had talked Lamont out of making a resignation statement. Cameron, too, had received much the same message when he phoned his old boss as Lamont was enjoying a last weekend in Dorneywood, the Chancellor's grace-and-favour country retreat – there would be no attack on Major from the backbenches. It is information that Cameron, concerned to show his own loyalty, would almost certainly have passed on to Number 10.

One of the reasons Cameron had been let go from the Treasury, so colleagues believed, was that it was felt he had gone too far in his efforts to present Lamont's exit in a favourable light to journalists after he ceased being Chancellor. In the strange world in which special advisers exist, it is sometimes wise for them to behave as civil servants do, that is with loyalty to the office, not to its occupant. Certainly Cameron was gravely embarrassed when Lamont launched a savage attack on Major in the Commons barely a week later. Amounting to a call for the Prime Minister's resignation, its most damaging passage contended that the Tories were 'in office but not in power'. It appears that even as his former adviser was concluding that he would not make a resignation statement, Lamont was composing the assault in his head as he walked through Dorneywood's gardens for the last time.

Worse was to come. Scarcely a month after his old boss had laid into Major, Cameron found that the Prime Minister privately believed his new one was a 'bastard'. The context, as ever with the Tories' most serious rows, was Europe. Major, weakened by Lamont's onslaught, had had a torrid time that summer seeking parliamentary ratification for the Maastricht treaty that enlarged the powers of the EU and was opposed outright by a rump of his party. On 23 July he called a vote of confidence – which he only just survived. That day he gave an interview to ITN's Michael Brunson declaring victory over the rebels. Afterwards, speaking privately, Brunson asked him why he did not sack Eurosceptic Cabinet ministers who had threatened to resign over the issue. Unaware that the microphone was still on, the Prime Minister said: 'You can think of ex-ministers who are going around causing all sorts of trouble. We don't want three more of the bastards out there.'

Howard was immediately considered a prime suspect as he had told Major he would quit if the PM signed Britain up to the Social Chapter of the EU enlargement treaty. It was an uncomfortable time to be in Howard's team, and for Cameron the embarrassment was personal as well as political. Laura Adshead, his former girlfriend, was one of Major's most senior advisers on Europe. She had earned the soubriquet Miss Maastricht in the press and was reported to have spied on gatherings of known Eurosceptics. Cameron may have feared that, having worked for Lamont, he would be regarded as a little too close to the rebel Eurosceptic fringe. In due course he took care to make a public display of his disapproval of his old boss's increasingly vocal opposition to Major's European policy. In his memoirs Lamont reports how Cameron 'cut' him at the Tories' party conference the following year after he had made a speech suggesting that the time might come when it would be right for the UK to leave the EU.

In the summer of 1993, however, the two men were still on good terms. The furore about Major's 'bastard' remark petered out with the parliamentary recess and, as Westminster succumbed to its traditional August torpor, Cameron left with friends for another rented villa in Italy, this time near Siena. One day Norman and Rosemary Lamont came over to have lunch with the young Tory set. One guest remembers that Lamont 'looked terrible'.

For the most part the talk was not of politics but of bridge. 'Endless bridge, from after lunch to before dinner and then after dinner long into the night,' complained one non-combatant. Cameron, perhaps by dint of his impressive job, was 'definitely the alpha male'. He and Samantha had one of the villa's largest and most beautiful rooms and, in the few daylight hours not spent over a bridge table, the couple lounged by the pool.

One day he drove her to Porto Ercole to see Woodrow Wyatt. Also staying with the Wyatts was the broadcaster Sir Robin Day. The visit was principally memorable for the attempts of Wyatt and Day to get the female members of the party to skinny-dip. Day, wearing a pair of tight blue trunks and nothing else, seemed particularly keen that Samantha should bathe naked in the Wyatt pool. In the car driving back towards Siena, Cameron's girlfriend asked, 'Who was that dirty old man in the blue swimming trunks?' On being informed that he had been, for decades, Britain's pre-eminent political interviewer, she said 'Of course!', and that she hadn't recognised him without his bow-tie.

It is interesting to note that the guest-list for this holiday – fairly typical of the time – included at least three people who are now successful senior journalists: Matthew d'Ancona, now a political columnist, Christopher Lockwood, a senior editor of the *Economist*, and Robert Hardman, a journalist on the *Daily Mail*. Just as he left for Siena another journalist friend, Alice Thomson, gave a fascinating glimpse into Cameron's circle in an article on the leading lights of her generation:

> If youth is oppositional, it should be natural for young people to search for an alternative to the status quo. In fact, they tend to go into Tory politics as a fast-track substitute for the Civil Service. There is no question of real spiritual commitment; they are impelled by an attraction to power. Since 1979, a clear path has opened out as aspirants join Conservative Central Office, then work as advisers for ministers and jump directly into the House of Commons. Michael Portillo is the best-known alumnus.

Added Thomson, herself only twenty-six at the time:

> David Cameron, 27, is current class leader and, like many, was at Eton
> and Oxford. (Young politicos from the state system prefer John Major's
> quiet-rise technique, and take lower profile jobs.) He moved from
> briefing the prime minister at PM's questions to being special adviser
> to Norman Lamont. In this position, from the election to the demise of
> his boss, he played a key role in policy making. After Mr Lamont's
> aggrieved departure for the back benches, Mr Cameron was wooed by
> Michael Howard at the Home Office.

Thomson then quotes 'Dominic Loehnis, 25, special adviser to Peter
Brooke, friend to David Cameron':

> When I went to Oxford, students were loud, heavy drinkers trashing
> curry houses. By the time I left, they were lounging around smoking
> dope, more open-minded. This generation exudes an air of responsi-
> bility, but I don't think there is any visionary feel or coherent philos-
> ophy. Most are critics rather than achievers. They hate the publicity
> that surrounds politics now and have opted for behind-the-scenes
> power in the media. But the young in politics have so much influence.
> I am on the cutting edge and that is exciting. You don't have to wait
> years for results.

In her article Thomson, who is now married to Edward Heathcoat-
Amory (himself a former staffer at CRD), then lists the other
members of Cameron's gang: 'Rachel Whetstone … is thin, wears
designer clothes and can hold her own in any political argument.
Laura Adshead … [is a] friend of Andrew Roberts and David
Cameron … Edward Llewellyn, 27, [is] also a graduate of the
Eton–Oxford–CCO production line.' Finally she includes 'Steve
Hilton, 23, the only Armani suit wearer of this group, [who] was one

of the few brave enough to leave, and is now at Saatchi's under a former Tory minister, working on the Conservative party's advertising, advising Boris Yeltsin on the referendum, and helping to sway the Irish and Polish election campaigns. "If you are good at something, nobody questions your age," he says.'

That summer Howard himself took one of the longest holidays of his political career, swapping his house in London with some Californian friends. There, in between lunch dates with Michael Caine and Sidney Poitier, he began mapping out his plans for the Home Office. He had with him two reports left over from the Clarke era, the Sheehy plan for police reform and the findings of a Royal Commission which had examined the criminal justice system. Confronted by what he saw as a defeatist attitude to crime endemic in the current system, combined with the political threat posed by Blair, Howard began to frame a wholesale revolution in home affairs policy that he believed would be too authoritarian for Labour to match. It was a strategy he knew would be achievable only if it were largely hidden from a department he thought too complacent, conservative and incompetent to oversee its own surgery.

As a result Howard trusted only a tiny circle that included Rock, Cameron and David Maclean, his closest ministerial ally whom he had made minister of state for police and criminal justice. 'I decided that radical change was necessary. And it became pretty clear in terms of these reforms that change was not what the civil service in the Home Office were used to and not what they approved of and not what in the early days they supported. So the first task I had was to impose my political will on the Home Office, and Patrick and David and the ministers, particularly David Maclean, were my closest allies in achieving that,' recalls Howard.

The Tory answer to Blair's 'tough on crime' slogan of January 1993 came that October at the party's annual conference, held that year in Blackpool's Winter Gardens. 'Prison works,' thundered Howard, to a rapturous reception from delegates. Few speeches in Howard's career were more important because, unusually for a conference address, the slogan was an adornment to real substance, not a mask to hide its absence. The new Home Secretary detailed no fewer than twenty-seven separate measures to fight crime. In addition to the headline pledge to build six new private prisons, there were crackdowns on ravers, hunt saboteurs and terrorists, new court procedures, new rules to boost rape convictions and – most controversially – a restriction of the right to silence.

Back in London, the Home Office's most senior civil servants listened aghast: none had had any idea of the range and depth of Howard's plans. Cameron and Rock had helped Howard bypass the whole system by cleverly parcelling the speech out across the whole department. 'No official in the Home Office saw the whole of that speech until after I had delivered it,' recalls Howard with evident pride. 'What we did was we worked it out together. We put the relevant bits to the relevant official at the Home Office to make sure there were no howlers in it, but no one saw the whole of it.'

Howard was the darling of the conference. His uncompromising message on crime was easy for delegates to understand and applaud. Cameron's own stock was clearly rising too, judging by an article in the *Financial Times* that appeared on the day of the speech. It tipped the young adviser – he would be twenty-seven that Saturday – to replace Gus O'Donnell as Major's press secretary. Cameron was a 'survivor', reported the paper, who 'combines amiability with a cool head and a firm hand'.

Major's Downing Street was certainly in need of some media-handling skills in the wake of the Prime Minister's own offering to the Blackpool faithful. Indeed Cameron could hardly contain his sniggers when Jonathan Hill (the man who had beaten him to the job as Major's political secretary) outlined the leader's 'back to basics' speech ahead of its delivery. He saw, as did a number of other special advisers in the room at the time, what a hostage to fortune such a moralising, retrospective slogan could become. But Hill and Tim Collins – another rival young Turk whom Downing Street had preferred to Cameron – got a large measure of the blame for encouraging newspapers to report Major's speech in terms of a call to return to Victorian sexual mores.

Howard was much more disciplined in his communication. Civil servants at the time have said how struck they were by the attention to detail he and his political team put into communicating with the press. Howard had cultivated a number of newspaper editors, including Peter Stothard at *The Times*. At his own level, Cameron was expanding his own journalistic contacts. With Michael Gove – one of Stothard's new young recruits – Cameron was a member of a dining club run by Martin Ivens, the *Sunday Times* deputy editor. Over fine food and wine at the Travellers Club, the keenest young blades of the right would meet and discuss the issues of the day. In reference to its venue and shared ideology, the club was known as the Fellow Travellers. While undoubtedly cerebral occasions, they – and other comparable gatherings – had their moments of guffawing intolerance. 'David was very right wing in those days,' says one who shared a dinner table with him, a remark which perhaps reflects his ability to meld into his surroundings as much as any firmness of view. Another acquaintance of the time remembers him being surprisingly squeamish about homosexuality for someone of his age. Anne McElvoy, who is now married to Ivens, has recalled Cameron from this time at a dinner in honour of John Redwood 'flushed with excitement, shirt hanging out and waving a large cigar while talking very tough about free markets'.

On one occasion during this period, a mutual friend arranged for him to meet the revered, ascetic Tory thinker and former MP Enoch Powell, before whom young Tories (particularly libertarian, Eurosceptic ones) would queue up to pay homage. As it happened,

Cameron outflanked Powell. Over the dinner table he spoke fluently of the need for the prison service to look to the market place to ease some of its problems. For Enoch Powell, the darling of the Tory right, this was too much. He felt it was one of the moral duties of the state to take charge of the penal system, and privatising any part of it would be a dereliction of duty to the public.

When it came to briefing journalists back in the office, Howard says that, while Cameron was involved, Rock did most of the media work, being the more experienced of the two. Indeed Rock spent so much of his time talking to his friends in the press that officials dubbed him 'Radio Rock'. Howard's biographer quotes 'a former colleague' as saying: 'He invented spinning before Alastair Campbell got out of bed.' Another innovation brought in under Howard and later aped by Campbell and New Labour was the use of a media management 'grid' to plot setpiece news events. The grid helps avoid two announcements competing for the media's attention at the same time. It can also help the cynically minded to 'bury bad news' by cramming that day's events with other newsworthy gobbets of information. 'Those who were working in the Home Office in 1997 said that the best preparation for New Labour was working for Michael Howard,' a senior official has said.

Perhaps unsurprisingly, Whitehall did not take kindly to Howard's methods. Barely a month after his successful conference speech, the *Guardian* reported officials complaining that the Home Office was being made into a 'PR machine for Mr Howard'. And in a clear reference to Rock and Cameron, Nick Cohen in the *Observer* quoted a senior civil servant saying: 'Howard just talks to young public school gentlemen from the party headquarters.'

It was around this time that another 'young public school gentleman' began his career. George Osborne, who had graduated the previous May from Oxford, was invited to apply for a job at CRD by his friend George Bridges. Bridges, the grandson of Sir Edward

Bridges, Winston Churchill's Cabinet Secretary, had started at CRD in 1992 and was now being called to serve in John Major's political office in Number 10. Osborne was given the job that Cameron had performed in the Political Section. Although Osborne's boss was Whetstone, he hardly knew her close friend David Cameron, whose career as a 'hot-shot special adviser' rarely took him back to Smith Square.

The pressures building up in the Home Office at the beginning of 1994 were to blow a huge hole in Howard's credibility some twenty months later when he controversially sacked Derek Lewis, the head of the prison service, in October 1995. Lewis, who had been brought in from the private sector, chose not to go quietly. With political support from Ann Widdecombe, he fought a bitter media battle that effectively ended Howard's hopes of being John Major's immediate successor as Tory leader. His revenge on Howard included a deeply unflattering portrait of his policy-making process in a book, *Hidden Agendas*, published in 1997.

Proposals for a new code of standards for the prison service were first presented to Howard in November 1993. The Home Secretary delayed the code's publication until the New Year when, Lewis claims, he told a large meeting of ministers and officials that he thought it would be perceived as a 'charter for prisoners'. 'One of his special advisers, David Cameron, then asked to see me in private,' writes Lewis.

> We talked through the difficulties we were having. Looking a bit sheep-ish, Cameron mentioned that Howard's wife, Sandra, had looked at the code's housekeeping standards, which concerned such matters as the frequency with which bed linen and socks were changed, and the standards for food provided. Mrs Howard, I was told, thought that the code's prescriptions for a balanced and nutritious diet were giving today's offenders more than they deserved.

When the book was published Michael and Sandra Howard denied the claim vigorously and threatened to sue. But no action was taken and Lewis's allegation remains on the record.

Rock, who insists that Sandra was far more liberal than her husband, says Lewis has misremembered the episode. He says one recommendation was that prisoners should have a change of blankets three times a year. 'As I understand it Michael Howard raised casually the blanket issue as an example of the contents of the proposed code and Sandra said something like twice a year is enough for the Howard household. For some reason I think that David must have heard of these comments and mentioned it in Derek's presence.' Rock goes on: 'I do remember David making the remark about a "healthy balanced diet" being better than specifying exactly what the diet should contain, but his intention wasn't in any way to denude the standards but to give less scope for frivolous litigation – and, frankly, to save us from public ridicule. There was never any suggestion that prisoners should be treated other than humanely; simply that Derek's proposals were too detailed.'

For all Howard's undoubted hard work in constructing and communicating a comprehensive overhaul of the criminal justice system, it failed in its key political objective. Blair persuaded John Smith, Kinnock's successor as party leader, that it would be madness for Labour to oppose the Criminal Justice Bill that contained many of the measures when it was unveiled in December 1993. When Cameron decided not to vote against Tony Blair's education reforms in 2005, he must have been mindful of how eleven years earlier Blair had slipped from the political noose that Howard had prepared for him. Cameron has accepted Blair's public service investment in order to neutralise the negative perception of the Tories as enemies of the NHS and state education, just as Blair accepted Howard's draconian crime-fighting measures to neutralise the public view of Labour as soft on crime.

Indeed, on occasion the shadow Home Secretary went out of his way to offer his assistance, for example when in April 1994 Blair helped Howard defeat a looming rebellion over so-called video nasties. When Blair suggested that he visit Howard at the Home Office, Cameron was despatched to greet the rising star and take him into the Secretary of State's room for a meeting to fix the compromise. Although the young Tory had watched Blair from afar from his first days in CRD, this was the first time he had actually met him. The special adviser was struck by how personable Blair was and how intelligently he dealt with the legal problem of banning titles like *Driller Killer*.

Relations between New Labour and Cameron were not always so harmonious. The previous month Cameron had been blamed for leaking to the press a story that Smith had secretly met with Major to discuss on what terms Labour would drop its policy of opposing the renewal of the Prevention of Terrorism Act. In what must qualify for an award in any pot-and-kettle name-calling competition, Cameron has the honour of having been accused by Peter Mandelson on the floor of the House of practising media dark arts.

The then Labour MP for Hartlepool demanded that Howard give 'an unambiguous undertaking that neither he, nor his officials nor his two special advisers, Patrick Rock and David Cameron, who are regularly seen operating in the press gallery, had absolutely no [sic] responsibility whatsoever for planting that story'. Cameron was, in fact, formally interviewed in an official Cabinet Office leak inquiry. Rock, who had been absent from the office at the time, was not. Although minor, the row came at a sensitive time for Cameron, who was waiting to hear whether he had been chosen to go on to the candidates' list of would-be MPs. When Mandelson came close to repeating the allegation outside the Commons chamber Cameron and Howard discussed suing him for libel.

The *Evening Standard* on 17 March had good news, albeit conveyed archly: 'Overcoming the handicap of being an Old Etonian, the Home

Secretary's special adviser David Cameron has taken the first vital step to becoming an MP. He has just been placed on the Candidates List after submitting himself for an "assessment weekend" at the Holiday Inn in Slough, thus notifying Tory constituency associations that he meets with Central Office approval.' The paper's diarist added that Cameron was a man of 'worldly sophistication', noting his membership of the Bullingdon and a holiday he had taken in Morocco before recording that he 'currently enjoys the affections of Samantha Sheffield, daughter of Sir Reginald, an 8th baronet. "He takes her to the races," I'm told.'

Getting on the candidates' list is a vital first step for the aspirant Tory politician. Cameron had been for some time on the threshold of becoming a politician in his own right. But first he had to make it on to that Smith Square list. Ideological belief and political ability were necessary but not sufficient conditions. Social polish was also needed – and it was this, as much as any other attribute, that was assessed at the Slough selection weekends. A former candidate who was selected at around the same time as Cameron describes the experience as a 'ghastly sort of house party where your every move is assessed. It's a sort of trial by snob.' The selection weekend was not a trial that David Cameron was ever going to fail.

By the spring of 1994, Cameron's personal and professional prospects were bright. Although Howard's reputation was beginning to suffer the attrition all Home Secretaries endure, there was nothing to suggest the internal Home Office convulsions ahead, and a safe Conservative seat at the next election must have seemed as good as certain. Blair and Brown were making political inroads but remained a limited threat while restricted to their home affairs and economic briefs. On the morning of 12 May 1994 Howard's office was concerned with smoothing the tricky progress of the Criminal Justice Bill through the Lords that day. Ministers were concerned that provisions for secure training units for young teenagers could be lost to a rebellion by Tory peers. Then came news of the sudden death of Labour leader John Smith. Rock recalls the day vividly. 'I remember going for a drink with David round the corner from the Home Office. We both agreed that Blair coming meant that we were fucked.'

Michael Howard was among the first Tories to have spotted Blair's potential. He and Sandra had invited the young, charming barrister and his wife for a dinner at their Notting Hill home shortly after he had arrived in the Commons in 1983. The fascination was shared by his young adviser: Cameron made a point of getting to know his opposite number, Tim Allan. Allan and the young Tory aide even had a number of dinners together as each tried to divine what the other really thought of their respective bosses. It was a relationship that deepened over the following years as Cameron's 'brat pack' Tories and the younger members of Blair's inner circle conducted a prolonged political flirtation.

Cameron's overt interest in the rise of New Labour begs an obvious question: how much of Howard's politics did he share? By his own admission he was a firm believer in the 'prison works' element of the Home Secretary's agenda and leaned to the libertarian right on questions of state regulation of individual lifestyles. 'When at the Home Office as a special adviser in the early 1990s, I wrote endless papers about scrapping our ludicrous [licensing] laws,' he later declared. 'The permanent secretary, who was also tiring of my missives about stiff minimum sentences for burglars, summoned me to his office and said: "Cameron, as far as I can see you want half the population in prison and the other half in the pub."' (His views on the licensing laws were to become a political difficulty during the 2005 leadership election, which coincided with a *Daily Mail* campaign against their liberalisation, something he had long argued for.)

Although Cameron has admitted he was 'only half-way' to being an 'inclusive' Tory while Howard's special adviser, at least one minister recalls doubting whether he shared the determinedly right-wing agenda of his boss. Sir Peter Lloyd was prisons minister until being sacked in 1994, presumably because he was opposed to most of Howard's policies. He remembers Cameron asking if he could visit a prison with him, an experience he felt would be useful as he helped the Home Secretary frame new policies. As they left Long Lartin, a maximum-security prison, the aide made clear how unpleasant he had found it. 'High-security prisons have a particularly oppressive, menacing atmosphere and I noted that it had affected him. As we left he commented on it. I was impressed that he had reacted first with his own humane instinct rather than some standard policy line,' says Sir Peter, who has continued to work for better jails. The former minister contrasts Cameron with Rock, 'a true believer', and says he wondered whether the former was 'one of those people who are just interested in politics but are not necessarily very ideological. I remember thinking in ministerial meetings, "He is a bright chap – does he really believe all this nonsense?"'

Howard himself says that Cameron never showed any signs that he disagreed with the direction – but would, occasionally, dissuade him from a course of action he thought wrong or politically unwise. Privately Cameron worried about some of Howard's more draconian measures. The crackdown on 'raves' struck him as illiberal – not least because his girlfriend was attending exactly the sort of dance events Howard wanted to ban. In general he kept his counsel, waiting to be asked his opinion rather than volunteer it. Howards explains: 'I talked to David and Patrick about what I was going to do. I reached what I would regard as a provisional opinion and then I would say this is what I think, what do you think? Do you think it would stand up? If I could be persuaded that it wasn't the right thing to do, I would think again. On occasion they persuaded me that the views I came to were wrong, that the risks were too great, the dangers were too great or it was just the wrong thing to do.'

Although he says he was too busy to socialise with anyone very much, least of all his special advisers, Howard does recall Cameron visiting his grace-and-favour house in Belgravia on at least one occasion when he held a party. Cameron's former headmaster Eric Anderson was, coincidentally, another guest (Howard's elder son Nicholas was at Eton at the time). 'What on earth are you doing here?' Howard recalls Anderson asking Cameron. 'Good God!' he exclaimed on being told that he was the Home Secretary's special adviser.

Howard makes no apology for his reliance on his tight inner circle, saying that Cameron 'worked really hard' and 'was involved in the whole of what I did'. 'It was lonely in the early days. It affronted the way in which the Home Office civil servants had done things for a very long time and it affronted the whole of the criminal justice establishment.' Rock says Cameron 'never gave the impression that he wasn't in tune with Michael Howard's agenda. When he came to the Home Office he was perfectly clear, as I was, that the remit was to shift the balance in the criminal justice system away from the criminal and towards the victim. He therefore worked to that agenda. It's obvious that David is somewhat more liberal on Home Office issues than Michael, but we both got on and did our job. I don't recall David ever raising with me any serious concerns about the general drift of policy while he was there, but then again I would have been surprised if he had done so.' His former colleague is also generous in his praise for Cameron's creativity in both speech-writing and policy-making. By way of example he says it was Cameron who came up with the CCTV Challenge policy that offered local authorities match-funding for proposed surveillance programmes. This simple measure helped both hasten the spread of crime-reducing technology and ensure its quality.

For Howard, though, Cameron's greatest talent was his capacity to do the sort of hard unglamorous work necessary if a politician is to achieve real change. 'The great difference between David and Blair is that whereas Blair is only interested in eye-catching initiatives and isn't interested in the nitty-gritty, David is prepared to roll up his sleeves and work hard and follow things through and will be a good Prime Minister for that reason. He is interested in delivery and is prepared to do what it takes to achieve delivery.'

ST GEORGE STREET
Carlton Communications 1994–1997

Michael Howard was not surprised when, in the spring of 1994, David Cameron told him he would be taking a job outside politics. The Home Secretary's young adviser was looking for a winnable seat and local Conservative associations tended then – and tend now – to mark down applicants with no experience outside Westminster. There was also the question of money. While Cameron had managed to increase his salary under Lamont, it was still well short of the income earned by most of his non-political peers.

He had a particular reason for wanting to speed his career: he and Samantha had become secretly engaged. He had wanted to marry her within a year of their courtship but she – at twenty-two – did not feel ready. Her mother had married very young herself and had got divorced just five years later. Samantha didn't want to make the same mistake, but she didn't want to say no. 'She couldn't really get her head round it,' says one of the two people in whom the couple confided. 'She needed about half a year to let the idea that she was going to get married sink in. She knew she wanted to marry him, but she also felt too young. She wanted to let the idea "I am getting married" settle in her head.' She might also have worried about the prospect of becoming a politician's wife, but Cameron was up-front about his ambition. Early in their relationship, he had told her that he planned to become an MP, adding. 'You must say if you think it is a problem.'

In the middle of 1994, as part of his campaign to woo Samantha,

Cameron sold his flat on Lansdowne Crescent and bought 3 Finstock Road. The house, in the less fashionable but quieter streets of North Kensington, cost £215,000. It was a sum he paid with the profit from his previous property, a bequest from his great-aunt Violet Critchley, some funds from his father and a mortgage. But the property had been divided into two flats at the time and needed a lot of work. Samantha, faced with deciding whether to sink her own funds into this project, finally made the commitment. The moment of their agreement to marry was, in Cameron's words, 'disastrous'. 'I kept taking her on a romantic walk or out for dinner and we'd always have some ferocious argument, so it wasn't the right moment. In the end, I proposed on the sofa as we watched a video of *Mean Streets*.'

Now all Cameron needed was a good position and a safe Tory seat. But how does a twenty-seven-year-old with no private sector experience land a well-paid, high-profile job from which to launch a political career? The answer was supplied by Samantha's mother, Annabel Astor, a friend and occasional holiday partner of Michael Green, chairman of Carlton, one of the most successful companies in Britain. She phoned Green with a proposition for her old friend. The pair had already discussed Cameron, whom Green had met. 'We agreed that to get anywhere in politics it was quite important to have some experience of the real world,' remembers Green. Annabel Astor had decided that Cameron and Green were well matched, and asked the Carlton boss whether he would like to employ her daughter's boyfriend. 'She's a very formidable lady with a very good sense of horseflesh, and when she says to me, "Do something," I do it!' says Green.

It 'wasn't a bad idea', Green agrees, for Carlton to help groom future politicians. And, although he does not say so, the fact that his friend and Cameron's prospective father-in-law William Astor had a chance of becoming a government minister would have done no harm. (He was not to know, of course, that, fortuitously, Astor was to enter the department responsible for broadcasting, National Heritage.)

Notwithstanding the encouragement from his friend, Green had his doubts. 'I remember David's interview vividly,' he says. 'I wanted to know how serious he was about business, making money, and politics. And to David's credit he was crystal clear. He said that he wanted to be an MP. That was what was important to him. I said that this could be a disadvantage at Carlton, because we looked for people that wanted to stay there for life. They may not stay for life but we needed people that breathed, dreamed and slept the company.' Cameron says that, to begin with, Green was explicit in trying to make it a condition of employing him that he would not fight the next election. 'He said the job was off,' says Cameron. 'Then he came back a week later and said here is another job, with lower pay, and I jumped at it, so I paid for my love of politics with a pay cut before I had even started.' 'David never ever wavered,' admits Green, either at the interview or over the next seven years they spent together. Carlton was always going to be an interlude from politics.

Those who know Green well will testify that he is not the easiest of men, and Cameron could be forgiven for thinking that the job he had taken might be a mixed blessing. The mogul's great friend Max Hastings, former editor of the *Daily Telegraph* and a confirmed heterosexual, once told Green that he would rather sleep with him than work for him. A former Carlton executive told Green's biographer that 'he has these moments of extreme temper – you know, like a child'. Some of these outbursts were understandable – others less so. One furious tirade is said to have been prompted by the lack of lights on Carlton's Christmas tree. Such stories were not untypical.

On top of this, not everyone was enamoured of Carlton. It was accused of producing down-market programmes, in breach of its franchise commitments. There was a perception that Green was offering 'pile 'em high, sell 'em cheap' television. Victor Lewis-Smith wrote disobligingly about the company in his acerbic television column in London's *Evening Standard* at least once a week. On one occasion he asked: 'What is the difference between Carlton TV and a bucket of shit? Answer: The bucket.' In 1994 Carlton was officially censured for its 'glib and superficial' output by the broadcasting standards regulator.

The Independent Television Commission handed that judgement down just before Cameron arrived at Carlton. In his seven years as its most senior communications executive he was to face plenty of similarly embarrassing rulings against the channel. In 1997, for instance, the ITC intervened several times over breaches of its programme code by the company. *Blues and Twos*, a police documentary, was censured for the fact that a film crew failed to identify itself when it accompanied police on a raid on a seventeen-year-old's home. *London Tonight* was criticised for inaccurate court reporting. A debate on the monarchy, filmed before an audience of 3,000, was of 'poor quality', said the regulators. More seriously Carlton had been handed a formal warning for breaching sponsorship rules, after *Now We're Talking*, hosted by Phillip Schofield, was completely paid for by British Telecom. In 1998 *Teargas and Tantrums*, a film about football violence, was condemned by MPs and the Football Association after it emerged that it had been made by a self-confessed former hooligan, and an award-winning drugs documentary was exposed as a fake. A public relations executive who worked frequently with Cameron at the time summed up his role thus: 'David was the acceptable face of Carlton.'

Publicly, of course, Cameron is admiring of Green. Lunch partners at the time attest that in private, too, he always made light of working alongside a man seen by some as something of a tyrant. 'I learned a lot from Michael Green,' Cameron told an interviewer just after he had launched his leadership bid. 'He is a terrific character – an inspirational, swashbuckling entrepreneur. He is leaps ahead of everyone else. He makes decisions quickly. He takes risks and is immensely charismatic. I think, I hope, I learned from him how to get things done, how to lead with conviction.'

Green was one of Margaret Thatcher's favourite businessmen and it is easy to see why. When he was only seventeen he and his brother bought an ailing printing firm and pioneered direct marketing before breaking into television production. Finally, and most dramatically, Green had delighted the Thatcher government by forcing his way into the cartel of commercial broadcasting. His victory, against all expectations, over Thames Television for the London franchise cemented his position as the free-marketeers' darling.

In 1994 it seemed quite possible, probable even, that Green would grow into a direct rival to Rupert Murdoch. He had added the Central franchise to his empire, had bought the Technicolor company and become a major shareholder in and chairman of ITN. When David Cameron arrived for work at Carlton's headquarters at 15 St George Street, Mayfair in September that year he was – according to Ray Snoddy, Green's biographer – just the latest in a succession of 'Tory boys' the mogul had employed in his empire. He did not start, as is sometimes reported, as director of corporate communication. His appointment was gazetted in *PR Week* as 'a member of the corporate affairs department'. The trade magazine added: 'It is believed he will act as PA to chairman Michael Green.' Nor did he immediately impress the company's executives. One, who later became a friend and supporter, recalls being taken to lunch by the new arrival. 'I remember thinking, "Oh God, another Old Etonian." I wasn't overly excited – he used to flush quite a lot.'

The top job was given to Jan Shawe, an experienced and professional operator who had been headhunted from the academic publisher Reed Elsevier. Starting a month after Cameron, Shawe found her basement office carpeted with bouquets of flowers from Green, clearly determined to charm his new acquisition. Her 'Day One' seems to have been the high-point of a remarkably short and unhappy tenure at Carlton. She resigned just over five weeks later, reportedly irritated at working 'in an office where all the talk among the courtiers was usually about what Green was doing and what his mood was on any particular day'.

Yet Green *was* Carlton. From his office way above them on the third floor of the then Carlton HQ in London's St George Street, he ran the company more like the family business it had once been than the FTSE 100 company it had become. He sat behind a small, polished wooden desk in a minimalist office. There were few signs of the entrepreneur's private life, but there were two prominent televisions on white plinths, one showing ITV, with the sound down, the other Carlton's share price. No one in his empire looked forward to being called into that office when Green was in a temper.

Almost as soon as Cameron arrived, he impressed colleagues with the way he dealt with Green and calmed him down. Rupert Dilnott-Cooper, then a senior Carlton executive, recalls one incident that he says shows Cameron's cool under fire. 'I was sitting in my office around about ten o'clock one morning and Michael rang and shouted at me.' Green was enraged by an article on Carlton in the morning's *Financial Times*, written after a briefing prepared by Dilnott-Cooper. 'I said to him, "A, it's a good story, and B, I cleared this through David." So Michael then proceeded to patch a call in to David Cameron. David came on the line and I wasn't expecting anything much, frankly. David was new to Carlton and I didn't know him at all well, but he was really brief, really good. He said, "Michael, calm down. This is a good story – I've seen it already, it's a very good story, kindly stop shouting at Rupert and shout at me."'

'David was the first person I'd ever come across who actually talked directly like that to Michael,' says Dilnott-Cooper. 'Michael is an entrepreneur who does not particularly tolerate "yes men" but nor does he like being treated to rude fight-backs. The only way to work for Michael was to be good at what you did, be polite but stand your ground when convinced you were right. You would not survive unless you had qualities of resilience, I mean serious resilience.' The story is endorsed by Martin Bowley, then in charge of Carlton's sales operation. Cameron, he recalls, 'would sit there and say "I think this" – then – bang – Michael Green would go: "You don't fucking tell me, you fucking idiot." And David would go, "Well, no, I do, I think this", says Bowley. And that was how it was done … Nothing comes close to Michael Green giving you a hard time, believe me. Nowhere near it. It is incredible.' 'Yes, he did stand his ground, he definitely stood his ground,' says Green today.

The truth is that, not for the first time, with Shawe's abrupt departure, fortune smiled on Cameron. He seized the opportunity with both hands. His sang-froid, his facility with words and his knowledge of the media all impressed Green. He denies, however, that Cameron's political connections were of any use ('I had access to government as the head of a media company'), and didn't need an ex-special adviser to lobby on his behalf. Yet there were those in the Opposition whom Green did not know, and whom he needed to meet, which Cameron was able to facilitate. Around the middle of 1995, the young aide set up a meeting between the entrepreneur and Labour's shadow Chancellor, Gordon Brown. Cameron, still not thirty, described Brown to his boss as 'going places'. Green certainly seems to have appreciated the encounter, calling it 'one of the greatest lunches ever'. The Carlton chairman and the shadow Chancellor had a good-natured but vigorous row about the merits of Labour's 'fat cats' campaign against corporate greed, he recalls. After the last of the coffee had gone cold, Brown was showing no signs of returning to Westminster, however. As the afternoon wore on, the restless Green muttered under his breath to Cameron: 'How do we close the meeting?' Cameron explained that 'The trouble with the Opposition is they've got plenty of time.'

Having weathered the initial storm and having shone since Shawe's sudden departure, Cameron had good reason to celebrate his first anniversary at Carlton. In a sign of his progress through the ranks,

Green invited him to begin attending 'prayers', a meeting of senior executives he held in his office on Monday mornings. The salary (around £80,000 a year, according to the estimates of colleagues) was much better than his £49,000 at the Home Office, and the work less onerous (although he showed a capacity for hard graft when it was needed). Apart from anything else, it was glamorous. 'He took tables at the BAFTAs to entertain journalists, he used to hang out in the Met Bar after work,' remembers one former colleague. The Met Bar, in Mayfair, was throughout the late 1990s one of London's most exclusive celebrity haunts. He would also go on occasional evenings gambling with his boss at the Portland Club, also in Mayfair, a celebrated cards club where his father was wont occasionally to bring cash to the table – although gambling appealed more to the younger Cameron's head than his heart. 'Dave used to be bricking it at the figures involved, and he always had his pot guaranteed by Michael,' says a friend.

The job as Green's aide meant frequent trips to the US, where he would visit Carlton concerns in Los Angeles and Las Vegas and talk to the money men on the East Coast. Green recalls how, to enliven the endless presentations to US bankers, Cameron and he would sometimes swap places – the young sidekick pretending to be the swashbuckling entrepreneur. Travelling the world at the side of a media boss and dealmaker supreme like Green, Cameron could have been forgiven for thinking that elements of his life resembled an airport novel.

In fact one 'bonkbuster', published just a year before by a university acquaintance, does indeed feature a character called 'David Cameron' who works in the media – albeit as a 'top war correspondent' ('He's survived bullets and bombs, but he's never met the right woman'). Tess Stimson, author of the book, *Hard News*, says her choice of the name was 'pure coincidence', although she admits she knew the future Prime Minister at Oxford and is a good friend of Robert Hardman, a long-time Cameron friend, whose name also appears in the book. Stimson, now a journalism teacher living in the US, admits that some of the parallels are 'hilarious'. The tale in which 'David Cameron' falls for a journalist colleague wrongly accused of taking cocaine certainly contains some sex scenes which cannot have failed to amuse Cameron and his girfriend. 'David pulled back, cupping her breasts in his hands. "Not yet, not yet, my darling my love,"' reads one of the tamer extracts from the book, which reached number five in the bestseller lists.

Progress in the romance of the real-life David Cameron was marked in less racy terms on 16 October 1994, in Nigel Dempster's diary in the *Daily Mail*. 'David [Cameron] proposed on a weekend when both the Astors and Sheffields were staying together,' trilled Dempster. '"There are eight children between the two marriages, and they are all the best of friends," says David, with relief. "Samantha is my younger sister Clare's best friend, so we've known each other for ages. But love really blossomed three years ago [sic] when we were all on holiday in Southern Italy to celebrate my parents' 30th wedding anniversary."' Cameron added: 'She's incredibly talented.'

What of Cameron's own cultural tastes? As befits the product of a decidedly 'county' background, they are unashamedly middle brow. His preferred reading has long been James Bond, and he has an immaculate collection of Ian Fleming's novels, even if he admits he prefers the films. His other preferences are also decidedly masculine. He has seen *Where Eagles Dare* seventeen times, has read all of Graham Greene's novels, adores Flashman (though, reluctant to amplify the comparison, doesn't advertise the fact), looks back fondly at Rider Haggard and cites *Lawrence of Arabia* as his favourite film and *Porridge* as his top sitcom. Also, rather charmingly, he refers to world-renowned actor Kevin Spacey as Keyser Söze, the name of his character in *The Usual Suspects*. Very demanding music is not his cup of tea, either. He's a fan of Pulp's 'Babies' ('a brilliant song to sing along to when I'm falling asleep in the car') and enjoys Bob Dylan's *Nashville Skyline* and *Blood on the Tracks*. When he was working for Norman Lamont one of his friends, amused and frustrated by his wilfully mainstream tastes, invited him to a performance of Richard Strauss's opera *Die Frau ohne Schatten*. A few days later a letter arrived from Cameron thanking his host for 'introducing me to National Socialism', but he had crossed out the last two words, replacing them with 'the operas of Richard Strauss'. Candidly, he added that he thought the composer 'a bit heavy for me'. He went on to say: 'At the moment I am listening to an excellent Callas compilation (which you would no doubt disapprove of as commercial) but we philistines have to start somewhere.' One friend has sighed that Cameron's musical tastes are well catered for by the old Virgin Radio, a claim his 2006 selection for *Desert Island Discs* did not disprove.

In December 1994 Cameron's search for a seat was proving to be less straightforward than he would have liked. One of his first attempts to be selected, for Ashford in Kent, ended in disaster. In a ritual that was to become grimly familiar for the young couple, they were invited by the local Conservative association to attend a drinks party with six other candidates and their spouses, chosen from 128 applicants. Over sherry and nibbles at the Ashford Post House Hotel, Cameron and his girlfriend worked the room, sticking closely to one another. More experienced political couples know that it is best to split up on such occasions, thereby projecting relaxed independence and doubling the opportunity for contact. Understandably nervous on this, her first outing as a prospective candidate's partner, Samantha had made the mistake of wearing a decidedly Notting Hill skirt with a large, leg-showing slit. On being told that that this would not be considered 'appropriate' in one of the crustier seats in the Home Counties, she felt obliged to borrow a safety-pin.

Despite these faux-pas, Cameron was shortlisted to go through to the next round with two other candidates, both now on Cameron's frontbench: Damian Green and Theresa May. The final selection, this time at the Ashford International, was to be held two days later. Cameron, however, made the mistake of arranging to travel to the

Kentish town from London by train – which was then cancelled. The hopeful candidate arrived, flustered, having begged a lift. Damian Green, a former Number 10 policy adviser, who had not trusted British Rail to deliver him to the good Tories of Kent, was selected instead.

Just as David Cameron was struggling to establish his own political career, another twenty-seven-year-old under the care of the future MP's father was heading for prison. The trial of Jeremy Gray for theft had all the elements of a truly gripping courtroom drama – and a headline-writer's dream: gay sex, drugs, betrayal, the Mafia and even British intelligence services. Had the journalists covering it known of its connections to politics those headlines might have been bigger. Jeremy Gray, son of a doctor from Tisbury, near Salisbury, Wiltshire, had gone into the City, where he became personal assistant to a senior stockbroker in the personal investments section of the respected firm Panmure Gordon. That broker was Ian Cameron.

On 1 March 1994 – around the time Cameron was being put through his paces by senior Tories at the Holiday Inn in Slough – Gray told his bosses that he would not be returning to work because he had been diagnosed as HIV positive. Some time that summer, it was discovered that Gray had moved £55,000 in treasury stock from his own father's account. Further searches uncovered an even more alarming theft – that of £3 million in US investments belonging to the British Heart Foundation charity. The profits had been siphoned off to a series of Swiss bank accounts. The swindle was a mortifying embarrassment to Ian Cameron, under whose charge Gray had been placed. Fortunately for all concerned, the Press Association report of Gray's case at Snaresbrook Crown Court on 5 October 1995 made no mention of the thief's supervisor.

Had it done so, eyebrows might have been raised when the court heard that Gray's father, Dr Michael Gray, had written to the Home Office passing on his son's claims that he was an 'unwanted leftover of British intelligence'. At first sight, Gray's claims seemed to be outlandish almost beyond words. He said he had become caught up in a drug-running and money-laundering ring connecting Dublin, Amsterdam and Bosnia after he had looked after a briefcase full of drugs as a 'favour' for a friend with Mafia connections. The young broker's godfather, Brigadier Charles Wright, told the court that he had had 'great difficulty' in believing the story but had found that it had 'some substance'. And then there is Dr Gray's letter to the Home Office. If Gray's claims had been complete nonsense, why did it receive an 'equivocal reply', as the court was told?

But more interesting still is the question of whether David Cameron knew about the case before it came to court – as seems likely. He had been in the Home Office when Gray's theft was discovered, but had left just before Dr Gray wrote to the department repeating his son's allegations that he had been caught up in a British intelligence operation. Whatever the truth, the case was a blot on Ian Cameron's otherwise spotless reputation in the City. Gray's father Michael says that Ian Cameron was entirely blameless ('I don't think he behaved in any way other than honourably'), but the fact that such money had been moved about on Cameron's watch did not reflect well on him. At the very least, the whole affair would have been a worry to him and his family, all the more so when – following an official investigation – Panmure Gordon was fined heavily.

Michael Green would have been sympathetic – for if there is one thing that the entrepreneur dislikes deeply it is adverse press coverage. There is a famous story about how Green ditched his former lover Jeanette Crowley when he fell in love with the young investor-relations executive and friend of the Astors, Tessa Buckmaster. The Irish actress, bitter at the way their relationship had ended, gave a newspaper interview in which she said there were only two things Green feared: 'poverty and personal publicity'. Green's relationship with the press – a mixture of fear and fascination – helps explain some of the animosity a number of financial journalists who covered

Carlton in the mid- to late 1990s have shown Cameron since he emerged as a leading politician. More than once the young PR man was instructed to deliver, as a former colleague put it, 'a Green bollocking by proxy'. None on the receiving end have forgotten the experience and a number have not forgiven Cameron.

Green once confided to an underling that he would like to have been the editor of the *Daily Telegraph*, and he once considered buying the Express Newspaper group and inserting Piers Morgan (former editor of the *Mirror*) as the daily paper's editor. One of the perks of his job as chairman of ITN was a pass to the Press Gallery of the House of Commons. Despite never having done a day's reporting in his life, the media mogul would use the journalist's pass to watch Commons events in which he was interested. He maintained friendly relations with a number of leading journalists, playing tennis regularly with Hastings at his country estate.

A former Green spin doctor recalls how a negative press article – even if fairly minor – could send him into a rage. Personally publicity-shy (Green would go to great lengths to avoid being 'snapped' by press photographers), he was nevertheless deeply interested in newspapers' content. Few weekends would go undisturbed by a call from Green to dissect in great detail the contents of the weekend's press. A negative piece about an enemy – Charles Allen, the head of Granada Television, for example – could win for the spin doctor his delighted congratulations: even if, as was usually the case, it had nothing to do with any briefing from Carlton. But with ill-deserved praise came unfair criticism. The trick, says another former employee, was to take the rough with the smooth and understand that neither would last for long.

In under eighteen months in the job, Cameron had gone from being the friend of a friend of his boss to being a 'member of the corporate affairs team' and thence to being its director. It helped that he had been taken under the wing of Piers Inskip, now Viscount Caldecote, and Edwina Paine, the well-bred head of investor relations.

Together they formed an aristocratic court around Green. 'Cameron was an upmarket guy,' recalls a former colleague, 'but they were all bloody upmarket ... they were all terribly posh. If they ever found a Labourite down there they would have hung him from the polenta machine in the kitchen.' Those working under Cameron at this time are generally supportive today. They say he had a keen eye for a story and was assiduous in finding out what was going on throughout the company. This last trait could have marked him down as Green's 'nark', but Cameron seems to have managed the company's internal politics as well as anybody. Those politics, to some extent, reflected national divides. Green and his inner court in St George Street represented the instinctive Tories (although he was to switch sides in 1997), while the fashionable television executives based in Carlton's other premises in St Martin's Lane were all for Labour. 'It was like a public school dorm – we wondered what they did all day,' says one of the latter camp of the former.

And, though teetering, the Tory administration was still in charge. Green accepts that Cameron's knowledge of Whitehall was an asset as he battled to change ownership rules to allow the take-over of ITV companies. For big fish like Carlton and its chief rival Granada, this was immensely important as it removed the protection given to smaller fry. ITV consolidation, as it was called, doubled the size of the biggest businesses at a stroke, since it was obvious which companies were going to prevail. More than in most industries, relations between media owners – particularly broadcasters – and the government are crucial. As Chris Hopson, David Cameron's opposite number at Granada, said at the time, 'there are few industries where your bottom line, or ability to grow, is so dependent on the actions of government and regulators'.

Because of Carlton's and Granada's shared interest in getting the 'no take-over' rule scrapped, the rivals worked together on the lobbying operation. It might have been handy for Cameron that his future father-in-law was a minister in the Department of National Heritage, which was responsible for broadcasting, but Hopson insists it didn't work like that. 'People sometimes imagine that what we do is have a long lunch with our old chum the minister, who returns to his department with rosy-red cheeks and announces, "Right we are going to change the Broadcasting Act."' In fact, said Hopson, 'you have to win an intellectual argument'. In this case the argument that Hopson and Cameron had to win was not only with the Department of National Heritage but also with the Welsh and Scottish Offices, and with the broadcasting regulators, all of which worried about the effect consolidation would have on ITV's regional output.

Among the many former colleagues and current friends whom Cameron could readily call on was George Bridges, by now John Major's assistant political secretary. Did Cameron feel a twinge of envy when he saw first Bridges and then in early 1997 Osborne take up positions in Downing Street? His friend Michael Gove says not – Cameron knew that by spending time in the 'real world' he was closer to building his own political identity. Indeed Bridges, four years younger than Cameron, was reported to have been lined up to replace him at Carlton when, as expected, the young PR finally became an MP. This planned extension of the political production line that began at Eton and ended in Westminster broke down, as we shall see, when the British electorate failed to create the necessary vacancy.

Cameron may have had another reason for feeling glad to be out of politics at that time. In mid-1995, when Major confronted his critics and called a leadership election, he invited his opponents to put up or shut up. All eyes were on Michael Portillo to see if he would stand, and at around this time, according to Cameron himself, he told Chris Patten that he believed Portillo would be the Tories' best choice as leader. 'I am not sure we are ready for a Spanish prime minister,' Cameron said Patten replied. In the event, Portillo didn't put himself forward.

For Major loyalists though, the immediate threat was John Redwood, admired by some for having the courage to stand against the Prime Minister, but loathed by others for his perceived disloyalty and Euroscepticism. Redwood, of course, hoped that the election would be the catalyst for a change of direction for the party. In the event, Major won and his critics were, for a while at least, thwarted. But the episode left traces of rancour towards those whom Major saw as having been disloyal. One of those who worked for John Redwood's campaign was Cameron's close friend and ally Steve Hilton. A university friend of Hilton said later, 'Steve has always had this sure sense that his time would come – he was just waiting for the right person to do it with.' He backed the right horse in Cameron. His choice of mount in 1995 was less well judged. (George Osborne worked on the Major campaign – a stint that won him the prize of becoming Douglas Hogg's special adviser at the Ministry of Agriculture, Food and Fisheries just before the BSE crisis hit.)

Major's attitude to Cameron is puzzling. Cameron briefed him twice a week for around a year before Prime Minister's Questions and almost every morning throughout the 1992 election campaign, but the former Prime Minister has let it be known that he has no clear memories of him. It is difficult to resist the conclusion that Major's silence is informed as much by a desire to be diplomatic as by any lack of insightful anecdotes about his successor. Cameron's social advantages were politically to his disadvantage (for years he was considered too posh), while the reverse was true of Major, who made political capital from his humble background. Yet class does not appear to have been an issue between them. Someone who knows them both well says that the 'chippiness' with which Major has occasionally responded to disdainful associates was never in evidence in his dealings with Cameron. 'For some Etonians class means so little to them they feel they are *beyond* class, which means that their dealings with people are unlikely to be contaminated by it,' says a former colleague, 'and I think

David is in that category.' An Oxford contemporary says he gets very stung by any suggestion of snobbery. Another says Cameron 'thinks class doesn't matter' (that is, shouldn't be thought to matter), but, being distantly aware of what a hang-up many Britons have about it, 'he's sophisticated enough never to actually say that'. Cameron was always careful to be seen as loyal, but in private he did call Major a 'loser' and disagreed with his European policy. Nonetheless, this didn't stop him from privately asking for the former leader's endorsement in the summer of 2005.

After his failure to win Ashford, Cameron missed out on a number of other seats, including Reading and Epsom, during 1995. Finally in January 1996 the race to Westminster must have seemed all but won when he landed the nomination for Stafford. It was a new seat created in a boundary review. The sitting MP, Bill Cash, had decided that a neighbouring berth was a marginally better prospect, leaving his former patch, considered fairly safe, up for grabs. His selection was another example of Cameron's good fortune – he was called to an interview at the last moment after two shortlisted applicants dropped out. Joy Richardson, still a stalwart member of Stafford Conservative Association despite advancing years, vividly recalls the meeting. 'I must admit that my first thought was that, at twenty-nine, he was too young. But then he spoke and it was so obvious that he was the best candidate.' Richardson remembers that his address to the local party was 'very simple, very intelligent, very friendly'. That Stafford was staunchly Eurosceptic (its constituency chairman later joined UKIP) will have helped. His stint as an adviser for Michael Howard probably did him no harm among activists regarded as being to the right of the mainstream Tory Party at the time.

He rented a farmhouse in a pretty village on the outskirts of the town, and started travelling up from London at weekends to work his patch. He kept the 'day job'. Green allowed him plenty of licence to cultivate the seat and promised him that if he failed to get into the Commons he could continue at Carlton. Samantha disliked the trips north but, nonetheless, went with him more often than not and, once there, worked hard on his behalf, albeit in her own way. Local party workers remember that her preferred tools of political communication were paint-pot, poster and ladder. Having repainted the local party's placards an appropriate hue, Samantha would then tour the town centre tying them to lampposts. It was not the only unconventional activity of hers that caused concern. 'We banned her from smoking in the headquarters – I think she used to roll her own cigarettes at the time,' says Joy Richardson, who greatly warmed to the young couple.

Samantha's own career was by now beginning to take off. At the start of 1996 she was working as a professional window-dresser and interior designer, having concluded that she could not make a living from being a professional painter (she had a studio in Kensal Rise for a while). She won a commission to redesign the interior of Smythsons on New Bond Street. Much like the Conservative Party, Smythsons was a once great institution in danger of being left behind by the modern world. Sigmund Freud's visiting cards, Queen Victoria's stationery and a letter from Charles Dickens apologising for his temporary use of some other stationery are displayed. Smythsons is 'probably the last British-owned and British-managed shop that's been on Bond Street for over 100 years', she has said. That, indeed, is one of the brand's big selling points. The old-fashioned, understated British style – what in Italy is known as *il look inglese* – is classy but also quite safe. 'I was itching to get my hands on the place,' she said later. 'Minimalism was coming in and I felt it needed a bit of attention to make sure it didn't get left behind.' Having refitted the shop, she pitched for the job as product development director, was successful and within six months was made creative director at the age of only twenty-five.

Perhaps in recognition of her dutiful trips to the Potteries, the couple had a holiday in the West Indies that March – their last together before the wedding planned for June. Then in May, while Samantha and her mother made the last adjustments to the plans, Cameron held a stag night, after an afternoon at the races, in a tent in an upland field in Lambourn, near Peasemore. Typically 'it was more like a marquee than a beer tent', recalls one of around thirty guests, who sat down to dinner while journalist Robert Hardman played the piano. 'As you might imagine with Dave, it was quite lavish, but there were no strippers or anything like that', said one who was there. His Heatherdown and Eton friends dominated – Charles 'Toppo' Todhunter, Tom Goff, James Fergusson. But his political gang was well represented too – Ed Vaizey, Michael Gove, Dean Godson and Steve Hilton. The best man, Dominic Loehnis, represented both sides. As an event, it conformed to custom in one key respect at least. 'We just drank a lot. There were speeches. I drank red wine completely throughout, from the moment of arrival to collapse,' records a stag, dimly.

The wedding itself – on 1 June – was just as traditional. Even the weather was true to form: it rained heavily. Despite the downpour guests remember an exceptionally happy and moving ceremony. In a reversal, perhaps, of traditional roles, after the couple had completed their vows and turned to walk down the aisle, the bride was her customary composed and sunny self, while tears streamed down the groom's face, a moment captured in a photograph now hanging in the Camerons' home. Michael Green, who had arrived late having nearly forced Michael Howard's ministerial car off the road in his haste to make up time, caused further mayhem after the service by leading a large number of guests' cars – including the Duke of Westminster's – in the opposite direction from the reception.

The wedding managed felicitously, and apparently effortlessly, to combine the importance placed by bride and groom on 'family' with the deftly political. Fortune, once again, seemed to play its part. 'I'm not saying Dave calculatedly married into a political family, or mar-

Mary Mount, second from right, at the age of 19 celebrating at the Coronation Ball, Sandhurst. Ian Cameron's wooing of Mary is a love story in which David Cameron takes great pride.

Annabel Astor, Samantha's mother and a successful businesswoman, poses in front of a portrait of Nancy Langham, another powerful woman who married into the Astor dynasty.

David Cameron (top row, second from right) photographed with team-mates from a Heatherdown cricket XI. He has said the school was a good preparation for life: 'We lost at everything.'

David Cameron was sent to prep school at the age of seven but seems to have been a generally happy, if hungry, boarder.

Cameron (with his sister Clare) rides at Peasemore without, it seems, a saddle or riding hat. Childhood seems to have been enchantingly rule-free.

LEFT: An innocent-looking 11-year-old Cameron at a Home Counties cricket match.

BELOW: Cameron, 19, in a Blues Brothers T-shirt and sarong on the Kenyan coast in 1986. The picture was taken by his then girlfriend Francesca Ferguson. She wanted to experiment, he didn't.

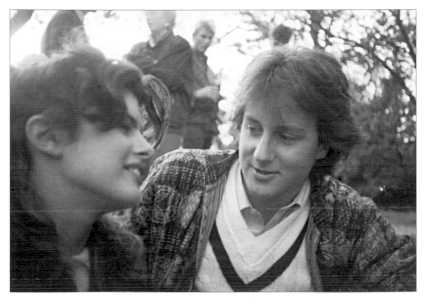

ABOVE: An attentive David Cameron at a party in Oxford. Note the sartorial appeal to both bohemia and tradition.

RIGHT: The young blade on safari, 1986.

1 The Hon. Sebastian Grigg, heir to the third Baron Altrincham and a Notting Hill neighbour. Married to former *Times* journalist Rachel Kelly, he is a partner at Goldman Sachs. 2 David Cameron. 3 Ralph Perry-Robinson, a former child actor who studied at the Prince of Wales's Institute of Architecture, he now lives near Salisbury, where he designs and makes furniture. 4 Ewen Fergusson, son of Sir Ewen Fergusson, a former Scotland rugby international who became British Ambassador to Paris and head of royal bankers Coutts. He is now a partner in the banking and financial division of City Law. 5 Matthew Benson, formerly with bankers Morgan Stanley, he is a director of Rettie and Co., an Edinburgh-based estate agent. 6 Marc Rowlands, Marlborough-educated barrister now specialising in contract law. 7 Harry Eastwood. Eastwood is commercial director of TV production company Monkey, where he works with fellow Etonians and Cameron friends Dominic Loehnis and Will Macdonald.

SEATED:

8 The Hon. Sebastian James, the son of Lord Northbourne, he became an entrepreneur whose business ventures have included a DVD rental business, Silverscreen, and an internet site selling rare books. 9 Jonathan Ford. Westminster School-educated, Ford studied modern history at Oxford and became a banker at Morgan Grenfell. He is a financial journalist. 10 Boris Johnson, former classics scholar and president of the Oxford Union debating society, he went on to become Mayor of London.

David Cameron, right, with Tim Collins, a colleague at the Conservative Research Department, on a visit to Germany shortly after the fall of the Berlin Wall.

David Cameron, regarded as a 'kid' by Treasury mandarins when he arrived, won most round. But his time at Number 11 taught him how rough a game politics can be.

Cameron looks on as Chancellor Norman Lamont delivers the words he helped craft earlier that evening, on the day that Britain crashed out of the ERM at a cost of more than £3 billion.

Michael Green, Cameron's charismatic but tempestuous boss at Carlton.

ried someone who would make a good political wife, but that is what happened,' said someone close to him. 'There was real feeling of political endorsement about the wedding, of it being a political clan thing,' said a guest. But nobody had any doubt they were doing the right thing. 'He's a cautious man, Dave, and would never marry recklessly,' says the friend. The occasion provided a perfect platform for Loehnis, addressing a marquee full of gifted public speakers, to bring the house down with his best man's speech, in doggerel verse, about the couple's courtship. As the day went on and the formality eased, further amusement was provided by Norman Lamont, and many others, pogo-ing vigorously to a nine-piece gipsy brass and string band long into the Oxfordshire night.

By the time he returned from their honeymoon in Italy and France, Cameron must have started to fear that his chances of becoming an MP were gradually slipping. It was by now clear that John Major's government, divided and exhausted, was going to lose heavily to Tony Blair's New Labour.

Green, too, began to see which way the political weathervane was pointing. He invited Baroness Jay, daughter of James Callaghan, on to the Carlton board, for example. Waheed Alli, the businessman behind Planet 24, was to become managing director of Carlton Productions, ensuring that the business was not too identified with the fading Tory regime. Alli was to be among the first businessmen to be ennobled by Tony Blair. (It is a small irony that among the aides he brought with him to Carlton were John McTernan, Tony Blair's last political secretary, and John Reid's son Kevin, who was given a job with Alli in the wake of a scandal about his employment in the Labour minister's constituency office. Both were unlikely colleagues for the aspirant Conservative MP and there is no evidence their paths crossed.)

That autumn Cameron found that increasingly his time was being taken up with the Stafford seat. The fear of losing an 8,000 majority had been easy to laugh off when he landed the nomination. Now it had grown into a nagging worry. No longer within the charmed circle of Number 10 and Conservative Central Office, he had to make do with snippets from friends like Bridges and occasional contacts with his former ministerial bosses. What they told him was not reassuring. The legacy of the recession, epitomised by Black Wednesday, had given Blair a golden political opportunity. He had convinced voters that Labour had changed and that the party deserved a chance. Cameron must have accepted that the Tories were heading for opposition – the question was: would he be joining them?

That autumn he made the requisite trip to the Conservative Party conference but this time as a PPC – prospective parliamentary candidate. From the podium in Bournemouth the former special adviser for Norman Lamont, who had worked behind the scenes on raising taxes three years previously, now argued passionately that they should be cut. What spare cash there was in the budget, Cameron told Ken Clarke, should be channelled to those hardest hit by recession, that is, 'small businesses where people took their own money out of their own pockets and put them into their businesses to keep them going'. In 1992 tax had been one of the key issues that helped the Tories hang on to power, but by 1997 it was becoming clear that even generous tax cuts wouldn't be enough to save Major's government from the consequences of years of recession.

At the end of the year, Michael Gove, by now a *Times* columnist, fulfilled his Christmas obligations by writing a largely light-hearted column about how Tory 'ultra-Eurosceptics', resigned to defeat, were looking forward to the purging fires of the looming electoral disaster. After such a defeat, Gove mused, the party would be reborn, shorn of its EU apologists. John Redwood would become Prime Minister, Michael Portillo would be Foreign Secretary and '1997 entrant David Cameron' would become Chief Financial Secretary.

The piece may have been whimsical in tone, but it did foreshadow an uncharacteristic public act of political defiance by Cameron. After

the Maastricht vote, Conservative candidates had an additional opponent to fight: the Referendum Party. Funded by the billionaire tycoon
James Goldsmith, its single policy was a referendum on continued
membership of the European Union. It was clear that this new party
would inevitably take more Tory votes than Labour and was therefore
a potentially disastrous drag in tight marginal seats like Stafford.

In the face of this threat David Cameron did something that he has
almost never done. He rebelled. Despite the fact that Major had not
ruled out Britain joining the euro in 1997, Cameron joined around
200 other Tory candidates who made it clear that they were opposed
to monetary union. His Labour opponent, David Kidney, was
delighted – it made it easier than ever for him to portray Cameron as
a creature of the Tory right. 'I simply labelled him as a right-wing
Tory, the kind of people you, the electorate, are currently rejecting. It
helped me that he was identified with a regime that the public were
saying no to. He said things like the national minimum wage would
cost millions in jobs but that was at that time the Tory Party line – and
he kept it very well,' says Kidney, a local candidate who pressed the
advantage to full effect.

With typical self-deprecation Cameron says that when he fought
Stafford at the general election in May 1997, 'Stafford fought back' (a
joke only a little spoiled by having also been used many times previously, including at the same election by Boris Johnson in Clwyd
South). In fact, the campaign itself was largely free of personal
rancour. The three main candidates met and agreed in advance that it
would be 'a clean fight'. Kidney admits he pushed at this agreement by
exploiting the fact that Cameron turned up very late to a hustings on
education funding. Labour's ensuing press release, 'Cameron plays
truant', irritates the Tory leader to this day.

Other than his stance on the euro, Cameron's own election literature for Stafford shows little deviation from the Central Office-
approved template of the time, right down to the 'Don't Throw It

All Away' slogan. The candidate evidently decided that having worked for Michael Howard was an electoral asset as his leaflets featured a number of photographs of Home Secretary and aide. Perhaps unsurprisingly given that the party was still trying to live down Black Wednesday and the Chancellor's subsequent rancorous departure from government, there were none of him and Lamont, and his time at the Treasury was not mentioned.

Friends, family and colleagues were pressed into service, the rented house in Tixhall becoming a dormitory, filling up after the arrival of the Friday-night train from London. Steve Hilton was a regular helper; Ed Vaizey showed up too, and even the journalist Edward Heathcoat-Amory, another friend and occasional holiday companion, did a tour of duty in the cause, as did his former economics tutor Peter Sinclair. From Carlton came Edwina Paine and others, while Mary and Ian Cameron travelled up from Peasemore – the latter wheeling himself around Stafford's main square handing out leaflets while the candidate's mother manned the phones at headquarters.

On 3 April, with less than a month to go to polling day, Cameron was endorsed by Howard on a flying visit to Stafford. While there the Home Secretary made the claim that Labour would put 24p on the cost of a pint – 17p came from the estimated cost of bringing in new glasses to ensure that drinkers got full measure (a Labour commitment) and 7p from the cost of the minimum wage. Cameron – who deployed the claim prominently on his leaflets – was delighted to find a pub serving 'Cameron's Strongarm' and consequently got Howard at the Castle Tavern 'quaffing ale from a traditional pint pot', as the PA report had it the next day.

Sadly for him the campaign fell flat. 'I just don't think he expected to win it,' said someone close to the campaign. 'He didn't strike me as having that inner confidence.' He was right. The drinkers of Stafford decided they knew froth when they saw it. Election night at Stafford's leisure centre on 1 May seems to have been a sour affair and Cameron evidently made little effort to pretend that he was enjoying himself. A number of ballots were spoiled, which prompted the Monster Raving Loony Party candidate, Ashton May, who was a little the worse for wear, to claim those votes as his, on the flippant grounds that anybody who had bothered to turn out to vote and had then spoiled their ballot 'must be loony'. Cameron was not in the mood for jokes, and his face turned sourer still when Ashton warned him, again light-heartedly, that he was in a position to prolong the evening's agony: if he didn't get satisfaction it was his right to demand a recount.

'On the night of the count when most people had clocked that Labour had won, quite a lot of the local Tories left and David was standing alone. He looked like a lonely figure,' recalls Kidney. Even Samantha seems to have deserted him. He has said she spent the night drinking in the leisure centre car park with the Monster Raving Loony Party. Attempts to verify this were thwarted by Ashton May's admission that 'There were various random people there, but I'd had quite a few pints by then, so I couldn't say.' The scene of pathos was completed when an elderly lady came up to Cameron in tears and said: 'I don't want to die under a Labour government.'

But the people of Stafford had spoken – and they had told Cameron to go back to London. Only just thirty, he would have other chances. Of the 51,722 who voted, Kidney polled 24,606 and Cameron 20,292. The swing from blue to red was 10.8 per cent, in line with the national average but slightly greater than those in the other Staffordshire seats. Although little personal blame was attached to Cameron – either then or now – he felt the defeat deeply.

The planned celebration party at the town's Tory HQ turned into a wake. The champagne, bought to toast success, drowned sorrow instead. 'He was terribly upset. We all were,' says Joy Richardson. 'We really wanted him to be our MP.' A friend says, however, that it was the beginnings of the making of him. 'One thing that others have said is that if there was a problem or issue that David had, it was that he was too smooth, too easy, and that confidence would come across as arrogance. But the puppyish self-possession of the arrogant twenty-something Cameron ended in defeat in Stafford.'

KNIGHTSBRIDGE
Carlton Communications 1997–2001

It was an altogether chillier world for David Cameron following his defeat at Stafford. Michael Green had held his job open for him at Carlton, but the next four years for both men would prove to be far tougher than they would have liked. Against a background of failed mergers and a disastrous foray into digital broadcasting, Carlton – and Cameron – began to make enemies among some of the biggest names in financial journalism. Cameron's conduct as a corporate spin doctor in the late 1990s was to come back to haunt him just as his bid for the Tory leadership caught fire in 2005. The allegations levelled then – that he was obstructive, bullying and on at least one occasion downright misleading – still resonate.

Commercial broadcasting in Britain in the late 1990s was convulsed by two big battles. Within the family of companies that made up ITV there was endless skirmishing over take-overs and mergers. The consolidation process meant that sooner or later there was only going to be one 'king of ITV'. Naturally enough, Green desperately wanted it to be him. But there was another battle – this time between the terrestrial broadcasters and the upstart satellite operators, notably the Rupert Murdoch-dominated BSkyB. The scene was additionally complicated by the advent of technology that enabled digital broadcasting and the subsequent distribution of franchises to exploit the new platform. No government could afford to be indifferent to questions of media ownership. For the press-obsessed

Blair administration the shakeout in ITV, the struggle for satellite supremacy and the shape of the future digital market were matters of the most intense interest and concern.

To help fight his corner, Murdoch cleverly recruited Tim Allan, who had worked for Tony Blair. For Cameron the message could hardly have been clearer – the future, in the City as in Westminster, belonged to Blairites. In fact he and Allan were on friendly terms. They had lunched together while Cameron was at the Home Office and Blair was shadow Home Secretary. Allan had been one of the 'Primrose Hill set' – Labour's answer to the clique of young Tories who would later become named after their habitat in Notting Hill – and had been present on those occasions when the two groups of 'young meteors' had socialised.

But there is little room for sentiment when billions of pounds of future revenue are at stake. Initially, at least, Carlton and Sky had been on the same side, joining forces with Granada to bid for the new digital channels in a consortium known as BDB. But in June 1997 the regulators ruled that the consortium would be granted the licences only if BSkyB were excluded from it. It was to prove a momentous intervention, forcing Murdoch to take ITV companies head on in the battle for customers. Over the next few years hundreds of millions of pounds were sunk into competing technologies and massive, loss-leading sports deals as the TV barons fought for the future of commercial broadcasting. Cameron's connections to the BDB camp, which later traded as ONdigital, went beyond his employment by Green. His father-in-law, Lord Astor, found employment after the Tory defeat on the consortium's board. George Bridges, who had seemingly been promised Cameron's job at Carlton when he expected to become Stafford's new MP, went instead from Number 10 to become BDB's spin doctor.

By now Carlton had moved to smart new offices at 25 Knightsbridge, and the senior TV executives were – much to their chagrin –

brought under the same roof as Green and his inner court. The building may have had its own chef but Green's modern art collection, some of it borrowed from the Saatchi brothers, wasn't to everyone's taste. 'You never quite knew what monstrosity was going to appear in your office next,' recalls one former employee, who says his least favourite work 'looked like a plastic bag glued to the wall'.

Cameron himself worked one floor below Green and his most senior executives in a 'rather scruffy' open-plan office. His working space was usually littered with business magazines. Gathered around him was a phalanx of mostly doting female staff including Edwina Paine. 'The atmosphere was not that of the factory floor,' says one occasional visitor to Cameron's realm. 'There would be much discussion of social events and shopping and boyfriends.' (Paine, who had a reputation for being unlucky in love, was rewarded by fate one day during her lunch break. As she crossed the road from Carlton's HQ she bumped into a Jeremy Herrman. She is now Mrs Herrman and her hedge-fund manager husband is worth an estimated £70 million. She gave Cameron's leadership campaign £10,000.)

Also joining Cameron's team in 1999 was his old CRD colleague who had succeeded him at the Home Office, Rachel Whetstone. Colleagues now say they were 'astonished' by Whetstone's arrival as public affairs manager at Carlton (effectively Cameron's number two). 'The line from him was that she was going to help handle the politics and press, but as far as we could see she had absolutely no experience of financial journalism whatsoever.' This is a little unfair. Whetstone had in fact already worked as public affairs manager for One2One, the mobile phone company, after leaving office with Howard following the 1997 defeat.

When he had a particularly good story to sell, there was a circle of trusted journalists who would receive a call from Carlton's head of PR. Most were Tory supporters. He could usually rely on the friendly ears of George Trefgarne, James Bethell and James Harding, for example.

These were journalist contacts that overlapped with his social scene, people he could trust and relax with; Harding, for example, was an occasional tennis partner. Cameron also seems to have had workable relationships with most newspapers' media editors. Ray Snoddy, then of the *Financial Times*, says: 'He was bright, good at his job, and I was impressed that he had a good working relationship with Michael Green, a trick that very few could pull off. Cameron knew the rules of the game, he could give you an off-the-record briefing. It was his master's voice – but delivered with a twinkle.'

Another broadsheet media editor says Cameron even began to sound like Green. 'Like a lot of people who worked for Michael Green he very quickly took on his distinctive sing-song intonation where sentences rise to a point and then fall away.' (A Carlton colleague recalls how Cameron's catchphrase was 'That's ridiculous!' delivered on a rising and then rapidly falling cadence.) 'He was one of a group of what I call "Super PRs". He was a step above a press officer – you knew he knew stuff because he was in the mix.' With those he knew, he could be a good gossip. 'When I see David Cameron today, it's not the David Cameron that I remember. Then he could have a slyly conspiratorial whisper or be somewhat hectoring, and there was no evidence of any interest in the sort of New Age stuff on show today.'

During TV industry gatherings in Edinburgh or Cambridge, Cameron always made a point of taking media editors out for a 'curry night'. Cocaine use is hardly unknown at these industry gatherings but, disappointingly for his critics, Cameron's chosen refreshment was lager, and that of a weak brand in moderate quantities. What did impress these specialist journalists was Cameron's detailed technical knowledge. He could talk for hours on such arcane matters as the 'inter-operability' of the competing broadcasting platforms. This propensity to immerse himself in and get a grip on fine details, attested to by both Carlton insiders and journalists, echoes observations by colleagues at CRD, the Treasury and the Home Office. Cameron works hard at making it look easy.

Portraying as a success the abject failure of ONdigital was beyond even Cameron's abilities, however. Allan, who has never been tribal, had been impressed by his rival's skill and brutality in dealing with the Lobby, as political journalists at Westminster are collectively known, but far less so by his attempts to protect ONdigital from Sky's sniping. The ITV package was marketed under the 'Plug and Play' slogan, but the message that customers would find it easy to install the receiving equipment was fatally subverted when a Sky-inspired nick-name 'Plug and Pray' began to stick.

Allan says now what he did to ONdigital wasn't even black propaganda – just what any rivals in a 'kill or be killed' commercial fight would do while staying within the bounds of propriety and legality. So when, for example, ONdigital released technical information about how many postcodes in Britain would be able to receive the new broadcasting service, it was – he says – a straightforward matter to commission research showing what proportion of Britain's population would not be covered, which, helpfully for Sky, was less than half. The reaction from the ITV consortium was not the full-blooded counter-attack Allan expected, but rather hurt bewilderment. 'Why are you being so horrible to us?' Cameron once plaintively asked.

By way of contrast to ONdigital's difficulties, Samantha Cameron's business was booming. She was revolutionising Smythsons' products. Her biggest success was the launch of the Fashion Diary, which carried listings for the sort of shops, restaurants and hotels that people in the fashion world might want to visit in London, Milan, Paris and New York. Meg Mathews (formerly Mrs Noel Gallagher) bought twenty-two copies as Christmas presents for her best friends. 'We were putting gold-stamped initials on them for people like Kate Moss and Naomi Campbell, and the great thing was that they all carried on using them,' Samantha has said.

Celebrity endorsement – an old political staple – worked wonders in updating the store's slightly fusty image. High-profile clients like Madonna, the Kennedys, the Clintons, the Blairs, Harvey Keitel, Catherine Zeta-Jones, Liv Tyler, Stella McCartney and Gwyneth Paltrow helped shift products such as an envelope-shaped handbag that costs £800. (It has been said that a Smythsons product is the perfect present for people who have everything except a sense of proportion.) The high prices seem to attract both the aspiringly stylish and Smythsons' investors. In 1998 the management bought the company from John Menzies, and Samantha was among those who acquired a slice of the shares. In 2005 they sold it for £15.5 million. That acquisition was orchestrated by Jonathan Green, a substantial backer of David Cameron's leadership campaign. The consortium includes Nicholas Evans-Lombe, an old Eton acquaintance.

Michael Green, David's boss at Carlton, is not only a longstanding friend of Annabel Astor but also invested in Oka, the company she now runs. In his capacity as a business investor, he also tried to buy Smythsons, and he says there is nothing remotely dilettante about Annabel's daughter. 'Samantha has her feet firmly on the ground. She was often at the office collecting David. She has inherited her mother's abilities in style and in business acumen. She's totally a together woman, and an important asset.' A friend of Cameron endorses the general view that Samantha embodies many of her mother's talents: 'Annabel is tough, fiercely ambitious, very powerful and incredibly attractive, but I'd hate to be on the wrong side of her. She gets ludicrous prices because she wraps men around her finger. She's very driven and Sam gets a lot of it from her.'

Meanwhile Cameron's media fire-fighting skills were being tested to their limits. Just before Christmas 1998 a showcase Carlton documentary on the Colombian drugs trade was exposed by the *Guardian* as a fake. *The Connection*, made by a thirty-five-year-old producer called Marc de Beaufort, had won a clutch of international awards when it was first shown in October 1996 watched by 3.7 million viewers. The producer and his crew were hailed as heroes for penetrating the notorious Cali cartel and exposing a new smuggling route through Heathrow. They told how they were blindfolded and taken by armed men to a secret location. The Independent Television Commission investigation concluded that the show had been 'a wholesale breach of trust between programme makers and viewers'. The 'heroin' shown was confectionary, the 'secret location' the producer's hotel bedroom and a 'gang boss' a retired bank cashier.

There had been embarrassments before, but the exposé of an award-winning Carlton documentary as a total fake was in a different league, that of the true PR catastrophe. Faced with the *Guardian*'s searching questions on the programme, Cameron desperately played for time, as the paper's media diary recorded. 'Cameron initially refused to take or return phone calls from *The Guardian*'s media correspondent four days in a row. Eventually, he seems to have inadvertently picked up his own phone. After *The Guardian* reporter introduced herself, she was confronted with the amazing sound of someone who sounded a lot like David Cameron maintaining that he was called "John Smith", and just happened to be walking past the 'phone.' The story finally broke just as Carlton was about to release an important set of results. Green's reaction was, although predictable, spectacular nonetheless. A senior executive present pays tribute to Cameron's cool during this episode. Eventually he calmed Green down enough to start working on a statement that put the best possible gloss on the fact that the company's award-winning drugs documentary was a pack of lies.

In the summer of 1999 ONdigital finally looked like it might be turning a corner. It had secured the exclusive rights to a number of European Champions League matches, thus striking at the heart of Sky's strategy. Partly as a result the platform had won an impressive 66 per cent jump in subscribers. But Cameron's efforts to wring as much good publicity out of the figures as possible earned him his first seriously critical notice. The 'Smartmoney' column in the *Sunday Express* anticipated the success on 19 September, prompting Cameron to phone around analysts to 'rubbish the story', according to its author David Hellier. It seems Cameron was annoyed that Hellier had stolen his thunder. For once ONdigital had a nice surprise to spring on the City and he didn't want it dribbling out into the market courtesy of a Sunday tabloid. When the figures were published three weeks later, and they proved to be just as good as the *Sunday Express* had said they were going to be, Hellier was moved to exact revenge on the man he described as 'Carlton's spin doctor'. 'Unsportsmanlike Spinning' reads the headline on a piece dated 10 October 1999. 'Carlton likes to "manage" expectations and was miffed by the accuracy of our story. City analysts may now be a little miffed with Mr Cameron and his Monday morning briefing three weeks ago.'

Hellier was among a growing band of financial journalists with a jaundiced view of the suave young spinner. Some say the PR man treated them with barely concealed disdain, and former colleagues bear witness to a tendency to look down on those he considered unimportant. 'He could be unfriendly, arrogant,' says one who frequently worked closely with Cameron. It is a complaint unfashionable contemporaries at Oxford and the Conservative Research Department might recognise. But another former colleague, who is not generally a fan, defends Cameron against allegations that he was needlessly obstructive. Because of the inherent interest in media companies – as opposed to say plastic manufacturing – he did not have to work hard to attract press attention. His role meant disappointing an awful lot of journalists. Indeed one of his principal functions was as gatekeeper, controlling rather than exciting press interest.

When Green did grant access to financial journalists, it was not always a success. One recalls an unsuccessful charm offensive, overseen by Cameron, when Green managed to irritate all and alienate many of the City's leading stock market reporters in a single lunchtime. Invited for lunch at Carlton's Knightsbridge HQ, this elite band accepted en masse, believing that Green must have something sufficiently important to say to summon them from their newsrooms. 'There we were with our gin and tonics waiting to go into the boardroom for lunch. Cameron was there schmoozing around and generally glad-handing when suddenly in walks the tiny figure of Michael Green in his stockinged feet,' recalls a bemused guest. 'Not only was he in his socks, but he was walking on the balls of his feet. Cameron either didn't notice or ignored it – the rest of us were gob-smacked.' Such eccentricity might have been forgotten, or at least overlooked, had Green not then shocked the room with his opening gambit as lunch was served. 'I've asked you all here', he began in his high sing-song voice, 'because I would like to find out where you get your stories.' One might as well ask an oil executive where his next big strike will be – or, indeed, a media mogul what profitable acquisition he is eyeing. 'I bet you would,' snorted one of the veteran market reporters.

Perhaps sensing the mood, Green then offered to 'answer any question you have about Carlton'. As it happened there was one matter that had piqued the interest of the market reporters. The previous weekend there had been speculation that the firm was about to take a significant stake in a rival. Naturally enough the first question bowled at Green was whether there was any truth in the rumour. In an echo of Cameron's own favourite refrain at the time, Green snapped back, 'I am not going to comment on market speculation.' 'At that moment he just lost the whole room,' remembers the reporter. 'We pretty much talked among ourselves for the rest of the lunch and went back to our offices with a poorer opinion of Carlton and Green than we had had when we set off.'

But Cameron was to make an error of far greater magnitude the following month when he took a call from Jeff Randall, then editor of *Sunday Business*. Randall, then as now one of the most respected financial journalists working in Britain, had picked up a tantalising rumour that two of the last big three ITV companies – Carlton, United News and Media, and Granada – were in talks about a possible merger. A trusted source had told him that Lord Hollick, chairman of United, had been spotted in Carlton's HQ. The exclusive revelation that Michael Green and Clive Hollick were about to join forces was a sensational story, but one that clearly needed confirmation from one of the two parties.

The precise nature of that conversation between Randall and Cameron is a matter of some dispute. There are conventions, though, in a situation where a journalist calls a spokesperson about a story which is true but which the PR doesn't want to confirm. Rule One, as Cameron has acknowledged, is not to lie. It is permissible to lead journalists off the scent, foster uncertainty, distract, browbeat, stonewall, bribe (with a better story), wheedle or even beg. The best press handlers will deploy all these methods and more and still maintain a reputation for truthfulness. Cameron has himself spelled out the difference between leading journalists off the scent and telling lies:

> I've spent some interesting times trying to handle the press for government ministers and large corporations – and I admit, I've had my fair share of media disasters. Most of them occur either when you don't know the answer to a question, or when you do but can't say. As well as actually saying: 'I don't know' or 'I can't tell you', we've all tried variants such as 'I'll get back to you' and then leaving the phone off the hook, or roaring with laughter and saying 'who on earth told you that?' But the one thing even the lowliest of spin paramedics is taught is that you must not lie: it means the end of your credibility and it should mean the end of your job.

Randall is an experienced journalist, for whom these sorts of exchanges are fundamental to his trade. He didn't get the confirmation, implicit or explicit, that he was looking for when he called Cameron about the merger story. He was left fuming when, weeks later, the proposed merger was announced to an astonished City.

When in 2005 David Cameron emerged as a frontrunner in the leadership race, Randall was waiting for him. 'I wouldn't trust him with my daughter's pocket money' was one early salvo. Writing in the *Daily Telegraph* late that year, Randall went for the jugular. 'In my experience, Cameron never gave a straight answer when dissemblance was a plausible alternative, which probably makes him perfectly suited for the role he now seeks: the next Tony Blair.' The key incident that motivated this attack was the merger story, says Randall, who is still angry about being misled. 'Whether or not he flat out lied, I won't say – but he went a very long way to leave me with the impression that the story was wrong. He put up so much verbal tracer that you started to lose your own guidance system. Your own navigational system started to wobble on the story. He put me right off it.' The deputy editor's hostility towards the Tory leader would hardly have been assuaged had word reached him of Cameron's response to his volleys. 'Who is Jeff Randall?' the former PR man is said to have asked rhetorically. 'A person of no consequence.'

Another senior journalist who dealt with Cameron extensively describes him as 'thoroughly unpleasant' and not a very efficient press officer: 'A good PR man will tell you stuff and give you insights and he never did that – which is why Carlton had rings run round it. If he'd been doing the job properly he would have said, "You have to make allowances for Michael [Green]", but he'd be just as abrasive.' Cameron's affable demeanour is only skin deep, he added. 'You see him now and he looks a charming bloke and for people who were meeting him for the first time he could be charming … [but] everyone's view of him has been coloured by subsequent events.' Cameron, he says, was a man who cultivated only those who could prove useful. 'I've only seen him once since [he became Tory leader] and he apologised for being such a wanker.'

Once he had secured the leadership, however, Cameron seems to have decided that he could ill afford openly poor relations with such a respected and powerful media figure. One day in early spring 2006 an emissary was despatched with an invitation to meet the Tory leader at 4 p.m. the following Monday. Randall was discreet about the approach, telling only a close friend that Cameron was 'suing for peace'. The meeting did not go well. First Cameron said he could not remember the disputed call – something that Randall found difficult to accept. The proposed merger was one of the biggest Carlton stories of Cameron's time, he pointed out. Cameron is said to have eventually issued a half-apology. 'If I lied then I am very sorry, but I honestly can't remember doing so.' Someone as bright as Cameron might regret saying such a thing, particularly in front of a third party – George Osborne was also in the room. It suggests that he might have been willing to contemplate lying (an impression which most people, even in politics and PR, would be anxious to dispel) and that it would not have been so unusual as to be memorable.

Of the merger story, Green says: 'David batted it off the way he was told to bat it off – the way you had to bat it off, where you can't say yes, you can't say no.' But Randall is not the only senior financial journalist with scores to settle. The day before Cameron was formally elected leader in 2005, Ian King, then business editor of *The Sun*, told the tabloid's readers that he 'wouldn't cut it':

Along with other financial journalists, I was unfortunate enough to have dealings with Cameron during the 1990s when he was PR man for Carlton, the world's worst television company. And a poisonous, slippery individual he was, too. Back then, Cameron was far from the smoothie he pretends to be now. He was a smarmy bully who regularly threatened journalists who dared to write anything negative about Carlton – which was nearly all of us. He loved humiliating people, including a colleague at ITV, who he would abuse publicly as 'Bunter' just because the poor bloke was a few pounds overweight.

A recent *Sun* interview with Cameron generously called him a former Carlton 'executive'. No, he wasn't. He was a mouthpiece for that company's charmless chairman, Michael Green, who operated him the way Keith Harris works Orville. The financial press had one thing in common with Cameron – he hated us and we hated him. Once, after talking to Carlton's unhappy City shareholders, I wrote a story reporting their complaints. Cameron went completely off the dial, writing to my boss, more or less inviting him to sack me. I dug out a clipping of the story the other week and guess what? A major aspect to the tale was that investors were worried about money Carlton was pouring into ITV Digital, then called ONdigital. Cameron claimed they weren't – insisting the business was perfectly healthy. Well, we all know what happened to ITV Digital. It went bust owing £1.2 billion.

Cameron's letter of complaint sent to King's editor at the time, the *Mail on Sunday*'s Bill Kay, does suggest a certain heavy-handedness. 'I have written to Bill Kay setting out the reasons why your article was completely unjustified. A full copy is attached,' Cameron wrote to King on 3 November 1998. 'If I make criticisms of your business you should see them. I hope you will adopt the same logic in future.' Speaking later, King defended his polemic. 'He seemed perfectly comfortable denying things which we, as reporters, knew to be true,' he said. 'Quite simply he was the worst press officer I have come across in the City. Neither he nor Green seemed to have the slightest idea of how newspapers really worked.'

One specialist media reporter who had frequent dealings with Cameron says their dealings were generally amicable and professional. 'I regarded him as a pro, and had no experience of being lied to by him, although I always regarded him as someone who was travelling through and was destined for politics. But I did have one bad run-in with him. I was writing a big piece on what Michael Green was doing and had been given good access. Basically, when the story appeared, I came to my own conclusions and didn't write what they wanted me to write. David called me up in a fury and slammed the phone down on me. I was quite surprised. It has only ever happened to me once in twenty years in journalism. We normally parted on a good note, but I thought that was unprofessional of him.'

Others, too, bear witness to Cameron's often difficult relationship with journalists while he was at Carlton. Chris Blackhurst, now editor of the *Independent*, says Cameron was 'aggressive, sharp-tongued, often condescending and patronising, but when awkward questions were put to him, frequently obstructive and unhelpful. If anyone had told me then he might … become Premier, I would have told them to seek help.' Patrick Hosking, of *The Times*, has also said he found him 'obstructive'.

Then there are the attacks on what Cameron spent seven years of his life defending: Carlton itself. With each speech the new Tory leader makes about corporate responsibility, he invites further scrutiny of his own track record in the field. He might, for example, have been wiser – before making his attack on a tie-up between W. H. Smith and Cadbury's – to remember what he himself wrote in a press release for Carlton when announcing a tie-up with the same newsagent chain. Hosking puts the case for the prosecution while seeming to express sympathy for the former PR man. 'His PR needs were many and varied but hardly likely to instil much dignity in a future statesman: defending the dumping of *News at Ten* to make way for a revival of *Mr and Mrs* with Julian Clary; arguing the case for commercials targeted at children; defending the screening of insalutary scenes from *The Vice* within minutes of the watershed; explaining how Carlton had come to screen a one-hour programme, conceived, sponsored and entirely funded by British Telecom.' One senior person with a good knowledge of how Carlton operates speculates as follows: 'My guess, and my understanding from talking to people there, is that David would have gone in to see Michael and told him the press was on to something and would have said, "What shall I say?" The ethos when working for Michael Green is that you do what Michael wants.'

Interviewed by the *Sun* in the crucial closing stages of the leadership race, Cameron gave what is to date his fullest defence of his Carlton record. 'I had a reputation for being quite tight-lipped. It is important not to lie to the press and sometimes I had to stonewall and be terse. I always try to be polite and friendly but I can be tough. Given a choice between being popular and being successful I would want to be successful. I would be prepared to be an unpopular Prime Minister as long as I got it right.'

Green defends his former spin doctor's behaviour in the face of a ravenous press pack. 'During good and bad times, David behaved very well. Every newspaper had three or four journalists that would spend all day thinking of a media story … [but] sometimes there were no stories, there was nothing to write.' The entrepreneur says Cameron would have seen first hand the vicissitudes of life lived in the public eye. 'We were heroes and geniuses one moment, absolute lunatics the next, and occasionally we just didn't know what we were doing, according to some newspapers. We were in and out of fashion. So we knew what it was to be popular and we knew what it was to be unpopular … And I'm a sensitive individual, I did take some of it personally, and therefore David certainly saw, learned what it is to get knocked, to see you up, to see you down, to see you fighting back, taking it seriously.' He adds: 'I think David enjoyed that – that I cared.'

Although Cameron had learned to pay attention to detail before arriving at Carlton, Green suggests he learned to be more careful still while working for him. 'We did think things through. David was sometimes surprised at my attention to detail. He learned that there was no point in bluffing. We did care about journalists, in particular bright journalists, because you can only bluff up to a point, but fortunately there is always somebody out there who knows our industry.' Most of all, suggests one analyst who covered Carlton throughout the 1990s, Cameron would have absorbed something that will stand him in good stead. 'David would have learned a lot about how to forge a brand from nothing but personality in working with Green. In many ways Carlton was a made-up company, only really there because of Thatcherism.'

WITNEY
Member of Parliament 2001–2003

It takes less than forty minutes to travel from Peasemore, the village of David Cameron's childhood where his brother and parents still live, to the Oxfordshire market town of Witney. Closer still is Ginge Manor, the country home of Annabel Astor, Samantha's mother. The seat is wealthily rural, its politics personified by the one-nation Toryism of Douglas Hurd, a Witney MP for many years. It is far enough away from London to escape the capital's pull and close enough to Oxford to benefit from that city's urbane influences. There can be few constituencies in the country better suited to Cameron and, luckily for him, he suited Witney. It became available when Shaun Woodward stunned his colleagues in 2000 by announcing that he was defecting to Labour. Woodward, a former colleague of Cameron's and fellow veteran of the 1992 campaign, quit ostensibly in disgust at Tory leader William Hague's decision to oppose the repeal of Section 28 which outlawed the 'promotion' of homosexuality in schools.

Woodward left behind a local Conservative party furious and embarrassed at what they considered an unforgivable betrayal – and, of course, he also left behind an inviting vacancy for a candidate of unquestionable loyalty. (He was to return to the Commons as Labour member for St Helens South.) The contest came down to two serious candidates, Cameron and Andrew Mitchell. Mitchell was a 'retread', who had lost his Nottinghamshire seat of Gelding in the 1997 landslide. He had the advantage of Westminster experience – he had been a junior minister under John Major – as well as having had a successful career as a merchant banker. The president of the local association, Lord Chadlington, recalls that there was a 'bigger buzz' about Mitchell on the eve of the selection meeting in April 2000. In fact Chadlington had begun the contest supporting Mitchell.

In the event it was Cameron who prevailed. Mitchell, magnanimously, insists that the future leader was obviously the outstanding candidate. But the selection was marred by claims of dirty tricks. Mitchell was unfortunate to have attracted the attention of Conservative Way Forward, a Thatcherite group set up to promote right-wing policies but particularly the cause of Euroscepticism. Among those active in the group were Dan Hannan and Doug Smith. In his book *Tory Wars* Simon Walters records how Mitchell's attempts to find a seat appeared to be the target of a covert campaign that 'followed him over the country. He went from one seat to another only to find the smears following him.' Mitchell was finally selected in Sutton Coldfield after an activist had claimed that Hannan had urged her to call Smith for 'more information' on the candidate. Cameron – on the same trail – had witnessed at first hand what was going on because he and Mitchell had been on the final shortlist at Wealden in Sussex the year before the Witney selection.

Cameron could hardly have had better local knowledge and support – Rachel Whetstone's parents Linda and Francis lived in the Wealden constituency and were leading figures in the local party association. In his book Walters records how a 'senior member of the local party' challenged Cameron's rival. 'Mr Mitchell, sleaze destroyed the last Conservative government. Since you were found guilty by a parliamentary inquiry of being involved in cash for questions surely it would be bad for us to have you as our MP.' The charge, as Walters adds, was grossly inaccurate – in fact Mitchell had been cleared of seeking improperly to influence an investigation into Neil Hamilton. Linda Whetstone, who does not deny that she and others had doubts about Mitchell's position on Europe, says she has no recollection of any co-ordinated efforts to frustrate his efforts to be selected. When it came to the final vote, Cameron lost out very narrowly to Charles Hendry. Mitchell did not make the final three.

In Witney, almost identical sleaze allegations surfaced again. In addition Mitchell was challenged over his claims to have been approached to serve Business for Sterling, the Eurosceptic campaigning group. Mitchell says that the claim – made to defend himself against the charge that he was a secret federalist – had been deliberately 'over-interpreted' by his enemies. Suddenly at the last run-off a letter from the group was made public disavowing a claim that Mitchell had been approached to serve on its national council. The letter had been procured by Doug Smith. Although there is no suggestion that Cameron, whose own Eurosceptic credentials were impeccable, knew what Smith had done to his rival, it is interesting to note that he went on to spend a period as one of his speech-writers.

It is quite possible Cameron would have won without the CWF operation. Not only did he speak fluently without notes – by now a staple selection-meeting performance – he also ignored a lectern that had been placed facing a horseshoe table of local party grandees. By standing in front of the lectern Cameron was able to address his audience both more directly and with more intimacy, as Lord Chadlington recalls. 'You do make your mind up in those first few seconds when someone walks in. He walked in front of the podium and spoke for five minutes in a very articulate and easy manner. He engaged himself with us – we felt we were engaged.' It was an accomplished performance – but, crucially, not too obviously polished. He has his wife to thank for spotting the difference. Cameron had by now learned to trust Samantha's instincts.

In the mid-1990s the couple went to a dinner with Shaun Woodward and his wife Camilla. Cameron and Woodward had been Central Office colleagues and were on fairly friendly terms. But driving home Samantha told her husband that he was absolutely not to trust Woodward, an intuition he waved away. When Woodward defected to the Labour Party in 2000, Cameron admitted to a friend: 'Sam was right, my judgement was wrong.'

He paid more attention when she told him why he had not been selected at Wealden. He impressed the committee with his evident ambition (he told them he wanted to be Chancellor of the Exchequer). But Samantha put her finger on what seemed to have cost him the selection: a subtle lack of spontaneity in his presentation. Linda Whetstone is more blunt: 'He made the most terrible speech and his wife told him so. He came off the platform saying, "Well that should have done it," and his wife said, "It will have done it!" and it did.' Nicholas Boles, a modernising Tory activist, says Samantha told Cameron that he had been 'too pat, too pre-baked' in his presentation. 'Then she came up with a formula which I've used and lots of people have used since, which is that in the answer to every question you must reference the personal, local, national in that order,' he says.

Immediately after securing the selection the Camerons accepted an invitation for lunch with the Chadlingtons, who then made them a proposition. There was a spare cottage on their estate. Why didn't the young couple use it as a weekend retreat and base to begin nursing the seat? No doubt grateful to be spared the inconvenience and expense of finding somewhere else, they agreed, moving into the cottage in Dean shortly afterwards. Cameron, mindful perhaps of Stafford, cultivated his new patch assiduously. 'He was always up, he was industrious, he really nursed the seat, although the chances of him losing it were virtually nil. It was interesting that he really cared and bothered. He had a full-time job but he came up on a Friday night and spent the weekend working hard in the constituency,' recalls Lord Chadlington.

That September in a letter to the *Daily Telegraph* Cameron signalled to local Tories that he shared their priorities as he ridiculed a decision by Woodward to abandon his support for hunting. Mocking his former colleague's claim that he was reacting to changing public opinion, Cameron rhetorically asked: 'Did Mr Woodward order a survey of local opinion about the issue that triggered his resignation – Clause 28 and the promotion of homosexuality in schools?' His choice of issue and the way he expressed it is interesting because it appears to be in marked contrast to his treatment of gay couples today. In his conference speech of 2006 Cameron won reluctant applause from delegates when he insisted that gay and straight relationships were equally valid. Yet as recently as 2003 he had failed to support the repeal of Section 28. It is an issue that Cameron now concedes he got wrong.

The following March, of 2001, Cameron was holding his own 'survey of local opinion' on Europe – actually a canvassing device in disguise – as he geared up for an election expected the next month. But the foot-and-mouth outbreak led Blair to agree to delay the poll until June, giving candidates an unexpected extra month. Cameron made good use of his time, and in the process accidentally stumbled across an effective political prop. In April the young candidate announced that he would undertake a charity cycle ride to every village in his constituency. Cameron hadn't ridden a bicycle 'for years' but thought it would get him around the constituency and garner some good publicity. The 'caper' worked and Cameron, ever the quick learner, cottoned on to the political benefits in getting out of the car.

The advent of his enthusiasm for cycling is known because of another profile-raising opportunity he was handed on a plate – a column for the *Guardian Unlimited* website. Cameron used his new platform to poke fun at his opponents and, occasionally, to admit to his own gaffes. Woodward was a repeated target of campaign mischief: Cameron delighted in the controversy over whether or not his predecessor employed a butler in the substantial constituency manor house he had bought with his wife Camilla Sainsbury, heiress to the supermarket fortune. Sometimes Cameron went a little far with his new column – he was forced to apologise for calling his Labour opponent an 'I-feel-your-pain rock-crushing bore'. Self-deprecating anecdotage quickly became a staple. When canvassing one day he wrote of an old lady who had told him she couldn't stop because she had just lost her dog. His ingratiating offer to help locate the animal backfired: the pet was dead. (One anecdote omitted was how on seeing his former headmaster Sir Eric Anderson shopping in Chipping Norton, the candidate ran after the venerable provost shouting, 'Sir, Sir, will you vote for me, Sir?')

In between such notes from the stump, Cameron inserted acute observations on the failure of William Hague's campaign to catch light. On 15 May he posed as a question what became the received analysis of the campaign's failure – its over-reliance on Europe at the expense of public services. Will Europe, he asked, 'remain high enough up the agenda to alter how people vote? Knocking on doors in the evening, the answer would probably be no. Education and the NHS predominate, where battle honours are more evenly shared.'

But when it came to his personal electoral battle on 7 June there was no doubting the winner. Cameron not only succeeded in winning a majority just shy of 8,000, he also increased the share of the Tory vote. It was not a bad achievement considering the way that Conservative voters in Witney had been treated by his predecessor.

Flying back to London from Harrogate through the dawn of 8 June, William Hague wrote a short but powerful speech. He delivered it, with considerable grace, on the steps of Conservative Central Office a few hours later. He hadn't done enough to roll back Labour's electoral tide, he said. It was time to let someone else try to revive Conservative fortunes. No sooner had David Cameron arrived in Westminster than he faced the choice of whom to back in a leadership race. But first there was one possible runner to eliminate. Himself. He told one confidant at the time: 'It is too early for me to stand, isn't it? Yes, of course it is.'

That one day he would run, though, was obvious, to him at least. He was canvassed by the *Daily Telegraph* just six days into the job. '[The Conservative Party] has to change its language, change its approach, start with a blank sheet of paper and try to work out why our base of support is not broader. Anyone could have told the Labour Party in the 1980s how to become electable. It had to drop unilateral disarmament, punitive tax rises, wholesale nationalisation and unionisation. The question for the Conservative Party is far more difficult because there are no obvious areas of policy that need to be dropped. We need a clear, positive, engaging agenda on public services.'

Apart from being strikingly similar to his message today, it was as clear a declaration of support for the modernising rallying cry of Michael Portillo as one could wish for. And yet David Cameron was a late and reluctant convert to the cause of modernisation. The ambivalence may also have been personal. One Tory MP who knows both Cameron and Portillo very well says that their relationship has been one of 'wariness'. Their rivalry began when both were at the Treasury together, despite the considerable disparity in status. Portillo the Cabinet minister saw early the potential threat of Cameron the special adviser.

Now an MP at last, by late June Cameron still hadn't made up his mind whom to back when he played in a cricket match between Labour and Tory politicos on the home turf of Chadlington village. The match, organised by Peter Oborne, then the political editor of the *Spectator*, was a chance for rival combatants to compare war stories in relative harmony. Ben Wegg-Prosser, whom Cameron had met through Ed Vaizey and who went on to become a key aide in the dying days of the Blair administration, was in the Labour XI, as were James Purnell and Andy Burnham, two rising ministerial stars. Playing for the blue team was a senior Tory figure who recalls how open Cameron appeared to be in calculating his self-interest in the contest. 'He sidled up and asked me who I thought would win the leadership election.

"Portillo," I replied. He said: "I'd better vote for him then."' It was a joke – if an incautiously cynical one.

By 27 June Cameron was being named as a 'possible' Portillo backer. The next day he delivered his maiden speech in the Commons. Unusually for a maiden it attracted a smattering of national coverage as sketch-writers wondered how Cameron would honour the Commons tradition that requires new MPs to pay tribute to their constituency predecessor in their first speech. 'Butlergate', which had served Cameron so well in his election campaign, was summoned into service once again. With finely judged malice he first listed the many distinguished Witney MPs culminating in Douglas Hurd, 'which brings me neatly to the hon. member for St Helens South ... he remains a constituent, and a most significant local employer, not least in the area of domestic service ... We are in fact quite close neighbours and on a clear day, from the hill behind my cottage, I can almost see some of the glittering spires of his great house.' The speech may have been well received in the press and among new colleagues on all sides in the Commons tea room – but it did not have the same impact on Mary Cameron. His mother's observation, having watched the speech on the parliament channel, was that her son needed a haircut 'to stop looking like Peter Mandelson'. She also admonished him not to 'wave your arms around while speaking'.

Finally, on 10 July, Cameron pledged his support for Michael Portillo less than a week before the ballot of Tory MPs. It did no good. Although he made it through to the second round, Portillo's vote was then fatally squeezed between the parliamentary party's right-wingers who voted for Iain Duncan Smith and its Europhile rump who supported Ken Clarke. Cameron's analysis of the failure of the Portillo campaign is instructive. 'Well, there we are. The Spanish armada goes down with all hands, including this particular new boy,' he wrote on 18 July, the day after Portillo was knocked out. 'What went wrong? Here was a leadership contender with buckets of charisma, a CV that included experience at the highest level of government and genuine cross-party appeal ... Our man had offered leadership, radical change and ideas that challenged the party both in parliament and the country. They simply weren't ready for it. In many ways it is a view I share.'

His scepticism was in marked contrast to the attitude of another rising star of the 2001 intake, George Osborne. Osborne, say friends, 'got it' some time before Cameron. When Cameron had been pre-occupied with Carlton, Osborne had been one of a set of Smith Square officials who had made the intellectual and emotional journey towards a modern Conservative Party. This group included figures like Danny Finkelstein, now executive editor of *The Times*, and Andrew Cooper, formerly director of Populus, now part of Cameron's Downing Street's operation. Cooper, when working under Hague as a Tory staffer, first crystallised the essence of the party's unpopularity when he commissioned polling that showed that voters liked Conservative policies – until they knew that they were Conservative ones. The problem wasn't the policies.

A close friend of Osborne says the experience of defeat is the key to understanding his instinctive perception of the Tories' predicament. He has summarised his own CV thus: 'I have not faced personal adversity, but on professional adversity I've got a record second to none. I joined the party the week Back to Basics fell apart. I worked in the Ministry of Agriculture when BSE hit. I was on John Major's campaign team in 1997. I then spent four years working with William Hague, and in the last Parliament I was fighting the election on the front line.'

Much is made of the similarities between Osborne and Cameron. Both come from wealthy backgrounds (Osborne is the heir to a baronetcy and a wallpaper fortune). Both went to Oxford, before working at the Conservative Research Department. But the similarity – as well as the relationship – is sometimes overstated. Although it is Cameron to whom the 'Notting Hill' tag has stuck, Osborne's background is more cultured and more metropolitan. His mother, Felicity, once worked as desk officer for Amnesty International, and the young Osborne would man the toy stall at the annual Amnesty International jumble sale (Bayswater Branch). His father had made his own fortune with the firm he co-owns with his brother, Osborne & Little. The young Gideon (he changed his name by deed poll as a teenager) was brought up among the *bien-pensants*. His parents knew writers, journalists and art dealers, and neither was a Tory (although his mother voted for Margaret Thatcher 'because she was a woman').

It was all a long way from Cameron's county set. While he shared some of the modernisers' analysis about the narrowness of the Tories' appeal in 2001, Cameron was dismissive of what he regarded as a tendency towards indulgent and sterile self-hatred. Friends say he is a cultural Tory who resented being told that it was people like his parents, his friends and to some degree himself that turned voters off. Perhaps most importantly Cameron had not had Osborne's experiences of the failing days of Major nor of the attempt by Hague to modernise, abandoned in favour of a sharp tack back to the right. It was these bitter lessons that helped Osborne to 'get it' and, when he entered parliament, to be acknowledged as Portillo's heir by the architects of his modernising message. Gradually, over the next four years, Cameron would shift his position towards that of Osborne, in time supplanting him as the modernisers' leader-in-waiting.

With Portillo out, Cameron had to decide whom to endorse in the final ballot of party members. Clarke might have been expected to win Portillo-backers, but Iain Duncan Smith was a hero of the party's Eurosceptic wing. Notwithstanding his wife's enthusiasm for Ken Clarke, Cameron chose to endorse IDS – a 'good egg'. In an unusually personal attack on the man who had dismissed him from the Treasury eight years previously, he laid into Clarke for being abusive about his rival. 'Mr Clarke's saloon bar habit of calling his opponents "head bangers" or "hangers and floggers" always gives me the shivers,' he wrote in his online column on 5 September. 'Mr Clarke's man-of-the-people, broad-brush approach has minuses as well as pluses. As a former adviser put it to me years ago: "The trouble with Ken's broad brush is that everyone else gets splattered with paint."'

The Tories made a net gain of just one seat at the 2001 general election. Failure in politics may be a certainty but it often carries its own consolation. The 166 Conservative MPs were not nearly enough to form a governing majority but their small number meant that each could hope for a greater share of the spoils of opposition, such as they were. David Cameron landed a good backbench committee place almost straight away. He was appointed, in July, to the Home Affairs Select Committee, one of the three most important in the Commons.

As a new member he might have been expected to bide his time, but Cameron wanted to make waves from the start. In his first meeting the new MP suggested that the committee launch an investigation into the problem of heroin addiction or 'options for changing the law towards cannabis'. 'On the drugs issue I am an instinctive liberal, disliking state bans on anything, but my worry has always been the very simple point that legalisation will make drugs more available and more people will try them,' he wrote the next month. Quoting a teenager who had told him that every pupil had tried cannabis by the time they reached the sixth form, Cameron went on to ask: 'Have we reached the stage where cannabis is so ubiquitous that decriminalisation or legalisation will not lead to increased availability of consumption?'

No sooner had he posed the question than David Blunkett, then Labour's Home Secretary, gave an answer. Called by the committee to give evidence in response to its drugs investigation, Blunkett used his appearance to spring the surprise announcement that he was considering reclassifying cannabis from a Class B to a Class C drug. Cameron was as surprised as everyone else at being outflanked by a Home Secretary with a strong reputation for being illiberal. His immediate response was to attack Blunkett for not going far enough.

So, while he welcomed the proposed downgrading of cannabis as 'sensible', he said it was 'feeble'. He asked 'why [the Home Secretary] wasn't addressing the real problem of cannabis being a black market drug, such as heroin and cocaine'.

Cameron went further when the committee resumed its investigation the following week, seemingly suggesting that the government should consider wholesale legalisation of cannabis. Cross-examining Sue Killen, the Home Office's director of drugs strategy, Cameron said: 'It would be disappointing if radical options were not, at least, looked at.' In the event the committee did not go as far as Cameron would have liked, but what emerged in May 2002 was nevertheless a highly controversial report. Among its recommendations was the downgrading of Ecstasy from a Class A to a Class B drug, as well as the trial use of so-called 'shooting galleries', rooms where addicts could inject with prescribed heroin in relative safety.

The report was too much for one Conservative member of the committee, Angela Watkinson, who disowned it – an unusual break with the cross-party spirit in which select committees are supposed to work. Cameron, however, took to the media to defend the majority findings with passion. In an article for the *Daily Mail* he wrote:

we are facing a drugs epidemic and every single one of us is a victim … It is no good preaching to young people, or telling them that all drugs are just the same. They won't listen. Ranking Ecstasy alongside heroin simply makes no sense. We want the police to concentrate on the drugs that do the most harm. In a typical year there are more than 80,000 arrests for possession of cannabis. As the paperwork for each one can take hours, and as around four-fifths of them end in a caution, is that really a good use of police time?

Cameron's advocacy of 'shooting galleries' and his strong support for the downgrading of penalties for cannabis and Ecstasy carried a political price. He was attacked at the time in his local paper and made enemies among some of his Conservative colleagues. It does not fit neatly with the caricature of the calculating careerist plotting his way to the top job. But perhaps Cameron, so long the mouthpiece for views that he did not necessarily share, allowed himself a degree of licence – once free to do so – on an issue about which he felt passionately. Intellectually, instinctively and personally attracted to practical measures to reduce the harm drugs do, he chose to ignore narrow political interest. He was to pay the full cost of that decision four years later.

As well as having the pick of plum select committees, the new Tory MPs of 2001 had an easier job of getting noticed by the press than those of larger intakes. Since Cameron had been serially tipped for great things when he wasn't even in the Commons, it was inevitable that he would attract early attention once at Westminster. Nor is it a surprise to find that it was Michael Gove who picked him out first. Gove had, after all, promoted him to the shadow Cabinet (in print, at least). This time the *Times* columnist was a little more circumspect. 'MPs are like wines – even a poor crop can produce a premier cru,' he mused in a column on 1 September 2001, pointing out that Tony Blair and Gordon Brown, 'MPs of exceptional quality', had been elected in 1983, a bad election for Labour. Gove picked out three new MPs of 'Downing Street quality'. David Cameron headed the list (Paul Goodman and George Osborne made up the numbers). Anticipating by at least three years the 'Notting Hill set' soubriquet, Gove also listed his friend's weaknesses thus: 'despite [his] Berkshire roots, [his] Notting Hill polish may make him seem too metropolitan for some'.

By now Osborne and Cameron were becoming more than just acquaintances. Their social circles touched a little: Osborne's wife, Frances, had known Cameron slightly at Oxford, and Whetstone had been Osborne's boss for a short while at CRD before she left to replace

Cameron at the Home Office after his move to Carlton. When Osborne, who had served as Hague's political secretary between 1997 and 2001, had been selected for the safe Tatton seat and Cameron had won the nomination for the equally safe Witney, it was obvious that they were going to be two stars of the 2001 intake. It made sense to get on.

Osborne's respect for Cameron's political nous was reinforced shortly after both had become MPs. Following the 11 September attacks in New York and Washington, Home Secretary David Blunkett introduced a set of new anti-terror laws. Because of the nature of the legislation it was dealt with on the floor of the Commons. MPs were to debate, line by line, measures as controversial as detention without trial. Osborne saw an opportunity to shine and began to attend proceedings that he knew would be the focus of media attention. Only one other new-intake MP was there: David Cameron had had the same idea. There is a parallel with Tony Blair and Gordon Brown, who in 1983 served together as newly elected MPs on a committee that examined what became the Trade Union Act 1984. Cameron and Osborne began sitting together through the long sessions on the Anti-Terrorism, Crime and Security Bill in November and December 2001. Since they lived near one another in west London, it was natural that Osborne began giving Cameron a lift home. (Later when Osborne decided to leave his Mercedes A Class at home and start cycling, Cameron, who had first taken up cycling again during the election, followed suit.)

Cameron was unabashed about his efforts to raise his profile, writing in his *Guardian* column that December, 'OK, so I'm a media tart. I spent a large proportion of last week negotiating with, preparing for and appearing on radio and television programmes.' Engagingly he doesn't try to defend heading for 'the studio lights, the green room and the powder puff' other than in terms of 'my bid for national recognition'. The column is an extraordinarily candid summary of the sort of presentational techniques politicians usually keep well from view. For years Cameron had been advising politicians and businessmen on media appearances. Now it was his turn to put into practice what he had learned from their mistakes. On preparing for the showpiece political panel show, Radio 4's *Any Questions*, he wrote:

> Don't drink anything at the dinner with Jonathan Dimbleby before the show; don't worry about the audience in the hall baying for your blood – concentrate on the folks at home. And try to sound reasonable.
>
> Michael Portillo once told me a tip he had been given: by being thoroughly rude and aggressive to the other panellists at the dinner you can wind them up into fits of indignation. They will then rant and rave on air and you will come over cool as the proverbial cucumber.

Turning to appearances on BBC television he boasted how he had fooled a producer into believing that he would deliver a right-wing rant on air only to change tack and be moderate and measured once the cameras were rolling. 'It wasn't great television but I was on and able to make my point.' His 'tabloid tips' were to read the television schedules and to 'have some jokes'.

If his liberal instincts led him to join with Labour MPs over the drugs issue, hunting was and remains an issue on which David Cameron is out of step with the sort of urban voters the Tories need to win back if they are to govern Britain again. His dislike of the ban on hunting with dogs is of a piece with his avowedly libertarian outlook. But there is more than just dry intellectual opposition to the ban: he himself has admitted it is one of the few issues that make him 'furious'. Normally a courteous parliamentarian, he made a series of abusive remarks during a key debate on the proposed ban. He called Sir Gerald Kaufman a 'pompous prat' and heckled Ann Widdecombe – the two leading proponents of the ban on either side of the House. (Cameron is suspected of shouting, 'You can take Widdecombe!' to

Labour MPs as his colleague spoke in favour of the ban.)

It is not, perhaps, surprising that Cameron feels the ban so passionately – horses, and country sports generally, are so integral to who he is and where he comes from. His father used to own a share in a number of racehorses (with, among others, Reggie Sheffield), and was an enthusiastic punter. Ian Cameron took his son to Aintree in 1977, giving the eleven-year-old an enduring memory of Red Rum rounding the Canal Turn to a famous Grand National victory. Cameron himself came to riding later than his elder siblings. Perhaps there was an element of the zeal of the convert in his support for hunting since he only took up the sport at about the time it started coming under threat. His next-door neighbour in his constituency village of Dean is the honorary secretary of the Heythrop Hunt, and it is with the Heythrop that Cameron has done most of his hunting (he told one newspaper at the time of the leadership election that he had attended only around ten hunts in his whole life). Famously, he rode Raisa, a retired working horse Rebekah Brooks borrowed from the police, and he has the use of a mount stabled at Ginge Manor, the home of his stepfather-in-law. Bart, a dark chestnut classic English hunter, is, at seventeen hands, large enough to accommodate Cameron.

It was presumably this animal that he rode when he went for a day's hunting with the Heythrop to show his support for the sport. 'I climbed on board a horse and went out for a day with the Heythrop hunt,' he wrote in his online column.

Nothing had prepared me for the sheer terror of a day's hunting. I battled in vain to control my powerful steed and careered through trees and bushes completely out of control. Trying to hover at the back of the field, I ended up at the front as a fox broke cover from behind. A 15-minute gallop along narrow paths in a forest followed, during which I thought death (for me at least) would be a release. The fox escaped. Having survived two-and-a-half hours without being unseated, I dismounted and collapsed in a sweating heap on the ground. My horse had hardly broken a sweat.

The day with the Heythrop might have been 'sheer terror' but it was a long way short of matching Cameron's scariest moment on a horse. That had come in the summer of 2001 when he, Samantha, and Dom and Tif Loehnis booked a horseriding safari in Kenya's Masai Mara. Cameron was near the head of a single file of riders travelling down a wadi when a lion leaped from cover and attacked the haunch of the seventh horse. Its rider stayed on but Tif Loehnis, travelling immediately behind, was thrown as her horse reared in terror. Cameron's horse bolted before he heard the roar or could realise what was happening. He turned his mount around in time to see an Argentine guide who had been bringing up the rear chase the lion away with nothing but a stick and curses.

When it comes to the British countryside, Cameron prefers the rifle and, recently, the fishing rod. He started shooting young – he and his brother took pot-shots at rabbits with an air rifle around Peasemore – and is regarded by his friends as a good shot. He has shot foxes in Norfolk and stalked deer on Jura with Michael Green. Several years ago he added fly-fishing for sea trout to his list of field sports when he took lessons on the Scottish island. Jura, say friends, is important to Cameron: it provides a total escape from the pressures of politics. The Astors' house, Tarbet Lodge, is perched on a remote sandy beach overlooking the Sound of Jura. The interior is comfortably snug, report visitors, who say the overall impression is of being accommodated within an elegant schooner as, more often than not, a gale blows outside. Annabel Astor provisions the lodge with pre-ordered delicacies that arrive, periodically, in parcels from the better shops of Edinburgh and London.

Cameron observes a singular ritual on Jura – he swims in the sea every day before dinner, regardless of the weather. His fondness for plunging into icy waters has been noted in other country estates where he has been a visitor. Charles Moore, then editor of the *Daily Telegraph*, recalls being a fellow guest with Cameron at a house party of their mutual friend Randal (Viscount) Dunluce at his home Glenarm Castle in County Antrim one November weekend in 1999. Cameron was his usual well-mannered self at dinner on Saturday, recalls Moore, who says that he 'seemed very comfortable in himself'. Cameron was considerably less comfortable the next morning, however, when he burned the toast, setting off the castle's fire alarms and thereby prompting a fire engine and seven firemen to race to the scene, bashing their way through the recently installed security gates in their needless rush. As 'penance', Cameron jumped into a local burn later that day.

This is Cameron's tribe, and it is clear that he feels its call on issues like hunting. But there is a far more important subject to consider in assessing whether his strongly developed sense of loyalty impairs his political judgement. It is Iraq.

Iain Duncan Smith's leadership of the Conservative Party began the day after the terrorist attacks of 11 September and from the start he offered strong support to what quickly became known as the 'war on terror'. Tony Blair's decision to stand 'shoulder to shoulder' with George Bush in the prosecution of that war presented the Tories with something of a political problem. Duncan Smith – who could fairly claim to know as much as any MP about international terrorism – was determined that the party he led would give unstinting support to Blair on this issue.

David Cameron, an MP for less than four months, admitted to admiring the way Blair handled the weeks following 11 September. As a member of the Home Affairs Select Committee he saw Blair at this time more than most of his colleagues since he was entitled to attend special briefings held by the Prime Minister in Downing Street on privy council terms. He intervened in the Commons debate prior to the decision to send British troops to Afghanistan, asking which other

NATO allies were sending soldiers – but the question was meant to be supportive, not to signal dissent. While few Conservatives would today believe it was wrong to support Blair on Afghanistan, the party's record on Iraq is a lingering embarrassment – and a political headache. Without the votes of Conservative MPs like David Cameron in the crucial Commons vote on the eve of war in March 2003, Blair would not have been able to overcome the rebellion in his own party. This fact, uncomfortable for all but the very few Tories who voted against the motion, severely limits their party's ability to benefit from the conflict's deep and enduring unpopularity. The added difficulty for David Cameron is that he advertised his doubts about the conflict repeatedly – but then, despite them, voted with Blair.

It was in August 2002 – a good seven months before the invasion – that Cameron first admitted to feeling uneasy about the seemingly inexorable march to war. 'I am an instinctive hawk about these things – and was about Afghanistan – but on this occasion have distinctively dove-ish tendencies. The question no one seems able to answer is the following: even if we believe that President Saddam now has lethal weapons, wouldn't an invasion make him more likely to use them, as he would be left with no way out?' It was not until the following February – the month before the invasion – that Cameron raised the issue in public again:

> Everyone knows that Saddam is a monster. Everyone knows that he has done dreadful things to his own people. Where they want to be convinced is that taking action is in the British national interest. The evidence of links between Saddam and al Qaida has so far been unconvincing. The evidence of weapons of mass destruction is more convincing. But people still want to know why deterrence is not better than a pre-emptive war.
>
> The Prime Minister probably can never give to us all the information from the security services and others that he has access to. But

if we are to fight a pre-emptive war in which lives will be lost, we need to know more. And we need to know it soon.

A few days later, Cameron listed four types of sceptical Tory: 'the "British interests first" brigade', the military types 'who are traditionally sceptical about most foreign expeditions', the 'Americo-sceptics, like Ken Clarke'.

Then there are the confused and uncertain, of whom I am definitely one. We are not peaceniks and are quite prepared to vote for war in the right circumstances. We loathe President Saddam and all his works. And we supported the last Gulf war with vigour.

We – the confused and uncertain – have listened carefully to the arguments and we have discerned two reasons for war. The first is that there may be links between President Saddam and terrorist organisations, including al-Qaida. We have waited patiently for proof, but none has arrived ... The second reason we have been given is that Saddam has weapons of mass destruction, such as chemical warheads, and a growing arsenal of missiles with which to deliver them. We believe this and understand that dealing with Iraq must be at the top of the international agenda. But that is where we become uncertain. How exactly should we deal with Iraq? All our political lives we have been nurtured on the theory of deterrence ...

Now we are being asked to swap deterrence with something new called preemptive war. I cannot be certain, but I suspect that many of us will not support preemptive war unless Blair can produce either compelling evidence of the direct threat to the UK, or a UN resolution giving it specific backing. The signs are that he hasn't got the first and won't get the second.

A month later, with neither fresh evidence nor second UN resolution, Cameron voted with Blair for war. In an article on the eve of the vote he explained why 'grudgingly, unhappily, unenthusiastically' he had chosen to support the war.

Having made the decision to support the Prime Minister, Cameron lavished praise on him. 'Blair himself has been masterful. It pains me to say so, but it's true. The speech in the great debate was a parliamentary triumph and it would be churlish to deny it. I've even sent copies to constituents writing to me about the war.' If that wasn't embarrassing enough, in a passage on the calculations for a comeback by Robin Cook, the former Foreign Secretary, who had resigned from the Cabinet rather than support the war without a second UN resolution, Cameron glimpsed the future. 'A long, unpopular war ending Blair's reign. A realignment within the Labour party – and perhaps even outside it. Conservatives tainted with support for the government's war.' That taint would dog the then leader of the Tories, his successor Michael Howard and – in time – Cameron himself.

By the spring of 2003 it was clear that Iain Duncan Smith's leadership was failing. He tried, as William Hague before him had tried, to accommodate the party's modernisers. And like Hague, he soon found it impossible to reconcile their demands for root-and-branch transformation with a recalcitrant and suspicious parliamentary and local party. David Cameron, who had supported him for leader over Ken Clarke, was brought in by Duncan Smith a year later to help improve his Commons performances. He was to be promoted by him the following summer and – when the end came in November 2003 in a bloody parliamentary coup – Cameron claimed that he voted in support of the embattled leader. But this conspicuous display of loyalty does not tell the whole truth of Cameron's relationship with one of his most recent predecessors. The truth is a little more complex.

Duncan Smith sent for Cameron, George Osborne and Boris Johnson in November 2002 when it was clear that he faced a potential leadership challenge. Officially the three young MPs were there to help coach him for Prime Minister's Questions, but Duncan Smith may also have hoped to share some of the lustre of the rising stars. The issue that prompted the crisis was his insistence that Tory MPs vote against proposed legislation that would allow gay and unmarried couples to adopt children. It was a policy that separated Duncan Smith and his band of supporters on the Christian right from the modernisers, who had been encouraged to believe that he supported their aims. Naturally enough, attention focused on Michael Portillo and his supporters, who made it clear that they intended to defy their leader and vote in favour of the measure and against the party line. The coincidence of the date, 5 November, wreathed reports of the clash in smoky conspiracy.

Despite being invited into Duncan Smith's backroom just the previous week, when the crunch Commons division came Cameron could not support the leader. He did not vote. A week later the *Sunday Times*, hunting through a wreckage for signs of life, named Cameron as a potential 'future Conservative prime minister'. The young MP himself chose to ignore the whole crisis. Writing his *Guardian* column on 15 November, he conceded that it had been 'a dreadful fortnight of media focus on leadership, backbiting and splits' but then with admirable optimism claimed that 'Tory tails are up'. To the leader himself he was always courteous – and punctual. Unlike Johnson, Cameron always reported for duty on time for the breakfast meeting on Wednesday morning that began Duncan Smith's preparations for PMQs. Other members of the briefing team noted how tired he looked. One recalls him quietly saying one morning that he had come direct from hospital where he had spent the night with his baby son Ivan. It cannot but have felt something of a chore on occasion for the young MP already struggling to balance the demands of a disabled child with his own career. He himself once recalled how one Wednesday he 'joined a subdued gathering at dawn in icy darkness' and added that he felt 'malnourished and tetchy' by the time he got to the Commons to watch Duncan Smith read his lines. But once inside the Tory leader's office in Speaker's Court just beneath Big Ben, Cameron would be dutiful and deferential.

In a pattern to be repeated when the pair resumed their role under Michael Howard, Osborne did the jokes while Cameron crafted the words. He almost always urged economy of expression on Duncan Smith, who liked to go 'off piste', as one of his former team puts it. The young MP drew on his time briefing John Major when he was at CRD as well as on his own far more limited experience of asking questions of Blair in his own right. Usefully for students of politics (as well as for his opponents) Cameron explained his technique in an online column he wrote just after asking his first question at PMQs.

'There are four types of question,' he wrote. 'First up is the "wife-beater". This is the question to which there is no answer. A typical effort would be: "What is the prime minister most proud of – the billion pounds wasted on the Dome or the million-pound bung from Bernie Ecclestone?"' He continued:

Next is 'the teaser'. This type of question looks limp and unexciting on paper, but can sometimes elicit the most interesting response by catch ing the prime minister off guard ...

Third is the *Daily Mail* special. Pick the issue that the middle-ranking tabloids are having kittens about and give it some oomph ... Make it on to the front pages and enjoy 15 seconds of fame.

Finally, there are the local issues. These are by far the most boring for everyone else to listen to, easily the most effective. Unlike national papers, local ones actually report in some detail what members of parliament do. A short question can be followed up with a press release, an endless round of local TV and radio interviews and a pro-longed burst of local stardom.

Thanks in part to Cameron's and Osborne's coaching Duncan Smith's performances began to improve. An attempted coup before the local elections in May 2003 failed, and when the Duncan Smith-led Tories did better than expected at the polls it seemed the danger to his leadership had receded. That summer Cameron – who, in July, voted for a Conservative motion to retain a version of Section 28 – was rewarded with his first frontbench job as deputy shadow Leader of the House. Cameron's putative boss, Eric Forth, was a close friend of David Davis, whose bid for the leadership Cameron had not supported and around whom opposition to IDS was beginning to collect. Forth was not, therefore, a natural ally, but the pair got on well enough.

Business Questions on Thursdays is a sketch-writers' staple. Like PMQs the day before, it is a forum where almost any topic can be discussed. Backbenchers are allowed to raise issues under the guise of demanding parliamentary time for its further debate. Both the Leader of the House and his shadow, therefore, can display their range and versatility as well as show off rhetorical flourishes in an atmosphere a lot less pressured than during PMQs. As Forth's deputy, Cameron could have expected no more than a bit-part role as his boss duelled with Peter Hain across the despatch box. But in a stroke of luck on just his second Thursday in the job Forth was called away and Cameron had to stand in.

At 12.31 on Thursday 10 July Cameron rose and placed his hands confidently on the despatch box for the first time. It was to be a triumphant debut, but he recalls how it very nearly went horribly wrong. Discomfited by some 'impromptu sledging' from Dennis Skinner, Labour's totemic MP for Bolsover, Cameron was momentarily lost for words, 'my mouth opening and closing like an ornamental Koi Carp'. He then made a minor slip when he tried to explain that the shadow Leader of the House was away, substituting the word 'deputy'. Skinner pounced: ''E wants the top job already!' Cameron quickly recovered and gave such a commanding performance that, reading the press coverage the following week, Duncan Smith may have concurred with Skinner. Quentin Letts in the *Daily Mail* described it as 'the best parliamentary debut I have seen', while Simon Carr in the *Independent* described him as 'future leader material'.

Most effusive of all was the profile of him in the following week's *Spectator* by his long-time friend and occasional drinking and holiday companion Bruce Anderson. Anderson, who can claim to have correctly tipped at least three future Conservative leaders, lavished praise on the thirty-six-year-old. His profile concluded: 'Successful politicians ought to have stamina, as well as intellectual ability, moral depth, commonsense as well as public relations flair. It is rare to find an individual who combines so many qualities, yet it may be that David Cameron does. They are bound to lead him to high office. In time, they will make him a candidate for the highest office of all.'

Cameron was quick to spot the danger of his sudden elevation to leadership candidate. He told his local paper four days after the article appeared: 'It's very flattering but often something like this signals the end of your political career rather than the beginning.' In saying this he was echoing Blair. On being promoted to the shadow Cabinet in 1988 Blair said: 'I'm acutely conscious of the fact that the history of politics is littered with the P45s of those who were supposed to be rising stars and ended up being shooting stars.'

That autumn was to be Iain Duncan Smith's last as leader. He was defeated in a leadership ballot triggered, in accordance with the rules, when twenty-five MPs wrote to the Chief Whip, David Maclean. Duncan Smith's allies remain convinced that he was the victim of a plot hatched by supporters of Howard acting in concert with modernisers such as Francis Maude. Since Cameron was known to have a close relationship with Howard (Duncan Smith was told that he was meeting with his former boss and Rachel Whetstone every week), as well as to be on good terms with many of the modernisers, he is suspected by some of having had a hand in Duncan Smith's downfall.

That autumn's conference, held in Blackpool, marked a new low for the party. On its eve the *Sunday Telegraph* had published claims that senior Conservatives feared that Duncan Smith's employment of his wife Betsy out of the public purse broke the rules on how MPs' office costs allowance should be spent. The nadir came when the shadow Cabinet was forced to bob up and down in a single phalanx seventeen times in the course of Duncan Smith's leadership speech – when 'the quiet man' claimed to be turning up the volume – in a singularly unconvincing display of loyalty. Cameron attended on only one day, forced for the second year running, he wrote, to spend conference week in hospital with his young son. Watching on a 'wobbly NHS television set by [Ivan's] bedside in St Mary's, Paddington', he must privately have despaired, although he wrote in his column, 'from this angle it all looks pretty good'.

Coincidentally, as Duncan Smith was being forced out of the Tory leadership, Michael Green was losing his battle with Charles Allen to control the merged Carlton and Granada. Rupert Dilnott-Cooper recalls that David Cameron was the only one of Green's former executive colleagues to speak up for him in the media. Listening to him praise Green on BBC Radio 4's *Today* programme Dilnott-Cooper remembers admiring his loyalty. 'What's the upside of doing that for a politician? Identifying yourself with the old chairman? It was an extraordinarily bold and decent thing to do.' Annabel Astor, though, would have expected no less.

Would Cameron be as stalwart a friend to Duncan Smith when the time for *his* exit came? His behaviour that day divides opinion. On the morning of 29 October 2003, Cameron and Osborne arrived as usual outside Duncan Smith's office to begin the weekly briefing. Their arrival was about the only usual facet of the scene. Over the weekend it had become clear that there would indeed be a leadership ballot since the requisite twenty-five MPs had demanded one. Duncan Smith had for days been under heavy pressure to stand down without a fight. Maclean told him, frankly, that he believed he had lost the confidence of the party. It was obvious why his enemies would prefer him to depart the scene gracefully. A ballot, although secret, would be divisive. It would also force into the open many of those who had been operating clandestinely. For that reason as much as any other Duncan Smith was determined not to be bundled from office despite the tearful entreaties of some of his closest aides not to fight on.

In an atmosphere of unreal formality, Cameron and Osborne began to prepare Duncan Smith as if it had been any other week. But at one point the Tory leader was called away for a few minutes, as often happened. As soon as Duncan Smith had left the room, Cameron said he believed that what he was doing was 'madness' and would only damage him and the party. When he was told that the leader was determined to stand in the ballot, as he was entitled to do, Cameron said that he would like to have 'a private conversation' with Duncan Smith. Behind closed doors he then begged Duncan Smith to reconsider, urging him to spare himself the humiliation of a heavy defeat. The former leader has told friends that Cameron said he should resign, but if he continued he could count on his vote. Allies ask why Cameron, then a very junior figure, took it on himself to speak so candidly to the leader. They question whether he was motivated by concern for Duncan Smith's feelings alone.

After PMQs – and, paradoxically, a much better performance than usual – Cameron chatted with a friend in the Commons smoking room. The Tory MP recalls that both were at a loss as to how to vote in the ballot due to take place in a room upstairs that afternoon. 'He and I sat in the smoking room together before going up to cast our votes and we both didn't know what we were going to do. We both sat there genuinely thinking this is a very difficult decision to make. He certainly wasn't involved in the pack that was after IDS and didn't particularly enjoy the spectator sport either.'

In the event Cameron voted for Duncan Smith (Osborne voted against). The result – 75 for, 90 against – was closer than expected. Why did Cameron vote for IDS when he thought he should resign?

Partly, say friends, because he was nervous of his constituency association whose grandees had made clear that, after Woodward, they would brook no disloyalty from a Witney MP. But also because it was obvious that IDS was going to lose. On this occasion, Cameron calculated, it was better to back the losing horse.

IVAN
Firstborn

Ivan Cameron was born in the Queen Charlotte's Hospital in London on Monday 8 April 2002. The birth was by Caesarean section, made necessary at the last minute because Ivan was the wrong way round in the womb. Otherwise it was a normal delivery of an apparently healthy baby boy. It was a joyful event but even then a period of mixed emotions: in nearby Hammersmith Hospital at the same time, David Cameron's godfather Tim Rathbone, Ian Cameron's schoolfriend and a significant personal and political inspiration, was having tests for cancer. He visited Samantha in hospital but was to die some weeks later. 'The fact that he was dying while my son was being born seemed to have some kind of symbolism. It made his birth all the more poignant and moving,' Cameron later told a friend.

Although Ivan was their first child, they quickly sensed that something was wrong. At Queen Charlotte's, he appeared to have occasional spasms. Otherwise, he seemed a very sleepy child and Samantha struggled with breast-feeding. But the health visitor paying the routine postnatal call to Ginge Manor, where mother and baby had gone after leaving Queen Charlotte's, saw no reason to be alarmed. Within a week it was clear that Ivan, still very sleepy, was losing weight. Sometimes his hand would spring open in a series of small but repetitive impulses. As first-time parents, David and Samantha Cameron had nothing to compare their son's behaviour to and, reassured by the advice of the health visitor, showed off their son to Dominic and Tif Loehnis that weekend.

But, as Ivan entered his second week, the jerks were becoming more pronounced. Annabel Astor had become sufficiently concerned to drive her daughter – on her birthday – and grandson to the local GP. The doctor's diagnosis was that the newborn was suffering from a kidney malfunction. He directed them to the Accident and Emergency department of the John Radcliffe Hospital in Oxford. It was here that the baby had his first major seizure in front of a doctor. The nature of Ivan's condition was beginning to be shockingly apparent. David Cameron, joining his wife at the hospital, shared her distress as their tiny child was subjected to forty-eight hours of blood tests, brain scans and lumbar punctures. Of all the tests, the one that was picking up the most identifiable evidence of Ivan's problem was the electroen-cephalogram (EEG). The EEG records brainwave patterns from the electrical signals emitted by the brain. This showed the high-voltage 'spikes' that occur in epilepsy, but they were followed by very little activity.

After one last confirming EEG, Mike Pike, a paediatrician, took the couple into a side room to talk. With ominous purposefulness, he placed a box of Kleenex beside them. He told them that this was very serious, that the pattern he had seen was consistent with 'a very poor outcome and severe disability'. Ivan, he said, would have 'very serious difficulties'. Cameron, struggling to take the gravity of the diagnosis on board, said: 'When you say he's got serious difficulties, does that mean he's going to have trouble doing his maths, or does that mean he's never going to be able to walk and talk?' Pike said simply: 'I'm afraid it means he probably won't walk or talk.'

Within a few days they had a name for Ivan's condition: Ohtahara syndrome. The National Institute of Neurological Disorders and Stroke (NINDS) provides the following definition: 'a neurological disorder characterised by seizures ... most commonly caused by metabolic disorders or structural damage in the brain, although the cause or causes in many cases can't be determined'. Most infants 'show significant underdevelopment of part or all of the cerebral hemispheres. The EEGs of infants with Ohtahara syndrome reveal a characteristic pattern of high-voltage spike wave discharge followed by little activity. This pattern is known as "burst suppression".' NINDS says that 'Antiepileptic drugs are used to control seizures, but are unfortunately not usually very effective ... The course of Ohtahara syndrome is severely progressive. Seizures become more frequent, accompanied by physical and mental retardation. Some children will die in infancy; others will survive but be profoundly handicapped.' Unsure whether Ivan would live for weeks or years, Cameron ensured that his son was christened at the earliest opportunity.

Cameron has said that the news hit him 'like a freight train'. A friend observes that the couple entered 'a very, very grim and difficult period'. Emotionally, they had to overcome the discrepancy between the elation they had felt at the birth of their first child and the reality of what lay ahead. 'You are depressed for a while because you are grieving for the difference between your hopes and the reality,' Cameron has said.

There were immediate practical issues to address, the most pressing of which was how best to manage his condition. Ivan went through further tests at Great Ormond Street and Queen Mary's hospitals in London as doctors experimented with cocktails of drugs. David and Samantha Cameron, taking it in turns to sleep beside their son on hospital floors, were given a brutal lesson in the reality of life as the parent of a disabled child. After his initial shock Cameron has described how he began to surface. 'There was a moment driving home from hospital and just thinking, "We are going to get through this. If we can't do a good job and look after him, then we have failed."'

Initially the Camerons tried to look after Ivan themselves, without the support of their local authority's social service department. For a year the couple struggled with the situation largely on their own, although they had help from a special-needs-trained nurse during the day. Three and a half months after Ivan was born, Samantha had returned to work for two days a week, and after five months she was back doing nine-day fortnights. It was a difficult decision. On the one hand she worried inconsolably about Ivan's minute-to-minute care, but, on the other, her career was important to her and she had always intended to carry on working.

Childcare was shared. Journalists spotted Cameron bottle-feeding his son in Westminster that summer and cited it as evidence of the changing nature of the Tory Party, not knowing the fullness of that truth. The young Tory MP also took Ivan to meetings at Carlton, where he remained a consultant. His former colleagues could hardly fail to notice a change. At Edwina Paine's engagement party, one said he seemed a 'different man ... he seemed much less frivolous'. Another senior colleague said: 'He'd walk around with that baby in a basket, he'd come to every meeting.' Where previously Cameron had appeared 'arrogant', 'this was a real leveller'. Giles Andreae has said that Ivan's handicap had given Cameron 'more humility'. Cameron has admitted as much himself. 'Having a severely disabled son does bring you into contact with a lot of other elements of life. You do spend a lot of time in hospitals, you meet a lot of other parents and families in the same situation. It's an eye-opener.'

At one point, Ivan's blood pressure shot up and he had to be rushed to the Renal Unit at Great Ormond Street. Cameron found that hospital visit in particular a strange experience. 'He was struck by the fact that there were all these kids there who had been on dialysis for months, being incredibly courageous with these awful, awful problems,' says a friend. 'I think it made him realise that there are other people in similar situations. On one occasion he was there all night, and at about 4 a.m. he was reading Jack and Jill to someone else's kids, and then had to go to Parliament early the next day to carry on with life as normal.' The MP saw too what a terrible strain it places on the relationship of disabled children's parents. 'One thing they were very determined about from the start was that they wouldn't fall apart, that come what may they would hold together,' remembers a friend. 'They were and are an incredibly close couple and they just decided they were going to have a happy family life, come what may. I think they were just very, very good to each other in that period.'

Samantha came to be particularly grateful for the support of her half-sisters Flora (Astor) and Alice (Sheffield). Others were good to them too, once the reality of Ivan's condition began to be appreciated. Rachel Whetstone, who was made Ivan's godmother, became a gate-keeper figure, offering support and passing on information to friends a little embarrassed by their stunned sense of inertia. 'She is much more pushy than all of us and would get in there and find out what was going on and disseminate info to the rest of us,' said one.

Whetstone and others were useful and kind, but one of those best placed to understand what the couple were going through was not an old friend but a new contact. Ian Birrell, then deputy editor of the *Independent*, had initially invited Cameron to lunch – before Ivan's birth – for professional reasons. By the time the engagement was finally fixed there was a personal motivation. Ian and Linnet Birrell's second child, Iona, then eight years old, also has severe epilepsy. She is effectively blind, is unable to walk or talk, is in need of round-the-clock care and suffers seizures on a daily basis. Instead of the usual Westminster gossip, the lunch ended up as an intense discussion about disability and parenting. Birrell shared his experiences of coping, and of the struggles that lay ahead, and as a result became close friends with Cameron and, later, with Samantha. 'The reality is that you come to realise that this is the child you've got and you learn to love that child, the child you hadn't expected to have,' said Birrell. 'Your love is very different but no less strong.'

By Ivan's first birthday the Camerons still had no state-funded domestic help, but they did have financial assistance with Ivan's care from Cameron's parents and Samantha's father. They were battling their grief and coping with a child in distress while trying to fulfil their professional responsibilities. At Parliament and in his Witney constituency Cameron was still working hard, showing little sign of what was going on at home. But the most gruelling aspect of all, he has said, was enduring his son's suffering. 'The really difficult thing is the unmanageability of the epilepsy,' he has said. 'He just screams. It's agony to watch, and you feel he's suffering. That's been the worst of it.'

In the spring of 2003, during the build-up to the war in Iraq, things began to reach a point of crisis. 'It was around then that I think they both began to wilt slightly under the tiredness and incredible stress of coping with everything on their own,' said Birrell. The couple made three major decisions. The first was to alter Ivan's feeding by arranging for him to take in food through his stomach. It had been proving impossible to get his food and medicine into him reliably, so they agreed to the insertion of a gastrostomy tube. Second, they decided to go to the social services. As Birrell attests, 'It is only when you get plunged into this world of disability that you realise, slowly, there is help available, poor and haphazard as it often is.'

And third, Samantha decided to go for counselling. She was worn out from lack of sleep, with nights spent at Ivan's bedside, and felt she was adding to her husband's burdens by talking all the time about Ivan, her worries and her exhaustion. She went to three or four sessions with an NHS family counsellor over a six-week period, largely to have someone who would listen, someone with professional experience to understand what she was going through. As a result of these decisions, combined with the advent of more respite care and the feeding tube, the Camerons' domestic life began to stabilise.

A subject that cropped up constantly between the two was whether to try for more children. Was there a genetic problem that might be replicated? Ohtahara syndrome is a convenient but imprecise term, and belongs to the wider family of epilepsy-related conditions.

Surprisingly little is known of the causes, although in Ivan's case the circumstances of his birth were not thought to have been at fault, as can be the case. Samantha has said that in a way she was relieved that the explanation seems to have been an 'act of God' rather than a birth problem, which would be more difficult to take. Beyond that, the doctors couldn't be sure. If the cause was genetic, they were told, the chances of it recurring were said to be one in four. If it wasn't, then they were one in several thousand. All in all, their genetic counsellor put the chances at about one in twenty. 'I remember them being worried when they heard that there was one couple to whom it had happened twice,' remembers a friend, which made them think the cause was genetic.

But Cameron's optimism was beginning to reassert itself: they decided that yes, they would take the chance. A few weeks after Ivan's first birthday, when the couple were near their lowest ebb, at last came some good news. Samantha was pregnant. The worries that went with that were undeniable, but the tests during her pregnancy were re-assuring. On 19 January 2004, Nancy Cameron was born. She was thoroughly healthy, a triumphant vindication of the couple's decision. Samantha Cameron felt the relief even more acutely than her husband. 'She was a different person until she had Nancy,' says a friend. 'Sam is so happy-go-lucky and giggly normally, but there is a deep-down sadness which will never completely go away. She has recovered to an enormous degree, though, since Nancy arrived. Dave really held things together. He just took a decision that it wasn't going to ruin things. He was so strong about it.'

By the autumn of 2003 Cameron was beginning to talk about his family situation publicly. In an article in his local paper he said, 'those families that do the most themselves to cope with the situation often get the least help.' The young MP really began to harness his political talents to the cause of disabled parents in a battle over the policy of 'inclusion', that is, of educating disabled children in mainstream schools. By May 2004 it threatened Ivan's own day centre in London. It was during a campaign to save the Cheyne Day Centre that Cameron spoke most directly about Ivan. In an article in the *Daily Telegraph* he wrote:

> [Ivan's] epilepsy [is] so powerful he can fit for an hour at a time, his small body contorted, often screaming in agony. And with the epilepsy comes cerebral palsy so severe that Ivan cannot move, sit up or hold on to anything or anybody. He cannot crawl, walk or talk and never will. Ivan is two – and he is my son. The point of writing this is not to seek sympathy. My wife, Samantha, and I have had that in welcome abundance. It is to tell a story about something that seems to be going badly wrong in this country.

Cameron explained the complex, under-resourced and unhelpful bureaucracies parents faced in getting any sort of education for a disabled child. 'Even I, with a university degree, English as my first language and three years as a member of Parliament, taking up complex constituency cases, am finding the process of getting the right school for my son an impossible battle.' In the most moving passage Cameron wrote: 'Ivan's only self-conscious movements are to raise his eyebrows and to smile. And his smile – slightly crooked, sometimes accompanied by a little moan – can light up a room. It never fails to make me both happy and immensely proud of him.'

He wasn't to know it at the time but even as Cameron wrote those words Ivan was losing his ability to smile. In his first years, there was a sense that his parents could communicate with him. They learned to make some sense of the slightest of signals. Little signs (a stretch, or a smack of the lips) seemed to mean 'more food'. Chief among these signals was his smile. Often Ivan would smile as soon as he heard one of his parents coming into the room. It was the sign that they were doing something right, that beyond the seizures and contortion, there were moments of mild serenity. Through this slender but vital channel of communication they found that he liked animals (they took him to a neighbouring farm either at Peasemore or at Dean), and that he enjoyed feeling the wind on his face (so they took him for plenty of walks in his specially adapted buggy) and going swimming (a constituency neighbour kept his pool suitably warm).

But now, awfully, the smile was fading. Over a three-month period when he was two he gradually stopped smiling. It went down to four or five times a day, and then to nothing. 'I once asked David if he thinks that Ivan enjoys life – it is, as I know, something that can be quite hard to tell,' said Birrell. 'And he sort of paused and looked up and then said, "Oh, not really, I think his life's very tough," and that's their main concern. It hurts them so much to see him suffer the whole time. They have not been concerned about the fact that he won't go to Oxford or play tennis at Wimbledon. What has bothered them above all has been trying to make his life as good as it can be.' Cameron was once asked whether he thought 'it would have been kinder' to let his child die. 'It's difficult. That is a conversation that we have quite often. What happens if he has terrible fits?' he replied, before bringing the conversation to a close.

'In terms of trying to "understand" what has happened, in some philosophical sense, actually I don't think you do need any explanation for it. I mean some people do, and it does affect their relationship, their religion, either strengthening it or weakening it, but I don't think in this case it has. His religion, while there in the background, is not the driving force in his life,' said Birrell. Cameron has described himself as 'a pretty classic Church of England "racked with doubt and scepticism" believer', although, until Ivan's arrival, it would have been hard to imagine Cameron being racked by anything. Indeed, Cameron's lightly worn Anglicanism is such that it has produced moments of unintended humour. The *Catholic Herald*, seeking to get a handle on the depth of his faith, asked Cameron if he believed in the resurrection. 'Yes, but I sometimes struggle with the big leaps,' said Cameron, as if coming back from the dead was a piece of cake. Cameron says he believes in God and is a Christian, 'and I worship – not as regularly as I should – but I go to church.' A close friend, asked whether Cameron's view of the world had been altered by the birth of Ivan, said: 'He believed in a God before it happened, and he believed in a God after it happened, but he was pretty pissed off with him.' When asked about it in late 2006, Cameron said to a journalist: 'A merciful God? These things are illogical. If anything it made me more religious. Obviously I pray for him. The truth is the first person who says "some good will come of this" you want to thump really quite hard, but actually some good *does* come of even terrible things like this.'

He used to take Ivan to a family church service where the boy would sit on his knee and he enjoyed being with other children and with his father. 'I get a good hour with him, and we bond,' Cameron said. Someone who saw him regularly in church testifies to the warmth of that bonding. Giles Andreae witnessed the couple's love for Ivan from close quarters. 'It's amazing, quite surreal, when you see Ivan sitting on their knee,' he said in 2005. 'He's huge, and they have him sitting like a little baby. There is utmost affection in their eyes. The way they have responded to that has been deeply and utterly extraordinary. You can only collapse into cliché. They think that every day is a bonus. The material affection is tangible. It's unlike the parent of a normal child. There's nothing he can do, so what manifests itself is a kind of angelic aura, supported by the fact that he has a very beautiful face – big dark eyes and big eyebrows and full dark hair. The set of his face is very composed, which you kind of translate as "sweet". He's like a great big angel. You're kind of drawn to that goodness. They are genuinely passionate about him. It's a really moving thing to see.'

As a parent in this situation, Birrell said, you either cope or you go under. And if you do cope, you reach a strange sort of normality, although it is not normality by most people's standards. 'If you listen to one week of what it takes looking after Ivan, it beggars belief. There are a million complications. It really is a staggering thing,' said Andreae in 2005. If the couple ever went away from home with the family, Ivan would have to travel in a van, and would have to have the full 'impedimenta – special this and special that', plus a ramp, to accompany him. 'Extreme epilepsy is very chaotic,' Cameron has said. Dr Mando Watson, Ivan's consultant paediatrician, said that with a patient like Ivan 'the important thing is to stabilise the condition. We try to control the seizures, treat any chest infections with physiotherapy and oxygen and also treat the disability – help them feed and make them comfortable so they can live as full a life as possible. The challenge is to enable these children to maximise every precious day. You have to get the balance right between having them in hospital and doing horrible things to them to make them better, which is also disruptive to the family, or saying: "This may help a bit, but it will mean several days in hospital, so let's leave it." Getting that balance is all important.'

Every morning soon after seven, Ivan would be collected from his basement quarters by his mother or father or brought upstairs by his night carer. His father, generally, would then apply Ivan's face creams, brush his teeth and hair, dress him, put him in his wheelchair and get him ready for school. Then Cameron would wheel him out to the ambulance and kiss him goodbye before he was taken, in the early years, to the Cheyne Centre. There Ivan had a special, protected environment, with physio, speech and music therapy, a special swimming pool and a full-time nurse, with whom he would spend much of the day before being driven home again. Sometimes he would have a convulsion and the ambulance driver would have to pull over and try to induce some calm. That routine lasted until 2007, when the centre, despite Cameron's lobbying, was closed. Then he attended Jack Tizard, a special school, in Hammersmith. Initially this was not a success as the vulnerable Ivan had to share a class with hyperactive children with autism. Ivan needed more help and protection, which, under a new teacher, he was soon given. He shared a class with five or six other children, some wheelchair-bound, most tube-fed like him, and had plenty of one-to-one attention.

The cost of Ivan's care was considerable, although the Cameron finances were bolstered by the parental help they were given and by a windfall Samantha received after Smythsons was sold. But the medical demands changed as, for example, Ivan's weight changed – or as his symptoms changed – and his twenty-one doses of medicine used to be recalibrated, often, of necessity, by trial and error. Even so he would awake screaming uncontrollably every night, or suddenly go red in the face as another seizure came on. Samantha, in particular, was reluctant to leave him for more than a few days at a time. Indeed Ivan could not be left for a moment on his own. He had someone with him round the clock, and at night time he was fed through a pump.

In the Cameron household, it became completely normal to have lots of people, carers and respite nurses and so on, wandering through. (The arrival of their third child, Arthur Elwen – now known to his family as Elwen – in February 2006 added to the chaos.) The Camerons did extensive work on their Edwardian terrace house, on King North Street just round the corner from Finstock Road, although the main press interest was in the environmental measures they took. They demolished the rear extension and had the basement redesigned to provide a room for Ivan (complete with pulley-and-hoist system to help lift him), a room for a carer, a playroom and a customised lift to take him upstairs and down.

'I know Sam worries about him, almost every second, every day,' said Birrell in 2006. 'She has told me that she is always thinking: Is he in pain? Is he happy? What's happening with the carers? The truth is that a severely disabled child does overshadow so much else in one's life.' With both parents having grown up in hospitable families, their inclination has always been to invite friends for a meal in the evening or at weekends, and they sought – for Ivan's sake and their own – to continue that pattern of life. Their gregariousness surprised some people, given the other demands on their time and energy. They used to tell friends that, just occasionally when they were the only two adults in the house, they would look at one another in amazement, as if to say 'Is it really true?'

The Camerons and their friends often discussed how much they should speak publicly about Ivan. Plenty of people – including some in the Tory Party – believed that they referred to him quite enough, and some even accused them of making political capital out of their misfortune. Charles Moore wrote that it would be 'creepy' if having fathered a disabled son made a politician more electable. Cameron's riposte was the family's 2008 Christmas card – a photograph which featured him looking at his elder son with fierce love. To any who felt squeamish about his candour the Tory leader said simply that Ivan is 'part of who I am'. Friends suspect that he would face just as much criticism if he had refused ever to speak about his son or about the issues surrounding disability. While some have said his family is so important to him that he might one day just walk away from politics, others think Ivan's influence has emboldened him. 'They'll never get over it, in one way,' said Dom Loehnis soon after Cameron became leader, 'and in another way it's the steel. It gives him the ability to say "it's a job" and to think there are many more important things in life, but be happy to take risks and be shot at.' Birrell agreed: 'I think what it does mean is that – and I've spoken to him about this – the worst thing that can happen to him in his job is that maybe he gets rejected by the party or suffers a cataclysm at the election. For any other politician that would be an absolute disaster, and of course with David it would be very upsetting. But having been through what he's been through, he has an unusual sense of perspective for a politician on his political life.'

Giles Andreae has said that Ivan gave the Tory leader 'a personal empathy with people whose lives have not gone as they would have liked. [The Camerons have] spent aeons and aeons waiting in hospitals. You can spin the Ivan thing if you want. You're damned if you do and damned if you don't. It's unnatural for someone in Dave's position to be required to show that kind of patience, but they've given it, in spades. We don't know the half of it. David has this quiet tolerance and patience – but there has been a big change in his nature. If his weakness was being seen as a posh narrow-minded twat from Eton, thank God that has passed.'

The Camerons had known within weeks of his birth that their son was likely to die a child. Just once Cameron had allowed himself to speculate about what it might be like for his son to reach adulthood when he was moved to tears after a visit to a residential care home for young severely disabled adults. 'I can't help [thinking] what it will be like if and when he's 18. We do our best to give him a good life, you sort of feel he's getting something out of it all … [but] profoundly disabled children, they often don't make it, to be brutal about it. They get a lot of chest infections, in the winter they're in and out of hospital the whole time.'

In one six-month period, Ivan had sixteen overnight stays in hospital. Two days after his sixth birthday Cameron cancelled a planned trip to Wales after rushing his son to hospital. On another occasion the boy's hip was broken during a particularly violent fit. Children with severe epilepsy are at constant risk that a seizure may go out of control, perhaps even fatally. And many of the sudden unexpected deaths in such cases occur at night. Ian Birrell put it starkly, 'Every morning you go downstairs and you are not sure if you are going to find your child alive or not in bed.' Ivan's fading smile wasn't the only sign of his condition's inexorable progression. By early 2006 he had lost the power to hold his head and could no longer cling on to a finger. In late 2008 there was an apparent breakthrough that seemed almost miraculous to Cameron – a new set of medicines unlocked Ivan's smile.

On Tuesday 24 February 2009, Cameron had a routine lunch with some journalists. Life was on as even a keel as he could have hoped, and Ivan had been going through a period of relative stability. Cameron had agreed to be home early to help make teatime pancakes with his children. Some time in the night Ivan began to fit. By 5 a.m. it was clear that the seizures were getting out of control. The ambulance arrived at St Mary's Hospital, Paddington, at 5.45 a.m. The medics tried for forty-five minutes to revive him but at 6.30 that same morning, 25 February – Ash Wednesday – Ivan was pronounced dead. Samantha and David returned to their home to find photographers outside. Pictures of the grief-stricken couple duly appeared on most of the front pages the following day, but in an uncharacteristic display of restraint the press, at the request of the couple, forbore from reusing the pictures the following Sunday and from printing a heart-breaking picture of Cameron with Ivan's empty buggy.

Ivan's death shook Westminster. Suddenly normal hostilities were an embarrassing irrelevance. Prime Minister's Question Time was cancelled, at the suggestion of Gordon Brown, whose daughter Jennifer, born prematurely, had also died shockingly young. 'The death of a child is a loss no parent should have to bear,' said the Prime Minister.

Three days after Ivan's death, the Conservative Party released a statement of thanks from Cameron for the condolences they had received. It continued:

We always knew Ivan wouldn't live forever, but we didn't expect to lose him so young and so suddenly. He leaves a hole in our life so big that words can't describe it. Bed time, bath time, meal time – nothing will feel the same again. We console ourselves knowing that he won't suffer any more, that his end was quick, and that he is in a better place. But we all just miss him so desperately.

When we were first told the extent of Ivan's disability I thought that we would suffer having to care for him but at least he would benefit from our care. Now as I look back I see that it was all the other way round. It was only him that ever really suffered and it was us – Sam, me, Nancy and Elwen – who gained more than I ever believed possible from having and loving such a wonderfully special and beautiful boy.

The following Tuesday, after a private funeral at St Nicholas Church, Chadlington, David and Samantha buried their son. Mourners were asked not to wear black.

His closest staff pay tribute to the way his team rallied round to give what support they could. The correspondence team, who handle the leader's mailbag, did particularly sterling work in making sure every one of the 11,500 messages of condolence he received was answered with fitting sensitivity. But nobody was under any illusions as to how much Ivan meant to the Camerons and how little they could really help. 'Dave had put so much into that child – he was their first child,' says one political intimate, who points out that the couple had been married six years before Ivan was born. 'Ivan was so much part of their marriage. He defined their familiness as opposed to their coupliness.'

Perhaps hoping his work would serve as a distraction from his grief, Cameron returned to the fray a fortnight after Ivan's death. Some time later, he admitted that perhaps this was too soon. If so, this surprises some of those closest to him. 'I saw he'd said that,' says one. 'I thought he was totally amazing. Grief comes in waves, and maybe he wasn't expecting so many of them. It probably took him by surprise that they kept on coming. As far as we were concerned, he really kept it together. When he came in he was very focused.' A senior Cabinet minister says: 'I don't think I saw it at the time. He came back to work but he was not enjoying it.' But a close friend from university admits: 'Not till the birth of Florence did it remotely heal, not that it ever can, of course, but not having the time to mourn may have slightly deadened his razor-sharp sense or sensitivity in the months that followed.'

And the sadness evoked by memories of Ivan can still ambush the Prime Minister. He was interviewed by Rosa Monckton for a television documentary about bringing up a disabled child. The encounter had moved him to tears, prompting Monckton, the mother of a Down's Syndrome child, to reassure him immediately that his upset would be excised from the aired version of the interview.

'Generally he's very good at holding it together, but every now and then something would trigger things off,' says a colleague. 'And even now (three and a half years after Ivan's death), if he does a hospital visit with Sam, he might see something that triggers things off.' It must be a loss for which, for others, it is impossible to make fitting allowance.

FINSTOCK ROAD
Preparing for the election 2003–2005

Notwithstanding the suspicions that Cameron was involved in the coup to unseat Iain Duncan Smith, he wasn't included in Michael Howard's campaign team. Indeed, Cameron was put out to discover from Greg Barker, a fellow 2001-intake Tory MP and friend, that he had not been invited to a meeting immediately after Duncan Smith finally accepted defeat. Howard had asked Liam Fox to be his campaign manager, supported by Oliver Letwin and Oliver Heald. He had also brought in Cameron's successor at the Home Office, Rachel Whetstone. Howard today insists that he didn't include Cameron in his preparations on 29 October 2003 because 'there wasn't really a leadership campaign'. Instead, he says, there was a small 'advance team'. 'David wasn't particularly involved in that.'

In Whetstone, Howard had found someone whom he could trust completely and who worked tirelessly on his behalf. One former head of news at the Home Office recalls that Whetstone would 'drop everything any time he called and do whatever he asked, even if it meant working through the night'. Whetstone had stuck with Howard, first through his bruising battles with Derek Lewis and then through those with Ann Widdecombe. He is reported to have told her that he wouldn't even stand for the leadership unless she agreed to come to work for him.

The impulse towards self-preservation that had motivated the Tory parliamentary party to rid itself of an unsatisfactory leader was not, for once, to fade the moment the deed was done. The cry was for unity. David Davis had to make the decision about whether to challenge a determined Howard. Davis knew, given the mood of both MPs and the grassroots, that he would be blamed for bringing about a divisive contest. He also calculated that if he stayed his hand he would be lauded by all and be in a perfect position to inherit the crown in the likely event of the Tories losing the next election.

Howard's launch speech, delivered in the appropriately modern setting of the Saatchi Gallery in County Hall on the other side of the Thames from the Houses of Parliament, became his acceptance address. It was written by Francis Maude and Nicholas Boles overnight in the latter's Westminster office and was delivered by Howard with almost no changes. (Maude's involvement was confirmation enough for the ragged band of IDS loyalists that Howard had been in on a plot.) Once again an incoming Tory leader from the right of the party promised to modernise it. 'There can be no no-go areas for a modern Conservative Party,' Howard said. And in a passage that could be delivered by Cameron today, he declared: 'We won't hesitate to give credit to the government when it gets things right. We won't oppose for opposition's sake.'

This was music to the ears of modernisers such as Andrew Cooper, the Tory staffer-turned-pollster whose analysis of the Tories' fading electoral appeal had made him a guru of the modernisers. He and others including Boles, director of the modernisers' favourite think-tank, the Policy Exchange, and Nick Gibb, who resigned from the Tory frontbench under IDS, had long been urging a 'new politics' that sought to position the Conservatives above short-term interests. How much of the modernisers' nostrums Howard really believed is questionable. By the time of the 2005 election he had abandoned much of the rhetoric, just as William Hague and Duncan Smith had done before him. 'I was probably in two minds during the whole of my leadership about the modernist [agenda], [the] need to change the perception of the party. I'm not the obvious person to put it into practice even if I agreed with the theory. But I was always in two minds about it. I wasn't totally resistant to it. I was resistant to some bits of it and I thought they spoil their case very often by going too far,' he says today.

What of Cameron, whom Howard immediately made a deputy chairman of the party? What – then – did he think of the 'new politics'? The evidence suggests that he was similarly doubtful. For example, he disagreed with Cooper's argument that it had been a mistake for the Tories to oppose legislation setting up foundation hospitals – exactly the sort of devolved power for public services which Conservatives had been advocating.

Cooper set out his thinking in an email to Cameron, Osborne and Boles following a dinner they had shared on 12 May 2003. It is worth quoting at length, showing as it does the sort of strategic thinking that Cameron then rejected but came to accept only two years later:

> Unless people feel that we are sincere in wanting the best outcomes for public services and those that rely on them, we won't move forward a square inch; if we are dumb enough to emphasise that we're only saying the things we are because we think that's what people want to hear, we don't deserve to move forward a square inch. Once we do get people to believe that we are sincere – and our values are properly aligned – we can be as robust and reformist as we like about public services (which George [Osborne] has rightly defined as a core part of the future Conservative proposition).

To this Cameron first replied, 'I don't agree about foundation hospitals ... the Bill is a complete and utter joke.' Then after another blast from Cooper, Cameron wrote: 'Still not sure I agree, but food for thought ...'

Boles, who is gay, believes that Cameron resisted the modernisers' message out of tribal loyalty to and affection for a party that had treated him so well. 'The Tory Party has been incredibly nice to David Cameron from his very first contact with it. It's given him the best opportunities that anyone of his age could ever wish for. And so it took quite a lot for him to be able to actually admit to himself that the Tory Party was in some way the problem. And that there were real, real faults ... not just things that weren't working in terms of they weren't winning elections but actually unpleasant things that were obnoxious or objectionable. It took him a long time – I think it even took him to after this [2005] election.'

There were 'lots of arguments', Boles recalls, 'about the specific issue of Section 28 over the years. And I remember Samantha "got it" much more and was much angrier about things like that. The fundamental difference between David and Tony Blair ... is that David is absolutely, cut right through him, a total Conservative. He was born into it, he loves it, it's embraced him, he's not the outsider. There is a neat metaphor that sums up the difference – Blair scaled up the Labour building from the outside and took it over at the top – that's absolutely not the case with David – he worked his way up on the inside floor by floor, which is why having to recognise that the Conservative building had to change dramatically was much tougher for him. George [Osborne] got there much earlier than David.'

A senior Conservative contrasts Cameron's 'gradual' espousal of the modernising agenda with Michael Portillo's sudden conversion. 'I think at least so far as the bystander is concerned, David's journey took longer. He was probably fortunate in the fact that he was a less well-known figure than Michael was. Michael's journey seemed to be very abrupt. It seemed that one minute you had Michael Portillo saying who dares wins and the next minute you had the touchy-feely Michael Portillo who was completely different, and that was quite hard to understand and to take. And this may be wrong. But David's journey was I think a more gradual one – if indeed it was a journey at all, because there are many aspects of his view on the world which have been liberal and conservative, as with his views on drugs.'

From the start of his leadership it became clear that there was a tension between Michael Howard and most of his closest advisers on the issue of Iraq. The death of the weapons scientist David Kelly in the summer of 2003 and the subsequent inquiry by Lord Hutton had exposed a wealth of embarrassing detail about the Blair government, particularly about how it had conducted itself in the run-up to the conflict in March. Lord Hutton had examined in detail the extraordinary allegation that Number 10 had deliberately exaggerated the intelligence on Saddam Hussein's weapons of mass destruction as it attempted to build public support for the war. That charge had become more politically loaded with each fruitless week US and British soldiers spent searching for the WMD that the Iraqi dictator possessed (as an infamous dossier had claimed). In a battle over the credibility of Andrew Gilligan, a BBC journalist who had first claimed that the dossier had been 'sexed up', the full weight of the government machinery as well as that of hundreds of journalists had come to rest on his source, Dr Kelly, with tragic consequences.

By the time Howard became leader, the issues of Iraq and Blair's trustworthiness had become entwined. It was an obvious political opportunity and one that Howard was determined to exploit. Shortly after becoming leader, he demanded to know what questions his party had asked Blair of his dossier on its publication. The answer – that Duncan Smith had ruled that it should not be queried at all – infuriated him. 'He went berserk. I have never seen him so angry,' recalls a witness. The Hutton Report offered some chance for the Tories to redeem their dreadful legacy on Iraq. The inquiry had thrown up much material damaging to the government and it became a commonplace assertion in the media that at least one Cabinet minister would have to resign when Lord Hutton delivered his verdict.

Some allowed themselves to become convinced that that verdict would condemn Blair himself.

Howard – remembering Cameron's grasp of detail and capacity for hard work – secretly asked him to begin preparing his brief for the longed-for day of the report's publication. Cameron set about combing through thousands of pages of evidence heard at the Hutton Inquiry. The intention was to help the Tories compile a dossier of their own – one that would help Howard maximise the government's pain. Michael Gove told his friend that he thought the project a mistake. Either Lord Hutton would deliver a knock-out blow to the Blair government or he wouldn't. If the former then there was no need for Tory help, if the latter no amount of Conservative reinterpretation of the case would make any difference. Indeed Howard could end up looking shrill and opportunistic. Gove's advice was waved away.

Some of Cameron's contemporaries were irritated when, almost immediately after Howard had secretly called for him, newspaper articles began to appear detailing his new job. One says he thought Cameron saw in Hutton a chance for personal glory: 'He was a hack on the make. Hutton was going to be the thing that made his name.' Less cynically, perhaps Cameron – who had recognised the pitfalls of the Iraq adventure but had decided, with the great majority of his party, to march on in lockstep with Tony Blair – saw an opportunity for a measure of personal redemption. Certainly those working with Cameron on his detailed analysis of the inquiry's evidence have only praise for his skills as a wordsmith and the effort he expended on the project. 'He poured a great deal of his energies into it,' said an ex-aide.

Samantha, by now heavily pregnant with their second child, and Ivan had to share Christmas 2003 with the written testimony of Gilligan, Blair, Alastair Campbell, Geoff Hoon, Sir Kevin Tebbit (Permanent Secretary at the Ministry of Defence) and hundreds of others. Cameron himself ruefully admitted: 'I'm one of the self-confessed anoraks who have read most of the hearing transcripts and the evidence provided to the Inquiry. I can't pretend I spent all of Christmas doing it, but there were times when … Hoon and Tebbit were competing rather effectively with family, friends, telly and shopping.'

The result was widely praised when the Conservative 'compendium' (for obvious reasons the word 'dossier' was not used) was published a few weeks before Lord Hutton delivered his report. It seems now, however, that the document was simply too successful. Cameron and his team had been so effective in convincing the media of Blair's guilt that they convinced themselves. 'At no point did the possibility of a complete whitewash [by Lord Hutton] get discussed. It might have been raised once or twice at meetings but as an option it was never taken seriously,' said one of those involved. Howard felt so confident that Hutton would condemn the Blair administration that he called for the Prime Minister's resignation.

On 19 January 2004 Nancy Cameron was safely delivered, but Cameron had hardly any time to spend with his new child as the publication date for the Hutton Report loomed. By 27 January he was chairing daily meetings of the 'Hutton prep team' with Guy Black, now Howard's press secretary. As is traditional on such occasions, the government had made arrangements for the Opposition to be shown the report a few hours before its publication. The facility, known as a 'lock-in', would start at 6 a.m. on Wednesday 28 January. Because it meant an especially early start, Cameron stayed with Howard at his home in Pimlico. It was a gloomy evening. Soon after supper the first edition of the *Sun* was delivered. It contained what looked like a genuine leak of the report. It was clear that, in simple terms, the judge had found for the government and against the BBC. Howard, admirable for his phlegm at times of crisis, announced that he was going to bed, leaving Cameron to fret about the morrow.

The 'lock-in' confirmed that the *Sun*'s leak had been accurate. For the Conservatives it was nothing short of a disaster. Both Howard and

Cameron looked ashen when they returned from the Cabinet Office to the Tory leader's offices in the Commons. Howard knew that in just a few hours' time he would be confronted by a gloating Blair in a Commons debate that he himself had demanded. At an emergency meeting of key Tories just before the debate, the option of rejecting Hutton's conclusions was never seriously entertained, something that surprised one of those present. Instead Cameron helped his leader fashion what he could from the report. From the moment Howard delivered his first sentence in the Commons – in which he said he and his party accepted Hutton's conclusions – his oration was drowned in Labour derision. Perhaps it was a mercy: Cameron had done his best, but his efforts to milk outrage from Hutton's rare and mild reproofs made Howard sound both desperate and mean-spirited. The fall-out from the Tories' ill-fated decision to talk up Hutton hit Cameron personally. He endured an uncomfortable appearance on *Newsnight* that week. 'What are you wittering on about?' Jeremy Paxman snapped at one point as the young MP sought to develop the Conservatives' response to Hutton.

The experience of Hutton scarred Cameron and has made him nervous of the Iraq issue ever since. Colleagues noticed that he soon began to side with those – Gove, Whetstone and Osborne – who thought Howard should abandon any further attempt to use the war's unpopularity to the Tories' advantage. Their opposition to Howard's desire to exploit Blair's difficulties over Iraq was ideological: they believed that the Prime Minister had done and was continuing to do the right thing. Cameron's opposition was more 'muted', recalls one witness. His opposition was on political grounds: Howard would gain nothing but contempt if he recanted over a war he had supported. It was a paradoxical position for Cameron to find himself in: he was urging his party to support a policy he had had grave doubts about. He had been a dove among hawks, and was now a hawk in the dove-cote.

The Tory leader had hoped that Hutton would give him a clear excuse for ending his party's support for Blair's policy. After the debacle surrounding the report's publication in January Howard at first accepted that he had no cover for such a naked U-turn. He increasingly had to resist attempts to 'stiffen' his foreign policy. One speech on foreign affairs, described by someone who read it as 'martial', was rejected by Howard. Others who saw the text Howard was supposed to deliver claim that 'it amounted to a call to bomb Iran'.

As the year wore on he became more convinced than ever that he should take on Blair on his weakest ground. Finally in an interview with the *Sunday Times* in July he said he would not have voted for the war had he known then what he knew now. The lawyerly justification – that the Commons motion had 'placed heavy emphasis on the presence of WMD ... I think I would have voted for a differently worded resolution' – was lost, as Howard hoped it would be, in the blaze of publicity this apparent recantation ensured. The reaction from most of those in his inner circle was fury, however. 'Cameron, Whetstone and that lot went mental, absolutely nuts,' remembers a witness. 'Cameron would get terribly huffy about Iraq and go around saying, "We shouldn't be doing this."' Sharp-eyed readers of Cameron's local newspaper would have spotted the division between the MP and his leader when he wrote in his occasional column: 'There are those who say that, having heard the flimsy intelligence base for the claims about WMD, they would not have supported the war. And there are those who – like me – still think that it was right to support our partner the US, uphold the UN, and get rid of Saddam.'

Howard and Cameron clashed again over Iraq when finalising the leader's speech to that year's party conference. The former special adviser, a veteran of many such speeches, succeeded at the last moment in neutering a damning critique of the war that Howard had planned to deliver. Such was the opposition of Howard's team to any attempt to realise the political potential of Iraq that, on at least one occasion, the Tory leader had to conceal from them his true intentions. The publication of a report by the Iraq Survey Group in mid-October that there were no WMD in Iraq offered an obvious target for the following week's PMQs. But the then Tory leader gave no indication that he was planning to raise the issue when, as usual, he was prepared for the weekly encounter by Osborne and Cameron. Once in the chamber he abandoned their script and went for Blair, demanding that he apologise for 'the way you misrepresented the intelligence you received'. 'Why', he asked, 'can't you bring yourself to say sorry for that?'

Not everyone in Howard's inner circle agreed with Cameron's position, as is obvious from a memo sent to Howard in early November 2004 and later circulated among other senior figures. The memo, written by Guy Black, begins: 'There is one subject that we resolutely (and wrongly) refuse to discuss – and that's Iraq. But we have to face it.' Black – who had first spotted Cameron's political potential at CRD – said he believed it was a 'real possibility that Iraq will turn out to be one of the dominant factors … in the election. We are not prepared for this in any way at all, and it would be insane to approach a general election without being so. There are a range of different views among your colleagues (and I suspect among your advisers) and an election time will not be the time to reconcile them. It's got to be gripped before.'

Howard – who agreed that the issue was 'extremely important and needs to be discussed' – called for a meeting of his most senior and trusted advisers in late November. Again Cameron insisted that Iraq would be a 'distraction' from the Tories' campaign message and ought as far as possible to be ignored. His view prevailed, and the Tories duly made little attempt to highlight the issue in the election the following year, something some believe cost the party dear. Today Howard is frank about his failures to do more to profit from Blair's difficulties over Iraq. 'I have great regrets about the way in which I handled things. It's one of my biggest regrets. We should have said again and again and again it was right to depose Saddam Hussein, it was wrong not to plan [for what happened afterwards]. Disbanding the Iraqi army was a cretinous thing to do. Blair could have persuaded the Americans not to do that, so he's partly responsible. And that [position] wouldn't have involved a U-turn, wouldn't have involved any flip-flop. Michael Ancram, the shadow Foreign Secretary when I wasn't the leader, had repeatedly been asking for a plan. So it wasn't just hindsight. It was an impregnable position and I should have banged the drum on that loudly and repeatedly, and I didn't – and that was a big mistake.'

That Hutton marked a low-point in Cameron's Westminster career seemed to be confirmed by the next job Howard asked him to do. While George Osborne's brief as economic affairs spokesman allowed him to range over the national scene, Cameron in March 2004 was appointed 'spokesman on local government finance and the council tax'. Cameron was at pains to point out to his local newspaper that he would 'continue his work as part of Mr Howard's Question Time team'. The subject might have been politically important, especially so since local elections were due in June, but it was hardly a portfolio for future leadership material.

It was also becoming clear that the polls would be tricky for Howard, whose honeymoon as leader was coming to an end. A series of policy launches under the slogan 'right to choose' had failed to catch light. Then Blair dramatically removed Howard's trump card by belatedly agreeing to his key demand for a referendum on the proposed constitution for the European Union. This presented a double problem for the Tory leader. Not only did it remove the cornerstone of his local election campaign, it also opened the party up to attack from parties like UKIP that offered outright withdrawal. Now that Labour and the Conservatives were offering the same policy, UKIP started to enjoy a surge in its support.

Cameron was involved in secret talks with leading anti-EU campaigners who were called in to persuade Howard not to change his policy radically to counter the threat. Howard wanted to propose a new referendum that would mandate a fundamental renegotiation of Britain's membership. The new policy would propose that Britain withdraw from the EU, ditch those obligations of membership such as fisheries policy that the Tories most disagreed with, and then campaign to *rejoin* the Union. Cameron and Whetstone, who were both appalled by Howard's idea, arranged a meeting with one of the businessmen who had led the campaign against the single currency. It was explained to Howard that, far from supporting him, many of those involved in the 'no' campaign would oppose him in any such referendum. Howard abandoned his plans.

Partly because of the UKIP surge, the local elections on 11 June were disappointing for the Tories. Although the usual sophistry was deployed to muddy the results, it was plain there had been no breakthrough. The early optimism of Howard's leadership now began to subside. In its place people began to wonder what would happen within Tory politics in the wake of a third successive defeat. The consensus was that David Davis was likely to succeed Howard, a prospect that so dismayed many in Howard's inner circle that he privately promised he would carry on even if defeated. But at some point, perhaps after the referendum on the European Constitution, he would have to make way for a new leader to fight an election in 2009/10. Who would it be?

In the summer of 2004 what was to become David Cameron's leadership campaign began to flow from two separate springs. The first had been bubbling quietly since the summer of 2002 when Cameron accepted an invitation to a weekend at the Sussex home of his fellow MP from the 2001 intake, Greg Barker. Barker, like Cameron, had worked for a while in public relations and had spotted his colleague's 'marketability' from the moment the two first met in the Commons. Although a protégé of David Willetts, the Bexhill and Battle MP became convinced within a year that Cameron was the future. 'I had come to the view that the Tory Party needed to skip a generation. We needed telegenic, charismatic, modern – not in a grumpy, tortured, Portillo way, but in a relaxed, effortless comfortable-with-themselves sort of way. And he seemed to fit the bill very closely.'

Barker decided to tell Cameron that he thought he should consider running for the leadership in the likely event of the Tories under their then leader Duncan Smith being defeated at the next election. 'I invited him down to my constituency in the second summer and I would say at that point I had come to the view that he was all that he was cracked up to be. I remember … we rode out together. I had a dinner party for him to meet Charles Moore, who is in my constituency and who was editor of the *Telegraph* then.' After the dinner Barker got down to business: 'I remember talking to [Cameron] after the guests left because we stayed up quite late. I made it quite clear what I thought. We were still under IDS at this point and we were anticipating that we would crash and burn at the next election. Dave was still very coy, saying that he would quite like to be shadow minister for the disabled. He certainly didn't go out of his way to wear his ambition on his sleeve. Dave didn't say "too soon", but he said that he hadn't really thought about it. "That's not my plan," he said.'

The next summer, in 2003, Barker invited his colleague from the whips' office, David Ruffley, whose loyalty to Davis was well known, to his home in Battle. In a good-natured way they began to argue about who would win a leadership election. Soon the pair were drawing up full-blown lists of the likely loyalties of every Tory MP. The result of what began as a joke exercise further convinced Barker that Cameron should run. 'I remember sitting on this bench in my garden and going through the parliamentary party lists and crossing off each name. Interestingly, when we looked at the votes, it was a pretty dead-heat situation … From that analysis it clearly didn't appear a done deal, but going through the numbers it said to me that it was entirely feasible.'

As Barker pondered his calculations Cameron was busy recruiting someone who was to become another key figure in his early campaign, his old friend Michael Gove, who had carved out a very successful career as a columnist for *The Times*. Over a lunch at his constituency home in Dean he stepped up a long-running campaign to persuade Gove to surrender journalism for the Commons. As Christopher Lockwood, a senior journalist on the *Economist* and a friend of many years' standing, looked on, Gove began to weaken. 'Dave did more than anyone to persuade me to apply to go on to the candidates' list … He would have sensed my initial crumbling,' says Gove.

Meanwhile another key figure was emerging from self-imposed exile. Steve Hilton had drifted away from the Conservative Party during its long years in opposition. His passionate interest in global capitalism's good works had led him to set up his own firm, Good Business. The firm – and a book of that title – offered a vision of responsible capitalism where brands are used to promote social as well as commercial goods. Hilton, who became an invaluable bridge to rich firms for a number of good causes, won many admirers for the clarity and power of his advocacy. He came to believe that Westminster politics could not match the transforming power of the market. Indeed he became so divorced from the Tory tribe that he voted for the Green Party in the 2001 election. The advent of the Howard leadership seems to have persuaded him to return to the fold. Maurice Saatchi, his former boss at Saatchi & Saatchi, had been made party chairman by Howard and Hilton agreed to work one day a week as his special adviser. He also became briefly enthused with the idea of becoming an MP himself and got himself on the candidates' list. The depressing reality of selection meetings soon dissuaded him from this course, however. (Hilton was among those Gove beat to the safe seat of Surrey Heath.)

The disparate elements of what was to become Cameron's leadership team began to come together in the late spring of 2004. In May Gove held a dinner in a Mayfair restaurant that he admits was a conscious effort to begin planning for the aftermath of the following year's general election. He invited the leading Tory talents of his generation – Cameron was an obvious invitee, as were Boles, Hilton and Osborne. The question of the leadership was not explicit – the subject of the discussion was what should be the themes of twenty-first-century Conservatism – but a guest remembers 'much jockeying'.

The dinners continued over the next twelve months with a shifting guest-list that had Cameron, Gove and Osborne at its core. Increasingly, the events were held at Cameron's home in Finstock Road in North Kensington. Looking back on this period it is tempting to speculate that Cameron was mentally preparing himself for a run at the leadership after the election. It was natural that the discussions should take place at his home: he had always been the leader of his gang, whose core members were Hilton and Gove. Osborne, who led a younger, more modernising gang of Cooper, Finkelstein and others, seems not to have been thinking in such tangible terms about his own leadership ambitions before the 2005 general election. Barker, who became a regular guest at the Finstock Road dinners, thought them frustratingly woolly in terms of concrete outcome. But gradually a leadership and headquarters were emerging from all the talk.

Comparisons between Cameron and Blair can be misleading but it is striking how similar is the make-up of their inner teams. Blair had a marketing guru, Philip Gould, a journalist, Alastair Campbell, and the other leading young star of his intake, Gordon Brown. Cameron has a marketing guru, Hilton, a journalist, Gove, and the other young star of his intake, Osborne who might also be said to perform the role as the Tories Peter Mandelson.

The extent to which Cameron and those around him were plotting to succeed Howard before the 2005 election is a highly sensitive subject. Whetstone's promotion of Cameron annoyed certain Howard aides, but what is indisputable is that many of those Howard employed within his inner office are now part of Cameron's backroom staff or kitchen cabinet – with one notable exception: Rachel Whetstone herself.

The close connections between Howard's young lieutenants came to public attention after one peripheral member of the set launched what appeared to be a well-briefed attack on a group of long-serving Tory MPs. George Trefgarne, the *Daily Telegraph*'s comment editor, reported in late July that a group of fourteen MPs were being urged to stand down and make way for some fresh faces. Fatally, among these 'bed-blockers' he listed Derek Conway, a famously pugnacious close ally of David Davis. Conway, who had been an implacable enemy of Duncan Smith, is not a man to trifle with, let alone summarily retire. He launched a full counter-attack on those whom he blamed for the briefing. 'This is what we call the Notting Hill set. They sit around in these curious little bistros in parts of London, drink themselves silly and wish they were doing what the rest of us are getting on with,' Conway said. It hardly mattered that none of the group would ever, as one put it, 'set foot inside a bistro', a form of eating establishment that is, in any case, a rarity within the W11 postcode. There was enough truth in Conway's caricature for it to stick fast.

The following day's newspapers contained a flurry of features, some replete with maps, detailing the overwhelmingly west London habitat of a collection of what had been a hitherto fairly anonymous group of staffers, junior MPs and journalists. In the best of these, by the *Guardian*'s Nicholas Watt, Cameron and Whetstone were described as the group's 'pivotal figures', while George Bridges (today Cameron's political director, at the time head of the Conservative Research Department), Ed Vaizey and Michael Gove, both speechwriters for Howard, were named as more junior acolytes. Watt wrung a rare quote from Hilton, whom he accurately described as a 'member of the set's inner circle': 'There is no point in pretending [that it doesn't exist]. We are mates. We go on holiday and have been doing this for years. We all worked together at Conservative Central Office in the run-up to the 1992 election. That was the origin of the friendship.' Hilton added: 'We're genuine mates first, and then comes politics. We have been around for a very long time. All this "bright young thing" stuff obscures the fact that we are actually old timers. I have been intimately involved in Tory election strategy for nearly 15 years.'

What was deeply ironic about the sudden press attention devoted to this close-knit group of friends was that it came just as the set was about to be torn asunder in a row that pitted Cameron's wife against his closest female friend. Something that Watt failed to mention in his otherwise comprehensive bestiary was that Hilton and Whetstone were more than just friends. The precise history of their relationship eludes even their closest confidants, but one of them believes they have been partners, on and off, for about a decade. At the time of writing the pair are together. But their relationship came under terrible strain on the morning of 17 August 2004 when a newspaper diary dropped a heavy hint that Whetstone was having an affair with Cameron's father-in-law, William Astor.

Richard Kay wrote in the *Daily Mail*: 'There is, I can reveal today, an intriguing romantic spring in the step of Rachel Whetstone, Tory leader Michael Howard's political secretary and queen bee of the so-called Notting Hill set of bright young Conservatives. The Benenden-educated brunette, who is one of Mr Howard's two most senior special advisers, has, I understand, formed a close friendship with a married older man who is a well-connected Tory grandee.' Kay then gave a hefty clue to the identity of this 'grandee': 'In her role as political adviser, one figure Miss Whetstone has helped promote is David Cameron, 37, the Conservative MP for Witney in Oxfordshire and a happily married father-of-two (with whom she is not involved romantically). Eton-educated Cameron ... is the stepson-in-law of

Viscount Astor, 52, a former government whip and Opposition spokesman in the House of Lords.'

Howard was away on holiday in France but Whetstone, typically, was at her desk in his suite of rooms at Westminster that day. Rather than hide, she decided to phone her friend and confess to the relationship with Astor immediately. Cameron, acutely conscious of the humiliation the article had heaped on his mother-in-law, not to mention on his friend Hilton, exploded. A tearful Whetstone fled Howard's suite of offices shortly after the call. 'David said some unconscionable things and ended by saying that he would never talk to her again,' claims a friend. Cameron wondered if there was any way of having somebody struck off from godmotherhood.

In the event Cameron did talk to Whetstone again – the dictates of day-to-day politics saw to that. She was, after all, Michael Howard's most senior political adviser. Hilton sought and achieved a partial reconciliation between his partner and his close friend Cameron. Samantha, however, whose mother remained with William Astor, felt deeply betrayed by a woman she had regarded as a close friend. Some had hoped that the marriage of Whetstone and Hilton – they now have two children – would help smooth things over, but the relationship between the two women remains difficult.

The growing resentment of Cameron, as evidenced by the reaction to the 'bed-blockers' article, was fuelled by his rapid rise in the summer of 2004. In the wake of the disappointing local election results Howard had removed from David Willetts the role of policy co-ordination and handed it to the thirty-seven-year-old neophyte MP. Willetts carried the blame for the failed attempt to communicate the Tory message on choice in public services that spring. Now Cameron had the job of rebalancing Howard's leadership, which he duly did, ditching much of the modernisers' rhetoric and many of their aspirations along the way.

One of Howard's former backroom staff says that Cameron was

brought in because the Tory leader had lost patience with Willetts's attempts to 'build something from the foundations up'. 'What Howard needed was someone who could get on with the job – there wasn't time to rethink twenty-first-century conservatism from the bottom up. There wasn't time to think through from first principles what public service reform should involve. In the time available what one had to do was to get a seaworthy platform together to contest the election.' The staffer continues: 'By the autumn I think the view was we can't spend our entire time talking about health and education and … our grand restructuring plans for them because people will just think that this is ideological and not about them.'

Increasingly there was tension between Howard and Saatchi, the party Chairman, although it was hidden from all but the innermost circle. Saatchi wanted a visionary Howard to inspire the voters towards a radical vision of a low-tax state; Howard just wanted to offer them practical solutions to their everyday problems and concerns. 'Michael was increasingly coming down to the view that actually it wouldn't suit him, it would be inauthentic and there wasn't time to be visionary. He would have to by default go into the election saying, I'm a practical man of action, I'm John Howard [the Australian premier], don't come to me for visions, come to me only for what is deliverable,' recalls a member of Michael Howard's team.

To underline the shift in thinking the Tory leader turned to the man who had helped his Australian namesake win four consecutive elections, Lynton Crosby, a campaign strategist and market research expert. He told Crosby he wanted a minimal campaign based on crime and immigration and to make a virtue of its simplicity and pragmatism in contrast to Blair's grandiloquence. Cameron was already a party to the change in thinking – so much so in fact that, had Crosby refused Howard's offer, the Tory leader was ready to sack Saatchi and replace him with the young Witney MP to drive through the campaign he wanted.

The tension that had been building up behind closed doors in the Tories' new HQ in Victoria exploded one day in late summer when Hilton reported back on focus-group research. He told Saatchi that, no matter how tax cuts were packaged, voters preferred adequate public services. Friends say the finding – deeply at odds with Saatchi's analysis that low tax was central to the Tories' appeal – heralded an epiphany for Hilton. Having sat out the skirmishing between Tory modernisers and traditionalists that had wrecked the leaderships of Hague and Duncan Smith, he now settled firmly on the side of the former. It meant a personal breach with Saatchi, who receives not one but two dedications in Hilton's book. For his part the great advertising guru had famously said that no one reminded him of himself as a young man more than did Steve Hilton. But after an unpleasantly abusive shouting match, Saatchi cut off his former protégé. Although he lacked the power to terminate his contract with the Tories he sent Hilton an email demanding that he not term himself Saatchi's special adviser.

Newly promoted to the shadow Cabinet, Cameron road-tested Howard's new message in his local newspaper column in September. 'The biggest problems today are cynicism and disillusionment,' he began, before laying responsibility for these political evils at Blair's door. 'Talk has always been cheap in politics and the soundbite culture of trying to get everything you want to do in just a few words just makes things worse ... The more people hear these statements and compare them with what they experience in their lives, the more infuriated, the more cynical and the more disillusioned they become.'

This was the message that Cameron repeated again and again that autumn, through the Tories' conference and into the TV and radio studios. In an unmistakable sign of his growing importance he was put forward to communicate the new message on BBC1's *Question Time* during conference week. It was a debut he described as 'terrifying', but a successful one. His celebrations of a successful conference and his thirty-eighth birthday the following weekend were marred by a burglary at Finstock Road. Thieves took a scooter and his family car. 'Things have changed,' he joked at the time. 'Ten years ago, they would have left my Skoda standing outside. This time they drove off in it.'

He was formally put in charge of writing the Tories' election manifesto the next month, provoking a fresh round of anonymous criticism. 'There is already deep upset at the way Howard has advanced his favourites. They are utterly untried and untested in difficult forums,' an unnamed Tory frontbencher told the *Daily Telegraph*. What particularly grated with allies of Davis was a claim in the newspaper that the promotion was confirmation that Howard had anointed Cameron as his heir. The piece seemed well briefed, but the former leader denies that he sanctioned anyone in his office to make Cameron his heir apparent. 'I saw him as my successor but not at that stage. I didn't authorise the piece in the *Daily Telegraph*. You are a leader of the Opposition with a million things on your plate, things are being written all the time about what you think. You can't get upset about every one of them. You can't take action every time. I didn't think it was serious enough. I wasn't privately furious at being used by Rachel [Whetstone] to promote the claims of David.' In fact, as we shall see, Howard's views on who should succeed him were not as straightforward as they might have appeared.

The Camerons had shared their Christmas the previous year with thick files of evidence from the Hutton Inquiry. This year it was lever-arch folders, bearing titles like 'tax' and 'health', that littered the floor. When they weren't at home they lined his office in the Commons. This was a pokey affair along a corridor known colloquially as the Yellow Submarine since the rooms have porthole-shaped windows. Cameron pinned to the wall a sheet of paper on which he had written, 'Is it good for people? Is it simple to understand? Will it work?' Immediately after Christmas he was joined by Gove, not yet an MP but selected for a safe seat, and the two divided up the work, emailing each other versions as they went along. 'It was genuinely like being a leader-writer or a script-writer. It was an effort to take all these serious thoughts of the leader and then synthesise them. The principal instruction [under which] we were operating is Labour will have a wealth of detail, [so] keep it short, concentrate on several clear values and several key policies,' recalls Gove. In a comment article for the *Daily Telegraph* published on 30 December, Cameron revealed that he had been plundering the back catalogue for inspiration. In tribute to his tribe he quoted approvingly Margaret Thatcher's introductory paragraph to the 1979 manifesto: 'For me the heart of politics is not political theory, it is people and how they want to live their lives.'

Cameron's role editing down Tory policy into this *de minimis* campaign – whose five pledges could be summed up in ten words – ruffled feathers. In the light of his subsequent espousal of the environment, it is ironic that some say this was one of the policies he helped quietly shunt to the sidelines. 'Crosby and Cameron wouldn't let Tim Yeo [the then environment spokesman] do any of his green stuff at all. They said it didn't fit in with the five pledges. Yeo got so cross at one point he threatened to walk,' claims an insider.

The full story is a little more complex. Yeo wanted to include in the Conservative 2005 manifesto a radical reform of the taxes on motoring. He presented to Cameron detailed plans showing how vehicle excise duty could be varied according to emissions. Gas-guzzling sports utility cars would pay more; smaller, more efficient vehicles less. It was just the sort of revenue-neutral (the overall tax burden is the same) but green measure that the Tories now embrace. But Oliver Letwin, as shadow Chancellor, disliked Yeo's plans intensely. He thought they would hit the rural and the rich – two key Conservative constituencies. That Crosby thought the whole environment issue something of a side-show didn't help either. Cameron did not, in fact, go out of his way to kill Yeo's policy, but nor did he do anything to help rescue it from Letwin's attacks.

Shortly after the Tories' launch, Cameron asked if he could have his rota of campaign visits slimmed down so that he could spend more time nursing his own seat. It was a request that prompted snorts of contempt from some other stalwarts. Some among Howard's supporters were furious that having finished his work on the manifesto Cameron appeared to be distancing himself from the leader. There was irritation, too, that Cameron seemed to enjoy more licence than his frontbench colleagues when it came to dissent. Just before Christmas he had abstained on the second reading of a Bill to pave the way for ID cards, arguing in shadow Cabinet that he had always opposed the measure. He also signalled his disagreement with his party's drugs policy when he appeared on ITV1's *Jonathan Dimbleby* programme in late March. He said the issue was 'slightly awkward' for him since he had supported calls for cannabis's legal classification to be downgraded.

Most infuriating for his detractors were newspaper claims that Cameron and Osborne were 'uncomfortable' with the Tories' focus on crime and immigration as campaign themes. Crosby, a veteran of elections in which immigration was a major issue, was not squeamish about its use, urging Howard to stick with a subject that had traction with the voters and ignore Labour's furious claims that he was 'playing the race card'.

What did Cameron privately think about the Tories' treatment of the immigration issue during the 2005 election? In public he chose his words carefully. His formula was that immigration had not been an issue in any general election in recent times but it had become one since Labour had 'lost control' of the system. It was not racist, he claimed, to talk about an issue that mattered to the British people, and he maintained that controlled immigration and good race relations were 'two sides of the same coin'. But he made almost no use of the issue in his own campaign literature, giving it fewer than fifty words in his main electoral address. More space, in fact, was devoted to his thoughts on the importance of international development. In private Cameron worried about the reaction to the Tories' use of the immigration issue among liberal, left-leaning newspapers like the *Guardian* and the *Independent*. Close observers say he was much more 'thin-skinned' about the criticism than Osborne. It was almost certainly Cameron who was the 'member of the Notting Hill set' quoted as saying: 'We've got to implement the strategy as well as we can but there's no way that I'd have done it this way.'

BLACKPOOL
Leadership election 2005

Sandra Howard and Rachel Whetstone settled down for a night in front of the television. As the leader's wife lay on the sofa of their constituency home in Folkestone, Whetstone sprawled out on the floor under a duvet. Howard himself announced that he was going to bed rather than watch the first results of the 2005 general election. It was a wise choice. Yet again Labour won a comprehensive victory. Its new majority, sixty-six, might have been reduced, but it was still forty-five greater than that won by John Major for the Tories in 1992. Nevertheless, Howard felt he had no reason to be ashamed as he was driven back to London on 6 May. He had arrived as leader too late to overhaul the party properly after the Duncan Smith disaster but had chosen instead to fight a campaign that would claw back some lost ground. And, in that respect, he had been successful. The tactics may not have been pretty, but fighting a minimal national campaign majoring on crime and immigration supplemented by an intense and tailored focus on marginal seats had at least avoided electoral melt-down.

Now, it was time for Howard to secure the second element of his legacy. First he called in at Conservative HQ in London's Victoria Street to thank staff. Then he quietly contacted Francis Maude, offering him the post of party Chairman. Most unusually for Howard, he made this major decision without consulting any of his senior aides. The appointment of Maude, an arch moderniser, was an unmistakable signal that Howard would do all he could to prevent David Davis from succeeding him. Howard had become convinced that the Tories would slide back towards electoral oblivion under a Davis leadership.

The two, never close, had become personally antagonistic within months of the start of Howard's leadership. Davis allies claim that he refused Howard's demand that he be pictured at Dover 'welcoming' the first wave of migrants from the so-called 'A8' group of nations that joined the European Union in May 2004. The shadow Home Secretary next led the internal opposition (which included Cameron) to ID cards. Then, shortly after the Tories' general election campaign launch, he found that the party's much vaunted pledge to recruit 40,000 extra police officers was actually dependent on a year's savings from the immigration budget. He felt that Howard had 'sold him a pup' and phoned the Tory leader just before midnight to tell him so. A shouting match then ensued which came to an abrupt end when one of the two men – it is disputed which – slammed down the phone. Such goodwill as Davis had earned with Howard for not standing against him in November 2003 was by May 2005 entirely spent.

Just in case new-intake modernising MPs had not got the message, Howard's closest ally, David Maclean, spelled it out. One newly elected Tory who went on to support Cameron recalls a phone call from Maclean the day after the election. The Chief Whip briefly congratulated and welcomed the new arrival – and then said: 'Some of us are wondering whether it isn't time for a new generation to emerge.' The MP was in little doubt what Maclean meant.

Maude's appointment was the first of a rapid series of moves Howard made in the immediate wake of the election to fix as far as he could the race to succeed him. His next was to fire the starting gun in that race – but to keep control of the distance over which it was to be run and the rules of the competition. In a surprise announcement made in Putney – where a young Tory woman, Justine Greening, had won a notable victory – he said that, at sixty-three, he was 'simply too old' to fight the next election and would be quitting. But then he added that he would not finally leave until he had honoured a promise to reform the rules on electing new leaders. Originally he had intended to set an explicit date for his departure but, in the car to Putney, he had come under heavy pressure from both Whetstone and his wife. The two women badgered him until he agreed to leave it vague.

Whetstone had taken a call from Osborne the day before who asked her to stop Howard resigning in the immediate aftermath of the expected defeat. Osborne had said that it would be bad for party morale. Although Whetstone couldn't stop Howard resigning she was at least successful in delaying his departure. She knew that if Cameron or Osborne were to run they would need as long as possible to raise their profile. The two had discussed in general terms what might happen after the election but had avoided a direct discussion about the leadership. It has been suggested that they wanted Howard to do badly so that one of them would succeed him, but in fact they both thought it was in their interest for Howard to do well enough to stay on and give them more time to establish themselves.

Now Howard had gone early and it seemed that one of the older, more established modernisers might seize the initiative. On the Saturday following the election, an agitated David Willetts warned an MP that Oliver Letwin was trying to persuade Cameron and Osborne to back Andrew Lansley. Lansley had a reasonable claim to the modernisers' candidacy. He had started out as a civil servant, albeit as Norman Tebbit's private secretary, had then become a director of the Conservative Research Department, had been elected an MP in 1997, had directed the 2001 campaign and had thereafter been a leading voice urging more representative candidate selection. Like Cameron he had come to the modernising message from the right but was untainted by association with the divisive figure of Michael Portillo.

Letwin, whose amiability belies razor-sharp political skills, had promised Davis when he had decided not to stand in 2003 that he would have his 'full support' in any attempt to succeed Howard. Now he was backing Lansley instead of Davis for a job that he subsequently helped win for Cameron. According to one MP, Willetts said, 'I'm very worried that Oliver is trying to get the new boys, Cameron and George [Osborne], to collect around … a modernising candidate to stop the David Davis bandwagon.' The next day Willetts met Osborne at his home in Bayswater to try to put a stop to any attempt at steamrolling the younger generation into backing Lansley. It was agreed that, for now, no one would declare support for anyone else, and when Letwin met Cameron and Osborne he came away without an agreement to campaign for their previous boss at the CRD. 'Oliver had the meeting and the Lansley thing disappeared into thin air,' said the MP.

Whether Cameron was ever seriously considering backing Lansley is questionable since that weekend he was making strenuous efforts to advance his own candidature and out-manoeuvre his rivals. The third feint in Howard's post-election anti-Davis operation was to reshuffle his top team. While not in a powerful enough position to sack his shadow Home Secretary outright, Howard could at least promote those who he felt had a good chance of beating him in the leadership election. He had initially thought he would give the most senior job, that of shadow Chancellor, to Cameron. Cameron, however, fought desperately to ward off the job.

Why did Cameron want the education rather than the more prestigious Treasury portfolio? It is true that he had become interested in the education of special-needs children. But while there is no doubting the sincerity of his interest in education, it is not hard to discern other motives for his rejection of the job of shadow Chancellor. Most obvious is that he wished to avoid a confrontation with Gordon Brown. Brown had already seen off six shadow Chancellors in eight years, and, since the economy showed no signs of faltering, the political opportunities of the post looked sparse. Perhaps also Cameron had seen the parallels between his situation and that faced by Brown under the leadership of John Smith. Cameron had served as a special adviser in a Treasury shadowed by Brown and then in a Home Office shadowed by Blair. He had seen how the latter gradually overhauled his rival to become Labour's leading moderniser from 1992 to 1994. He had done so despite the fact that Brown, as shadow Chancellor, was the senior figure, and that Blair's own portfolio, home affairs, was traditionally a weak one for Labour. As Blair's biographer, John Rentoul, has written: 'Gordon Brown's accession to the shadow Chancellorship ... while logical and much desired by him, was to hold him back.'

Ever since Cameron and Osborne had emerged on the national scene the year before, newspapers had been dubbing them the 'Tories' Blair and Brown'. But which was which? For Cameron, in particular, the comparison was dangerous. As the older, more experienced man, he could well imagine how history could be made to repeat itself as he became bogged down in a series of unseemly rows about taxes, in which he would inevitably be presented by Brown as an enemy of good public services. Education on the other hand offered an attractive platform on which to develop his modernist credentials and – like Blair before him – redeem for his party what had once been a negative issue.

The former leader admits he was puzzled by Cameron's attitude. 'I didn't offer David the shadow Chancellorship because I was told he wanted to be shadow Education Secretary. I was surprised he didn't take the shadow Chancellor job. I was surprised he didn't want a higher-profile job,' says Howard. Cameron prospered and rose rapidly under Howard's leadership. Although not in his embryonic leadership team (possibly out of understanding for Cameron's family responsibilities at a difficult time), he had helped the new leader prepare for the Hutton Inquiry, overseen a policy review, been promoted to the Shadow Cabinet and written the Conservatives' 2005 election manifesto. Perhaps, most importantly, Howard had done nothing to correct a widespread assumption that Cameron was his chosen successor. By the end of the election campaign, however, he was having serious doubts about whether Cameron was the right candidate to stop Davis. He told senior aides that he believed that Osborne would be a better successor than Cameron. He had been angered by his former special adviser's criticism of the campaign's focus on immigration and further irritated to be told by Whetstone that he didn't want the shadow Chancellorship. By contrast – despite inaccurate reporting to the contrary – Osborne had shown no squeamishness about the immigration issue, which he accepted was one of the best cards the Tories had to play.

On Sunday 8 May Osborne, who had just agreed with Willetts not to back Lansley, received a call from Rachel Whetstone. She told him that Howard was going to offer him the shadow Chancellorship – but there was a condition attached. She said: 'He wants you to run, George.' Osborne's reaction was stunned disbelief followed by trepidation. He was just thirty-three and hadn't even made it to the shadow Cabinet. He thought that at best he might be made shadow Home Secretary in a post-election reshuffle. Now he was being asked to take on Gordon Brown and David Davis simultaneously.

With just under twelve hours to make his mind up he phoned two of his closest friends in politics. They both told him the same thing: take the job but don't commit to running. The following day, Monday 9 May, Howard invited Osborne to take his pick – he could have either the shadow Chancellor or the shadow Home Secretary briefs – and was pleased to see that he did not choose the easier course. Then the outgoing Tory leader urged Osborne to stand. Osborne said that he wouldn't rule out running but it wasn't what he wanted to do.

Did Cameron know of Howard's rejection of him in favour of Osborne? It would appear from his reaction to the news that Osborne was going to take the shadow Chancellorship that he did not. Cameron had been waiting that morning in a room in the Commons with Whetstone while Howard prepared to reshuffle his team. In due course Maclean entered and announced: 'George has been persuaded.' Cameron punched the air with delight.

Later that morning he took a call from his old university friend Andrew Feldman, who was now running his family textile firm Jayroma. Feldman was blunt: 'Are you going to run?' He had a reason for asking, he said. Lord Harris, the carpet magnate and Tory donor, wanted to meet him if he was considering throwing his hat in the ring. Cameron, who was on his way to a celebratory lunch with his father at White's Club, said he hadn't made up his mind. Later that day he called Feldman and said that he would be happy to meet Harris. At his house in Eaton Square the Tory peer told Cameron that he was the man to rescue the party. Cameron demurred. He said that he had very little experience. He had, for example, been at the despatch box on only a handful of occasions. After the meeting, Harris was more convinced than ever that Cameron should run.

In public at least Cameron was batting away any talk of a challenge. The day after the election he told his local news media: 'It's not on my horizon at all. I think Michael Howard did a very good job and I want him to remain as leader.' In private too, even among close friends, he gave the impression of wrestling with the decision. Michael Gove recalls meeting him and a mutual friend, Tania Kindersley, for a drink in a hotel in Soho, about a week after the election. Gove says his friend was 'playing his cards close to his chest'. At around the same time Gove phoned Hilton, who was on holiday in Berlin, to update him on the situation back in London. He agreed that Cameron should run. Cameron had in fact already spoken to his parents and siblings about doing so and had received strong encouragement. Later, he would claim that Samantha, too, had urged him to run, when he had had doubts. 'You wake up in different moods on different mornings. But my wife, Samantha, said to me, "If you can't do it now, then you won't be able to do it later, so go on, do it."' He has said that he finally decided to run while in his garden at Dean. 'I remember walking around talking to Sam and thinking "Come on."' Samantha understood – and shared – his professional drive. She had, after all, continued to work hard at Smythsons (where friends have learned not to call her).

But Cameron had got himself into a tangle in an interview the previous October when he was asked if, looking in the mirror, he saw a future Prime Minister staring back. 'In politics, there is a mixture of egotism and altruism in all of us. I think it is on the whole a pretty healthy mixture and I think all of us, if you scratch us, dream of our party winning power and being in government. I don't think we all wake up and think, "If only I were Prime Minister." It takes a very special sort of person to want that sort of responsibility.' He was then asked if his answer meant he was ruling himself out of running for the top job. The question seemed to throw him. 'No. I mean yes. I mean no. I don't think I'm one of those people, is what I'm saying. I really don't. I look at Blair and Thatcher and Major. I think of the enormous responsibility they had on their, um, shoulders, and I just think that you've got to be … It's a different game.'

Those who know Cameron best speak of slight and extremely well concealed intellectual and social insecurities, but now, when the opportunity was really at his feet, he was determined to take it. The only remaining obstacle was Osborne, whose spectacular promotion to the shadow Chancellorship had caught almost everyone by surprise. Suddenly, for the first time, he was being talked up as a leadership candidate in earnest. Osborne himself admits he 'did think for a couple of days whether it was something I should do'. In fact it was almost a fortnight after the reshuffle that he announced he wasn't going to run. It wasn't just in deference to Howard that he didn't rule himself out straight away. The young MP actively canvassed opinion on his possible candidature. He asked Lynton Crosby, who told him, bluntly, that he was too young. It is likely that he asked William

Hague. 'George thought about it immediately after being made shadow Chancellor,' says Michael Gove. 'I think there was always an understanding that if one of them stood the other one wouldn't. And I think that George thought about it and then quickly realised that, for a variety of reasons, Dave would be better. There was about twenty-four hours immediately after George was appointed [when] some people said, "Oh maybe [it] could be George." But then internally between George and Dave it was agreed that there could only be one and it was understood that it was Dave.'

Friends say there were a number of telephone discussions between Osborne and Cameron, but the details of those calls are as yet known only to them. The pair, acutely conscious of the damage suffered by both Blair and Brown as a result of leaks about the various accommodations they have reached, have since strenuously denied that they made a 'Granita-style deal'. The only arrangement that was entered into was that, if Cameron ran and Osborne didn't, the latter agreed he would be Cameron's campaign manager. Tellingly he did not ask Cameron to make the reciprocal commitment. One friend says that Cameron was more 'psychologically prepared' to challenge for the leadership. Certainly in the days following the election the younger man's mind was taken up with thoughts of his looming first encounter with Brown in the Commons debate that would follow the Queen's Speech.

Finally on Thursday 19 May, after ten days' reflection and canvassing, Osborne made his decision. In a further proof against suspicions of secret deals he phoned not Cameron but Toby Helm, a journalist on the *Daily Telegraph*, with the news. 'There has been some media speculation about what I would do but I am making it clear I will not be a candidate,' he told Helm. 'I have a big enough job being shadow chancellor, opposing Gordon Brown and developing an economic policy that broadens the appeal of the Conservative Party.' Next Osborne told Cameron himself, who said that he still hadn't finally made up his own mind but repeated that should he stand he wanted Osborne to be his campaign manager. It seems likely that Osborne simply reached a conclusion that he was, as Crosby and others had told him, too young. And youth, after all, is a self-correcting defect: had Davis won in 2005 Osborne would have been well placed for the next contest.

Having settled the Osborne issue, Cameron next tried to address what he knew would be his biggest vulnerability in the forthcoming campaign, his privileged background. Was he, as he himself put it, 'too posh to push'? Class would always have been an issue in a Cameron leadership bid, just as it was when Douglas Hurd, another Old Etonian, fought John Major for the job in 1990. And, like Hurd, Cameron faced an opponent whose life story was not one of gilded privilege, of nannies, swimming pools and friends in the City. Davis, son of a single mother, had been brought up on a council estate. He had come into politics via commerce and a stint in the territorial SAS. When Davis had worked near Westminster as a young man it was wiping tables at the Royal Festival Hall, not rubbing shoulders with Cabinet ministers in Smith Square.

Cameron began to address the issue of his background head-on, giving a series of interviews, in which he knew he would be asked if he were 'too posh'. His answer was to turn defence into attack. 'In the sort of politics I believe in it shouldn't matter what you've had in the past, it's what you are going to contribute in the future, and I think that should be true of everybody, from all parts of society, all colours and ages and races, and I hope that goes for Old Etonians too,' he said just ten days after the election. The portrayal of Old Etonians as just another minority to be welcomed within the rainbow coalition that was the modern Conservative Party was one that even some of his friends found less than convincing.

Nicholas Boles recalls staying at Cameron's home in Dean in October 2004 with Osborne. After dinner Boles told his friends that both were simply too privileged ever to lead their party. Not surprisingly they vigorously disagreed. It was an argument that rumbled, more or less good-naturedly, long into the night. Now that it wasn't just theoretical banter among friends but a real issue in a real campaign, Boles felt no less concerned that Cameron's background would cloud the modernisers' message. In an article for the *Evening Standard*, he wrote: 'It may well be the case that someone from the Right of the party, especially someone whose personal history exemplifies a modern classless Britain, will be better placed to persuade more traditional Conservatives of the need for radical change.' In the event class was to be much less of a factor than they feared. Indeed perhaps the worst damage done by Cameron's background was that it kept away potential supporters like Boles from his campaign when he needed them most.

Cameron kept to his official brief throughout the months of May and June, evading questions about his leadership intentions in a way that encouraged speculation that he would run. In his first Commons speech of the new parliament on 24 May he deliberately echoed Blair. 'I agree with the Prime Minister about one thing – there is no more important issue in this country than education.' In the words of the *Financial Times* he 'staked his claim to be the standard bearer of the Tory modernisers by invoking the spirit of Tony Blair's slogan, "education, education, education"'. While Cameron was making gains in the media war, the reality of his campaign was rather more modest – as became evident when in June he called a secret meeting in his office. He later joked that at the start of his bid he could have fitted his campaign team into the back of a taxi. He might have added that a minibus would have been sufficient for his initial parliamentary support.

Although relocated to rather more spacious quarters in Portcullis House, a smart annexe to the Palace of Westminster, there was still plenty of room for the gaggle of MPs that came to pledge their loyalty. There were fourteen of them: Hugo Swire, Andrew Robathan, Michael

Gove, Boris Johnson, Richard Benyon, Peter Luff, Oliver Letwin, Hugh Robertson, Greg Barker, John Butterfill, Nicholas Soames, Ed Vaizey, George Osborne and Peter Viggers. Looking at the list it is immediately obvious that Cameron's core parliamentary support was blue-blooded. At least four went to Eton. The Newbury MP Richard Benyon, in particular, comes from a stable similar to that which produced Cameron. The Benyons, like the Mounts, are a grand county family which has produced a long line of MPs. Indeed Cameron's mother is among Benyon's constituents and his forebears among Benyon's predecessors. William George Mount became Newbury MP in 1885 and was succeeded fifteen years later by William Arthur Mount. (Other families to have held the seat since include the Hurds, Clifton-Browns and Astors.)

Once he had gathered together these flowers of the English aristocracy, it seems Cameron had an attack of diffidence, that blight of the upper class. It was not a successful meeting. Cameron was 'reticent', according to one present. He said that, while he was very grateful they had all come, he was still considering his options. Since some of them, including Viggers, who had already signed Davis's nomination papers, had risked a good deal by coming to Cameron's office, this was not the sort of call to arms that had been expected.

Immediately afterwards Robathan, one of the few not to have been born into a great family, asked to see Cameron alone. The MP, a former soldier (and another veteran of the SAS), told him that he had failed utterly to rally his troops. If he wanted loyalty he had better lead from the front. Cameron had asked Swire to 'keep the book', that is to maintain a tally of pledged and possible supporters and to seek to convert the latter into the former. The East Devon MP, a fellow Old Etonian, concealed from Cameron how thin his support was for fear of damaging his confidence. 'Greg [Barker] and I used to hide the truth from David – this is sort of June now. It was only ever those fourteen. We couldn't get beyond that for ages.'

Willetts, Lansley and Yeo were more experienced and had longer track records in espousing the modernising message. It was also, arguably, their last shots at the top job – an argument that holds surprising sway among MPs, if not with the public. In contrast, Cameron could bide his time, a point made with maximum condescension by Andrew Mitchell. 'Someone recently gave me a few bottles of Chateau Latour 2000. I think it would be wiser for me to leave it in the cellar for quite a few years yet before I open it, and I would give the same advice to some of the younger leadership contenders.'

One vintage that was certainly ready for drinking – had indeed been decanted twice before – was Kenneth Clarke. Clarke had declined to stand against Howard in 2003, saying: 'I'm not going to give up any of my other bad habits, but coming second in Conservative leadership elections is something I don't intend to do.' Some addictions are too hard to kick. Cameron was invited to Clarke's Commons office – just a few doors away from his own – for a private chat. One of Cameron's friends recalls: 'Ken rather grandly offered David the chance to be his running mate.' It was an offer that Cameron had little hesitation in turning down.

His parliamentary support might have been tiny but Cameron had managed to create sufficient media buzz to attract backers at the bookmakers. By mid-June they had made him second favourite behind Davis (evens) on odds of 5/1. (Clarke was 10/1.) Cameron was also proving successful in raising cash. His old university friend Andrew Feldman started making approaches to potential supporters on his behalf. Swire says that Gove was 'doing all the speeches and tactics' in the early part of the campaign and that Oliver Letwin was also a 'key' figure. (Osborne 'became active', says Swire, 'especially after the party conference'.) With Gove and Letwin, Cameron crafted a speech which he hoped would unify both the modernising and the traditional Tory agendas and which could mark the 'soft launch' of his campaign. While the formal campaign couldn't be launched until there was a contest that autumn, this was an attempt to build momentum towards the objective that, by the end of the summer parliamentary term, Cameron should be regarded as the main challenger to Davis.

But his chosen theme, the family, left some of his audience distinctly unimpressed when he delivered the address to Boles's think-tank, the Policy Exchange, at the end of June. One bright young Tory thinker was heard to remark after the event how disappointed he had been by Cameron's performance. 'He reminds me of Willie Whitelaw,' the young intellectual sniffed. 'A lightweight with bottom.' After the event Feldman sought reassurance from Hilton that the whole Cameron campaign wasn't about to bomb. Norman Lamont, meanwhile, was 'very surprised' that his former special adviser was standing for the leadership of his party. 'I told Michael Green that I thought that he shouldn't run. I didn't think that it was in his own best interests and I didn't think that he would win.' The following month a Davisite passed one of the small band of 'Cameroons' in the Lobby. He observed 'with genial malice' that he understood that the candidate's parliamentary support had made it into double figures. It was a cruelly accurate estimate. By the time MPs broke up for their long summer recess at the end of July, the Cameron campaign had failed to attract a single extra MP.

Even loyal lieutenants like Gove began to worry that Cameron was giving the impression that he was running not to win but to position himself for some future contest. His worries would not have been eased had he overheard the discussions around the Camerons' dinner table the following week. To recharge his energies for the fight ahead, Cameron had taken his family to Jura in the last week in July and invited Swire and his wife, Sasha, to stay with them. 'There was a lot of talking and David was leaving all his options open,' says Swire, although he adds that it was, to him at least, 'perfectly clear from day one that he was going to run'.

Soon after his return from Jura, Cameron held a meeting in the Piccadilly offices of Robert Fleming, a merchant banking constituent who was helping bankroll his campaign. He summoned Hilton, Feldman, Letwin, Osborne, Gove and Vaizey to discuss what should be the campaign's slogan and main themes. Hilton, leaping about with his customary energy in front of a whiteboard, underlined the social-responsibility message. Letwin, meanwhile, was pushing a slogan that would have Cameron promising to 'make Britain more civilised'. It fell to Feldman to point out that his friend was going to have to say whatever it was thousands of times. He had better be thoroughly comfortable with it. 'I felt that if it wasn't consistent with who he is, with his temperament, he wouldn't be able to say it with conviction,' says Feldman.

At last a slogan emerged under which Cameron could confidently campaign for the leadership and then campaign for office: 'modern compassionate Conservatism'. The slogan had at first been rejected on the ground that it would be associated with George W. Bush's campaign for the US Presidency, which had also made great play with compassion. Eventually it was decided that Cameron was sufficiently different from Bush to render any comparison meaningless. Cameron's own insight was that he should act as if he were already the leader and do and say those things necessary to help the party win the general election. In proving that he could win the latter contest he would win the first and spare himself the contortions of tailoring different messages to MPs, the party faithful and the country at large.

Throughout August Cameron delivered a series of speeches and interventions that started to mark out a discrete agenda. While Davis, still basking in the praise for his response to the 7 July terrorist bombings in London, adopted a policy of 'magisterial silence' (as Barker puts it), Cameron made the best use he could of a media struggling to fill space during the summer months. In a series of well-received speeches he spoke on social enterprise, constitutional reform, foreign policy, community relations and, more generally, improving the quality of life. By the end of the month he could point to what he called a 'Cameron manifesto'. Its overarching theme was 'modern compassionate Conservatism'. In a speech delivered in Devon that presaged much of his agenda in his first year as leader he said: 'Modern compassionate Conservatism means recognising there's more to human life than getting and spending money.'

But for all the praise from commentators – India Knight called him the first Tory she could imagine voting for – Cameron was struggling to keep his campaign alive. In late August he launched a charm offensive among Tory grandees and newspaper magnates in an attempt to neutralise the growing threat of a Clarke campaign. He arranged a private meeting with Lord Heseltine, but the peer refused to back him, a rejection that then leaked. When a profile-writer sneaked a look in his diary and spotted that he had an appointment to see Jonathan Harmsworth, owner of the *Daily Mail* and *Mail on Sunday*, his prospects in that quarter looked no less tentative: the *Daily Mail* was clearly backing Clarke, having decided to put to one side his views on Europe. By the beginning of September, despite winning plaudits from commentators for his speeches, the Cameron campaign looked to be in deep trouble.

A poll of Tory MPs in the *Sunday Times* on the first weekend in September revealed just how little parliamentary support he had. Of one hundred members canvassed, the newspaper could only find nine backing Cameron, a figure that actually inflated the number of firm pledges. Most damaging of all was that Liam Fox, the darling of the Thatcherite right, who had made a dramatic late entry into the race the day before, was backed by more MPs (albeit only one more). The newspaper quoted Alan Duncan, a shadow Cabinet moderniser, calling on Cameron to pull out of the race. 'We are coming to the endgame here with Clarke versus Davis. I think Cameron can now go away,' he said.

The newspaper would have been read with particular interest at the home of Andrew Mitchell, where the man who was to become Davis's campaign manager was entertaining two rather surprising guests: George Osborne, earmarked by Cameron to be *his* campaign manager, and Hugo Swire, who had been his 'numbers man'. Their decision to accept Mitchell's social invitation (their wives were also guests) may have been perfectly innocent, but Cameron regarded it with considerable suspicion, as did some of his closest supporters. One referred to the house party in Mitchell's smart Nottinghamshire home as 'George's night in Transylvania'. Both Osborne and Swire received a number of text messages that weekend demanding to know whether they were about to jump ship. Mitchell did indeed try hard to win Osborne over to the Davis camp. (Osborne meanwhile took the opportunity to review Mitchell's visitors book, fascinating reading for a rival campaign manager.)

One of the key actors in this drama does not deny that Osborne was unconvinced that Cameron would win. 'Did George have a wobble? George grew more committed during party conference. And George is a politician to his fingertips – part of him thought, "This could be me." And had he been older it most likely would have been.' Another says that Osborne's 'mild frustration' at this time was that Cameron hadn't shown enough commitment to his own cause. Cameron's very English distaste for aggressive self-promotion was undermining morale, as even close friends admit. 'My concern was David was trying to win it on the basis that he was the younger Douglas Hurd and the Tory Party would be safe in his stewardship. That if [he tried] to win on the basis that "I'm a bit nicer than David Davis and a bit younger than Ken Clarke" it wouldn't work,' says one.

Just when the Cameron campaign team thought things couldn't get any worse, Davis landed the surprise endorsement of Willetts, who backed the frontrunner after folding his own leadership bid. Barker says the following fortnight was 'grim'. 'We were getting by far the best media profile. The question was … to what extent MPs [were being] turned by that.' It didn't help that Cameron chose this time to take a second holiday, leaving his team to face the growing threat from Clarke and Fox. 'We had actually spent quite a few of our rounds in July and August … so we didn't have a great deal to fight back with. It did get quite depressing.' Things got so bad that the possibility of pulling out of the race and cutting a deal with Davis was raised. On his return Cameron rejected it out of hand (on the ground, according to a close observer, that he could not trust Davis to deliver on any promise made in return for his withdrawal). Liam Fox put out feelers, offering Cameron a senior job if he would pull out and offer his support, but Cameron was not tempted.

To eradicate the sense of malaise, Cameron held a dinner at his house in mid-September for his core team. He asked what he needed to do to get his campaign back on track. Osborne told him bluntly that he had to step up a gear and make the case for radical change more aggressively. With his back against the wall Cameron decided to go for broke and stage a high-profile event for the launch of his formal campaign. He told Feldman that he thought it would cost about £20,000, throwing into chaos his old university friend's carefully apportioned campaign accounts.

As MPs began to drift back to Westminster through September they were also met by a much sharper parliamentary operation. It was still unclear whether the leadership election was going to be run under the system set up by Hague, under which successive ballots of the parliamentary party whittled the field down to two candidates who would then be presented to the grassroots. An alternative plan drawn up by Howard that proposed to give MPs the final say and so avoid the lack of a parliamentary mandate that had hobbled IDS was itself the subject of a membership ballot, the result of which was still not known. Whichever system was used it was clear that, at the very least, the winning candidate would need to be in second place among MPs.

Responsibility for 'running the book' had passed to Andrew Robathan. Swire is gracious enough to admit that a more experienced hand was called for. 'I had never run the book before and we had only been in politics for four years. It was very difficult for me to go to some of the older, trickier [MPs] and say, "What are you doing?"' The task of garnering MPs' support had not been made any easier by Cameron's refusal to cut deals with individuals or tailor his position to suit factions. 'If you win the election on the basis of tacking in order to please existing party opinion then you will win on that basis and never have the freedom of manoeuvre to be a successful leader,' he told his supporters.

By contrast, Swire said, 'The Davis campaign was a classic template of how not to run a political campaign. It was intimidatory, promissory: all the things that we weren't. David really can as far as I know put his hand on his heart and say he promised nothing to anyone. Our campaign was always open, very friendly, not clubby. I think that was terribly important.' Another MP ally concurs: 'The interesting thing about Dave all the way through the leadership campaign [was that] he was very, very level-headed and I never really saw him get angry or tetchy. He can be a bit sullen, withdrawn, but you never ever saw him tear people off a strip or lose his rag in the way that David Davis was legendary for doing.'

While admirable, Cameron's demeanour and tactics were least effective when it came to the most inexperienced Tory MPs. Davis's lieutenants found it relatively easy to persuade an impressive number of the new intake that they were backing a winner. To counteract this, Cameron and his wife invited groups of new MPs to Finstock Road for dinner parties to win them over, but gained precious few converts over the claret and lasagne. He seemed to be paying for a common perception among the 2001 intake – that he had been over-keen on impressing his seniors and that he was aloof and dismissive towards those of his peers not necessarily blessed with talents on a par with his own. By contrast the growing tally supporting Davis – advertised almost weekly by this time – created an impression of unstoppable momentum.

Meanwhile Clarke was doing his best to bounce Cameron out of a race he presented as a two-horse contest between himself and Davis. 'We're at the moment still slugging it out,' he said. 'I've no idea which of us is going to attract David Cameron when he finally decides that he'd better join one or other of the main contenders.' For good measure one of Clarke's supporters, John Bercow, added: 'In the modern world the combination of Eton, hunting, shooting and lunch at White's is not helpful when you are trying to appeal to millions of ordinary people.' But it was Fox that Cameron was most worried about. He was confident of being able to win a three-way fight for the MPs' votes if it was between Davis, Clarke and himself, but he needed to get there first. Fox, by drawing on the same pool of MPs for whom neither Davis nor Clarke looked an attractive option, risked pushing him into fourth place – and elimination – in the first ballot. Sir Malcolm Rifkind, whose decision to stand for the leadership after two terms out of parliament had not yet been exposed as vainglorious, made up the numbers.

In the last week of September all five candidates formally declared. Clarke dispensed with a formal launch but instructed his party that it was 'Time to Win'. Fox also had no formal launch but set out his stall with a pledge to pull the party out of the right-of-centre but federalist EPP grouping in the European parliament. Cameron, seeing the danger to his right flank, decided to break his 'no promises' rule and matched this sop to the Eurosceptic right. It may have helped counter the attraction of Fox among some Tory MPs but – as he had himself predicted – this 'tacking' was to haunt him as leader.

Meanwhile Hilton was at his obsessive best in planning the official launch of the Cameron campaign on 29 September – which was also the date of the Davis launch. Initially Davis's camp tried to harry

Cameron off 'their' launch date but he stuck firm, calculating that by generating extra media interest the clash would only do him good. Nothing was left to chance – especially not the candidate himself. As Cameron worked on his bearing and delivery, Hilton secured the venue, backdrop, music and lighting for an event on which the survival of the leadership bid itself depended. By now the campaign was being run from a small office in Greycoat Place just round the corner from Conservative headquarters. Two former CRD colleagues, Ed Llewellyn and Catherine Fall, had quietly been called to the colours. George Eustice, who had resigned from Conservative HQ to run Cameron's press operation, helped complete a youthful and generally professional team.

When, on the morning of launch day, Cameron arrived at the venue, the Whitehall HQ of the Royal United Services Institute, he was on edge. Eustice's mobile telephone, which hardly stops ringing even on quiet days, kept competing with the candidate's attempts to rehearse – an irritation Cameron found unbearable. Cameron is a cautious player of politics – until the moment for action arrives. Having judged that a risk is worth running he tends not to hedge thereafter. He had already as good as staked his candidacy on this launch but, late on, chose to add another element of chance and speak without notes. The decision had been taken the day before at a practice run. Cameron suddenly resolved to abandon his script and speak off the cuff, as if giving an answer to the question, 'What is wrong with the Conservative Party today?' The question-and-answer format is his favourite method of communication. Why not, he said, give the answer without waiting for the question? It was more authentic than reading from a prepared text, but it was high-risk.

Journalists arriving hot-foot from the Davis launch earlier that day were handed strawberry smoothies and chocolate brownies. As they settled in their seats, they took in the room, white and circular, and the ambient music – 'lots of little chimes and bells', wrote Ann Treneman in a sketch for *The Times*. 'I am only surprised that we weren't handed little white towels and lavender eye-pads.' It was all very different from David Davis's launch that morning in the fusty oak-panelled surroundings of the Institute of Civil Engineers on Great George Street. Davis's message might have been 'Modern Conservatives', but that was just a slogan: this *was* modern.

Osborne then introduced his 'good friend Dave'. Earlier worries about Cameron's diffidence vanished as he gave a controlled but spirited performance. Taking on Davis's claims to be a moderniser, he said that only he would see through the necessary reforms. 'The choice for the party has got to be who do you think really believes it? Who will really stick to it when the going gets tough and the press attack you after a couple of years and say this is not distinctive enough, it isn't attacking enough?' It sounded fresh because it *was* fresh. For large chunks of the presentation Cameron was improvising, albeit around a meticulously prepared theme. In his most quoted passage, he confronted the issue of his relative inexperience. 'I believe that if you have got the right ideas in your head and the right passion in your heart and if you know what this party needs to do to change, then you should go for it. That is why I am doing this.'

Osborne, sitting next to Samantha Cameron, was genuinely impressed – and genuinely surprised – by his candidate's performance. Very late in the day and when it was really needed, Cameron had shown he had steel and charisma. It was the official launch, not the more widely remembered conference speech a week later, that was the turning point of the Cameron campaign. The launch communicated confidence to his team, to the watching journalists, to other Tory MPs – Cameron was going to 'Change to Win' – the bolder slogan now supplementing 'modern compassionate Conservatism'.

Having seen the formal campaign successfully launched after so many doubts behind the scenes, Cameron and Hilton holed up in Finstock Road and started working on the candidate's conference speech. Now that they had at last built up some momentum, this had to be the address where Cameron overhauled the favourite. One witness of the collaborative process between Hilton and Cameron describes it thus: 'It's not that Steve does his speeches and Dave says, "I'll take that." Steve interprets what Dave wants to say. They are almost finishing each other's sentences in terms of speech-writing ... bouncing ideas off each other.'

The annual conference – held that year in Blackpool – was Howard's last gift to a 'stop-Davis' candidate. He had so arranged the timing of his departure that the gathering would become a beauty parade in which the candidates would be judged on the quality of their speeches. Davis was a relatively poor conference performer, as Howard well knew. Arriving at Blackpool, Cameron and Hilton split up. While Hilton took a room in the main conference hotel, the Imperial, Cameron himself stayed at a less expensive but more private establishment a short distance away.

Cameron knew that in just three days' time he would be making a speech that would make or break him – but, before he could do so, his wife insisted that he smarten up his wardrobe. Samantha had already taken him to a tailor, a sortie he agreed to only after coming under heavy pressure from both his wife and Caroline Balcon, his secretary. The result was a new suit, designed by the fashionable tailor Timothy Everest, who also designs Gordon Brown's suits. Cameron, who shows no great interest in expensive clothes or indeed cars, subsequently moaned to friends that 'no suit is worth four figures'. So it was Samantha alone who went to Blackpool's M&S on the eve of the big speech. She returned with a new pair of shoes and a collection of ties, including a lime-green number that was to become her husband's 'lucky tie'.

Cameron himself worked the conference hard from Sunday to the day of his speech, the following Wednesday, attending all the key receptions. When he had a moment he would return to Hilton's room at the back of the Imperial, kick off his shoes and lie on the bed and attempt to take a short nap. But sleep in such an environment was not easy. Hilton's was a small room overlooking the hotel kitchen, its stuffiness compounded by the fact that no one could work out how to turn off the radiator. At any point there would be half a dozen members of the campaign team either standing around or sitting on the floor.

Hilton, meanwhile, sat at his desk in front of a computer and high-quality printer, bashing out text and issuing orders. He had had the much admired idea of producing a daily Cameron campaign newsletter to be distributed throughout the hotel. It was a typically simple but smart marketing tool that reached a high proportion of the party's most important figures. In a nod to US political conventions, Hilton also had hundreds of 'I ❤ DC' badges made to be distributed among delegates, the younger and better looking the better. The Davis team's stunt – posing large-breasted women in T-shirts bearing the legend 'It's DD for me!' – managed, by contrast, to look both cheap and dated.

At last on the morning of Wednesday 4 October David Cameron took the main stage of Blackpool's Winter Gardens and began, 'We meet in the shadow of a third consecutive election defeat.' The speech delivered essentially the same message of the official launch: that the Conservatives needed 'fundamental' change, not just 'slick rebranding'. Cameron said later that he owed the start of the speech to a chance conversation he had had with the journalist Matthew Parris. 'You need to understand people's respect for the history of the party, and the contribution previous leaders have made,' said Parris. So Cameron balanced an attack on the party's complacency with a restatement of Conservative achievements, principles of freedom, support for aspiration and patriotism. The middle section reclaimed education as a Conservative priority, attacked Gordon Brown for standing in the way of progress and gave precedence in foreign policy to places like Darfur above traditional Tory hobby-horses like Gibraltar.

But it was in the final section that the speech caught fire as Cameron zeroed in on his principal asset. 'There is a new generation of people taking on the world, creating the wealth and opportunity for our future. We can lead that generation.' In cadences that recalled Blair's choppy oratorical technique, he went on: 'Changing our party to change our country. It will be an incredible journey. I want you to come with me.' Finally he hailed 'modern compassionate Conservatism' as 'right for our times, right for our party and right for our country. If we fight for it with every ounce of passion, vigour and energy from now until the next election, no one and nothing can stop us.'

The hall erupted in applause, the ovation extended by several minutes by the arrival of Samantha on stage. Cameron bent down to pat her pregnant stomach, giving photographers an iconic shot of the 'next generation'. He whispered something in her ear which several newspapers took to be a touching 'I love you'. A friend of Samantha's rang the next day and mentioned how sweet it was that he had done that. Samantha feigned fury: 'He didn't say, "I love you." He said, "Am I sweating too much?" I told him, yes he was!' The enthusiastic reaction to the speech was genuine enough but had been cleverly given a helping shove by Hilton and his aides. With a small but effective organisational sleight-of-hand, the Cameron team had managed to persuade the conference's organisers – officially neutral between the candidates – to reserve the front seats. Naturally enough supporters were encouraged to make use of this allocation that just happened to be in camera shot. The initial broadcast reports – usually crucial in moulding how such events are subsequently covered in all media – were duly highly favourable.

Such tricks should not detract from what was a remarkable performance. It was a performance that Cameron had long been preparing for. Just as he had done to win his seat in Witney, he dispensed with the lectern. And absorbing the lessons of Norman Lamont's autocue disaster some twelve years earlier he had learned his speech – the germ of which had emerged from a lunch in London with Steve Hilton, George Osborne, Danny Finkelstein and others – by heart. This last feat almost cost him dear: he suffered a moment of terrible panic about halfway through the address when he forgot a line, but he recovered in such a way that no one noticed.

The speech was a triumph, but Clarke, Davis and Fox were still to come. (Rifkind had opened the 'beauty parade' on the Monday with a speech, charming but anachronistic, of oratorical flourish.) The former Chancellor was the afternoon attraction. He gave the speech of someone who knew this was his last chance. 'We are searching for a leader who will be seen by the public as a prime minister in waiting,' drawled the old war-horse, failed candidate of two previous leadership contests. 'Oh boy, have you kept me waiting.' Clarke cleverly tapped into a collective guilt felt among the Tory grassroots who had rejected him in favour of Duncan Smith in 2003.

Cameron, meanwhile, was still struggling to win over the key newspaper executives. He had made an apparent gaffe at a dinner with senior journalists and managers from the Telegraph Group the night before the speech when he said that he considered himself 'the heir to Blair'. The remark, probably inspired by Osborne who was at his side, was in fact meant to set Blair in a Conservative continuum that starts with Thatcher and ends with Cameron wresting the mantle back from 'Tory Blair'. It was an idea that was too clever by half. Martin Newlands, then the editor of the *Daily Telegraph*, is reported to have replied, 'David, I would not repeat that outside this room.' Unfortunately for him, someone did repeat the remark outside that room. He would, of course, have been compared to Blair whatever he had said in public or private, but the remark is as damaging as Newlands feared it would be because it implies admiration for a man who had so comprehensively bested the Tory tribe for a decade. A dinner with News International editors, at which candidates were required to rotate from one title to another in between courses, went no better. It was made perfectly clear that Fox, not Cameron, was the favoured candidate of the *Sun*.

But cheerful news was reported back to the Hilton Base Camp by Greg Barker, who had happened to be sitting in a hotel corridor when Davis walked by with aides the night after Cameron's triumph and before his own trial. Davis was overheard to sigh, 'God, I've been so busy, I haven't even started on my speech yet.' Bravado or not, the truth is that the press reaction to his subsequent effort was overwhelmingly negative. It is today argued that the speech and its delivery were actually rather good. In fact it was neither any worse nor any better than Davis's normal efforts. And that was some way beneath Cameron's par. But again the press reaction was given a helpful steer, this time by Alan Duncan, who had recanted his earlier advice that Cameron could 'go away' and leave the field clear for Davis and Clarke. Duncan informed journalists immediately after the speech that he had intended to declare for Davis but was now planning to support Cameron instead. Such interventions helped ensure headlines like 'D-Day, A Dismal Day for Davis' in the next day's papers.

Alongside post-mortems of Davis's speech, however, were a few lines recording a fringe event that Cameron had attended later that same day. There the journalist Andrew Rawnsley had asked the candidate whether he had taken drugs at university. 'I had a normal university experience,' Cameron replied. 'So that's a yes, then?' pressed Rawnsley. 'There were things that I did then that I don't think that I should talk about now that I'm a politician.' Cameron's denial was – and remains – mysterious. Why did he not deploy the standard refusal to discuss drug use, a line all politicians know very well? His answer virtually invited further inquiry. Friends say Cameron thought that the Eton cannabis incident would come to light during the campaign.

Perhaps he believed that a complete refusal to have answered the drugs question would then look shifty and prepared an alternative, more honest refusal. Cameron's formulation does make more sense if one believes that he was at that time braced for his school disciplinary record to be unearthed.

The great irony, of course, is that the story did not surface despite the best efforts of dozens of journalists set on his trail. The following week was to be Cameron's first taste of the press pack in full cry. His supporters were impressed by how determined he was to stick to his line even as it began to be suggested that he had taken cocaine, not just cannabis. He repeated his formulation in a television interview on the Sunday. 'I did all sorts of things before I came into politics which I shouldn't have done. We all did.' Nowhere did the story of what drugs Cameron had used and when fascinate more than in the bars and clubs of Notting Hill Gate. One west Londoner reprogrammed his mobile phone so that, when he receives a call from his cocaine dealer, he proudly shows his friends the caller ID. It reads 'David Cameron'.

But the *Daily Mail*, at that time still backing Clarke, saw no reason for levity, demanding day after day that Cameron 'come clean' about his drugs past. The screw was turned by the other leadership candidates, Davis, Clarke and Fox, who all issued unequivocal statements that they had never used drugs. But by Thursday the tide began to turn. Cameron was again asked whether or not he had taken drugs. He refused to give in to the media 'witch-hunt' because 'that was all in the past'. 'I'm allowed to have had a private life before politics, in which we make mistakes and we do things that we should not – and we are all human and we err and stray,' Cameron said on BBC1's *Question Time*. 'And I think if you want to have machines as politicians who have never done anything wrong, I think that is a very sad day and we should not be driven by the media on that.' More significant than his response, however, was the fact that it drew considerable applause from the audience. The public, Cameron sensed, were on his side against what they believed was a bullying and intrusive media.

The next day the *Evening Standard* splashed on a story that a 'close relative' of Cameron had received treatment for drug addiction in South Africa. He immediately issued a statement: 'Someone very close in my family has had a dreadful problem with drugs. They have been through it, been through rehabilitation, and I'm incredibly proud of them.'

Even the *Daily Mail* softened, sensing, perhaps, that it was getting on the wrong side of public opinion. The following day Cameron was offered a slot in the newspaper headlined, 'The truth about my attitude to drugs'. 'I know there's a suspicion that, because of my age and backgound I have a tolerant attitude towards drugs,' Cameron wrote. 'Nothing could be further from the truth. I've seen the dreadful damage that drugs can do.' Cameron had kicked drugs into touch, for now.

By 18 October Robathan could hardly keep up with the flood of MPs signing up for the Cameron camp ahead of the first ballot that afternoon. Howard's alternative leadership rules had been rejected, so the contest was to be held under Hague's model whereby MPs choose two candidates who are then presented to a membership ballot. Most Tory MPs had kept their counsel over who they were backing until before the party conference. Now many were coming under pressure from their local associations to back this exciting new prospect Cameron. It was pressure to which most were only too willing to submit. The easiest and safest way to back a winner in politics is to wait until one emerges. (That is why Cameron supporters are ranked by those with the best claim to be 'true believers' according to the month in which they declared allegiance.)

That Robathan was still working hard for the cause at this time is to his credit. Now that Cameron looked likely to win, Robathan had every reason to expect that the new leader would make him his Chief Whip. He had, after all, sharpened up the parliamentary operation considerably and had been steadfast when others had wobbled. Cameron signalled instead that he would choose Patrick McLoughlin, the existing Deputy Chief Whip. It was a canny choice – McLoughlin, a former miner, is liked and respected across the parliamentary party. The putative appointment – briefed to a Sunday tabloid – was a clever way of reassuring MPs that Cameron would not rule by clique. But it was hard on a loyal colleague, as well as another breach of his 'no promises' rule. Cameron did not find the decision easy and it took him three days to make up his mind. But he concluded that McLoughlin would help maximise his chances of victory.

It was Clarke who fell first. He polled just 38 votes, behind Fox, 42, Cameron, 56, and Davis with 62 votes. Even though he topped the poll, the result was an all-but-mortal blow to Davis. The next ballot confirmed to the country what Westminster already knew, that Cameron was now the runaway favourite to win the leadership. It saw him attract the support of ninety MPs as against Davis's fifty-seven. Fox, who had given a creditable performance in Blackpool and had powerful media support, managed a surprisingly good showing of fifty-one but was out of the race.

Had Howard been successful in giving MPs the final say, Cameron would have been crowned there and then. But his proposals had been narrowly defeated at the end of September. Thus Davis and Cameron now faced a second electorate, this time the party's rank-and-file members. The winner of this ballot, to be announced six weeks later, would be the next leader of the Conservative Party. There is a lingering suspicion among Liam Fox's supporters that Cameron sent some of his votes over to the Davis camp to keep Fox out of second place. They are right that Cameron feared running against Fox more than he did Davis in the membership elections. Cameron discussed with two of his most senior lieutenants whether or not they should vote for Fox but concluded that it was 'psychologically impossible' to vote against oneself.

Before the national campaign got properly under way, the earlier drugs controversy threatened to flare into life again. With Cameron the clear frontrunner all eyes were on the following Sunday's newspapers. What 'drugs shame' would they rake up on the Tories' blue-eyed boy? Under the headline 'Top Tory, Coke and the Hooker', the *Sunday Mirror* carried claims from a former acquaintance, Jennifer Shackleton, that she had seen a 'top Tory' snort cocaine. But it wasn't Cameron in the frame – it was Osborne. The front-page article was accompanied by a picture of Cameron's campaign manager with his arms around Shackleton. On the table in front of them was what appeared to be some powder. Osborne denied taking drugs but acknowledged the woman he had known as Nathalie Rowe, a prostitute, saying she had been the lover of a friend who had then become addicted to drugs.

In fact, Osborne had suspected that Shackleton was trying to sell her story for months. Before the election he had received, out of the blue, a series of calls from her – calls he suspected were being made to prove their connection to a newspaper. It seems at least possible that his knowledge that this story was about to break contributed to his decision not to stand against Cameron for the leadership. In the event – because he wasn't a candidate – the story did little damage to either Osborne or Cameron, who again refused to talk about drug use in his past.

Cameron chose an inner-city backdrop to launch his national campaign with a message that identified the regeneration of the party with regenerating inner cities. It was followed a week later with a major speech on the environment. Although he had touched on green issues over the course of the summer, it wasn't until the end of October that he spelled out his new policy. It was a classic example of 'new politics'. Climate change was too important to remain a political football, he said, it was time that an independent body, like that which governs interest rates, was set up to fix statutory carbon emission reduction targets.

Davis was not quite finished yet, however. He scored a points victory over Cameron when, on 3 November, the two went toe to toe in a special edition of BBC1's *Question Time*. Michael Gove takes responsibility for the below-par performance of his candidate. Rehearsing before the show, Gove played the part of Davis. He did so with as much aggression and malice as he could bring to the role. But the real Davis prefaced his first answer with a homily to the importance of civilised debate, and went on to behave, initially at least, with mildness and good manners. Cameron, pumped up from his sparring with Gove, struggled to get the measure of the new Davis and lost the audience. He had also been advised by an image consultant, Anthony Gordon-Lennox, that he should stand further back than he had been expected to stand. This stance, used by John Kerry in the 2004 US presidential election, was a mistake. Cameron looked not relaxed, but strange.

Cameron had seen the danger of the head-to-head with Davis at least a week before. For so long the outside bet, he now had to deal with the perils of being a frontrunner – and Davis had little to lose. What was needed was an insurance policy: a good headline to play the day after the debate to swamp any coverage of a poor performance. Towards the end of October, Barker told Cameron he had found just such a card to play – Willetts was ready to defect to his camp from Davis. Willetts had been rueing his endorsement almost from the moment he had made it. Now three weeks after the Blackpool conference he sat with Barker and wrote a letter resigning from Davis's campaign and endorsing Cameron. Just as he was about to hand it over, Willetts had second thoughts, however. He told Barker he owed it to Davis to explain to his face what he was about to do. That interview left Willetts more agonised than ever after Davis made clear the enmity his exit would leave behind. Finally, he decided he would lose more credibility by ratting on Davis than by enduring the consequences of his foolish endorsement of him.

Meanwhile, George Osborne, sensing Willetts's weakness, wanted to brief the newspapers about the defection in order to box him in. This course of action was vetoed by an agitated Letwin, however. Cameron made his displeasure clear: when Willetts phoned his office to explain himself, he refused to take his call. Later he joked to a Davisite that Willetts had been caught 'on the Berlin Wall'. 'We had his arms, you had his legs.' The story of Willetts's serial indecision was spread rapidly through Westminster, thereby inflicting just the sort of damage to his reputation he had wanted to avoid. The message to others thinking of messing with Cameron was made abundantly clear.

On 9 November, Davis appeared to have dramatically overhauled Cameron. A poll of Tory Party members suggested exactly half supported Davis, and just 37 per cent backed Cameron. It seems that the survey was a rogue poll as subsequent surveys accurately predicted that Cameron would win by two to one. Liam Fox, who had kept his powder dry since being knocked out a month previously, endorsed Cameron on 13 November. This, surely, would bring a clinching number of votes to the Cameron cause.

Certainly, there was confidence in the air. A week before the leadership election, one of Cameron's more cerebral lieutenants approached Frank Field, the widely respected, deep-thinking but disaffected Labour MP, to ask if he would chair a new policy forum. Field was offered the chance to appoint experts to look into policy across the board, on the understanding that the findings of this body would be available to all political parties. The plan, if Cameron won, was for Field's appointment to be announced in Cameron's acceptance speech. In the event, Field told the Tories that such a position was inconsistent with his role as a Labour MP, and the plan, which seems to have been tailor-made for him, was shelved.

But victory was not certain as long as there was an interview with Jeremy Paxman to be faced. Cameron, showing his experience of television, and appearing after Davis had performed badly in his own clash with Paxman, insisted on bringing his own make-up team and lighting experts to the Nottingham studio where he insisted the interview be recorded. 'I rang the BBC and said I did not want to look like David Davis did,' he admitted later.

Paxman did his best to scrape through the greasepaint with a first question designed to unsettle Cameron. 'Do you know what a Pink Pussy is?' he demanded. Cameron thought it might be a nightclub in Ibiza to which he was relieved he hadn't been but said he didn't know. 'What about a Slippery Nipple?' Paxman continued. Cameron, by now cottoning on to the line of questioning, replied that it was a drink. It was, as Paxman pointed out, a drink served by the jug in bars owned by Urbium, of which Cameron was once a board member. Blaming Cameron for the evils of under-age and binge drinking because he had once been involved in a company that ran bars was never going to have the candidate on his knees. But the way Cameron dealt with first that sally and then with Paxman's follow-up attack on tuition fees was impressive.

He later admitted that he had pre-prepared his first counter-attack, delivered after he had been interrupted several times. 'This is the trouble with these interviews, Jeremy,' Cameron said. 'You come in, you sit someone down and you treat them like they are some sort of a cross between a fake and a hypocrite and you give them no time to answer their questions.' Paxman was taken aback when a few minutes later Cameron returned to his theme, after he had again been interrupted. 'Jeremy, this is farcical! Why don't we have an agreement? Give me two sentences and then you can interrupt.' Watching politicians of every stamp must have been willing Cameron on as he turned the tables on their tormentor-in-chief. As soon as the show was aired his phone began to throb with incoming text messages. Lord Chadlington – a PR man of some experience – immediately sent him a congratulatory text, as did Nicholas Soames whose text asserted that Paxman 'doesn't like it up 'im'. For Cameron it was sweet revenge for having been accused of 'wittering' by the interviewer after publication of the Hutton Report.

On 6 December 2005, at the Royal Academy of the Arts in London, Sir Michael Spicer, chairman of the Tory backbenchers' 1922 Committee and returning officer for the leadership election, announced its results. David Davis had polled 64,398 votes while David Cameron had attracted 134,446. His winning margin was, thus, more than two to one.

Earlier, in the Commons smoking room, Cameron had put the last touches to his acceptance speech. It was a moment's calm during which he could reflect on a remarkable journey from new back-bencher to leader that had taken four and a half years. In that time he had seen three leaders fail. Each had arrived promising to bring change. Each had turned from that path and been defeated. In his first address as leader he was determined to make clear that he would not follow them. 'I said when I launched my campaign that we needed to change in order to win. Now that I've won we will change.'

Top of his list of things that needed to change was the 'scandalous under-representation of women in the Conservative Party'. Next was the party's attitude to inner cities; third, he said he would end 'Punch and Judy politics'. 'When the government does the right thing we will support them.' He then took his audience through the challenges Britain faced: economic competitiveness came first, then reform of public services, and then 'quality of life', under which safe streets, home ownership and climate change were grouped.

He concluded by identifying the 'final challenge ... at the heart of all the others'. At the time this passage was reported only as an attack on Thatcherism. It was not, in fact, so meant. It does capture, however, the core of what Cameron, with Hilton, is trying to achieve:

It is having social action to ensure social justice and a stronger society. I want to set free the voluntary sector and social enterprises to deal

RMAN SHAW SOUTH

of the Opposition 2005–2007

eader of the Opposition David Cameron's overriding
to convince voters that – this time – the Conservatives
aged. And was true that he represented a significant
the strength of his commitment to the
e pas sal free healthcare and education. But he also
unive ate and wants to reduce the demands made on
ma duals to take responsibility for their own welfare.
evious Tory leaders he also believes that exhor-
rred to legislation, devolution to centralisation. He
neously to convince voters that the Conservatives
e reassuring the party that, in essence, they had not.
ook as long as it did for him to run into difficulties
d an exceptionally long honeymooner core
s first major crisis – bins – remained close
fund of useful his shadow Cabinet,
essential if team were either given
team xtent to be concealed.
Davis was retained as

with the linked problems
drug abuse, family breako
ronments, high crime. We
broken society. There is su
thing as the state.

It was only after the speec
dawn. Among those calling
World editor Andy Coulsor
names of the new head
undoubtedly need. Another
him and George Osborne fo
Blenheim estate. Suddenly
arrived at the Royal Academ
leader of the Opposition. A
swept down Piccadilly driv
known as Howard's govern
believe at last.

On becoming l
imperative was
really had char
break from th
provision of
believes in a s
it by requirin

In common
tation is the sta
had ged whil
wonder it t

He may have h
months before h
William Hague, a
private office was
of his leadership
Gove and Geor
at hand, Go
public. The
meant th
Defeat
new

shadow Home Secretary, and Hague was persuaded to return, taking from Liam Fox the job of shadow Foreign Secretary with Fox compensated with the defence brief. David Willetts was so comprehensively forgiven that he was handed Cameron's former job as shadow Education Secretary.

Cameron may have been open-handed in his distribution of shadow Cabinet jobs, but in the construction of his private office he appointed only those he trusted. For his chief of staff he chose Ed Llewellyn, whom he has known since Eton. Both claim that their relationship really dates from the 1992 general election. Llewellyn, who had also been at the Conservative Research Department, was Cameron's linkman to John Major when the then Prime Minister was on the road campaigning. After the election he had served as Chris Patten's adviser in Hong Kong before working with Paddy Ashdown in Bosnia Herzegovina (where the former Liberal Democrat leader had been appointed UN High Representative). Patten – his former boss at CRD – holds him in high regard. Llewellyn's neat, bespectacled figure is rarely far from the wings when his leader performs, a small, ironic smile sometimes visible in the shadows. Cameron also recruited another Old Etonian veteran of the Major era: George Bridges, the man he had lined up to replace him at Carlton in 1997. Bridges was not only of the Establishment – his grandfather had been Churchill's private secretary – he was on the sceptical wing of the modernising project. Both features made him a useful foil to Hilton's iconoclastic eccentricities. Cameron's gate-keeper remained Catherine Fall, a scion of the Establishment and yet another former CRD colleague.

But the most important decision Cameron made about his private office was related not to personnel but to location – or rather co-location. Cameron and Osborne had often discussed how the damaging divisions between Tony Blair and Gordon Brown might have been avoided. The new Tory leader had worked for a chancellor, his lieutenant for a prime minister: both knew that the tensions were institutional, not just political or personal. Their solution was to share a suite of offices, on the second floor of Norman Shaw South, one of the House of Commons' more functional buildings. The heart of the Tory leadership in opposition lay in the room between Cameron's and Osborne's offices where both Llewellyn and Matthew Hancock, Osborne's chief of staff, had desks. Llewellyn's open-plan arrangement facilitated easy consultation as well as reducing the scope for mischief-making, muddle and misunderstanding. The most important meeting of Cameron's day – usually at 3.30 p.m. – was with Osborne and Llewellyn.

Before the office arrangements could be finalised Cameron had his first Commons clash. He has said that he couldn't enjoy his leadership victory because no sooner had he won than he had to start rehearsing for his first Prime Minister's Questions. Osborne and Hague helped him prepare. Hague's advice was to drink a heavily sugared cup of tea, to coat the larynx and provide an energy rush. Cameron, who hates sweet tea, followed the advice but felt sick. He needn't have worried: he scored a direct hit on Blair, on whose premiership the clock was ticking. 'You were the future once,' he mocked. In the words of one who helped craft it, the phrase was intended to introduce the theme of 'an inevitable generational shift'.

The new leader took control at an ideal moment to demonstrate commitment to the 'new politics'. Blair was facing a Commons defeat at the hands of Labour backbenchers angry about the dilution of local council control over schools. Cameron supported Blair, the outnumbered centrist reformer of public services, against his left-wing rump. (Two years before, Cameron had rejected calls for just such a symbolic show of values over opportunism when Blair was confronted by a Commons revolt over giving hospitals more autonomy.) Although the tactic of supporting the government when they were right was invaluable in reassuring voters, it didn't give Cameron much of a distinct political personality. He was, after all, supposed to be offering change, not continuity. But laying the emphasis on responsibility too soon risked seeming harsh, reviving memories of Tory 'wars on single mothers' or 'welfare scroungers', and sounding too gloomy for the youthful new star. Cameron needed to win permission to be heard – in the jargon of political experts – before he could truly develop that theme. He needed a vehicle to drive home the message of change – and found it had two wheels.

If there was one issue that defined Cameron's first year as leader of the Opposition, it was the environment. He could credibly claim that solutions to climate change require conservative values of individual responsibility and efficiency and it fitted his emerging localist agenda. But best of all it was a gift to his image-maker-in-chief, Steve Hilton. A willing media lapped up pictures of Cameron cycling to work, wearing shoes made from recycled material and – the high point of this strategy – dog-sledding in the Arctic Circle to inspect at first hand the effects of the warming planet. Cameron even made the environment the theme of his first electoral test, fighting the local council elections under the slogan 'Vote Blue Go Green'. But the freewheeling hit a bad bump in April when his official chauffeur, Terry, was pictured following behind carrying his shoes. Cameron admitted that, although he had been cycling from Finstock Road to the Commons, his official car had been ferrying clothes and documents. 'It was a mistake,' he lamented later. 'It happened two or three times. I now have panniers.'

While the environment was his main message to voters, candidate selection was his priority with the party. Hague had fought a bloody but largely unsuccessful war with local Conservative associations to get them to select more women and non-white candidates. Duncan Smith and Howard, too, had declared that the party had to become more representative of the population at large. Yet white, mostly wealthy men overwhelmingly dominated as candidates in winnable seats. Within two weeks of Cameron's victory, the Tories moved ahead of Labour in the polls for the first time since the fuel crisis in 2000. By the end of the year the party was recording its best poll positions since 1993 and Cameron was determined to use his power as the new leader to succeed where Hague had failed. He introduced a so-called A-list of centrally approved candidates to be considered for seats. John Hayes, a junior education spokesman and a right-winger currently under reconstruction, was incautious enough to voice publicly the private opinion of many of his colleagues. The A-list, he said, was 'a bizarre theory of people who spend too much time with the pseuds and posers of London's chi-chi set and not enough time in normal Britain'. The A-list itself was quietly dropped a little over a year later, but a requirement that local associations' shortlists should be at least 50 per cent female began to change the nature of the party's candidates. By the end of 2008 the Tories could claim that a third of winnable seats had female candidates and around 5 per cent of their candidates were people from ethnic minorities.

Efforts to foster a sense of ownership of the Cameron project through grassroots participation were nevertheless among the least successful of this early period of his leadership. In February 2006 he set to work on a mission statement which would be put to a membership vote. The manifesto, entitled *Built to Last* and launched ahead of the party's spring conference, was designed to flush out opponents on the right. Their opposition would allow Cameron to win both publicity for his message and a mandate for reform from the grassroots. It was another idea that was too clever by half. The right, spotting the trap, stayed silent and the document was mostly ignored. It had to be relaunched in August just before the proposed referendum, prompting Labour jeers that it should be retitled *Built to Last a Bit Longer*. The next month, when the result of the referendum was announced, Cameron stood on the steps of Leeds Civic Hall proclaiming a 'big exercise in party democracy and an overwhelming vote'. The figures showed a different story. Only a little over a quarter of those eligible to vote – 26.6 per cent – had bothered to do so. Commentators were quick to draw an unflattering comparison with Blair. When he had tried the same trick the year after his election as Labour leader in 1996, he secured a turnout of 61 per cent for his document *New Labour, New Life*.

Nowhere were the conflicting demands to rebrand and to reassure in such acute competition as they were over crime. Alongside the issue of the environment, Cameron spent the first half of 2006 tentatively sketching the responsibility theme. His first target was business. 'Britain faces an obesity crisis, why does W. H. Smith promote half-price chocolate oranges at its checkouts instead of real oranges?' he asked in a speech in January 2006. But altering the location of confectionery in shops was hardly going to heal Britain's 'broken society', the phrase that Cameron had lifted from Fox's leadership bid and made his own.

Ever mindful of the need to balance traditionalists with modernisers, he had brought in Danny Kruger to partner Doug Smith – now transformed as an ultra-moderniser – in his speech-writing team. Kruger, a softly spoken, likeable ideologue, had worked with Duncan Smith on his version of compassionate conservatism. His agenda of active citizenship, volunteering and fraternity, rooted in the Christian right, tallied with Hilton's vision for the Cameron leadership. Stressing a collective, moral responsibility for healing the 'broken society' offered a way of reintroducing, detoxified, the traditional themes of law and order. When Kruger, in his first speech for the leader, attempted to do just that, it proved to be Cameron's first critical disaster. The subject matter, youth crime and its causes, was tricky enough, but Cameron's message that anti-social youths needed to be led to emotional maturity through love proved too much. When reminded of his speech to the Centre for Social Justice in July 2006 Cameron never fails to point out that he never said 'hug a hoodie', the headline used by a Sunday newspaper and picked up with glee by Cameron's critics. His actual words, nevertheless, remain startling:

> Crime, drugs, underage sex – this behaviour is wrong, but simply blaming the kids who get involved in it doesn't really get us much further. It is what the culture around them encourages ... If the consequence of stepping over the line should be painful, then staying within the bounds of good behaviour should be pleasant. And I believe that inside those boundaries we have to show a lot more love.

Sir Nicholas Winterton, then Tory MP for Macclesfield, voiced the mood of perplexed concern among the grassroots when asked for his comment by the *Daily Telegraph* the next day. 'I'm not sure what my leader is seeking to do. Perhaps he is trying to be more inclusive but that does not mean pandering to people who are anti-social.'

By the time his first party conference as leader came round that October, Cameron had decided he had to take on his party while his mandate was still fresh. Osborne was facing increasing heat from right-wingers who wanted him to make firm commitments on reducing tax, and the discontent over the A-list rumbled on. Worse, the drafts of his main leader's speech were a mess. Samantha, who came to three final speech meetings, 'tore the thing apart'. 'No, no, no! You can't say that. You want to say it like this.' One figure remembers a furious Hilton, in T-shirt and jeans, staying up all night chain-smoking, to knock the speech into shape. The contrast with Cameron's approach is illuminating. 'David's reaction was, "Well, it's not great, but it'll have to do."' (Hilton sometimes doubts the extent of Cameron's zeal.)

Early in his leadership Cameron had reached a key strategic decision: to make the health service his number-one priority and to settle for good any suggestion that the question of its funding could be reopened. On reappointing Andrew Lansley to the health brief when he became leader, he had told him that winning voters' trust on the health service was an 'overwhelming strategic priority'. 'From the moment David became leader we all knew that establishing our credentials on the NHS was absolutely essential,' says a senior aide. Cameron chose to educate his party in directly personal terms:

> When your family relies on the NHS all the time – day after day, night after night – you really know just how precious it is ... For me, it's not a question of saying the NHS is 'safe in my hands'. My family is so often in the hands of the NHS. And I want them to be safe there ... We will always support the NHS with the funding it needs.

His commitment to public services – particularly health and education – doesn't fit neatly into the script of those who see Cameron in purely class terms. Ivan meant he had more experience of the NHS than most but his schooling was as far from state education as is possible in this country. Although he believes in the universality of both services, there is a second difference: his prescriptions for the health service are largely conservative while those for education are radical. 'There is a world of difference between the schemes for improving the health service drawn up by fit young men in their thirties who've never been anywhere near it, and the experience of anyone who's actually had to rely on the thing,' says one ally. He adds that Cameron's view is that 'The Conservative Party has never had to rely on it, as I have – therefore I understand it better than the rest of the party, and better than – or at least in the same way as – the rest of the country.'

Cameron cannot, of course, speak from the same personal experience when it comes to state education, but friends insist that, if anything, he is even more passionate about that issue. He is known to have had long, disapproving conversations about the policy adopted at the 2005 election when, as a colleague puts it, the aim was to get individuals to opt out of the state system, rather than to persuade institutions from outside the state system to opt in and so provide opportunities and challenges for those educated by the state. It was Cameron's passion for raising educational standards across the board that helped persuade the carpet millionaire and philanthropist Phil Harris to endorse his campaign for the leadership. 'He is genuinely bewildered by the way in which Tory local authorities take educational underperformance for granted. Samantha is incensed that Conservative councils in London tolerate the poor level of educational performance that they do,' says a colleague. 'What he absolutely thinks is, rich people overwhelmingly buy an education for their children, which enables their children to more easily pass examinations and then make the sorts of choices that they want. The problem for poorer people is that the well-meaning say, "Ah yes, well, you need a different sort of education" from the sort they would necessarily buy for their own children, and as a result you have this terrible situation whereby poorer children have been let down by not having access to an education of the same rigour, quality, standards, level of aspiration and ambition.' The sincerity of this belief would explain why he finds charges of snobbery so wounding that he developed a blind spot in relation to his background – a blind spot that concealed a disaster fast approaching.

In an interview with the *Daily Telegraph* to mark the end of his first year as leader, Cameron said: 'I don't go out of my way to annoy anybody but I want to change the Conservative Party and get us back to the centre ground.' But, given the relentless pace he had set himself and in his heavy reliance on the same, increasingly weary advisers, the balancing act between rebranding and reassurance was beginning to wobble. The great irony of 'grammargate' was that it concerned a fight Cameron thought that he had already won. When during his leadership campaign he broke with the previous Tory policy of encouraging grammars to 'survive and thrive', it caused a minor stir.

He had, after all, helped write the grammar school policy into Michael Howard's manifesto and subsequently had supported it as education spokesman. But it had not caught light as an issue.

So when Cameron's successor in that post, the cerebral David Willetts, announced that he wanted to make a key speech, the only concern was that it lacked an obvious headline. 'Our main fear was that it wasn't really newsy enough,' recalls one of those charged with reading Willetts's intended text for an address to the CBI. Another says that Cameron himself flicked through a draft and 'had a conversation … about how to make it more interesting'. The shadow Cabinet at which the speech was discussed was not in fact chaired by Cameron (Hilton had persuaded him to spend two days as a teaching assistant in Hull). Willetts is absolved by a colleague of misleading the meeting when he said that the speech's primary intention was to set out new policy on making it easier to set up academy schools free from local council control.

Nevertheless one of Cameron's aides was aghast on hearing a radio interview with the shadow education spokesman on the morning before the speech. 'He was saying things that he'd never said in any of the meetings I'd been at.' Although Willetts was subsequently deeply shocked, he had intended to be provocative. In explaining his motives a friend says that he was convinced that only by making a dramatic renunciation of selection could the Tories hope to be heard, and believed, when they spoke about education. Somehow no one in Cameron's office had spotted that Willetts was picking a defining fight with the traditionalists – as well as core supporters – when he claimed that grammar schools serve only the middle class whose children dominated their intake. The key passage read: 'We must break free from the belief that academic selection is any longer the way to transform the life chances of bright poor kids. We have to recognise that there is overwhelming evidence that such academic selection entrenches advantage, it does not spread it.'

The backlash was immediate. Members of Cameron's staff recall the 'warning lights going off all over the place'. MPs, candidates, activists began bombarding the Tory high command in protest almost as soon as Willetts had sat down. Ominously, at least one front-bencher, Graham Brady, promptly and publicly rejected the central claim that grammars did nothing to help social mobility. To give an impression of party discipline Brady was reprimanded by Patrick McLoughlin, the Opposition Chief Whip and former miner, but the real fury in the whips' office was directed at Willetts himself. The Tory leader, still in Hull, was persuaded that Willetts should be made to explain his speech to a meeting of the Tory backbench 1922 Committee. Far from allowing for a managed deflation, the meeting in Committee Room 14 turned into a ritual humiliation. After Willetts had given his account and two MPs had spoken in his favour – Ed Vaizey and Stuart Jackson – the condemnation began. Dangerously, his critics came from all sections of the party. Sitting in the front row and looking sulphurous was Michael Howard, who loudly banged the desk in support as the blows rained down. Howard was proud of being a grammar school boy and as a Kent MP served a constituency that still had state-funded selective schools. The former leader was so angry that the next day he began to write a piece for the *Daily Telegraph* attacking his successor. It was only the intervention of Rachel Whetstone, his former chief of staff, which prevented a full-frontal attack. Instead Howard 'told friends' in a Sunday newspaper that weekend that he was 'livid'. He added, 'I can remain silent no longer' – both a threat and a rebuff to Whetstone's charm offensive.

Cameron called round his key allies that Sunday. Hilton, who vowed never to talk to Howard again, was for confrontation, as was Oliver Letwin, who attacked the whips for 'hanging Willetts out to dry' at the 1922. If the party wanted a fight, it would have one. At a press conference the next week Cameron gave his critics a 'clear and uncompromising message'. Pledging to build more grammars, he said, would be an 'electoral albatross' and those who said otherwise were 'delusional'. 'This is a key test for our party,' he said. 'Does it want to be a serious force for government and change, or does it want to be a right-wing debating society muttering about what might have been?'

His most senior supporters now believe that this escalation was a serious mistake. In impugning the good faith of his critics, Cameron opened himself up to a personal line of attack. What right had an Old Etonian to deny others a selective education? The question was posed by John Humphrys on the *Today* programme and then again and again in leading articles and comment pieces, particularly in the *Daily Telegraph* and the *Daily Mail*, where Cameron's enemies scented blood. The irony, of course, was that the decision to engage in the grammar school debate had been taken in order to soften the party's elitist image. Hilton believed that it was vital that Cameron showed that he cared for all children – not just the middle classes.

As the row dragged on into a second weekend the Tory leader hit back at those who had used his background against him: they were, he insisted, 'inverse class warriors'. He added that the row over grammars was 'over'. But nobody had told Brady, who produced evidence in *The Times* the next day which, he said, disproved Willetts's claim that selective schools damaged social mobility. To underline how weakened Cameron's authority had become, Brady was reprimanded (again), and he resigned the next day after authorised briefing suggested that he would be sacked in the approaching reshuffle. It was Dominic Grieve, the shadow Attorney General, who dealt the killer blow when he used forensic skills honed by years at the Bar to point out that the official Conservative policy in fact allowed for more grammar schools to be built in those areas that already had them. The Tory leader had apparently gone to war with his party over a misreading of his own policy. Hilton wanted Cameron to sack Grieve, but Brady was already being hailed as the grammar school martyr. Besides, what exactly was Grieve supposed to be sacked *for*?

Throughout the controversy Cameron had denied that this was his 'Clause IV moment' – a reference to Blair's symbolic fight with his party. Blair had selected his ground and had fought a battle on it that he knew he would win and be shown to have won. A key lesson the Tory leader learned from grammargate, by contrast, was that he had allowed himself to be tempted into a fight not of his choosing where 'victory' lay in not abandoning a policy he had announced more than a year before. Reviewing the episode later, one senior Tory reached for a domestic analogy: 'In any relationship if the husband takes the wife for granted there will be one thing trivial in and of itself, an act of thoughtlessness, which will lead the simmering resentment to come to the boil and that's what happened.' The thinness of Cameron's parliamentary and media support came as a shock. The vehemence of the *Daily Telegraph* in particular brought home the realisation, in the words of one Cameron ally, that that newspaper was being run by an 'uneasy coalition of Brown worshippers and Thatcher nostalgics'.

The inquest focused on the failure to spot the dangers when Willetts had submitted his original draft. 'We knew there had been a massive breakdown,' said an insider. 'Everyone thought someone else had done the bit of work to actually check what was going to be asked, what the answers were to specific questions. Meetings had taken place [where] everyone had a different understanding about what the purpose was … and what we'd agreed.' For one key player it had been only a matter of time before the bandwagon that had been careering along for almost two years would come to grief. 'Given how fast we'd been moving, we'd actually been managing to avoid most if not all such traps. This was the first one we fell into and it was one hell of a trap.'

Grammargate had raised the issue of class. During the Conservatives' leadership election Blair had told a newspaper editor at a private lunch: 'The Tories need to understand that the back-story doesn't matter, it's the message that counts.' In the event the Tories rejected David Davis's council-house, single-parent back-story and elected an Old Etonian who admits that his CV is 'corny'. But since in Britain class, like the poor, will always be with us it was inevitable that it would return. Newspapers began noticing just how many fellow former pupils of Cameron's old school inhabited his private office and frontbenches. The publication of the Bullingdon photograph in the first edition of this book drew further unwelcome attention. The image was subsequently withdrawn by the copyright holders for future newspaper use, prompting allegations that it has been suppressed.

Perception of wealth could be as much of a problem to a party leader as class. Their own personal finances suggest that David and Samantha Cameron are, by most voters' definition, well off – but by the standards of most of their friends they are disadvantaged. When they bought their house on on King North Street on 11 May 2006 they paid £1,125,000 without a mortgage. They bought a second home in Dean, Oxfordshire for £650,000, this time with the help of a mortgage. The couple made a profit of just under a million pounds on Finstock Road. Cameron also had a windfall, but a much more modest one, on his purchase of 100,000 shares in the bar business Urbium, on top of his £28,000-a-year fee for being a non-executive director of the firm. Samantha Cameron's stepfather, Viscount Astor, sat with David Cameron on the board of Urbium. Indeed it had been his step-father-in-law who got him the job. John Conlon, the firm's head concedes the 'recommendation was important. But, quite frankly if David had not been up to it he would not have been taken on, whether Lord Astor was his father-in-law or brother or whatever.' In 2005 Samantha made between £250,000 and £400,000 when the management buy-out team sold Smythsons for £15.5 million. She said the sum was 'nothing life-changing, that's why I'm still working'. Cameron might not be embarrassingly rich, but class was still liable to trip him up. 'Hug a hoodie' had shown how easily a single speech could be caricatured. Grammargate had shown how Cameron and Osborne, two 'posh boys', were in danger of themselves being lampooned.

The Tory leader had known for some time that he had two significant personnel gaps in his operation: a press secretary to protect him from the media and a chief executive to get a grip on the party machine. But both recruitments had proved far from easy. George Eustice, who ran Cameron's press operation from the moment his leadership challenge was launched, was never likely to be Cameron's Alastair Campbell. In June 2005, as Cameron was preparing to stand for the party leadership, Eustice, a senior Conservative Party press officer, had agreed to join the team but it was always assumed that it wouldn't be for ever and that one day they might need to bring in 'a Nick Robinson or somebody'. After Cameron became leader, the idea was mooted in Cameron's office of hiring someone to liaise with 'opinion formers' – editors, comment editors and columnists. Cameron, Osborne, Hilton and George Bridges, both together and separately (which was not without its difficulties), set about finding a suitable candidate.

The *Sun*'s outgoing political editor was approached, but he turned them down. Sarah Sands, who had been editing the *Sunday Telegraph*, Martha Kearney of *Newsnight* and Ian Birrell of the *Independent* were also sounded out, before Guto Harri emerged as the likeliest to say yes. Harri had got to know Rachel Whetstone, Michael Howard's former chief of staff, when he was covering the election campaign of 2005, and impressed Steve Hilton when, in November of that year, Whetstone had invited Harri – by then working in New York – to a Google conference in California.

Steve Hilton persisted in pushing Harri's claims, which culminated in the full Cameron charm initiative (a family barbecue at Dean). In a characteristically self-mocking manner, Cameron warned Harri that moving back to the UK from the US was a big step to take to work for someone whose three most recent predecessors had barely troubled the scorers, but that he should go away and think about the matter over the summer. In fact the courtship was over, with Harri left hanging.

In early 2007, with Harri's position still undetermined, the game changed. A major (but unannounced) shift of strategy was in the offing. In earlier times, Cameron's media team, led by Eustice and Hilton and with the support of Oliver Letwin, had adopted a strategy of arms' length engagement with the press. Hilton was among those who believed that no longer was the printed word a major leader of public opinion. People were now less deferential to thunderous editorials from on high. They made up their own minds, thank you, with the help of TV channels, information from the internet and their immediate surroundings. Bolstered by opinion data, some of it provided by his partner Rachel Whetstone, Hilton and Eustice had sold his boss the idea of a new arrangement with the press barons, whereby a greater, healthier distance was kept and the democratic process would be all the better for it. Television was to be the new battleground. There was to be 'no more sucking up to Murdoch' because there was no need for it. It was a defiant and refreshing departure from the Tony Blair textbook.

There were to be other, tougher aspects of this new approach, and they had largely been vindicated, not least when a well-prepared Cameron outfoxed Jeremy Paxman during the leadership campaign. Cameron and his team had taken a muscularly non-committal approach to mounting calls to 'come clean' on whether the leader had ever taken Class A drugs. Editors in supportive papers who offered to 'do the drugs story sympathetically' were politely told that Cameron was allowed to have a past, before he became a politician, that was free of scrutiny. Similarly, when the *Daily Mirror* followed Cameron on his bike and filmed him going through red lights, his office toughed it out, saying 'this is not a story' and refusing to comment, which effectively killed it. In other words, Cameron's people expressed a novel 'no thanks, we'll play this game our way' attitude. And it seemed to be working. In August 2006, the Tories had established a good lead in the polls. Such insolence was not appreciated by the Murdoch-owned *Sun*, which asserted in its leader column that Cameron did not deserve his lead. Murdoch's critics took this to mean 'we have not endorsed him yet.

But the plan was to turn out to be no more than an experiment. By early 2007, the sunny hopes for a new politics were already fading. Cameron was struggling to convince a great many in his party that he was a Conservative at all, and with the Labour government anticipating a rise in their poll ratings with the expected accession of the comparatively untainted figure of Gordon Brown, the arms' length relationship with the Murdochs looked needlessly bold. The previous summer he had made the notorious proclamation that became known as his 'hug a hoodie' speech. The press reception had been hostile, but for Eustice and Hilton this was no more than was to be expected. 'Yes, yes, we'll carry on,' said Cameron, evidently less convinced than his aides. At their encouragement, 'to show we wouldn't be bullied', as one confidant put it, he followed up with a speech of comparable tone and surprise value. Cameron was the object of yet more consternation from his natural supporters and their mouthpieces in the press. When his closest media advisers proposed a third such speech, Cameron, in a typically Cameronian way, said 'I'm *sure* you're right … but how much more of this do we have to do?' To emphasise his declining faith in the new approach, he invited comparison with the never-say-die 'invincible knight' from *Monty Python and the Holy Grail*, whose bravado led him to having all his limbs cut off but who insisted on shouting fatuously at his triumphant adversary 'Tis but a flesh wound!'. This was Cameron's lighthearted way of saying enough was enough.

In fact he felt things were getting very serious. With the austere but principled Gordon Brown waiting to sweep away the perception of Labour as polished but shallow, Cameron needed to be at the top of his game. Indeed, what would happen if Brown was to call an early election? Cameron knew Brown had good relations with both Rupert Murdoch and Paul Dacre, Editor-in-Chief of the *Daily Mail*. Why should either newspaper group go against the personal preference of its most senior executive and endorse Cameron? Charlie Brooks, who at that point was at the start of his relationship with Rebekah Wade, told a friend that Rupert Murdoch – whose pedigree in picking winners was second to none – believed there would never be another Etonian in No. 10 again. The thought occurred to Cameron that he could be out of his job by the end of the year. 'David got very tetchy at around that time,' says Cameron's friend. 'His apparent breezy confidence often hides a lack of exactly that, and David had a really major wobble that spring.'

'We tested the new strategy to destruction,' remembers George Eustice. 'But the knowledge that Gordon Brown, the ultimate licker-of-the boots of the Murdoch regime, was coming in meant that Cameron was likely to be portrayed as loftily out of touch rather than right, so we had to abandon the experiment. David stuck with my strategy as long as he could,' remembers Eustice, 'but having reluctantly abandoned the "keep your distance" approach, he then embraced the "OK, let's do what everyone else does", and let's do it properly stance.' Someone else close to Cameron's thinking added: 'George Osborne in particular, and to a lesser extent Michael Gove, thought it was part of the New Labour playbook to get Murdoch on side. Keen on the traditional idea of wooing the media. We might not like it, it's just the way of the world. However unpleasant these people may be, however much you may not like them, you have to play their game and go to their parties.'

So, notwithstanding Cameron's previous coolness to Murdoch, a legacy of Carlton TV's defeats at the Australian's hands, it was all systems go to get Murdoch on side. The brave talk ('We don't need bloody Murdoch!', as one of Cameron's strategists had put it privately) was set to one side, and every opportunity to impress News International was to be grasped with alacrity. As luck (if that is the word) would have it, there seemed an admirable way of killing two birds with one stone close at hand.

Rebekah Wade, then editor of the *Sun*, was among those who could see how a problem might turn into an opportunity. George Osborne suggested to Cameron that, rather than take Harri, he should give the job to Coulson.

Although Coulson was not a notably political figure, his tabloid experience plugged an obvious hole and his Essex background was an obvious plus. To a clique of public schoolboys terrified of seeming out of touch, Coulson was perfect. He was *a real person*. He was in touch with real people, or so the Cameron inner circle liked to believe. His influence with the media helped keep Cameron's right-wing backbenchers at bay. (One MP was to remark much later that Coulson was 'the only real Conservative in Downing Street', evidently unaware – as were many in the party – that Coulson had been a Blair voter.) He would also be able to tell the leader, for example (as he did some months after the 2010 election), that it would not help Cameron's quest to show he understood the concerns of 'ordinary people' – not least those in his own constituency – if he was to allow his third home, his base in Dean, to be sub-let. To compound the insensitivity, the prospective lessee was an Old Etonian friend. While the dangers of this might seem obvious to some, to those close to Cameron it was merciful evidence that no one would accuse Cameron of being out of touch while Coulson was around. The snag was his recent past. That January, the *News of the World*'s royal reporter Clive Goodman had been sent to prison for four months for intercepting hundreds of mobile phone messages left for aides of senior royals. Also involved was Glenn Mulcaire, a 'security consultant', who was sentenced to six months for his part in these and other phone interceptions. Coulson resigned as editor, saying that Goodman's actions were entirely wrong 'and I deeply regret that they happened on my watch'.

His resignation might have drawn a line under the affair but it also had the effect of closing down further scrutiny of the newspaper's operations. Until the matter was formally settled, the *News of the World* refused to say whether Coulson had known what Goodman and Mulcaire were doing. The question was not invalid. It emerged in the court case that Mulcaire received an annual salary of £104,988 for research and 'surveillance'. But it was further alleged that he had also received an illicit £12,300 for phone tapping, paid by Goodman from fiddled expenses. One former *News of the World* employee says, 'You can't buy a sandwich on expenses without somebody questioning it in that office.' Coulson's friend Piers Morgan, who himself had had to resign from editing the *Mirror*, said: 'As for Clive Goodman, I feel a lot of sympathy for a man who has been the convenient fall guy for an investigative practice that everyone knows was going on at almost every paper in Fleet Street for years.'

Cameron's mind was made up and in late May 2007 he appointed Coulson as his Director of Communications.

The effect was instant. The operation acquired a more professional and hard-nosed demeanour. Journalists not notably friendly to the Cameron project, who previously had enjoyed an easy-come, easy-go relationship with the leader, found access more limited. In policy decisions, too, Coulson could be relied upon to provide a dose of down-to-earth realism to counter, for example, some of Steve Hilton's more fanciful and easily ridiculed notions. Relations, initially at least, were more respectful than some have suggested, but the pair were cut from a wholly different cloth. One of those intimately involved in their relationship denies they had major fallings out, but said there was a dysfunctional atmosphere. 'Steve felt that because so many of the main players had known one another so long, they could easily have robust arguments about work in the context of basically liking and admiring one another, but that was never the case with Andy and Steve,' he said.

As a press minder, Coulson was considered a great success. As far as most of the media was concerned, he was what David Cameron had needed, even if he didn't necessarily make their jobs any easier. There was little criticism of his competence – as Cameron was to claim a little desperately later on in the saga – or, indeed, of David Cameron's decision to appoint him. The *Daily Mail* welcomed the arrival by the Tory leader's side of 'an able and likeable professional'. Lance Price, a former media minder for Tony Blair, could see the sense of appointing someone who retained Murdoch's respect. 'The Tory leader,' wrote Price, 'knows that, as yet, Murdoch doesn't take him seriously. It must sicken Cameron to see the News International titles giving such generous coverage to Brown, a man whose redistributive tax regime, pensions policy and so much else is anathema to them.'

With the arrival of Coulson, traditional Tory themes (crime, immigration, lower taxes) came to appear more in Tory statements. He discouraged (some would say prevented) Steve Hilton from making public utterances, and had a major hand in the distribution of portfolios among special advisers, which didn't endear him to some. Cameron welcomed Coulson and on occasion took his advice unwillingly in order not to offend him. But some of Cameron's long-term circle were resentful. 'He took him into the inner circle and allowed Coulson an influence that some around the cabinet table felt was undue,' said one. And Coulson took a little while to come to terms with the style of his new boss. When Tony Blair made his famous 'feral beasts' speech about the media, Coulson suggested Cameron make a speech denouncing Blair, which would be a way of winning favour with Paul Dacre of the *Daily Mail*. But other voices at Cameron's side pointed out that in Blair's speech there was not much with which Cameron could disagree, and he ignored Coulson's advice. Coulson also struggled to convince his master over the leader's truncated trip to Rwanda, as well as of the wisdom of meeting a number of B-list celebrities offering little obvious traction to the Tory leader.

Not only was grammargate the end of Cameron's honeymoon, he knew that Brown was preparing to enjoy his own romance with the voters. To complicate matters further, the six policy-formulation groups set up the previous year were now finalising their reports. The groups had been, in part, Cameron's way of involving figures like Ken Clarke and John Redwood without giving them shadow Cabinet jobs. Now a blizzard of policy proposals, many unhelpful if not downright eccentric, was coming his way. Cameron's response was to add another layer of consultation. 'Stand Up Speak Out – the Nation's Despatch Box' was launched in mid-June, billed as the public's chance to inform the next manifesto. The fears of some in Cameron's office that the project was an expensive waste of time, as doomed to failure as other innovations like the mayoral primaries or *Built to Last*, were to be largely justified as it slowly sank without trace despite a bill thought to be around £250,000.

Although the Tory leader was keener than ever on 'political cross-dressing' – the phrase Blair had coined partly to describe Cameron's appropriation of the left's language and symbols – he was careful to include tweed, twinset and pearls in the wardrobe. On 18 June 2007 he gave a speech in Tooting designed to position the Tories as 'progressives' while reassuring traditional supporters that the idea of 'social responsibility' rooted his project firmly in Conservativism. In the *Daily Telegraph* Simon Heffer called it 'philosophically naive and vacuous'. The *Guardian* leader meanwhile drily noted, 'David Cameron yesterday compared reconstructing the Conservative party to building a house, and if the metaphor is correct then he must now be staring at heaps of rubble, cement and copper piping, hoping that the architect's plans come together before the first tenants move in.' It was worse than that. The policy process meant there were dozens of architects and hundreds of plans; an accident on such a building site wasn't just likely, it was guaranteed.

Cameron asked Osborne quietly to oversee Letwin, who was supposed to be making sure the policy groups stuck to the task of realising the Tory leader's vision – not, as they appeared to be doing, indulging their own preoccupations and prejudices. The attempt to get a grip came too late, alas, to save Hugo Swire's career, which was ruined when he agreed to speak in advance about what the policy group on culture was considering. His artless suggestion that the Tories would allow museums and art galleries to restore admission charging reignited the issue of class still smouldering from grammargate. Yet again an Old Etonian was seen to be forbidding the poor entry to improving institutions. Hilton, who had never liked the urbane Swire, forced the shadow Culture Secretary to repudiate his own words and insist that the policy was still under review. Two weeks later Cameron sacked one of his earliest supporters and closest political friends in a reshuffle. 'I thought it the right thing to do,' Cameron later said of Swire's ejection. 'I will probably have to fire many friends,' he added. Willetts too paid a price, although he was only shunted sideways to be replaced by Michael Gove. Jeremy Hunt, Grant Shapps, Nick Herbert and Sayeeda Warsi were brought in to 'freshen the team'. The last appointment required Warsi's elevation to the House of Lords – despite his reforms Cameron couldn't wait for the articulate Muslim Tory woman to be selected in a winnable seat.

David Cameron was at his best on Tony Blair's last day as Prime Minister. He paid generous tribute to a man he admires more than it is sensible for him to admit publicly. Blair, he said, had 'considerable achievements to his credit', and he then urged his own MPs – some of whom complied only reluctantly – to their feet to give him a standing ovation. Few quotes have caused him as much trouble as his claim at a private dinner in October 2005 to be the 'heir to Blair'. The remark was supposed to set Blair in a Conservative tradition which Cameron was determined to reclaim. Instead it has ensured that he is endlessly compared to Labour's most successful leader and is accused of simply aping his methods to win power. Critics suspect mutual admiration. It is extraordinary just how many of Blair's backroom staff towards the end of his regime were on good terms with the Conservative leader. John McTernan, a former director of political operations in Blair's Number 10, was a former colleague of Cameron's at Carlton and has called him 'genuinely talented'. Ben Wegg-Prosser, Number 10's director of strategic communications, numbers Cameron in a circle of Tory friends that includes Ed Vaizey and Hilton. And Philip Collins, Blair's former speech-writer and a novelist, has as his agent Tif Loehnis (wife of Dom Loehnis). A Labour friend of both Cameron and Blair recalls Cameron's repeated expressions of admiration for the political skills of Blair (and Mandelson) throughout the 1990s. By contrast he was said to have called Major a 'loser'. For his part Blair remarked on the speed with which Cameron had taken to his job. 'He's been impressed with how quickly he's got his head round PMQs.' One figure in regular contact with Blair in the last months of his premiership said he was 'fascinated by the phenomenon of David Cameron'.

But in Cameron's first year as leader the imagery of the conflict between Cameron and Brown was already pugilistic. Blair described the Tory leader as a 'flyweight' who would meet a 'big clunking fist' when Brown became Prime Minister. Cameron also replied with violent similes, repeatedly borrowing from George Orwell to describe a Brown government as 'like a boot stamping on a human face – for ever'. An overheard exchange between Cameron and Michael Heseltine on the eve of Blair's departure gives a flavour of the private view. 'We're quite happy Blair's going. He's trying to get out of the shit and can't. Brown thinks he still can, so we have to push his face back in it.' 'That strange man in Downing Street' was how Cameron described Brown in an interview with *The Times*. The animus on both sides was real – or in a phrase that Cameron sometimes likes to employ, 'not just political, but personal'. Aside from Brown himself, Ed Balls attracts particular vitriol from the Tory leadership. Balls is an exact Oxford contemporary of Cameron and also read PPE – Balls got a higher first-class degree, something that will matter to both of them. (Balls was briefly a member of the Oxford University Conservative Association, a body that Cameron avoided.)

Cameron knew that Brown had spent months if not years planning for the moment when power passed into his hands. Within hours of leading the applause for Blair he was given a taste of what was to come when he was handed a letter from Quentin Davies, a Tory MP for twenty years, who had set his face against the new leader. 'Although you have many positive qualities you have three, superficiality, unreliability and an apparent lack of any clear convictions, which in my view ought to exclude you from the position of national leadership to which you aspire,' wrote Davies in a polemic that could have been written by Brown himself.

If Cameron was right to wave aside the Davies defection as a one-day wonder he could not so easily ignore the incursions into traditional Tory territory clearly designed to fracture his base support. Over the coming months Brown invited Margaret Thatcher for tea in Downing Street, ditched super-casinos, distanced himself from twenty-four-hour drinking and cleared the way for the reclassification of cannabis as a Class B drug. The strategy was clear: Brown was aggravating Cameron's strained relationship with his base while smothering the centre ground with a series of announcements and appointments that spoke to themes of moral purpose and national unity.

The death of the Labour MP Piara Khabra in June 2007 posed an electoral test of this attempt to squeeze Cameron. The Conservatives had come only third in Khabra's Ealing Southall constituency at the

2005 election and the seat had not therefore featured much on the party's target lists. Cameron had to choose whether to write the seat off and appear defeatist or rise to the challenge and throw all he could at it in an attempt to take the gloss off Brown's honeymoon. Cameron chose the latter course, visited the seat five times, allowed his own name to be put on the ballot paper – and was defeated. The week before the poll on 19 July the Conservative candidate, Tony Lit, was revealed to have attended a very recent Labour fundraising dinner. Columnists declared the campaign a hubristic shambles: despite all the hype, the party had come third. Cameron had shown his inexperience in believing what he was told about how well the campaign was going. Deborah Mattinson, Brown's pollster, previewed what would become Labour's key attack line when she said the result proved that while 'slick communication skills may have been enough to put him on the map a year ago the electorate has moved on and such slickness is simply not enough now'.

And when it rains, it pours: summer floods hit Witney almost as soon as the votes had been counted in Ealing. With large portions of his constituency under water, this was not an ideal moment for Cameron to fly to a remote African nation. But scores of Tory volunteers who had given up two weeks of the summer holidays to volunteer in Rwanda were waiting in Kigali – along with the Rwandan president and half a dozen journalists sent to cover the trip – for Cameron's arrival on a long-arranged visit due to start that Sunday. Cameron hurriedly arranged a constituency excursion during which he wore Wellington boots, a suit and a concerned expression. The broadcast media ignored the tour. If the Tory leader had any remaining doubts about how unfair politics can be to an underdog they would have been settled by that Sunday's papers. One columnist mused that Cameron might be, not the Tories' Blair figure, but their Neil Kinnock. Most damaging was a report in the *Sunday Telegraph* that at least two MPs had sent letters to Sir Michael Spicer, chairman of the 1922 Committee, asking for a vote of no confidence. Although twenty-seven short of the number needed to trigger a vote, the letters were, the paper asserted, the 'first concrete evidence of rebellion'. Cameron had had a ring-side seat at Iain Duncan Smith's defenestration and knew only too well how self-fulfilling stories of rebellion could become. Was this, a moment of high danger, really the right time to hand his critics a stick with which to beat him?

As Dean, like the rest of central England lay under sodden skies, Cameron put off the packing of his tropical kit to make a series of telephone calls. Andy Coulson, making his first significant intervention, wanted him at least to delay departure to enable a second floods photocall. Steve Hilton was keen that the Rwandan trip should go ahead but supported the idea of a delay. George Osborne was also in favour but urged Cameron to cancel a second trip to Pakistan due to take place shortly after he returned from Rwanda. Coulson agreed that the Pakistan trip should be ditched. Hilton did not. Andrew Mitchell, whom Cameron had made shadow international development secretary, had led the advance party to Rwanda. He was patched into one conference call as he travelled by bus to a genocide memorial and, surrounded by journalists, was alerted to the possibility that Cameron might delay or cancel.

George Eustice, however, argued that the Tory leader would exacerbate rather than alleviate the panic if he changed plans. Cameron was due to address the 1922 Committee on the following Wednesday, Eustice pointed out, making it impossible to delay the trip to any useful extent. The only way to ensure that he could fly out and come back in time would be to hire a private plane. Everyone could see the presentational issues that would arise if he landed at Kigali airport in a Learjet. It came down to a simple choice: go today or cancel. In the end Cameron believed that Eustice was right: the greater risk lay in not going. If he went, he would be portrayed as abandoning his core supporters for the sake of a cynical media stunt; but if he stayed it would be worse. So Cameron went, but the issue divides his team to this day. Osborne has changed his mind and believes it was the wrong call. Eustice, Mitchell and Hilton all believe he was right to stick to his guns. Cameron says in public that it was right to go, but is much less certain in private.

Faced with the increasing likelihood that Gordon Brown would cash in on a 10-point poll lead and call an autumn election David Cameron curtailed his summer holiday. During such time as he did spend away from Westminster he reflected on what had gone wrong – and on what he could do to put it right. Grammargate, Ealing and Rwanda had so alienated him from core Conservative support that he had been brought to the edge of a serious leadership challenge.

It was time for a change of direction. The most urgent need was to reconnect with his base. If that reduced Brown's lead to the point where it killed speculation about a snap election, so much the better. Cameron, whose embrace of the modernisation project was always more pragmatic than ideological, realised that if it was a choice between being accused of lurching to the right and crashing to defeat it was time for a sharp tug on the wheel. Hague, who was on hand to ensure that Cameron did not repeat the same mistakes he had made in pursuing what is known as a core-vote strategy, said it was a matter of 'riding the dip'.

But it was left to another former leader, Iain Duncan Smith, whom Cameron had put in charge of the social policy review, to show the way. IDS's prescriptions of radical welfare reform, promotion of marriage and action on debt, gambling and drink had mostly been adopted, but it was his description of the ailment that was most useful: Britain, he said, was a 'broken society'. As already noted, the phrase had in fact first been used by Liam Fox in the 2005 leadership race, but it was during the summer of 2007 that two shocking murders brought it into focus. The deaths of Garry Newlove, a forty-eight-year-old father kicked to death by drunken teens, and of eleven-year-old Rhys Jones, shot coming home from football practice, induced a moral panic. Cameron's rhetoric about family breakdown, about generations of worklessness and about a state that had abandoned the moral sphere suddenly resonated as never before. Sensing that he was catching the national mood, Cameron made three speeches on crime in as many weeks, winning the first approving coverage in months from newspapers like the *Sun* and the *Daily Mail*.

One speech in particular has become regarded internally as a definitive statement of his appeal for a new 'social covenant'. Large sections were written by Cameron himself after he and Samantha had watched a television news interview with the parents of Rhys Jones. 'He has a very natural way of realising where the public are on these things and he felt this was a big one. So that night he rewrote the speech, as I remember, sat up to God knows what hour, sending round a draft in the early hours,' recalls an insider. Cameron did not conceal his feelings. 'What his parents said yesterday, when they spoke of their loss of their boy, of their child, and what he meant to them, was so powerful and moving,' he said. The usual political response of summits, crackdowns and beefed-up legislation, he added, were not enough to avoid such a tragedy happening again. 'I promise you, unless we choose to change, that is exactly what will happen: our shock today will turn into a shrug tomorrow, just a kind of impotent ache about the state of the world. Or we can start saying to ourselves and to each other: "I've had enough of all this."'

Immigration too, long a modernisers' taboo, suddenly made a reappearance with Cameron embracing the idea of a cap on non-EU migrants. On tax Osborne embraced (gingerly) the findings of the economic competitiveness policy review led by John Redwood, which included a proposal to cut inheritance tax. Osborne left the door open to this possibility but signalled that he had yet to be convinced. Finally the Tory leadership sidestepped the vast 'Quality of Life' report by ostentatiously rejecting a minor recommendation that supermarkets be made to charge for parking. The report was the environmental chapter of Cameron's policy-review process – headed by John Gummer and the glamorous Zac Goldsmith, pin-up boy of affluent environmentalists – which was supposed to be the distillation of Cameron's greenery. To some modernisers, all this looked sickeningly like the mistakes made by Hague, Howard and IDS when each had reverted to the core vote, concentrating on what one termed the 'old ladies' of crime, immigration and low taxes and thereby alienating centrist voters.

They worried, too, that Cameron was in danger of ruining his own brand, that of the bluff can-do optimist. Coulson, who had played a large part in plotting the summer offensive, dismissed the objection. Cameron *is* an optimist, Coulson argued, and his warnings of a 'broken Britain' – or, for the benefit of a front-page headline in the *Sun*, 'anarchy in the UK' – had all the more force from the mouth of someone whose disposition was so sunny. The party's private polling seemed to bear Coulson out. The last week in August 2007 saw a dramatic improvement in Cameron's personal rating. Asked whether the Tory leader shared their values, 20 per cent more voters disagreed than agreed. After articulating public disgust at the Newlove and Jones murders, that figure dropped to 10 per cent – a hugely significant shift.

Despite such encouraging signs it was clear to all in Cameron's inner circle – or almost all – that an autumn election was more likely than not. Hilton, alone, maintained that Brown would not have the courage and declined to take part in election-planning meetings chaired by Osborne in the party's new HQ in Millbank, which temporarily replaced Norman Shaw South as the leadership's nerve-centre. At his Bayswater home, meanwhile, the shadow Chancellor held a secret meeting with Michael Gove, who tried to talk him out of cutting inheritance tax. Such a move, he argued, broke faith with a key guiding principle that tax cuts should benefit all sections of society, not just the well off. Cameron, however, agreed with Osborne that the most pressing need was to energise the party faithful and give them a policy they could take to the nation's doorsteps.

Besides, Osborne had an answer to the chorus of outraged liberals accusing Cameron of 'doing a Hague': they would match Labour's spending totals for the next three years. The policy would not only thwart the attack used successfully for the last three elections that the Tories were hell-bent on cutting spending on schools and hospitals, it would balance out the tougher messages on crime and education. Furthermore, because Labour had announced unexpectedly tight totals, matching them would be consistent with the policy of spending less than the economy grew – or, as the slogan had it, of sharing the proceeds of growth.

The announcement of the new policy, described as 'unilateral economic disarmament' and 'the worst blunder' of his leadership a little over a year later, barely registered when it was made in the first week in September. Brown's media machine managed to stifle it with the much less significant story of the defection from the Tories of a disaffected donor – to Osborne's intense irritation. By the time Labour delegates gathered in Bournemouth at the end of the month most of them expected that they would be sent home from the conference with a war cry from their new leader. It didn't happen – and few were more relieved than David Cameron.

He had put Conservative Campaign Headquarters (CCHQ) on a full war-footing. Michael Ashcroft, who had moved his target-seats operation in-house that summer after delicate negotiations with Cameron himself, was directing below-the-radar campaigning and monitoring the scores of tracking polls that he funds directly. The peer's sizeable contributions to the party and his strong opinions about campaigning methods ensure that he remains a difficult figure for Cameron to manage. But all thoughts of reducing his influence were forgotten now as the election loomed. The manifesto was being cobbled together under the direction of Oliver Letwin. Leaflets were printed and additional personnel hired. Hosting a pre-conference meeting of the shadow Cabinet, Cameron told them they had to mount the 'biggest political fight and comeback of their lives' over the coming week. Labour had hoped that the Conservatives would fracture under the threat of the election, but it had the opposite effect – a defiant *esprit de corps* began to flow from Cameron through the shadow Cabinet.

When he invited the key players to the conference war room – a suite in the Imperial Hotel in Blackpool – on Saturday 29 September, hopes were beginning to rise that Brown might have missed his chance. 'We always thought that his best chance of calling the election was before our conference,' recalls one key figure. 'But we also knew that weekend that no pollster would be able to tell him with certainty that he would win an overall majority.' Cameron did his best to project sangfroid. Reviewing another negative set of headlines predicting that the Tory conference would descend into a festival of internal feuding, an aide suggested that surely this was 'rock bottom'. 'Oh, no,' Cameron replied, 'we've got tons of bedrock to go – and then there are miles and miles of molten lava. I know that I'm supposed to "ride the dip" but this is turning out to be a journey to the centre of the earth!'

The start of the conference the next day proved his cheery pessimism correct. A faulty microphone meant that the official welcome couldn't be heard. Some representatives, dismayed by this evidence of their party's incompetence, began to barrack the stage. Gleeful journalists predicted that an epic political disaster was about to unfold. And then, suddenly, it all went right. Hague gave a brilliant, rallying speech and then, the next day, Osborne had what Ann Treneman, *The Times*'s parliamentary sketch-writer, dubbed his 'million-pound moment'. His announcement that a Tory government would abolish inheritance tax for all homes worth less than £1 million was met with such a storm of approval in the hall that the shadow Chancellor looked stunned. Then came a stroke of luck. Liam Fox's speech on defence coincided with a trip to Iraq by Brown, where he signalled troop withdrawals but failed to announce them explicitly. According to Ashcroft's polling, Fox's stinging rebuke that Brown was cynically using serving British soldiers as a khaki election backdrop resonated strongly with voters.

Cameron had started the conference intending to give a standard speech from notes. As the week progressed, however, he grew in confidence and started to contemplate a stunt he and Hilton had toyed with but rejected. He would, after all, speak from memory, thus repeating the feat performed in his 2005 speech during the leadership race – delivered in the same hall – but on a far greater scale. It was a typical Cameron gamble: an unashamed look-at-me, high-wire act of political theatre. He calculated that the contrast with Brown's plodding delivery of a list-laden text the previous week would be irresistible to the media. He doesn't often admit to bouts of self-doubt, but he has said that he was 'incredibly nervous' in the hours before he took the stage at the Winter Gardens on 3 October. To clear his head, he and Samantha gave his police and media minders the slip and, letting themselves down the hotel fire-escape, went for a walk on the beach early on the morning of the conference's last day.

Then at last he stepped on to the podium, placed his watch and a sheaf of reminders on the lectern and began. 'It may be messy but it will be me,' he began. When asked a year later what was the best moment of his political life to date, Cameron cited the moment during the 2007 conference speech when 'I knew I was going to be okay. There was a wave of relief.' The subsequent gush of positive coverage overlooked the fact that the address was indeed messy – and very long. It ranged from MySpace to Swampy via Iain Duncan Smith and many other points in between. But the finale was stirring. So Mr Brown, he said, what's it to be?

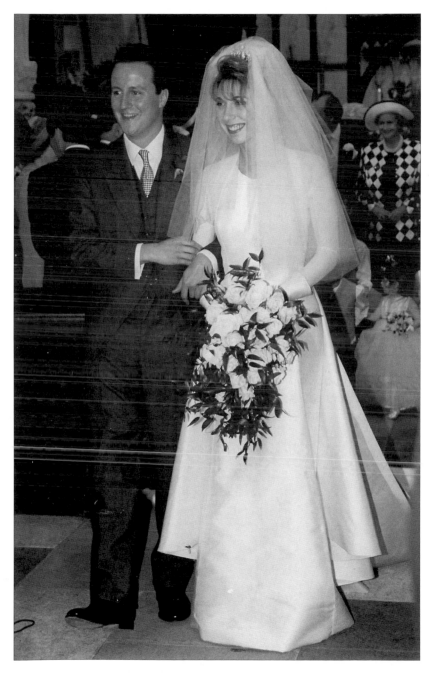

David and Samantha Cameron on their wedding day in June 1996.

ABOVE: David Cameron (far left), in fetching plus-fours, stands next to an armed Charles Moore in a shooting party at Glenarm Castle, County Antrim. The host, Viscount Dunluce, is third from right.

BELOW: 'Oops'. Cameron looks suitably abashed after, having burnt the toast, he set off the fire alarm and caused the fire brigade to smash down the gates of Glenarm Castle.

LEFT: A tanned Cameron takes a break from 'endless games of bridge' in Siena, Italy.

BELOW: Cameron has a Labrador-like tendency to jump into water, no matter how cold. This was County Antrim in November. Charles Moore is among those not tempted.

ABOVE: Left, Steve Hilton and right, Andy Coulson, who brought a harder edge to Cameron's dealings with the lobby.

BELOW: Anything you can do … George Osborne, the original cycling moderniser, and Cameron riding to Westminster in May 2006.

ABOVE: The press feeds on a new star. The shoes followed in a limousine.

BELOW: What do we do now? Boris Johnson and David Cameron celebrate unseating Ken Livingstone as Mayor of London.

ABOVE: Steve Hilton, right, the brilliant, obsessive strategist, and the man who 'invented' David Cameron. The more he stays in the shadows the greater the media's interest in him. George Eustice, former head of press, is on the left.

RIGHT: David Cameron celebrates his first anniversary as Tory leader on 30 September 2006. Seen here with his family in Portobello Road, London.

Samantha, David, Arthur, Nancy and Ivan (clockwise), at the wedding of
Samantha's jeweller half-sister, Flora, in September 2006.

ABOVE: Nick Clegg and David Cameron in the Number 10 rose garden on Wednesday 12 May 2010, explaining to the world how their differences aren't that great after all and what a good idea the coalition is.

BELOW: Follow me: David Cameron in a rare public photograph in the company of Rebekah Brooks, then editor of the *Sun*, at Charlie Brooks's book launch in April 2009.

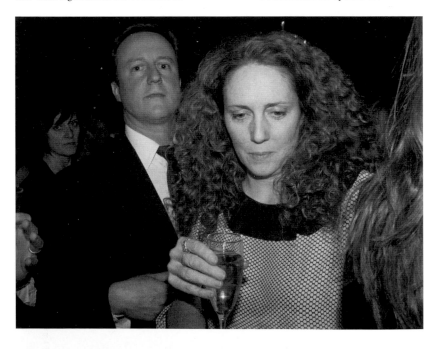

Let the people pass judgement on ten years of broken promises, let people decide who's really making the arguments about the future of our country. Let people decide who can make the changes that we really need in our country. Call that election. We will fight. Britain will win.

Hague had told Cameron in early summer that if Brown were to call an election he would do so on 4 or 5 October. The days passed with no word from Downing Street but plenty of evidence that Labour was still gearing up for the fight. By Friday the 5th Cameron had on his desk data marked 'Field-work: Daily Tracker'; it was Ashcroft's polling and it couldn't have been more encouraging. Not only were the Tories closing the gap on all measures, it was clear that the inheritance tax announcement had been a smash hit – an astonishing 22 per cent were able to cite it without prompting.

On Friday Cameron had lunch with the German Interior Minister Wolfgang Schäuble at the Carlton Club, a once grand but stuffy gentlemen's club on Pall Mall. Although Schäuble has a reputation as one of the starchiest, most conservative of European politicians, Cameron managed so well to feign interest in the complexities of the German domestic political scene that he was congratulated by his guest for his good manners. In truth everyone at the table knew that the Tory leader was on tenterhooks. Llewellyn received a text message halfway through the lunch with the latest poll figures. He passed the information on to his leader: it was neck and neck.

Then on Saturday 6 October word came through from Coulson that Brown had summoned Andrew Marr, the BBC journalist, to Downing Street for an announcement. Coulson also told Cameron that his former newspaper, the *News of the World*, was carrying a poll showing the Tories ahead in marginal seats. Taken together, the information could mean only one thing – the election was off. The next day came the Marr interview, during which Brown's agony was there for all to see. Cameron was jubilant, but because of Dean's terrible phone reception he had to keep running into the garden to take the calls from Osborne and others on his mobile. They had – as Cameron had urged them to do – staged the political fight-back of their lives.

MILLBANK
Leader of the Opposition 2007–2009

Gordon Brown's decision to call off the early election in October 2007 came at the end of a week that marked what one pollster called the 'most violent earthquake in public opinion for 25 years'. Not since the Falklands War had a government's popularity changed so dramatically. Brown's personal ratings suffered a catastrophic slump, compounded by his contemptuously far-fetched claim that his decision to call off the election had had nothing to do with the polls. Cameron – who claims with comparable implausibility that he would have won – felt deflated after the initial euphoria. As part of his humiliating retreat Brown had ruled out a poll in 2008 and it seemed all but certain he would go the full five years. Cameron, already leader of the Opposition for almost two years, was doomed to another eighteen months in what Margaret Thatcher described as the worst job in British politics. The compensation was that the extra time would allow proper planning for a first Conservative term of office and an increased likelihood of the sort of landslide win – and therefore mandate – to implement genuine reform. At the start of 2008 Francis Maude was tasked with setting up an 'implementation unit' which, in addition to some policy work, was to recruit sympathetic former civil servants and identify future special advisers and frontbenchers for government. The creation of the unit was used to bolster the impression of the inevitability of the forthcoming victory. What six months previously might have appeared at best presumptuous now looked like sensible preparation.

Faintly at first, but then ever more strongly, Conservative MPs began to smell fear wafting from the Labour benches, particularly following Brown's performances at PMQs. He had been poor from the start but it was only when the Commons returned after the summer recess, and against the backdrop of slumping approval ratings, that his own side started to appreciate how outclassed he was by Cameron at the despatch box. The contests became so one-sided that Cameron would exchange high-fives with some of his staff on his return to Norman Shaw South.

But even as polls swung behind Cameron – indeed, even before Brown called off the early election – a financial disaster was brewing that would change the nature of the election and determine the character of British politics for many years to come.

In August 2007 few in Britain paid much attention to the rising default rates in the so-called 'sub-prime' US mortgage market. Their significance was brought sharply home on 13 September 2007 when a run on the Northern Rock building society showed what turned out to be just the leading edge of the storm to come. Brown's desperate searches for a private buyer and his final, reluctant acceptance that the lender would have to be nationalised – or 'placed in temporary public ownership' – seemed at first a gift-wrapped opportunity for the Tories. What more obvious proof could there be of a clapped-out administration retreating to its statist core?

Osborne declared that nationalisation of the Rock was a 'monumental failure'. Yet in opposing direct government intervention on Northern Rock, Cameron and Osborne were open to the charge that they too were retreating to the past, to the laissez-faire economic policies of past Tory administrations. Critics have said they should have thought through the full implications of the freezing up of the credit markets, realised that state action would become a necessity and positioned themselves more carefully in late 2007.

The one politician who was well placed to take political advantage of the credit crunch was Vince Cable, the temporary replacement for

Sir Menzies Campbell – the second Liberal Democrat leader to be deposed in the course of the parliament.

Cable, a former economist, had been warning about an approaching crisis for some time. The 'Sage of Twickenham' not only supported full nationalisation of Northern Rock from the outset but also ensured that Brown did not make much political capital from the crisis. His quip on 28 November that Brown had undergone a 'remarkable transformation ... from Stalin to Mr Bean' did more damage with gentle humour than any of Cameron's occasionally histrionic PMQ performances at the time.

If Cable's success was an early warning of the threat posed by the Liberal Democrats, the arrival of Nick Clegg saw it recede. Cameron first patronised and then simply ignored Clegg.

Meanwhile, Osborne redoubled efforts to woo the liberal media. There was talk of a 'progressive alliance' and the claim that the Tories were now best placed to secure 'progressive ends through Conservative means'. To his distress Clegg found that his political persona as a young, modern family man and his political space were already occupied by Cameron.

Cameron, in turn, was more worried by a Conservative than a Liberal Democrat rival. On 1 May 2008 he held Boris Johnson's hand up as a proud trainer might his triumphant boxer – showing off the new Conservative mayor of London. This picture of unity belied a much more complicated truth for, in fact, it was only long after Cameron's search for a candidate to take on Ken Livingstone had descended into farce that he had turned to Boris.

Officially, the Tory leadership was neutral; unofficially the modernisers had a candidate in Nicholas Boles. Boles, defeated in the 2005 election, had even given up his job as director of the Cameron-leaning think-tank Policy Exchange to take a run at the mayoralty. Although fresh-faced, personable, intelligent and gay, he was not the sort of high-profile figure who would be able to compete for the media's attention with Livingstone. Frankly, Cameron wasn't confident he could win. Behind the scenes the Tory leader began to take charge of the search. Sebastian Coe, Lord Stevens of Kirkwhelpington (formerly Sir John Stevens, head of the Metropolitan Police), Derek Laud, radio presenter Nick Ferrari and Sir John Major were all considered or approached but fell by the wayside.

The hunt became humiliating when Cameron approached Sir Menzies Campbell to discuss the idea of a joint Lib Dem–Conservative candidate, the former BBC director general Greg Dyke.

Then, at the end of June 2007, Boles became ill and pulled out. Cameron was now without even a default candidate: it was time for desperate measures. Until that moment David Cameron could scarcely have done less to help Boris Johnson's political career. The two men had known each other for almost twenty-five years. At Eton, at Oxford, in the media and in politics their lives had touched, diverged and touched again. Their contacts have been marked by competitiveness rather than collegiality. Boris's swashbuckling brilliance was admired by Cameron, two years his junior, but he was more amused than impressed. Boris, a scholar, was a member of Pop, a pupil-elected elite: the schoolboy Cameron was not. In debating circles at school and university, Boris had played for laughs and deftly concealed his gifts behind a buffoonish exterior, while the more contained Cameron had played a longer game. As a fellow member of the Bullingdon Club, Cameron was comparatively strait-laced. It was Boris, not Cameron, who developed a friendship with Darius Guppy. Guppy, who later went to prison for fraud, prided himself on his brilliance and his disdain for convention. Rules were a bit bourgeois. They applied only to the little people.

Cameron's first job had been at the Conservative Research Department after being turned down by a number of blue-chip employers. Boris, on the other hand, had been interviewed by CRD six weeks after Cameron, and they had been keen to have him: Boris told them that his first preference was a traineeship at *The Times*, which he landed. Although that job ended in the first of his many disgraces, by the time Cameron was doing well at CRD, Boris – as the *Daily Telegraph*'s Brussels correspondent – was said to be Margaret Thatcher's favourite journalist. And when Cameron joined the media world working for Carlton – not the most prestigious outfit – in the 1990s Boris capped a decade of brilliance with the editorship of the *Spectator*. He was still only thirty-five.

It was not until both were elected to the House of Commons in 2001 that Cameron finally began to haul himself on to equal terms. Even when both, along with Osborne, were asked to help Iain Duncan Smith prepare for PMQs it seemed that Cameron was to be cast as the drudge. Struggling after Ivan's birth, he nevertheless strove to do his duty by Duncan Smith, in contrast to Boris's lackadaisical and dilatory appearances. Cameron and Osborne shared the whips' view that their colleague lacked both seriousness and application. While for many the clever, funny, lovable Boris has enlivened the political landscape, Cameron saw a man who, carried away by his own verbal brilliance, was forever having to issue apologies for his lack of restraint. Who was sacked from *The Times* for inventing quotes? Who, in a famous phone call, did nothing to dissuade Darius Guppy from having a journalist beaten up? Whose extra-marital affairs resulted in at least two abortions and deep distress to at least two women? Whose idealism and loathing of priggishness prevented him from understanding why his mistress would not be happy to go on a Johnson family holiday? Who lied to the press and to his boss about an affair?

So it was a surprise only to Boris that, on 9 December 2005, three days after becoming leader, Cameron omitted Johnson from his shadow Cabinet. Boris, as *Spectator* editor, had been one of the earliest supporters of Cameron's leadership campaign, his natural competitiveness overcome by an assumption that Cameron's elevation could do him nothing but good. 'Although he regarded Cameron as gifted but nonetheless not his equal intellectually, I think he just assumed that, with "the chaps" in charge, he would do well out of it,' says someone who knows him well.

Boris, it seemed, would have to wait his turn, labouring in the post of shadow spokesman for higher education. He resigned from the *Spectator* and addressed himself with some earnestness to a brief which, he would have had to admit, did interest him. If the 2005 snub to Boris was remarkable only to its victim, its repetition eighteen months later was publicly more obvious. When Cameron reshuffled his team in July 2007 he promoted three MPs from the 2005 intake. Boris, an MP since 2001, stayed with higher education. To Boris, the reason sometimes offered – that Cameron could not afford to promote yet another Etonian – was not good enough. This wasn't what he had left the *Spectator* for, and it was a stunning rebuff.

A month later, now that Cameron needed him, Boris was going to make him sweat. A few weeks before Boles's withdrawal from the mayoral race he resignedly told a friend, 'When they've tried everyone else, oh well, it'll have to be me.' Even when it became obvious that there was no other option, the Tory leader couldn't face asking Boris to run himself – he asked Coulson to sound him out. Boris wanted to remain as MP for Henley even if he acceded to the London mayoralty, and friends of Boris have claimed that he secured such a promise (subsequently broken) from Cameron. In any event, after a couple of days of playing hard to get, Boris affected a fitting bashfulness and agreed to stand.

Initially, Cameron's reluctance to allow Boris a run at the job seemed to have been justified as a poor campaign failed to get off the ground – not least because the candidate appeared too busy completing a television series and other commitments. By December Johnson admitted privately that his campaign was not equal to the task. 'He started to worry, I think, that he couldn't win it,' an observer said. Osborne, who was handling the London mayoral campaign at Tory HQ, had been despairing of the Boris campaign for some time – even briefing the Tory activist website ConservativeHome about the leadership's 'concerns'.

The leak was part of a series of efforts to force Boris to accept a key appointment to relaunch his stuttering campaign: that of the bull-like Lynton Crosby. The Australian political consultant and architect of the Tories' 2005 election campaign was a controversial figure. He was blamed by some for Michael Howard's overemphasis on the issue of immigration, and his occasionally abrasive style had left more than one nose out of joint. Cameron himself did not escape the odd fusillade. But Howard's successor knew a professional when he saw one and had already tried to bring him back, sending George Bridges and Francis Maude to Sydney in January 2007 with an invitation to return as the party's chief executive. The four-day visit was followed by an invitation to Dean during Crosby's next trip to the UK when he and Cameron discussed terms. Although that appointment fell through – a failure that some believe was to have significant consequences for the national election campaign in 2010 – Crosby did now agree to try to rescue the mayoral campaign.

Once he had submitted to Crosby Boris knuckled down and on 1 May 2008 won.

His victory opened a new chapter in the Johnson–Cameron relationship. Someone who knew them both at university laughs at the media's occasional portrayal of them as friends. 'The only thing they have in common is ambition,' he says. One might add a reluctance to take one another seriously – hence the occasional jocose, double-edged, for-the-cameras sparring – and disbelief at one another's success.

Having won London, Boris was better placed than ever to win Britain. Cameron could hardly express anything other than delight at a Conservative victory. Certainly a Tory victory in London was a milestone on the way to Downing Street, and he let it be known he felt that 'you take what you can get' in politics. But Cameron also knew it heralded the arrival of a serious rival.

Although aides claim both men have maintained a friendship of sorts, it is not a relationship of equals, at least as far as Johnson is concerned. A friend who knows Boris extremely well says he believes himself to be the most intelligent person in the world, 'and I'm not really exaggerating'. With self-esteem of that order, founded on a belief in your own near-infallibility, people are bound to get upset, whether by accident or design.

'Boris despises David. He doesn't respect his intelligence, thinks he's conventional and safe and unimaginative, and he can't understand how he's got the top job,' says an old acquaintance of Boris.

Cameron, when explaining that he was glad he hadn't joined the *Economist* because he was not a natural journalist, added: 'I sometimes think there are people in politics who ought to be in journalism and there are people in journalism who should be in politics, but I'm certainly not going to say who.' If he, seeing himself as one of life's dutiful, was not referring to Boris Johnson, he might as well have been.

Johnson, who controversially kept his £5,000-a-shot column in the *Daily Telegraph*, used it to skilfully to needle Cameron all the while under the pretence of slavish loyalty.

Sometimes he went too far. 'If you believe the politicians, we have a broken society, in which the courage and morals of young people have been sapped by welfarism and political correctness. If you look at what is happening at the Beijing Olympics, you can see what piffle that is.' Even had Boris been as sleepy as he sometimes pretends to be, he would have known how important the 'broken society' is to the Cameron message. A sharp phone call ensued from Cameron's office, although publicly the leader adopted the indulgent 'Boris is Boris' approach.

Although Boris's victory attracted most of the media attention, the hammering Labour took in the rest of the country was more significant. In England alone the Tories had won almost a thousand new council seats and taken 40 per cent of the vote. Labour, on 27 per cent, only just managed to avoid being beaten into third place by the Liberal Democrats, who won 26 per cent of the vote. Most encouragingly for Cameron the Tories were clearly regenerating outside their core areas in the south-east of England.

Further confirmation came with victory at the Crewe by-election where Labour's attempt to paint Cameron and Osborne as 'toffs' had failed miserably. Cameron read the last rites over New Labour, asserting that Brown had run the 'most negative, the most backward-looking, the most xenophobic, the most class-war sort of campaign they could have done and it completely backfired'.

It was now Brown's turn to teeter on the edge of a leadership election. Desperate to reassert his authority and exploit the one issue on which voters preferred his stance to Cameron's, he made a Commons vote on a new counter-terrorism bill a test of his leadership.

The issue was tricky for the Tory leader, it split his party and was a wedge between his traditional voters and the Liberal Democrat-minded supporters he was wooing. The appointment of David Davis, a passionate libertarian, as shadow Home Secretary had helped paper over the cracks.

Cameron was proud of how he had handled Davis after beating him in the leadership election. He had given him a plum brief and always treated him courteously despite the occasional display of disloyalty. Davis hadn't, for example, concealed his contempt for the 'hug a hoodie' speech nor had he been noticeably supportive during grammargate.

In Opposition and during the first months of government Cameron liked to think of himself as akin to the chairman of a capable board who had, he believed, contained his former rival's ambitions and harnessed his skills. He agreed with Davis that Brown was guilty of cynical politicking over seeking to extend the period terror suspects could be held without charge.

But despite holding firm and running Brown very close to a Commons defeat on the issue, Cameron was poorly rewarded by Davis.

Emotions still running high, Davis suddenly announced that he intended to quit his seat and fight a by-election – the campaign, he said, would serve as a national referendum on the balance between civil liberties and security.

Cameron's response was a master class in the politely lethal putdown. Davis, he said, had made a 'very courageous and brave' decision, but a 'personal decision, and not one of the shadow Cabinet or Conservative Party'. Although Davis was duly returned to the Commons, the Haltemprice and Howden by-election was – just as Cameron had foreseen – an embarrassing sideshow that proved nothing except perhaps the poor judgement of the man who had triggered it. The strange episode seemed further proof of Cameron's good fortune. Just as a new rival emerged so an old one self-destructed.

On 7 July 2008 Cameron delivered a speech that in some senses marked the completion of the detoxification project. Standing in a Glasgow church, he delivered an unabashedly moral sermon that linked the themes of responsibility and of the need to heal a 'broken society'.

Society had been too circumspect in failing to judge the behaviour of others, he said. It was time for him to speak out against 'moral neutrality'.

He gave examples:

We talk about people being 'at risk of obesity' instead of talking about people who eat too much and take too little exercise. We talk about people being at risk of poverty, or social exclusion: it's as if these things – obesity, alcohol abuse, drug addiction – are purely external events like a plague or bad weather. Of course, circumstances – where you are born, your neighbourhood, your school and the choices your parents make – have a huge impact. But social problems are often the consequence of the choices people make.

It was a long way from 'hug a hoodie'. The previous November, Cameron had made a thoughtful speech about immigration, taking on the notion of multiculturalism in measured language that won praise from Trevor Phillips, head of the Equality and Human Rights Commission.

Now he had won back for the Tories the right to make the case bluntly that it was time to help people to help themselves.

Gordon Brown did not say that it marked a return to John Major's 'back to basics' because he would not have been believed. At last he was winning the argument on the 'broken society'.

Events – momentous and trivial – were about to combine to call into question the Tory leadership's judgement in matters foreign, financial and personal, however. Almost certain that there wouldn't be an autumn election, Cameron and Osborne urged their staff to take a proper summer holiday – with luck, they said, it might be their last chance for years. Cameron himself ostentatiously supported domestic tourism by holidaying with his family in Cornwall, but before he left on his real holiday – a two-week cruise with what he calls the Sheffield/Astor gipsy encampment in Turkey – he flew to Georgia to protest against Russia's invasion of the disputed territory of South Ossetia and to call for full NATO membership to be granted to Tbilisi immediately. The intervention, which appalled some senior figures in his shadow Cabinet, provides an illuminating case study of why

Cameron has struggled to forge a coherent, credible foreign policy. The Iraq legacy hangs over all those Conservatives – Cameron included – who voted for Blair's decision to support the US invasion.

Decontaminating the Tory brand meant distancing it from George W. Bush, as Cameron did on the 2006 anniversary of 9/11:

> I believe that in the last five years we have suffered from the absence of two crucial qualities which should always condition foreign policymaking. Humility, and patience. These are not warlike words. They are not so glamorous and exciting as the easy soundbites we have grown used to in recent years. But these soundbites had the failing of all foreign policy designed to fit into a headline.

While this grated with those, like Osborne and Gove, who were still prepared to defend the Iraq invasion, they saw the political necessity.

As one Tory neo-con put it: 'Just part of having a civilised conversation with most people in this country was to show that you grimace appropriately when George Bush's name was mentioned. David had to set his features in the appropriate way at the mention of Bush in order to get a hearing on anything else he said on foreign policy.'

But simply gurning at the Bush presidency didn't make for a very distinctive profile, and, two years later, with Bush's presidency drawing to a close, Cameron's foreign policy was judged to be one of his weakest flanks. It wasn't just the legacy of Iraq that limited his room for manoeuvre – the shadow of Maastricht still falls over the Tories.

Although Europe was a handy way of rallying the party's base from time to time, Hague had tested to destruction the notion that the cause of resisting the march of EU federalism was much of a vote winner.

Soon after his leadership victory Cameron had to break his pledge to pull the party out of the centre-right but federalist European People's Party grouping in Strasbourg and to do so 'in months not years'. (The deadline for withdrawal was put off to June 2009.) Even Brown's refusal to honour a pledge to hold a referendum on the reworked EU constitution offered at least as much downside as it did up. Hague, as shadow Foreign Secretary, skilfully contained the Eurosceptic right during a parliamentary debate deliberately extended to ventilate Tory tensions. Cameron said he would 'not let the matter rest there' if the constitution were not fully ratified by the time of a Cameron administration but managed to avoid spelling out further what action he would take to renegotiate the UK's relationship with the EU.

Denied the trappings of office, Cameron's globe-trotting had been *ad hoc*. His trip to Rwanda, though seen by some as an ill-advised stunt, did at least suggest that he had the guts to put international development ahead of immediate political expediency. He repeatedly visited British troops in Iraq and Afghanistan, but while these are no doubt useful fact-finding tours, they did not offer much chance of definition. (On one occasion in detailed conversation with a soldier, he asked revealingly, 'What does Tony Blair think?')

He promised a defence review after the election, which deflected difficult questions over the proper future shape and funding of Britain's military.

But in seeking to find a balanced, pragmatic tone on foreign policy, Cameron verged on the vacuous, for instance describing Blair as 'a humanitarian interventionist without putting any kind of practical brake on these impulses. I think you do need that sceptical, enquiring sense when it comes to foreign policy.' In a speech in Berlin in October 2007 he sought to define what he called liberal conservatism:

> Liberal interventionism – the idea that we should just get out there into the world and 'sort it all out' – was the right impulse, was morally correct, but failed to strike the right balance between realism and idealism. I think the right balance can be found in what I believe in: liberal conservatism.

The speech, delivered near the Bundestag, was given a polite round of applause from the invited audience of politicians.

His biggest 'big idea' was to develop a 'partnership for open societies'. 'We don't have to say to those countries you have to adopt democracy tomorrow,' he has said,

> but let's form an organisation that isn't led by the West, that is led by you but involves countries like India and China and Japan and others, that believes in the steady progress of the rule of law, human rights and more open societies. That would be a good way of engaging some of the moderate states of the Middle East.

At about the time he became leader, a political ally, acknowledging he had some ground to make up internationally, said of him: 'The trouble is, David doesn't think about these things very deeply. His political interests lie elsewhere.'

Like every other senior politician, Cameron scrambled to be associated with Barack Obama during the presidential candidate's tour of Europe in the summer of 2008.

But other than the obvious presentational bonus of associating with the young, black charismatic 'change' candidate of US politics, Obama's arrival helped free Cameron from the Iraq legacy.

With Bush leaving the White House, it was no longer so necessary to distance himself from the US. At last he could contemplate attacking Brown from the right on foreign policy. In August 2008, an opportunity seemed to be presenting itself when the Russian tanks trundled across the border with Georgia. There was general condemnation of the Russian use of force, although the Tories' initial statement, by foreign affairs spokesman William Hague, was decidedly muted, urging restraint, caution and so on on all sides. But David Cameron saw an opportunity to make some political capital. On Wednesday 13 August a vigorously anti-Russian opinion article, written by the Tory leader, appeared in the *Daily Telegraph*. 'This is not some quarrel in a faraway land. What happens in Georgia directly affects us,' he wrote. The first concern he cited was energy security, followed by a wish not to allow aggression to go unpunished. Following the article's publication, Cameron was invited by the Georgian government to visit the country, which he did the following Saturday. There he repeated his view that Georgia's application to join NATO should be 'accelerated'. Cameron's stance was a more radical position than has been generally thought. In the first place, the British government, while deploring Russian aggression, had shown no great desire to offer a strategic guarantee to one of Russia's more volatile neighbours, and was keeping it as a possibility for the future. Cameron's move caused consternation on two counts. By calling for an 'acceleration' of Georgia's application to join NATO, he was asking for something which NATO's member states, just four months earlier, had effectively rejected. Cameron was demanding something which simply wasn't going to happen, making him look both high-handed and ill informed. The term 'accelerate' was dropped from subsequent statements.

Secondly, the views he expressed were closer to those of shadow defence spokesman Liam Fox than to those of his foreign affairs counterpart William Hague. To some in Cameron's circle, it looked as if Fox – who has made something of a study of the geopolitics surrounding Russia's energy policy – had 'got at' the leader, although Fox was not the only person Cameron consulted that week. One adviser to the Georgian government expressed surprise at Cameron's haste, while a source much closer to him in London called the visit 'ill advised and hasty'. In the press, Max Hastings was not alone in suggesting it was 'folly' to offer security guarantees (which NATO membership would entail) that the West did not have the will to enforce.

Was the 'Georgian folly' an example of inexperience, impetuosity, and a triumph of partisan expediency over national interest?

With the benefit of his decision to press for NATO action in Libya for guidance, might it instead have been early evidence that Cameron harboured more interventionist instincts than he thought it wise to show?

After Tbilisi, Cameron headed for Corfu where, with George Osborne, he had been invited to celebrate the fortieth-birthday party for Rupert Murdoch's daughter Elisabeth, hosted by the Rothschilds. The details of that fateful party, the shadow Chancellor's decision to board Oleg Deripaska's superyacht and hold whatever discussions he did about a donation from the controversial Russian tycoon might never have come out had Osborne not tangled with Peter Mandelson.

Yachtgate – as the Oleg Deripaska affair inevitably became known – was wounding for three reasons: it reminded voters that both Cameron and Osborne are from wealthy backgrounds, it exposed their carelessness about fundraising and it created tensions between the two central figures of the Tory leadership.

When Osborne's own dealings with the Russian – including the claim that he had tried to solicit a donation from him – were revealed, the shadow Chancellor was pilloried as hypocritical and arrogant. The affair also shone an unwelcome light on a world of privilege usually screened from voters, not least because newspapers printed a new Bullingdon photograph showing Osborne and the club members of his day posing with almost pantomimic arrogance. Among the most damaging details of the affair was that Osborne had taken a brief break from the opulence of marbled villas and superyachts to fly back to London to make a speech on poverty.

But unlike grammargate – the last time class had reared its head – this time the toxic issue of party funding was involved. Andrew Feldman, the university friend Cameron brought in first as fundraiser and then as the party's chief executive, had joined Osborne on Deripaska's yacht because he regularly took his holidays nearby. Both denied Rothschild's claim that they had solicited a donation. Neither could deny, however, that a conversation about a cash gift from a UK company controlled by Deripaska had later taken place. The Tories' account maintains that this suggestion – which flouts electoral law – was rejected out of hand.

A chastened Osborne announced that he would in future take no part in direct, private fundraising. Cameron's aides did not deny that the affair had strained their relationship. They suspect that the shadow Chancellor had not told Cameron he had been on the Deripaska yacht before the Rothschild letter was published. It was noticeable that Coulson took immediate and total control of the handling of the affair, effectively suspending Osborne's own press operation. 'Andy's view was the first requirement was to protect David,' observed one who witnessed his damage-limitation exercise.

The Deripaska affair put Osborne out of action just when Cameron needed his strategic gifts more than ever to adapt Conservative economic policy to the dramatically changing conditions, the collapse of the giant US bank Lehman Brothers in September having sparked worldwide financial turmoil. Before the recession took hold, David Cameron liked to say that he would do for Britain's 'broken society' what Margaret Thatcher had done for its 'broken economy', a vainglorious comparison crafted for him by Oliver Letwin. 'I'm going to be as radical a social reformer as Mrs Thatcher was an economic reformer, and radical social reform is what this country needs right now' was a typical boast. Much of Cameron's early project was predicated on the assumption that sustained, stable economic growth was a given. As he said in May 2006:

We should be thinking not just what is good for putting money in people's pockets but what is good for putting joy in people's hearts. When politicians are looking at issues they should be saying to themselves, 'How are we going to try and make sure that we don't just make people better off but we make people happier, we make communities more stable, we make society more cohesive?'

But voters fearing for their jobs and homes no longer wanted to hear about the General Well-Being Index, a measure and economic model of happiness developed in the Himalayan kingdom of Bhutan and endorsed by Cameron.

It is true that Cameron had all but dropped the environment as an issue and substituted spiralling public debt. But the severity of the crunch as evidenced by the Lehman collapse raised some uncomfortable questions about their own economic policy. It was all very well sounding the alarm over the affordability of Brown's programmes, but hadn't the Tories pledged to match his spending at least until 2011, and perhaps beyond? And what, precisely, happened to their promise to 'share the proceeds of growth' in a recession when by definition there was no growth? The reply – that it would hold true over an economic cycle – begged at least as many questions as it answered.

Then there was the legacy of Northern Rock. Nationalisation looked less of a 'monumental failure' as governments around the world began throwing taxpayers' cash around in a bid to prop up their stricken financial institutions. The Tories' early criticism of state action to bail out the banking sector became increasingly embarrassing. In truth the political value of the matching pledge had dramatically diminished as soon as the election was called off in October 2007, but, because it was too embarrassing to jettison it immediately, Osborne was left pointing out that he had allowed room not to match the last year of the three-year cycle, 2010/11.

As the 2008 party conference approached, the shadow Chancellor took evasive action – giving the broadest of hints in a newspaper interview that the matching policy was coming to the end of its useful life. It didn't stop the economic crisis wreaking havoc with the party conference, although it was events outside the Birmingham venue, not activists' anger within, that made that year's conference slogan, 'Plan for Change', ever more apt. Cameron had hoped to use his conference speech to nail the recession on Brown once and for all. But, with the world holding its breath for the future of global capitalism, the time wasn't right for party politics – so plans changed. By the time of Chancellor Alistair Darling's pre-budget report the next month, Cameron confirmed that he was ditching the matching pledge and set out what he acknowledged was a stark choice. The Conservatives would support monetary intervention – that is, interest rate cuts – and state intervention to facilitate lending. But they would not back tax cuts paid for with borrowed cash.

The political risks of 'doing nothing' were obvious and Brown lost little time in accusing the Tories of returning to their 'nasty party' past. In fact, Cameron had no alternative. It was possible to evade Brown's attempt to impose a dividing line over public spending during years of growth. A recession – fuelled in part by ballooning public debt – made further such efforts impossible.

What remains surprising is that it took the Tory leadership so long to abandon the matching pledge. Some of Cameron's friends hint that he found the decision one of the most difficult of his leadership and complained he did not share his colleagues' relish at the prospect of taking an axe to public spending. 'That's not what I came into politics for', one recalls him saying.

On 23 January the Office for National Statistics confirmed what everyone already knew – Britain had plunged into recession. The news darkened through the remainder of that winter and into spring. But far from inducing a sense of political crisis, the financial storm offered a measure of respite for Brown.

It provided what New Labour strategists liked to call a key 'dividing line'. Cameron may have abandoned his earlier policy of matching Labour's spending plans and brushed up his credentials as a fiscal conservative but it was neither convincing nor comfortable.

The world's largest economies were united in agreement that debt-funded government spending, either through infrastructure projects or tax cuts or both, would have to pick up the slack caused by the credit freeze and subsequent collapse of private sector economic activity.

Cameron and Osborne – who had just committed themselves to radically reducing state spending – found themselves isolated and exposed on the central question facing the world. Unlike Vince Cable, neither was able to claim to have seen the crash coming. The Tory leader even issued an apology in mid-March for failing to spot the signs and urged Brown to do the same.

He, of course, did nothing of the sort but dismissed Cameron and his party as 'do nothing Conservatives' at every opportunity.

Although it suffered diminishing returns, in the early months of 2009 it hurt.

With the newly elected US president Barack Obama reluctant to make saving the world economy his first defining task, the world stage was clear for Brown. In a further slice of luck it was Britain's turn to chair the G20 group of finance ministers, a hitherto obscure, not to say dreary, sop to those not invited to the more important G8 group of the world's largest economies.

Brown – with the help of Mandelson – turned it into geopolitical show business. He toured the world ahead of the 'London Summit' of world leaders on 2 April.

Cameron mocked the prime minister's self-portrait of an experienced and judicious economist dashing into the fray and by swift and decisive action saving Britain – and indeed the world – from total economic collapse as ludicrous. But as he hosted President Barack Obama on his first international summit and brokered deals between the US and China, Brown did, fleetingly, look the part.

And then it all went very badly wrong. Brown's most trusted press chief Damian McBride, known to lobby journalists as 'Mad Dog', was exposed as having plotted to smear senior Tories with malicious falsehoods, including one involving George Osborne's wife, Frances.

The distance between the image of a principled 'son of the Manse' and his brutal and unsavoury backroom was left gaping. Cameron, Osborne and Hilton felt thoroughly vindicated in their personal hatred for Brown and his team: now, the public could see, too, what they had always known, they said to one another. For Coulson it was another opportunity to bond with his boss. For months afterwards Cameron would tell senior journalists that the difference between himself and Brown was that 'Andy' would never have done anything like McBride.

But it was Coulson's role in the next disaster to hit Brown that really made him a bullet-proof member of the team.

When Derek Conway, a Davisite who had coined the term 'Notting Hill set', was found to have employed his son from the public purse for no obvious public benefit, Cameron's first instinct was to deny Labour a scalp. Perhaps because he was on the hoof, or perhaps from mulishness, he did not deploy his usual process of taking soundings and initially refused to withdraw the whip from Conway. It was only after heavy lobbying from allies that the Tory leader read the full account and realised his gaffe. As Cameron says of himself, he's quick to learn from his mistakes.

From as early as February there had been rumours about a leaked computer file containing the expense records of every MP stretching back years. In a stunning scoop in late March, the *Sunday Express* reported that Jacqui Smith, then Home Secretary, had claimed for a pornographic film on her expenses. The corroborating detail was extraordinary.

But even though Number 10 was well aware that the file was being hawked around Fleet Street it did not take evasive action.

Over in Norman Shaw South, however, considerable attention was being paid to how to deal with the approaching crisis. For one thing Cameron knew that he had little to fear personally, although, rather charmingly, he sought reassurance that his purchase – after he became party leader – of a tray, some tea cups and a teapot for constituency use, would not be regarded as profligate.

Although he had claimed the maximum allowable for mortgage payments on Dean he had not, unlike his more careless colleagues, padded his claims with extra, embarrassing items. The worst detail was an invoice to prune some wisteria and fix a leaky radiator.

Cameron had further insurance in that the newspaper that ended up buying the file was the *Daily Telegraph*. After an embarrassing not to say eccentric flirtation with Brown, the *Telegraph* was looking to find a way back to its natural home as the Conservatives' paper of choice in time for a return to power.

Neither it nor Cameron could know on the eve of publication of the first set of claims – of Brown and the rest of the Cabinet – what a spectacular success the 'expenses scandal' would prove for both.

The next two months showed Cameron at his most adept and most ruthless. He got on top of the story early and stayed there by sacrificing friends, flattering the media and channelling public anger.

In the first week of the crisis he called the media to a press conference announcing a parallel investigation into MPs' behaviour in which they would be judged not by the letter of the parliamentary rules book but by the court of public opinion.

I want to start by saying sorry. Sorry that it's come to this. And sorry for the actions of some Conservative MPs. People are right to be angry that some MPs have taken public money to pay for things few could afford. You've been let down. Politicians have done things that are unethical and wrong. I don't care if they were within the rules – they were wrong.

It proved a smart move, allowing Cameron to take some control over a messy process and project authority over his MPs. It also gave Coulson something to barter with in negotiations with the *Daily*

Telegraph. As the paper dripped out material day by day, the ever-accommodating Llewellyn ran the inquisition but it was Coulson and Cameron who would decide on the fate of that day's target.

At the time of the Jacqui Smith revelation Cameron had said she had failed the '*Daily Mail* test' – a judgement of tabloid perception rather than whether rules had been followed. Now he applied the *Daily Telegraph* test on his MPs – in effect, if the paper thought it worth a story, the MP should at the least apologise. Where cases were considered particularly egregious Cameron undertook to fire frontbenchers and even deselect the culprits deemed worst.

Friends and allies like Gove, excoriated for claiming a child's bed among other items considered by the *Telegraph* improper, were humiliated as Cameron 'got tough' on expenses. Andrew MacKay, an old-stager who insinuated his way into Cameron's outer circle as his parliamentary adviser, was sacrificed along with his wife and ex-*Telegraph* lobby journalist Julie Kirkbride, for the truly indefensible ruse, theoretically allowable to MPs married to one another, of billing the taxpayer for both their main and second homes.

But as the weeks – and the allegations – dragged on, Cameron appeared to have helped fan a firestorm that would devour the whole of his party. In the Commons tea room, where agitated MPs sheltered, dreading a call from one of the *Telegraph* journalists assigned to the story, he was not popular.

It was notable, said critics, how many of and with what speed Cameron's internal enemies were hurried into the line of fire. There was indeed some glee at the discomfort of long-despised Tory squires who thought nothing of making the taxpayer foot the bills for duck houses, moats and manure. For uber-modernisers the purging flames of 'expenses' offered the chance to burn out the last of the contamination of the Tory brand. The scandal made in vivid terms the case for a 'new politics', a phrase Cameron had been pushing since 2005.

Cameron emerged from the expenses scandal with more authority over his party while Brown was a dramatically weakened figure. From the start he seemed to regard both the crisis and its solution as a parliamentary issue, not seeing that the public did not make the distinction between MPs and government. His belated and clumsy attempts to get on top of the story were quickly lost in the minutiae of parliamentary procedure. Cameron and Nick Clegg easily slipped from ineptly laid traps and in the process built the beginning of a relationship, although the Lib Dem leader was as wary of Cameron as he was of Brown.

Labour strategists said that it was inevitable that the party of government would suffer the most from public revulsion at the antics of incumbent MPs of whatever stripe. A better, braver, more nimble Labour leader might, nevertheless, have done more to compete with Cameron to 'own' the crisis and refract public anger through a Labour message.

Although the Tory leader may have had a good 'expenses', most of the rest of his party were nervous wrecks. Even Osborne, 'cleared' by the *Telegraph*, found himself the subject of an official investigation and was subsequently censured. More than once that summer Cameron found himself 'cut' by Tory MPs who felt he had betrayed them for his own ambition. Sir Peter Viggers, one of the first to have backed him in 2005 and the owner of the duck house that came to symbolise the crisis, was typical of those who felt badly ill used and made sure that he let him know. An anonymous letter was circulated complaining of actions designed to assert a 'Stalinist hold over the party'. Less hysterically, media supporters like Fraser Nelson, the editor of the *Spectator*, wondered at the brutality of Cameron's behaviour.

Cameron must have been relieved, therefore, to be able to throw the Tory right a bone. And there are few bones the Tory right likes as much as those of a European federalist. On 22 June, while most mainstream media attention was focused on the election of a new Commons Speaker, Cameron formally withdrew his party from the European People's Party (EPP) group in Strasbourg, honouring the pledge, made in a panic to block Liam Fox, during the leadership contest. The creation of the new grouping of non-federalist mostly Eastern European parties had taken years of delicate negotiations with partners, some of whose views were to say the least embarrassing for a modern British politician. Cameron had also had to endure repeated lectures from Angela Merkel and Nicolas Sarkozy about the folly of withdrawal. He could not resist a 'comedy German' accent in relaying Merkel's sermons to friends while Sarkozy's passionate tirades he found simply alarming.

In the end, however, the separation did exactly what he hoped it would: shore up his position with both MPs and activists while attracting small and largely predictable criticism of some of the more unsavoury new bedfellows from the left.

While Cameron may have consolidated his position as party leader through the first half of 2009, he was privately dismayed at what he might inherit in power.

He could be powerfully scathing about Labour's failures, for instance, in his response to the 2009 Budget. The 'fundamental truth', he said, was that all Labour governments run out of money.

The last Labour government gave us the Winter of Discontent. This Labour government has given us the Decade of Debt. The last Labour government left the dead unburied. This one leaves the debts unpaid. They sit there, running out of money, running out of moral authority, running out of time. You have to ask what on earth is the point of another fourteen months of this government of the living dead?

Writing in the *Financial Times*, Philip Stephens called it the performance of a 'politician on the threshold of Downing Street'. Barely two months later, however, the same commentator was complaining that he still didn't know what the Conservatives 'were for'. 'The big danger for Mr Cameron is that the promised austerity lacks convincing context.'

Cameron had a twofold problem in providing that context. On the one hand he wanted a proper mandate for the subsequent remodelling of state spending which would require the party to be as honest as it could about the cuts it planned to make – but he did not want to scare voters away. Secondly, he was determined not to abandon a commitment to improve public services even as he was in effect serving notice there would be less money for them. He needed a credible explanation of how this would be possible.

The Tory leader was to try again and again to resolve these twin issues over the next year, without success. Part of the problem was that he himself was – and perhaps remains – unsure of what the proper 'context' of austerity ought to be.

Cameron made an early bash at squaring the circles when he addressed the Conservatives' 2009 spring conference in Cheltenham. 'There are deep, dark clouds over our economy, our society, and our whole political system. Steering our country through this storm; reaching the sunshine on the far side cannot mean sticking to the same, wrong course. We need a complete change of direction,' he said.

But the coming 'age of austerity' wasn't all pain, he said. 'We are not here just to balance the books. There's more to our mission than coming in like a bunch of flint-faced accountants. The question is: how does government help achieve these wider aims in the age of austerity? And the answer is: by delivering more for less.'

There was to be a return to traditional public spending control, a 'new culture of thrift' in government, social problems were going to be cured not just treated and lastly innovative use of new technology in public service delivery. Each shadow minister was tasked with finding savings to contribute to 'a spending review' overseen by Osborne and Philip Hammond. The exercise was as much to hide as to reveal Conservative intentions. The decision to abandon Labour's spending plans had been caveated – the party would maintain planned levels of spending on health, education and international aid. The second commitment was later all but dropped and the third was a tiny proportion of government spending, but the first – the commitment to the NHS budget – had the effect of jacking up the pain for all other spending areas. A comprehensive spending review was a blanket that could smother any question of detail.

Cameron accepted there was no need to answer Labour's demand to set out exactly what the party would cut – after all, he had had first hand experience of Smith's disastrous shadow budget in 1992 – but wanted at least a sketch in broad outline. Osborne was more cautious. In a running argument between the men over the summer, Osborne presented voluminous examples drawn mostly from US politics together with polling results that backed his claim that the public weren't ready for the full consequences of what a proper fiscal consolidation would mean.

Hilton was for as much honesty as possible and as the inner team began to prepare for the party conference – the last big showcase before the long election campaign – it became clear that Cameron was going to have his way. Osborne, therefore, began to work on a series of cost-cutting measures that it was hoped would do just enough to draw the sting of Labour's criticism that the Tories were masking their intent but not so much as to allow themselves to be painted as crazed ideologues bent on slashing where they could. It wasn't an easy job. One of Osborne's friends recalls him saying that it was '"doing his head in", which is an un-George thing to say'.

(Labour's high command, too, was having trouble deciding how straight to be with voters about the scale of Britain's woes but the roles were reversed. Brown shared Osborne's view of the electorate's limited capacity to absorb bad news while Darling insisted that the credibility of not just the party but the country demanded a fuller response than had been given so far.)

Although Osborne had accepted the need for an 'honesty' strategy on the cuts he was still very nervous about how it would go down. Polling continued until just before the Tories gathered in Manchester for what Cameron told the shadow Cabinet would be a sombre, businesslike gathering. Any hint of presumption, jollity or entitlement on display at the party conference would be stamped on. (Although that didn't stop Cameron, while preparing his own address, digging out the eve-of-an-epoch conference speeches of Margaret Thatcher, from 1978, and Tony Blair from 1996).

Boris Johnson, not being in the shadow Cabinet, didn't hear that lecture, not that it would have made any difference if he had. It's possible that when Johnson called on Cameron to issue an explicit pledge to hold a retrospective referendum on the Lisbon Treaty he didn't mean to cause trouble; possible but unlikely. Johnson, always keen for definition, would have been aware that even his indulgent party admirers wouldn't forgive rank disloyalty during an election campaign. This, therefore, would be his last chance to discomfit Cameron and court the party for at least six months.

The issue was ticklish; in his pursuit of the backing of the *Sun*, Cameron had issued a 'cast-iron guarantee' that there would be a vote on the Lisbon Treaty. He had, it is true, always refused to be drawn on what might happen if the treaty – a further surrender of national sovereignty in exchange for a less sclerotic, expanded EU – had been ratified in all member states.

But while there were sound reasons to avoid spelling out the position it looked at best evasive and at worst dishonest. Johnson's intervention was, to say the least, unhelpful.

Wrangling with the right over Europe wasn't the start to the sober, 'rolling up our sleeves' sort of a conference that Cameron had hoped for. An echo of the histrionics in Tory high command was by Boles, not yet an MP (he had been selected for safe-as-houses Grantham) but a loyal handmaiden to the leadership. 'La vendetta è un piatto che va mangiato freddo,' he texted in the early morning; 'revenge is a dish best eaten cold'.

Osborne won back control of the conference by spelling out the first details of the Tories' deficit reduction plan presented under the refrain that 'we're all in this together'. The most eye-catching was the bringing forward of a rise in the pension age. The other element to the new economic message was the warning that, unless action was taken, Britain would lose it creditworthiness, an economic disaster that would make its borrowing more expensive and risk plunging it into a tailspin ending in default and humiliation.

At the time the evidence for the claim was sketchy at best; only one of the international credit agencies had sounded an alarm and then only in an extreme set of circumstances. Moreover, it might be regarded as a self-fulfilling prophesy of doom as well as a surrender to the bond markets. But Osborne needed to justify the scale of the cuts and the risk to Britain's 'AAA' rating was something that could be easily understood.

After Osborne had laid out the hard road to get over the top of Britain's debt mountain, Cameron intended his speech to give voters a view of the other side. Hilton had, as usual, refused to test any of the messages with focus groups, trusting instead on Cameron's ability to communicate naturally. The rhetoric borrowed heavily from Martin Luther King by way of Neil Kinnock.

But Hilton's insistence on authenticity paid off in the sense that the speech came alive not at the expected clap lines but when Cameron lit into Labour's record on poverty. 'Who made the poorest poorer?' he demanded. 'No, not the wicked Tories ... you; you're the ones that did this to our society. So don't you dare lecture us about poverty.'

Cameron had good reason to feel in good heart as he celebrated his forty-third birthday in an Oxfordshire pub later that week. The party was registering double-digit poll leads, he had finally secured the backing of the *Sun* and he had got the Tories' economic message into a position on which the party could confidently campaign during the election.

FALLING SHORT
General election campaign 2010

George Osborne had warned that the Tories would pay a price for giving voters a taste of the economic medicine to come and, ten days before Christmas, David Cameron learned what it was.

An ICM poll showed that the Tories' advantage over Labour had narrowed to nine points. It was the first time in a year that the Conservatives had not enjoyed a double-digit lead. Other surveys confirmed the trend.

Cameron, who watches polls much more closely than he ever admits in public, scrutinised the survey for clues.

What was horribly unclear were the pace and scale of the tightening. Had he erred in hastening and amplifying the austerity message? In over-reaching for credibility, had he handed his enemies too much ammunition? Women reaching retirement age and those in receipt of child tax credit had started receiving Labour pamphlets warning of 'Tory cuts' within days of Osborne's conference speech.

Cameron, who relies so much on momentum, was spooked that the spell of an inevitable Tory victory was beginning to be broken. To regain the initiative a New Year policy blitz was planned for the start of the so-called 'long campaign' – the period of electioneering that precedes the formal calling of the poll.

Coulson told shadow ministers to prepare three or four key policies to be repackaged in a rolling operation that would run through January, soaking up as much media space as possible.

When accused of travelling light Cameron parried that there was too much Tory policy, not too little. The real trouble, he believed, was that the press had paid insufficient attention to what had been announced.

Highlighting key policies also gave shadow ministers the chance to quietly prune their programme ahead of the full manifesto launch. But it was a panicky and chaotic affair and was soon abandoned.

What might have been dismissed as a false start instead set the tone for the election campaign to come. Looking back on its failure the key members of Cameron's team all choose to highlight different facets. For some the problem was that it was too negative, for others that it was insufficiently inspirational, while for some the cardinal error was not seeing the dangers posed by the TV debates.

All agree, however, that its inadequacies are well illustrated by the poster advertising campaign that was supposed to launch the January blitzkrieg. Thousands of sites throughout Britain had been booked months in advance. In the weeks leading up to Christmas the Tories' advertising agency, Euro RSCG, had sent a steady stream of suggestions to Hilton. He didn't like any of them. It wasn't the fault of the agency but reflected a deep three-way split in the campaign team.

Hilton wanted to start the New Year on a positive note, setting out why voters should choose the Conservatives. Osborne, however, was adamant that it would be a mistake to stop hammering away at Labour. 'To keep our foot on Gordon Brown's neck as he always put it,' recalls one insider. It was a position broadly favoured by Coulson.

Stephen Gilbert, in charge of the so-called 'ground war' in the marginal constituencies, argued that the Tories should use their financial advantage to address head-on voters' worries that the party could not be trusted on the NHS. The need to reassure voters meant, also, that Cameron's own face should feature prominently on the posters, he believed. Others wanted to hold back that asset – Cameron was and remains more popular than his party – until later in the campaign.

Cameron, 'grumpy with the realisation they didn't agree', took charge of a compromise-reaching process over the Christmas and New Year holidays. Thus, with just days to go before the launch of their 'long campaign', its key offensive was still being cobbled together on Hilton's laptop. Inevitably the result was a mess.

'We can't go on like this,' a tieless Cameron solemnly intoned from a thousand poster sites across Britain. 'I'll cut the deficit, not the NHS,' he added in jarring juxtaposition.

Within hours of the unveiling it was clear that it was going to be a critical disaster. Not only did it fail as a piece of propaganda, Cameron faced questions until polling day and beyond over whether his picture had been airbrushed. Superficial, false and evasive: it was not the image they had hoped for.

'The face with that glassy-eyed stare was the opposite of compassion. It was cold, severe, weird-looking,' shuddered a friend.

'The internal view was that it was the poster which started the drift and they lost momentum because they took their foot off Gordon Brown's throat,' says a close observer. 'The lack of clarity caused some internal tensions and they were introspective for a period and that is when they lost momentum.'

Cameron has always prided himself on managing 'internal tensions'. He has been compared to a conductor waving a baton, now at the horns, now at the strings, as he makes music out of what would otherwise be competing sounds. The trouble was, just as the orchestra most needed direction, the conductor seemed to lose focus.

Cameron and his wife started bracing themselves for the anniversary of Ivan's death on 25 February. Although Samantha was by now pregnant again, the couple were still grieving the loss of their son, a process of emotional recovery delayed, in Cameron's case, by his public exposure, says a close friend. Of that time, he says, Cameron 'was not quite as on it. He was not quite engaged.'

The disengagement was to some extent also deliberate and

institutionalised. In an election campaign the 'principal' has to be kept away from the day-to-day minutiae. The trouble was that Osborne – who was supposed to be in overall charge – was not recognised as such by Hilton, nor even Coulson.

Osborne confessed to a friend that he was 'hating every minute' of his role as election coordinator. He had brought back George Bridges to shore up his position but, although Bridges did his best, the campaign team was becoming quarrelsome and dysfunctional.

Matters weren't helped by the fact that Cameron himself wasn't always consistent about policy or even about the scale of the austerity he thought Britain should endure. To Osborne's irritation he used a speech to business leaders at the World Economic Forum at the end of January to say that the cuts in the first year of a Tory government would not be 'particularly extensive', adding later in an interview that 'we are not talking about swingeing cuts'. The shadow Chancellor could see that, having chosen to stand and fight on fiscal conservatism, there was no point in soft-pedalling that message now.

By mid-February the right-leaning newspapers were drumming their fingers. In one of a rash of football analogies on the general theme that the complacent Tories should be more than a goal up a *Times* leader grumbled: 'They think it's all over, it isn't.'

The *Daily Mail* blamed Cameron's inconsistency. 'Voters don't like politicians who tack and trim, constantly changing their minds. The Conservatives have done it on Europe, marriage and their strategy for a draconian cutback in spending. With the election only months or perhaps weeks away, this confusion is hugely counterproductive.' In the *Wall Street Journal*, Melanie Phillips wrote of Cameron's 'egregious opportunism'.

Efforts were made to get a grip; Hilton and Coulson were required to share a room in Millbank; Gove, who had been watching the mess in quiet despair, was drafted into an ad-hoc election campaign team. The question it had to address was how to balance attacks on Brown with a more positive message which raised the most urgent issue – exposed by the poster debacle – of how to frame the Tories' positive offer.

As the spring conference season approached, Cameron summoned the key players to his house in King North Street. It was not a successful meeting. He texted participants the next day to say that he had not found the 'navel gazing' useful and instructed the team to continue to highlight both Brown's failures and the 'message of change'. Bridges and Coulson boiled the latter down into six bullet points, duly enumerated by Cameron in his speech to a restive party in Brighton at the end of February.

The Conservative vision for Britain, he said, was to boost enterprise, deal with the deficit, clean up politics, raise school standards, maintain the NHS and back families. On the last he surprised a listening Osborne by committing the party to a marriage tax break within the next parliament, by accident. (For all his discipline, Cameron does occasionally blurt his true intentions.)

By now the polls were looking ominous – one dramatic survey released on the eve of Cameron's speech had Labour within two points. The news was delivered to Cameron over dinner with Coulson, Feldman and others. 'There was real anxiety at that point,' recalls one diner.

Worse was to come. Just when Cameron was first aware that Michael Ashcroft was not domiciled in the UK for tax purposes is still not clear. What is beyond doubt is that for more than four years as leader he chose either not to inquire or not to bring the fact into the light.

On 1 March, Gordon Prentice, the former Labour MP who finally forced Lord Ashcroft's tax arrangements into the open through a freedom of information request, recalls meeting Cameron as he strode through the House of Commons. 'Well, you've got your answer now,' he said without breaking stride.

The breeziness was an act. Cameron knew full well that the disclosure and its timing were a disaster. The issue of Ashcroft's tax status had, like toothache, caused the Tories a dull pain for more than ten years, ever since the then Treasurer's nomination for a peerage had been rejected on the grounds that he kept the bulk of his fortune, estimated at more than £5 billion, offshore.

After an agreement, brokered by Hague in 2000, the then Tory leader told Tony Blair that Ashcroft would pay 'tens of millions' of pounds more in tax as a result of becoming a UK resident. In fact the deal struck with the Cabinet Office was that Ashcroft would become a 'long-term', not 'permanent', resident of the UK, a change that allowed him to persuade the Revenue to allow him to keep his fortune in countries like Belize, untaxed by the country in whose legislature he served.

There were plenty who suspected as much but Ashcroft's reputation as an aggressive litigator and the confidentiality of individual tax arrangements in British law frustrated attempts to get at the truth for a decade.

Ashcroft had become a Labour obsession thanks to his strategy of identifying marginal seats for generous and long-term funding. While the relative value of his donations, made through a UK-listed company in an arrangement criticised by the Electoral Commission, dwindled over time, he maintained far more influence than most donors. This was in part inspired by the personal loyalty of those like Stephen Gilbert, whom he had employed after Gilbert – now Cameron's political secretary – had been sacked by the party in one of its many internal purges. A former, very senior, member of the party's hierarchy also admits that 'everyone was scared of Michael'. 'We all just danced around the bonfire, including David.'

Cameron, whenever asked about the tax arrangements of the man he had made Deputy Chairman in 2005 and had brought back into mainstream operations two years later, made full use of the sanctity of an individual's relations with the taxman. But when the Liberal Democrats proposed a new law that barred 'non-dom' peers, Cameron, who professed to be a champion of 'new politics', had no choice but to back it. Conservative press officers said that such a law would cause Ashcroft 'no trouble'.

Cameron has so far not said when he knew that was, at best, misleading. His aides say that he found out in late January when Ashcroft – at Hague's insistence – had phoned the Tory leader to confess the truth. For his part Hague said that he only became aware 'over the last few months' that his billionaire friend did not pay UK tax on all of his foreign income.

Even had Cameron only discovered in January, the uncomfortable truth was that Ashcroft, a major figure in the Conservative Party, had not done what it had been assumed by the wider public he had promised to do.

The person Cameron held responsible for sorting it out, William Hague, either did know or should have known. It looked bad for Cameron and worse for Hague.

The 'Ashcroft scandal' lasted more than a week, long enough to remind voters that the Conservatives were still funded by a relatively small group of wealthy business backers. Although Gordon Brown and Labour, discredited as they were with their own recent history of funding scandals, were unable to benefit much from the fallout, could there be another young, fresh, personable politician who might offer 'change'?

On 6 April, to no one's surprise, Brown called the election. Cameron, competing with the gravitas of the drive to the Palace, borrowed the backdrop of the House of Commons for his response staged on the South Bank. To an audience of party workers he appealed to the 'great ignored' who 'work hard, pay taxes and obey the law'. The Nixonian echo of the 'silent majority' was dropped immediately but other elements of the first day of campaigning set the model for the next month. Immediately after the South Bank campaign launch Cameron travelled to the West Midlands and Yorkshire, the two main battlegrounds. There he gave short speeches to audiences of party workers in open-necked white shirt with the sleeves rolled up which alluded to his youth, a fresh start for the country and the multiple failures of Labour's debt-fuelled misrule. For most of the next month the same format would be repeated in almost all of the Tories' list of 'target seats' using to the full the cash advantage which had enabled the hire of a plane.

Election accounts show it spent £270,000 hiring the twenty-eight-seater Dornier A328 turboprop. (It also spent £10,000 on 'counter-espionage', essentially vetting campaign staff and securing communications – an investment no doubt approved of by Coulson.)

All parties were well aware that the traditional tools of the constituency visit and daily press conference had been made much less relevant, perhaps even obsolete, by the advent of full television debates between the leaders of the three main parties.

Cameron had first called for TV debates when he ran for Conservative leader in 2005 and had not wavered in his support as the logic for such a gamble disappeared with Labour's poll lead. Coulson enthusiastically supported Cameron in his belief that he could only benefit from a platform which would allow voters to make the comparison with Brown, a poor television performer.

Indeed, both men were so eager for the contest they agreed to a lengthy list of demands made by Labour as well as accepting that the Liberal Democrats had to be given equal billing.

What remains surprising about Nick Clegg's barnstorming performance in the first television debate on Thursday 15 April was that the Tories were surprised at all. It had been obvious from the first rehearsal that Cameron was going to have to fight the Liberal Democrat leader for the 'change' mantle. A team led by Jeremy Hunt, who played Clegg in the mock-ups, correctly anticipated how Clegg would lump both Brown and Cameron together as a discredited status quo. After the first rehearsal, Anita Dunn, one of two US political consultants brought in to sharpen the campaign, said: 'Well, I'm voting for Nick Clegg.'

George Bridges recalls: 'The first day we had the full-scale run-through it became blazingly obvious that we'd been going round saying, "We are the change" and suddenly here's this guy who *is* the change.'

It would be untrue to say that, having identified the problem, Cameron did nothing about it. He worked with Bill Knapp, the other American drafted in, on parrying the Clegg challenge. Knapp was impressed with Cameron's natural facility as a communicator (a session to prepare Osborne for the shadow Chancellor's debate, by contrast, had him in despair). The party also polled extensively to find resonant ways of illustrating the most powerful issues. Finally, Cameron spent more time on rehearsals than Brown, although not as much as Clegg.

Bridges says that the 'love-bombing' strategy pioneered in the Crewe by-election and subsequently used nationally had left the Conservatives with few options to deal with the 'emotional' appeal of Clegg. 'I question whether or not we'd thought through the whole Lib Dem threat enough. I know that I hadn't.'

The Tories had had a reasonable first week. Borrowing from the New Labour playbook, they had produced an impressive array of business endorsements and had scored modest hits with attacks on Labour's 'jobs tax' – a rise in National Insurance that Alistair Darling had announced. But this was the 'phoney war'; the real hostilities weren't due to begin until transmission began in the Manchester television studio.

Cameron prepared for at least one of the TV debates by having a sleep, according to an aide. His remarkable ability to switch off is one of his gifts as a politician. But on the night of the first TV debate –

arguably the biggest of his political career – his nerves got the better of him. 'From his point of view he was the person with everything to lose,' said an ally, adding that, unusually, he had failed to synthesise adequately competing advice.

The format of the debate didn't help: because of Brown's poor eyesight he was placed on the left of the stage where he would be least disadvantaged. Clegg had drawn the other spot, leaving Cameron stuck in the middle. Usually a master of working an audience, he was hemmed in further by the rigid time limits. In striving to be folksy he overreached and too many anecdotes created an impression of falsity. The worst moment of a poor performance came in an answer to a question about immigration.

'I was in Plymouth recently and a forty-year-old black man … said, "I came here when I was six, I've served in the Royal Navy for thirty years, I'm incredibly proud of my country. But I'm so ashamed that we've had this out-of-control system with people abusing it so badly".'

The intention had been to connect with voters who believe immigration should be curbed without appearing racist. The effect was to give the impression of a man mildly surprised to have stumbled across a 'black man' for the first time in his life – and 'in Plymouth' of all places.

Clegg, by contrast, was a revelation. 'Who could have known that Nick Clegg had *that* in him,' marvelled one of Cameron's allies more than a year later of the Liberal Democrat's hitherto unsuspected television presence. Britain woke up the next morning to the thrilling realisation that, against all expectations, the election was going to be fascinating and potentially revolutionary.

It was a long weekend in the Conservative campaign headquarters. Cameron, fine on Friday, was by the weekend distraught. One close ally says he was 'catatonic with depression'.

'I felt terrible about it all. I felt guilty by association, that I'd been part of the team that had utterly failed to prepare him for this.'

It was notable that the HQ in Millbank was virtually empty in the three days that followed the debate. Some well-informed Tories believe that the campaign was close to an implosion as a slew of polls in the Sunday press confirmed a huge surge in Lib Dem support. The *Sunday Times* reported that Nick Clegg was more popular than Winston Churchill. In its leader the paper said that the decision to take part in the debates 'could turn out to be the biggest political gaffe since Mr Brown's failure to call an election'. A tetchy postmortem on Monday failed to lift the sense of gloom but by Tuesday Cameron appeared to have recovered some of his equilibrium.

With the wind in their faces, panicky Tory candidates were soon complaining that the approved campaign book wasn't working well enough on the doorstep. In particular they disliked the phrase Big Society, coined by Hilton to capture the essence of a Tory government led by Cameron that would use and devolve power to facilitate the spread of individual and collective responsibility for social goods. Building a big society squared the circle between commitment to public services and a fiscal conservatism which necessitated deep cuts in public spending. Less state funding was consistent with better public services and a better quality of life when better citizens took more responsibility for themselves and others.

An outing, in a speech just before the election was called, had been received well enough, at least in the comment pages of sympathetic newspapers. It featured heavily in the election manifesto launch, a modish affair in Battersea Power Station. The manifesto's title, *Invitation to Join the Government of Britain*, sought to enthuse voters for this idea which Cameron said was both ambitious and modest. Letwin and Hilton (with James O'Shaughnessy, then head of policy, caught painfully in the middle) had bashed out the text.

But for many voters the latest formulation of the 'more for less' promise smelled fishy. It didn't help that the phrase had not been market-tested (Hilton has said that to have done so would have been 'preposterous' since it had never been intended to be a slogan), nor had any efforts been made to blend it into other campaign messages. The failure to coordinate the Tories' efforts to deliver a positive message is perhaps the campaign's most glaring failure. The dissonance meant, if anything, that the efforts were counterproductive, the message appeared to many dishonest if not downright vacuous. Previous admirers like Polly Toynbee had already abandoned what she called the 'head-swivellingly empty oxymoron' of 'progressive conservatism'.

Although some senior Labour politicians privately agreed with Cameron's critique of its over-reliance on spending and desertion of the moral sphere, they gratefully accepted more grist to mill their message that the Tories could not be trusted.

A relentlessly, negative, no-frills campaign dominated by the single, easily understood message that the Tories were hiding deep spending cuts about which they were ideologically excited was working better than some of its architects had dared hope.

Andrew Cooper, who at that time was director of Populus, the polling organisation used by the Tories, said: 'I think in some ways Labour fought a brilliant campaign, given they had no resources and were led by a lunatic. The ground campaign was very, very targeted and ruthless.' Specifically, Labour worked on the fears of key segments of voters who relied on the NHS and benefited from tax credits. The latter in particular was a weak spot since Osborne *did* very much want to trim the benefit payments, particularly for middle-income earners, but could not admit as much.

Cooper says that although voters were largely persuaded that it was time for a change, Labour was succeeding in preventing significant numbers to reach the further conclusion that it was time to change to the Conservatives.

Those, like Osborne, who defend the Tory campaign in 2010 insist that despite the shaky start the TV debates did end up benefiting the party, not least since they provided some shelter from Labour's 'hard pounding' on the cuts theme.

The second TV debate, hosted by Sky in Bristol, went a little better. Themed on foreign affairs, Cameron held water, although the instant polls showed a dead heat.

With a fortnight to go it was becoming obvious that if the Tories were to win a majority at all it was going to be a small one. This in turn made another looming election of critical importance to Cameron, although to most voters it was totally obscure.

The post of chairman of the 1922 Committee had become vacant with the retirement of Sir Michael Spicer. His successor, as the foreman of Conservative backbenchers, would be elected by rank and file Tory MPs in the first few weeks of a new parliament. Whoever it was would wield huge influence in a parliament with a small Tory majority. The leading candidate was none other than Graham Brady, Gove and Cameron's nemesis from grammargate.

As a youthful, personable, northern, urban, lower middle-class, vocally Eurosceptic Conservative, Brady was representative of the sort of backbencher the leader's clique had frozen out – which, of course, made him all the more attractive to other MPs who felt overlooked.

Gove had been worrying about Brady for some time and now Cameron too began to see the threat. Having to negotiate with Brady and a rump of mostly right-wing Tory MPs for the day-to-day survival of his government was not an attractive prospect for either Cameron or any of his inner circle. They believed that the sort of compromises that would have to be made with the Tory right would undo most of, if not all, the work that they had done in Opposition to move the party to the political centre. The difficulties of managing relations with the European Union with such an outcome did not bear thinking about.

The question was, what to do about it? Letwin, true to his wonkish nature, had spent the weeks after the publication of the parties' manifestos analysing all three. Osborne had a more practical interest. He told Cameron the party had better prepare for the eventuality of a hung parliament. Cameron agreed but insisted as leader that he should be kept out of the discussions.

On the night of Sunday 18 April, Oliver Letwin, William Hague and Ed Llewellyn arrived at Osborne's town house in Notting Hill. Had they been asked they no doubt would have said they were simply having dinner with a friend. If the media – or even other members of the shadow Cabinet – had been aware of what was being discussed that night it would have changed the course of the election and Britain's history.

In front of them lay copies of the Liberal Democrat manifesto, the Conservative Party manifesto and transcripts of everything Clegg had said about what he and his party would do in the event they held the balance of power.

Letwin, a copy of the Tory manifesto in his hand, went through it chapter by chapter, assessing what the Lib Dems might accept and what they would insist was junked. By the end of the night there was a set of scribbled notes. These were to become the first draft of what was to become the coalition agreement.

Two days later the Tory leader invited Osborne over to King North Street for dinner on the eve of the second TV debate. The two chewed over the campaign before turning to the question at hand.

Cameron then set out his position. In the event of a hung parliament he wanted to publicly dangle the prospect of a full coalition with the Lib Dems, what he was to later call a 'big, generous offer'. 'Either they'll reject it in which case we'll be on the high ground, or it might work and we'll have a much better majority,' he said.

Curiously, despite Cameron's preference for a 'full coalition' when the team met at Osborne's house for a second time on the Sunday before the election, they discussed a possible Lib Dem deal in terms of a so-called confidence and supply agreement, a sort of non-aggression pact that would allow the Tories to govern day-to-day.

Less than five days after the private dinner he shared with Cameron, Osborne made a rare appearance at a press conference to denounce the dangers of denying a single party an overall majority. He unveiled a faux election broadcast for the fictional Hung Parliament Party in an attempt to raise the spectre of the horrors of coalition government.

Given that they were preparing an attempt to make just such an arrangement work the text is, to put it politely, ironic. A hung parliament would mean that 'under-the-table deals will be the order of the day', it claimed, 'more dithering policies' and the 'risk of killing the economic recovery'.

Although the debates squeezed the life out of most of the rest of the campaign, it managed to summon moments of traditional election hurly-burly. The day before his dinner with Osborne, Cameron confronted and unmasked the *Daily Mirror*'s 'chicken' in Tamworth, a hapless, costumed reporter tasked with fowling Cameron's visits. Two days later he was pelted with an egg in Cornwall. The sequence settled once and for all the question of which came first, he joked (frequently).

For a man on the edge of losing an election that until recently had seemed in the bag, Cameron gave a good impression of enjoying himself as the finishing line hove into view. Cooper recalls that the leader was in 'an amazingly confident mood, [he] seemed to be quite enjoying it'.

The task of looking relaxed became easier after the third and last TV debate, hosted by the BBC in Birmingham. An aide says Cameron found the preparation for the debates tiresome and the debates themselves restrictive, and had been badly shaken by his failure in the first. He was judged to have 'won' the final bout, however, and professed himself delighted at the prospect of a return to real campaigning.

After their surge the polls suggested some of the wind was coming out of the Lib Dem sails as voters began to pay close attention. An ill-advised policy of a limited amnesty for asylum seekers had given the Tories the chance to raise the issue without risk of a blowback. Labour's 'comeback' narrative had died in the aftermath of Brown's disastrous encounter with Gillian Duffy, a pensioner in Rochdale, whom, courtesy of a forgotten radio mic, he was heard to describe as 'a sort of bigoted woman'.

On Bank Holiday Monday all three leaders addressed an event in Westminster Central Hall. Brown, well suited to the pulpit, did well but so did Cameron and Clegg.

Cameron then geared up for what was briefed as an epic twenty-four-hour whistle-stop tour of key constituencies. It was a gimmick designed to keep the rolling news channels fully occupied with images of a youthful, dynamic leader right up until polling day but it served another purpose.

Given what he feared was coming, he needed to be able to show that he had done everything humanly possible. Failure, if that's what the voters delivered, wasn't going to be for the want of his personal efforts.

'I think it's fair for someone in the last twenty-four hours of campaigning to spend all their time, all their effort, all their energy trying to win people over for an overall majority,' he said.

After watching the sun rise over Grimsby Fish Market, Cameron ended the campaign in a rally in Bristol. Following a few hours' sleep he then headed, by prior arrangement, to Steve Hilton's farmhouse close to his own home in Dean.

Already gathered around Hilton's modern kitchen table were various aides, Osborne and the Chief Whip Patrick McLoughlin. The presence of 'the Chief' hints at the meeting's original purpose, planned right at the beginning of the campaign, which was to start to thrash out the finer details of the Tory government structure and its first actions. That wasn't how it turned out. 'Elections are very curious days for politicians,' says one who was there. 'You are working at 150 per cent and that day – it's tumbleweed. So we sat there.'

To pass the time Cameron, Osborne and Hilton all gave their predictions: all were within a few seats of the final result. They hadn't made it.

Despite the best-ever funded campaign against a deeply unpopular leader with poor communication skills, at the tail end of an administration that was racked by scandal and recession, Cameron had come up short. Why? Each of the main participants gives a slightly different answer which is itself an explanation. One of the key figures says it was the failure to coordinate what became rival and contradictory efforts. 'There were four or five campaigns within the one. [There was] a campaign around the manifesto, the campaign around the advertising, the campaign around how to attack Labour and then other bits and bobs. There was no core, central message.'

70 WHITEHALL
Coalition negotiations 7–12 May 2010

'You should get hold of Danny now!' Cameron barked into his mobile phone as he was driven from his count in Witney in the early hours of Friday 7 May. Back in the party's HQ in Millbank, Ed Llewellyn did as he was told and texted Danny Alexander, Nick Clegg's chief-of-staff.

As he did so he could watch helicopter-shot TV coverage of his boss's progress down the M40 towards London. Footage inside the car would have shown a distraught figure.

'He was barely functioning,' a close aide was quoted as saying of Cameron in a newspaper account a week later. 'His mind was whirring. All he could think was how, after five years of the change agenda, he could have failed.'

Earlier in the day at Steve Hilton's house it had been agreed that the main imperative in the hours after the polls closed would be to prise Gordon Brown out of Downing Street no matter if it were obvious the Tories had fallen short.

In his address after regaining Witney (with an increased majority), Cameron said Labour had 'lost its mandate to govern' but the party just hadn't won enough seats for him to credibly demand Brown's resignation.

Now, in the car on the way to the campaign HQ, he began to face up to what failure might mean. Arriving in Millbank, he headed first to a party for high-rolling donors. Many had believed that victory was certain and the atmosphere was unpleasant. Cameron made a speech, stayed for as short a time as was decent, and then retreated into the office on the building's north-east corner usually used by his friend and Conservative chief executive Andy Feldman.

Ashcroft – incredibly among those in Tory HQ on election night – slipped out to give a TV interview hinting heavily that the decision to take part in the debates had cost the Tories a majority. The vultures were already circling.

'He knew right away. His bollocks were on the line. He had to think very quickly how he and George were going to get out of this alive,' said a friend. In Feldman's office Cameron didn't have to disguise his distress. 'He did feel that we should have done better,' admits one at the meeting, tactfully. But since things were in flux there was still a chance to shape events, he said. Llewellyn told the meeting that Alexander had responded to his text and further contact had been arranged for later that morning. Osborne, who had opposed the approach as premature, was aghast. He and Hilton bickered over whether the Lib Dems would form a coalition with Labour until Cameron, desperately tired, called time. It was 6.00 a.m. – well after a dawn Cameron must have hoped he would be spending on the doorsteps of Number 10. Instead he grabbed a few hours' sleep in a suite on the twelfth floor of the Westminster Bridge Park Plaza Hotel.

Four hours later, by prior appointment, the key figures trooped in to receive their instructions. Samantha had returned to the family home after a troubled, sleepless night. In subsequent interviews Cameron has given the impression that he woke, refreshed, in his hotel room on 7 May with the idea that he would pursue a full coalition with the Lib Dems. He may have woken with renewed determination to pursue that goal but, as we have seen, the notion of a maximalist offer to Clegg had been in his mind since the first TV debate had made a hung parliament the most likely outcome. 'He thought a minority government would mean another election, probably within months. He knew he had misjudged this election campaign – and that was after five years of preparation. Everyone was saying that another election in the autumn would give us a decent majority, but he couldn't see any reason why they'd necessarily do any better. A full coalition would protect him not only from the electorate but from his own mutinous backbenchers, a lot of whom were furious about the way the campaign was handled.'

Was Osborne one of those who thought a second election – held after a short period of minority government – winnable and therefore preferable? Or was his reluctance based on a more personal calculation? But if Cameron was to be hounded out for failing to win the election there was little to no chance the enraged party would turn to the campaign coordinator to lead it. Perhaps it was just that, for once, Osborne's reading of the political landscape was blurred by exhaustion.

In any case on Friday morning Cameron would brook no disagreement about the way forward. 'He behaved as if he had had ten hours' sleep instead of two,' said one aide, 'and was amazingly focused.' He instructed Hilton to draft the text of his 'forward leaning' offer and told Osborne to prepare for negotiations.

He has said that his shadow Chancellor's job was 'to get us out of Opposition and into Government. He was going to drive the chariot as fast as he could, leaving the leader of the party to make the final decision on whether the deal was the right one.'

But still Osborne cavilled at the tone of Cameron's offer even as it was being prepared. Hilton was sent back to redraft after he objected to the frequent use of the word coalition in the original text. In all, for that and other reasons, there were at least five drafts of the speech.

Cameron, meanwhile, covered his back with a ring around. While grandees like Sir John Major and Michael Howard received a personal call to alert them of what he was planning to do, most of the shadow Cabinet learned they were being asked to share power via a conference call. Dominic Grieve started to object but was ignored. Later two other figures from the party's right, Chris Grayling and Liam Fox, also registered opposition.

At 1.40 p.m. Cameron broke off from his calls to watch Brown address the nation. Initially he was statesmanlike – insisting that he was there only as prime minister not as Labour leader and that Cameron and Clegg should be given all the time they needed to discuss a deal. But then came the sting: if the talks 'came to nothing' he would, of course, be ready to talk to the Liberal Democrats. A Lib-Lab deal, moreover, would result in 'immediate legislation' on electoral reform 'to restore people's faith in politics'.

The game was clear, and now it was the Tory leader's turn to play. Cameron was handed the final text of his announcement as he left for St Stephen's Club. This had been the venue for Cameron's crisp execution of expenses wrong-doers almost exactly a year earlier. Now, again, he generated the impression of a man taking command of a fluid set of circumstances and turning them to his advantage.

He started with a defence of his campaign. The Tories, he said, had gained more seats than in any election in eighty years, more than Margaret Thatcher had ever won, and insisted he was proud of that achievement.

'But we have to accept that we fell short of an overall majority,' he conceded, quickly moving the focus to the threats Britain faced as a nation, its military campaign in Afghanistan and the sovereign debt crisis then just beginning in Europe. 'So we must all rise to this occasion. We must all show leadership.'

He thanked Clegg for being clear that the Tories, as the winner of the largest number of seats, had the chance to form a government. He said one option was a Tory minority government bolstered by a confidence and supply arrangement but made clear he was unenthusiastic about an option 'we can try'.

It may be possible to have stronger, more stable, more collaborative government than that. There is a case for going further than an arrangement which simply keeps a minority Conservative government in office. So I want to make a big, open and comprehensive offer to the Liberal Democrats. I want us to work together in tackling our country's big and urgent problems, the debt crisis, our deep social problems, and our broken political system.

Cameron spent the rest of the speech in effect opening negotiations, marking red lines as Europe, immigration and Trident but then stressing shared ground on education, tax reform and the environment.

The critical issue of electoral reform was fudged. And the opening offer was very low, just 'an all-party committee of inquiry on political and electoral reform'.

The markets, disappointed that Cameron did not use the word 'coalition', dived in the minutes after the address but the Cowley Street headquarters of the Lib Dems were able to read political code better than the traders.

One senior Liberal Democrat was astonished by Cameron's speech. 'We'd assumed that Cameron would have trouble responding quickly,' he recalls. 'We were stunned by the speed of Cameron's response. Whatever Nick had done, Cameron had done too. It's the mark of a big hero to be able to be knocked back by events and to read it right and his big offer did that. It was not a perfect speech, but it was a bloody good speech given the fact they were knackered. That showed me he has an extremely good sense, a very good reading of the territory around him. He has an instinctive touch of a very high order.'

Then Cameron returned to Norman Shaw South, went into George Osborne's office, picked up the phone and set about doing all he could to charm Clegg.

Despite – or, perhaps, because of – the similarities in their backgrounds of relative privilege and careers as professional politicians, the two young leaders had largely avoided one another until this point. Shortly after his election as Lib Dem leader, Cameron invited Clegg and his wife, Miriam, to join him and Sam for dinner at their home. When Cameron told journalists how Clegg had declined the invitation he did so in a manner that claimed indifference had trumped mild surprise.

Privately Clegg was much more exercised by the two men's competition for the same political persona. 'Nick was seriously discombobulated by Cameron,' says a confidant. 'Every time I met him he'd say "bloody Cameron, what can I do about him?" These were two "young Lochinvars". [Clegg] became obsessed with it; two siblings of the political system, two people of the same ilk struggling for the same space in the public mind.'

Clegg also knew that Cameron's office had a poor opinion of him. The view in Norman Shaw South was that the new Lib Dem leader had poor decision-making, poor judgement and was wasting his time and energies on the wrong issues.

A member of the inner circle challenged over Clegg's championing of the environment, an issue which had once helped define Cameron's leadership, was dismissive. 'He can have *that*, we were doing youthful vigour a couple of years ago … we're on to flags and fireplaces now.' Only one leader needed to bother to look prime ministerial – and it wasn't Clegg.

Profile writers sent scouring for shared history had little to go on. A forty-minute chat while waiting for the opening of the Supreme Court building and talks on how to evade Brown's attempts to trap them over expenses reform seemed to be the total of their private dealings thus far.

But what they did share, when they spoke at 4.00 p.m. on Friday 7 May, was a sense of profound disappointment. Neither had achieved the promised breakthrough. Clegg has described candidly how he felt 'bruised' by the scale of his party's failure. Voters recovered from

Cleggmania almost as rapidly as they had contracted it – the party had, in fact, lost seats.

Here, in the shape of Cameron, was one man who still wanted – needed – to 'agree with Nick'. The fifteen-minute call was described by Clegg's aides as 'businesslike, efficient and warm'. Clegg said later that he 'knew he could do business with' Cameron after the initial call, but, perhaps by way of putting up a fight against the charm offensive, told the Tory leader he thought it important that the talks be 'policy-based'. 'What matters is getting it right,' he said, 'and that depends on policy rather than personalities.'

Having spent so long in the waiting room of national politics, the Lib Dems were not going to fall in with the first suitor to offer them a ride. In any event, for most Lib Dems a deal with Labour, while dismissed by some as being a 'coalition of losers', was the most ideologically congenial. But whatever the eventual outcome, if the party was to get the best price for its favours, it needed more than one credible bidder.

So half an hour after Clegg had finished his call to Cameron, he was on the phone to Gordon Brown, who was putting up a fight to end all final-reel fights. The prime minister felt he had a decent chance of staying in Downing Street. Cameron's speech, he felt, was that of a man who would say anything for office, lacking the strength and stature that the public was looking for, and he told Clegg as much. Peter Mandelson, though, felt differently. He said later: 'I must say I couldn't see the error in what he was doing at all. I felt this guy knows what he's doing and he's going to motor.' Much has been written, and disputed, about the manner Brown adopted in dealing with Clegg during negotiations, some to justify the eventual outcome of the talks. The important point, though, is a simple one. Cameron made himself a much more appealing (more respectful, optimistic and less presumptuous) suitor than Brown. Cameron is a man who enjoys making people feel at home. As the then Cabinet Secretary Gus

O'Donnell put it: 'You could observe from the body language that there was a high degree of trust.' If party-hosting had been the issue, the deal would have been done by sunset.

Clegg's caution notwithstanding, Cameron was delighted, particularly since the Lib Dem leader had agreed that the parties' negotiating teams could meet that evening, ensuring a sense of momentum. A Tory aide said: 'We were all thinking about putting the family pictures back on the desk, thinking we were going to be in opposition for some time to come. But when Dave finished talking to George, he was very positive. Already he and Nick were talking like old friends. They are both young men, with similar backgrounds. But what really drew them together is that they were both men in highly stressful situations.'

The venue of the talks, 70 Whitehall, chosen from a menu offered by the civil service, was no accident. 'It was important to establish almost literally a bridgehead to No. 10 from the off – it gave the right message about our intention,' said a Cameron aide.

Having made his play, Cameron ascended out of view. As the negotiations dragged on over the coming days his life appears to have been surreally relaxed. He returned home to his wife and excited children almost as if he had been away to war. 'He walked through the door and just gave Sam the most enormous hug,' recalls a friend. He hosted a junior colleague's birthday dinner party on Saturday night, whose guests included Gabby Bertin and Andy Feldman.

Although he spent a good part of the weekend speaking on the phone or sending texts about the nation's future, Cameron did his best to have a low-key weekend unwinding. He left the media appearances to his juniors, with Michael Gove, for example, appearing on *The Andrew Marr Show* that Sunday morning, speaking sunnily about the talks, and even light-heartedly offering to give up his presumed education brief to David Laws if that was what a deal required. But generally the media had few scraps to feed on, leaving much scope for speculation and supposition. As one of the negotiators put it, 'I remember it as a very pleasant part of my life. We just got on with the talks, and, with due respect, enjoyed not having to talk to the press at all.' On Sunday, while the nation surmised and plotted the permutations, the Camerons, seemingly impervious, unwound with a family lunch with Michael Gove, his wife Sarah and their two children. As the Goves left after lunch, their minds briefly relieved of the cares of the previous few weeks, they were assailed with questions from reporters excited by Gove's offhand remark to Andrew Marr. 'Have you just resigned, Mr Gove?' they asked. 'No, we've just had lunch,' he replied, astonished and amused.

In fact, although the occasion had been mostly social, Cameron and Gove did discuss what would happen if the deal fell through. 'He knew that if it didn't work out he would be blamed by the entire Conservative family and movement for blowing this historic opportunity,' says an ally.

Cameron continued the low-key theme of the day with a game of tennis, occasionally checking in with his negotiators about the talks.

The two teams, Osborne, Hague, Letwin and Llewellyn for the Tories, Danny Alexander, Chris Huhne, Andrew Stunnell and David Laws for the Lib Dems, had made excellent progress, but at no point during the weekend was a deal with Labour ruled out. On Monday they hit a seemingly insuperable obstacle.

Electoral reform was always going to be the most tricky area for the Conservatives. Indeed, Brown had changed his position at the end of the last parliament to exploit just this division between his opponents.

It was received wisdom in Westminster that the Conservative parliamentary party could never agree to the possibility of a new voting system which, it was feared, would permanently lock it out of power.

A referendum on whether to keep the traditional winner-takes-all, or first past the post, proved to be a non-negotiable price for Lib Dem participation in a coalition in the end-game of the talks. Labour had a manifesto promise to hold a referendum on a move to the Alternative Vote system – matching this was the least he could do.

Cameron told Clegg this was undeliverable. Clegg, after consulting his MPs, told him that in that case he was opening formal talks with Labour, although it was possible they still might be able to do a confidence and supply deal. Cameron was left looking, at best, at the misery of a minority government. At worst it suddenly seemed that Brown might, incredibly, pull off a deal with the Lib Dems himself. Although Clegg had always said he would talk to the party with the greatest number of seats first, the Lib Dems had never ruled out a deal with Labour, the favoured partner of most of its MPs and activists. One source reports that Clegg told Gordon Brown, with Ed Balls and Mandelson listening in, that he needed to deal with Labour, otherwise Lib Dem party members 'will leave in droves'.

Whether in reality this was a bluff to put pressure on the Tories or not, talks with the incumbent party suddenly appeared to have assumed substance, especially after Brown seemed to have been persuaded that he would resign if that was the price of a deal.

Just how Cameron shifted his party over the electoral reform sticking point and himself into Number 10 remains controversial. Crucial to the key passage of play in the five-day negotiations is what – according to the official account at least – was a misunderstanding. With the chances of a deal with the Lib Dems slipping away on Monday, Cameron told first his shadow Cabinet and then a meeting of his backbench MPs that he understood Labour had offered Clegg a change in the voting system without a plebiscite. The Labour offer dramatically changed the odds and made it imperative that Cameron be allowed to offer the concession that would allow a Lib Dem/Tory coalition to come into being.

The only way to defend the current electoral system – on this account – was to give the Lib Dems a deal in which any change was put to a referendum. Conservatives, further, would be free to campaign against the change. That successful appeal proved to be the pivotal moment in the negotiations.

Only some months later did it emerge that Labour had never made such an offer.

How did this falsity arise? Did Clegg lie about the nature of Labour's offer to Cameron? Or did Cameron invent it to push his party into the vital concession? Or was the Tory leader himself given the false information by someone else? It would be an understandable card-player's bluff for Clegg to make out that he still regarded the other bidder as viable, even though by that time he had concluded privately that Labour, whoever was its leader, would not have the parliamentary support and authority to deliver on an expansive deal. In any event, Clegg has denied ever telling Cameron that Brown had offered AV without a plebiscite, and presumably Cameron would not be naïve enough to rely on the word of one bidder against another's. Challenged, Cameron has said that he had good reason to believe it was true. He was asked some weeks later if he had misled his MPs. He replied: 'No, because I was absolutely certain in my own mind that that was the case. I think I had good reason to be certain.' He said he had also had a conversation with Clegg in which he'd said it would be 'wrong' to change the voting system without asking the public.

In the account given to Rob Wilson, a Tory MP who wrote a book on the negotiations, Cameron was led to believe it by Osborne who had had the information from 'lots of different sources' in the media.

A senior Cameron minister confirms that Osborne was Cameron's principal source. 'George in particular relayed the rumour, the view ... I don't know that we knew that it was the case, that Labour was prepared to offer AV to the Liberals. By that time we'd cleared away an awful lot of the rest of the undergrowth ... *We perfectly well knew that we didn't know.* We had come to the view that it was very possible and

David came to the view that we should ask [the party] ask for permission.' (Italics added.)

Deliberate falsehood, gross exaggeration, caveatted surmise or convenient misunderstanding, it did the trick.

Allies, perhaps seeking to insulate Cameron from the charge that he was less than honest, assert that Tory MPs agreed to the coalition on the basis of their own self-interest.

Recalling the critical meeting one said: 'One of the first things he said was, "We've got this agreement with the Liberal Democrats. One of the key things is that if this agreement goes ahead we will have a fixed-term parliament", and then looking at several people who had just won their seat, he said, "That means there will be no new general election for another *five years*." At that point the deal was sealed because there was an emotional connection between leader and audience.'

Shortly after seven o'clock on Monday night Hague was able to announce that the Tories – in the interests of national unity – had gone the extra mile. Just over twenty-four hours later Cameron would be in Downing Street.

Labour peer Andrew Adonis later said he saluted 'David Cameron's strategic brilliance' over those few days but, perhaps typically, some on his own side felt he had been outmanoeuvred by the Liberal Democrats. Former Liberal democrat leader Lord Ashdown appears to think he was. 'Looking back on it, it is remarkable that we ever thought a deal with Labour would work, because it wouldn't, and it is even more remarkable, extraordinary actually, that the Tories thought it was a realistic proposition. If I'd been a Conservative I think I would have seen through it straight away. I would have said, "Go ahead, do a deal with Labour". a) it wouldn't have lasted, and b) Labour had no enthusiasm for it, c) it would have been an abnegation of the wishes of the nation, and as such seen as a grubby, dirty deal. It would have been a death knell for the Lib Dems.'

10 DOWNING STREET
The coalition's honeymoon

David Cameron arrived in Number 10 in the twilight, a consequence of Gordon Brown's determination to be photographed leaving his office in daylight.

Nick Clegg, still trying to lever concessions from the Tories, begged Gordon Brown not to end negotiations. Labour's prime minister, however, was persuaded to salvage a little pride with a dignified exit in the company of his family and in the afternoon sun.

Consequently, Cameron received a call from Sir Gus O'Donnell saying he should be ready to go to Buckingham Palace at any moment. He called Samantha at King North Street where she was helping Nancy with her homework. 'Well, you'd better get your frock on as we're going to the Palace.' Samantha at first thought he was joking: the previous night, deflated, he had told her over supper that he doubted the coalition could be agreed.

The first Conservative outrider into Number 10 was Liz Sugg, Cameron's visits supremo, who was sent ahead to prepare for her boss's arrival. Soon others made the short trip across Whitehall to their new home in time to 'clap in' the new Prime Minister.

Since Brown had resigned before the coalition deal had been finalised, Cameron was careful to tell the Queen only that he hoped to share power with the Liberal Democrats.

On the steps of Downing Street he said he thought a coalition would 'provide this country with the strong, the stable, the good and decent government' it needed. Then, using words that were to become the slogan of the new coalition government, he added: 'Nick Clegg and I are both political leaders who want to put aside party differences and work hard for the common good and for the national interest.'

After a quick briefing from his old colleague Jeremy Heywood and a congratulatory call from the US president, Cameron returned to the Commons to address a jubilant meeting of the parliamentary party.

Through the early hours of the following day Cameron, Osborne and Hague – who had already been appointed Chancellor and Foreign Secretary – worked on the shape of the new Cabinet.

Cameron opted to be generous in victory and agreed that Clegg should be Deputy Prime Minister. Four other Lib Dems were to get Cabinet jobs, Danny Alexander, Chris Huhne, Vince Cable and David Laws. It was slightly more than their share of seats allowed but Cameron wanted to show a host's magnanimity and, in any case, didn't want to start his new government with a row.

After some sleep Cameron and Clegg presented their new coalition to the world, posing first for pictures at the door of Number 10 and later holding a press conference in the rose garden.

The waiting press pack saw the two rivals, both aged forty-three, emerge from the back door of Number 10 and walk, lock-step, deep in conversation down a garden path hedged by flowering wisteria and magnolia. Comparisons to a gay marriage proved irresistible.

'Today we are not just announcing a new government,' Cameron said as Clegg looked on approvingly. 'We are announcing a new politics.'

Almost as astonishing as the sight of the two former rivals laughing in the garden of Number 10 was the document which underpinned their alliance. Ten days later a full coalition agreement, developed with the help of the civil service, was published. In return for the AV referendum and other constitutional reforms there was Lib Dem support for a commitment to accelerate efforts to pay off Britain's structural deficit. Later it would emerge that the parties had agreed to wipe out the debt by 2015. The plan went further even than the Tories' election claim to remove 'the bulk' of the debt in a parliament.

Clegg, the leader of a centre-left party, had guaranteed his support for deep cuts to public spending over four years which would entail a dramatic and lasting remodelling of the British state.

The rest of the document was a synthesis of the parties' manifestos as hammered out by the negotiating teams, which gave plenty of scope for widespread public service reform in education, criminal justice and welfare. The Lib Dems could point to a package of tax reforms that was broadly in their favour but had to concede upgraded civil and military nuclear programmes. The Tories had to sacrifice bills to shore up national sovereignty from further predation from the European Union and European Court of Human Rights but kept the politically vital pledge to reduce immigration.

Success would mean pulling off the impressive feat of having paid off Britain's crippling overdraft while upgrading its public services. For Clegg there were two additional attractions, the prospect of electoral reform and a definitive proof that coalitions could work.

Clegg, although given the title of Deputy Prime Minister, was given a set of rooms in the Cabinet Office. 'It's *pretty* close together,' Cameron had insisted in the rose garden. 'This is not going to be a partnership where we have to book meetings.' Yet despite all the marriage analogies this was coalition, not merger, and the two great offices of state were both held by Conservative politicians. It was to be a Tory Downing Street.

Cameron stamped his mark, doing away with Brown's open-plan war-room. The format of study, private office and den were restored as the three main elements of the Prime Minister's inner office. The link back to Cameron's previous period in government was embodied in the figure of Heywood. The Treasury official with whom he had worked as a special adviser was asked to stay on as Downing Street's most senior official and given a desk outside his study. He was becoming an increasingly pivotal figure in Cameron's Number 10.

Continuity with Norman Shaw South, meanwhile, came in the shapes of Kate Fall and Ed Llewellyn, sitting at two desks in the private office. A third, circular, table towards the centre of the room is used to hold meetings.

They instructed the rest of Downing Street's machine in the ways in which he liked to work. Cameron received submissions on paper, not email, they said. He would then annotate them in the top-left corner, and this copy would be scanned and distributed. He won an early victory against the civil service capture by insisting that he keep his personal mobile phone (although he had to submit to an additional level of security).

On the walls of David Cameron's office, where most of his meetings are held, are two large, modern prints of a south coast estuary, a picture of Sir Winston Churchill and several views of Oxford. The office is also notable for an enormous number of chairs, both comfortable and functional ones, and pictures of Cameron's wife and children by his desk.

Sam Cameron was reluctant to leave the house in which they had lived with Ivan but had accepted before the election that there were overwhelming reasons of security and convenience for the family to live 'above the shop'. The couple agreed on the need for a thorough refurbishment of the flat above Number 11, which, since Blair, has housed the Prime Minister's family.

The world was given a glimpse of her efforts when Michelle Obama came to see them during a state visit. A room used by the Browns as a bedroom became a 'white-walled, high ceilinged family room', according to one visitor's report. There was also 'a stainless steel galley kitchen' and a pair of 'chunky matching mustard sofas'.

The revelation that £30,000 of taxpayers' money had been spent on the refurbishment caused controversy but visitors speculated that the remainder – paid for by the Camerons themselves – would have been much more. The investment suggested a degree of confidence that they would be there for a while.

Before they had a chance to move in, the fourth Cameron child arrived. Florence Rose Endellion Cameron was born on 24 August, a month ahead of the due date. Her second middle name is a nod to the Cornish village where the Camerons were holidaying when she made her early appearance.

Cameron's family life had been disturbed in any case but, once they settled into the newly refurbished flat in the autumn, he established a routine of rising at 5.30 a.m. to exercise and clear overnight work before the first 8.30 a.m. meeting of Number 10 staff. This meeting, held while Clegg was still commuting from his home in Putney, was a Conservative-only gathering, allowing Cameron the freedom to be purely political and not worry about coalition etiquette.

Cameron's first big set-piece Commons appearance came in June with the publication of the Saville Inquiry, which had been set up in 1998 by Tony Blair. The report's findings into the 1972 shooting of thirteen civilians by the Parachute Regiment in Derry, Northern Ireland, clearly warranted an apology.

Cameron delivered it simply but sincerely to a stilled chamber.

I am deeply patriotic. I never want to believe anything bad about our country. I never want to call into question the behaviour of our soldiers, whom I believe to be the finest in the world. But the conclusions of this report are absolutely clear. There is nothing equivocal. There are no ambiguities. What happened on Bloody Sunday was both unjustified and unjustifiable. It was wrong.

Praise for his performance helped Cameron grow in confidence and stature. He was helped, too, by the absence of a Labour leader although Harriet Harman, as stand-in, succeeded in needling him once or twice during PMQs.

Ed Miliband was elected Labour leader that autumn, his narrow victory over his brother David delivered by union votes courtesy of the party's electoral college. He was immediately caricatured as a captive of the left, hopelessly associated with Brown, for whom he had worked most of his adult life. It would prove a hard tag to shake.

Four months after the failure to win the general election had left Cameron facing an ignominious exit from politics, he was the Prime Minister of a stable government opposed by a party that seemed to have charted a course away from the centre ground. What could he make of this opportunity?

'TOO MANY FRONTS'
The domestic agenda 2010–2012

Tony Blair, finding himself alone with Cameron during the Remembrance Sunday commemorations in 2006, is said to have delivered a piece of advice wrapped in an insult. Blair, by then knowing he would have to hand over to Gordon Brown the following year, told Cameron that he, Blair, had been a much better leader of the Opposition. But, he added, were Cameron to become Prime Minister the Tory should move more swiftly than he had done in 1997. Cameron took the words of the man he and Osborne jokingly referred to as 'The Master' to heart.

By the time he took office the implementation unit under Francis Maude had done extensive work with the civil service on a smooth transition. A new Conservative government wouldn't, like Blair, waste the precious first months when political capital was at its highest with overcaution or logistical muddle. Cameron also liked to contrast his own style with the 'control-freak' Gordon Brown. He would trust his own ministers to get on with the job without fear they were about to be reshuffled. His aversion to changing the portfolios is a marked feature of his leadership. In six years he has had only one major shake-up.

Similarly, the civil service would be restored to its rightful position and the number of political appointees, or special advisers, which had grown remorselessly under Labour, would be limited. The Institute of Government, an independent non-government organisation, had provided discreet cover for pre-election meetings between senior civil servants and their new political masters in its comfortable offices a short walk across St James's Park in Carlton Gardens.

Getting the machinery right was one thing: actually governing was another.

The familiarisation process notwithstanding, some senior civil servants believed the Conservatives were 'cocky' when they arrived in office. 'They felt they had little to learn,' said one Whitehall figure.

After the whimsy of the rose garden, Osborne delivered an 'emergency Budget' on 22 June. It was an exercise in political 'shock and awe'. The political message was a continuation of his 'we're all in this together' refrain before the election. The cuts were 'tough ... but also fair'. The theme informed a comprehensive spending review which followed. Tough because departments other than health and international development had to cut their budgets by a quarter and public sector workers were given a two-year pay freeze, fair because a range of middle-class benefits, including child benefit, were also slashed or frozen.

Surveying the grim prospect of fights with vested interests on almost every front, senior Tories were reassured that the decision to reprieve the NHS spared them a battle on their weakest ground. Such comfort was misplaced.

A Health Bill promised in the Queen's Speech which followed shortly afterwards had promised to replace a 'top-down approach' with the 'devolution of power and responsibility to doctors and patients'.

This was a surprise since it was neither in the Conservative manifesto nor the coalition agreement. Where had it come from?

Andrew Lansley had been desperate to restore an element of GP fund-holding for years but had been forbidden from being explicit by Cameron, convinced of the paramount importance of reassuring voters that the Tories could be trusted on the NHS.

Now in government, the Health Secretary got clearance for a huge shake-up. Most controversially, the plans required the abolition of a whole tier of NHS bureaucracy despite the fact that Cameron had repeatedly said in Opposition that there was to be 'no more top-down reorganisation of the NHS'. Lansley had successfully worked Cameron's fear of repeating Blair's mistake of putting off difficult public service reforms until it was too late to implement them without fatal compromise.

It was a time when ministers were competing with one another for recognition as radical reformers. 'There was definitely a reforming zeal in those first few weeks,' says a Number 10 aide. 'In order to be part of the programme you had to define what you were doing in revolutionary terms.'

Some in Downing Street saw the dangers straightaway. The plan in Opposition had always been to use education – where the Tories had a well-developed and popular reform agenda – as the bridgehead. Health was a long way down the batting order. 'It was partly the first flush of government,' says one senior Tory. 'There was an enormous amount going on, we were taking a lot of big decisions.' 'No one said … this is a big reform of the health service, who supports this, who backs it up? There was no sustained effort to get the health professionals on board.'

Sure enough, the reaction to the plans when they were at last published was overwhelmingly hostile. 'We paid the price for having been reassuring on the NHS during the election campaign,' said one of Cameron's closest aides. 'Whereas we spent two years preparing the ground for cutting the deficit, on health reform all we managed to do was fritter away any support we might have had from the professionals.'

Another close friend of Cameron recalls being aghast at learning he had given in to Lansley's pleading. 'I felt like one of those German generals in 1941 on the Western Front. We were doing quite well and then the Boss says, "When are we going to invade Russia?"'

As opposition continued to build through the autumn, Cameron called a meeting of senior ministers and officials and asked Lansley once again to explain why his complicated set of reforms was necessary. Heywood was later heard to complain that the lengthy meeting had been a failure. Everyone who had been in favour came out more enthused while the doubters took away aggravated concerns, reported Downing Street's chief civil servant. A number of participants, including perhaps Cameron himself, didn't 'understand what the hell [Lansley was] talking about'.

Cameron decided to 'outsource' the decision to Letwin, says a friend, adding, 'it's not a mistake I suspect he'll make again'. But Letwin gave a judgement on whether the reforms would work, not whether they were politically sensible or correctly presented. Although Osborne has told friends that he regrets not 'killing' Lansley's plan when he had the chance, ultimately responsibility belongs to Cameron.

An ally says he and Osborne came to realise they were throwing away the 'precious commodity' of trust on the NHS 'for a bunch of reforms that no one understands [anything] about except that the health service is against them'.

Friends defend him against the charge that he is influenced by polling but do not deny he shows an almost obsessive interest in the raw data of politics. To the chagrin of some strategists, he is a frequent visitor to political betting websites, not to place bets but to keep abreast of the latest debates on polling methodology. On the issue of health the numbers were unambiguous.

In late spring 2010 he announced there was to be a 'pause' on the proposed reform as suggested by his new head of media Craig Oliver. The pause was presented as a listening exercise but also gave Number 10 and Lansley more time to build a consensus of health professionals behind the bill.

The problem was that it went to the head of an already embarrassingly long list of U-turns. The tone had been set early when

Cameron ruled out the scrapping of free milk for primary schoolchildren the previous August. Other notable about-turns included the abandonment – at Prime Minister's Questions – of a plan to sell nationalised forestry land. Cameron was caught between two evils: if he pressed ahead with the bill he risked losing public confidence that the Tories could, after all, be trusted with the NHS. And yet if he abandoned it he would hand Labour a victory and risk damaging his own reputation as a strong leader.

By the summer of 2011 Downing Street, having launched what one figure billed a 'political rescue' of health policy, was also engaged in a running battle with Ken Clarke, who Cameron had brought back to the frontbench in 2009 partly to shore up the Tories' credibility in the City after Osborne's Deripaska misadventure.

Clarke, who accepted the justice beat with some reluctance, addressed it with the same independence of mind and reforming zeal displayed by Lansley. He appalled the right-wing press with a number of reforms to prisons and the judiciary. Constitutionally respectful of his elders, Cameron's patience was nonetheless sorely tested by Clarke's intransigence.

There were two big spending departments where Cameron's hands-off approach was paying dividends, however. Iain Duncan Smith was given his head to radically overhaul welfare, eradicating the many perverse incentives baked in by decades of meddling and bouts of social engineering. Osborne baulked at the cost of introducing a universal benefit, the key reform that was supposed to ensure that work really did pay. But Duncan Smith won Cameron's support at a political cabinet in Chequers in September 2010 and the policy was launched at the subsequent party conference.

Cameron's late entry into the battle over the policy was typical. Close observers say he avoids personal confrontation, preferring to hang back until a resolution has been reached which then receives his benediction.

Michael Gove – after a rocky start – also repaid his prime minister's faith, freeing schools from local government control with an expansion of the academies programme and enabling parent groups, charities and other organisations to establish so-called 'free schools'. But here, too, the new Tory-led government was given cause to reconsider the lessons it had chosen to learn from Blair. Within weeks of Gove's arrival he was hit by a series of damaging leaks that could only have come from inside the department. His struggles with a machine, inert and hostile by turns, led to an increasing reliance on special advisers which in turn worsened relationship with his officials.

Steve Hilton, too, was finding the civil service machine infuriating. Cameron hinted at his own anger in his speech to the Tories' spring conference in March 2011. In 1999 Tony Blair had said of the public sector, 'I bear the scars on my back after two years in government and heaven knows what it will be like after a bit longer.' It took less than a year for Cameron to say of 'anti-business bureaucrats', 'If I have to pull those people into my office to argue this out myself and get them off the backs of business then, believe me, I'll do it.'

As the anniversary of the coalition drew near, it was becoming obvious that Cameron needed to increase significantly his oversight of and control over the rest of Whitehall. Until now he had made confident delegation a defining characteristic of his leadership. But while the government's divided political loyalties had been glossed over under the banner of national unity, the rhetoric seemed to have deadened some Tory ministers' political instincts while encouraging others to pursue their own agendas. The list of U-turns masked a deeper problem – the coalition risked becoming an unhappy mix of the managerial and revolutionary.

Cameron sharpened up the political operation, bringing in Andrew Cooper, the pollster who had done so much to get the Tories to realise how much voters disliked them. Structures were overhauled so that potentially troublesome policies could be identified and called in much earlier. Blair and then Brown had used a team of policy-orientated special advisers to shadow individual departments for just this purpose. As part of his 'chairman of the board' style Cameron had initially dispensed with the need for a full Number 10 policy unit. Now, stuck with his self-imposed cap on the number of special advisers, the Prime Minister had to beef up his own department with what one ally called 'bright officials and secondees from outside but not political people'.

Cameron had hoped to take what he considered the best of Blair, while learning from his mistakes. There have been some successes, notably he and Osborne have avoided recreating the dysfunctional duopoly that wrecked New Labour. But he has also misapplied and misunderstood many of the lessons of the man whose heir he once claimed to be. He inherited power in an utterly changed economic situation. By their own admission, a set text of the Cameron set was Philip Gould's 'Unfinished Revolution', which has been called the Blairite playbook. In fact that era *was* finished.

At the end of November 2011 Osborne admitted that the coalition would not, after all, pay off the nation's overdraft by 2015. Indeed, the country was going to have to borrow another £111 million, partly to pay for unemployment that would brush the three million mark. Moreover, additional cuts and pay freezes would be needed to convince moneylenders that Britain was still AAA rated.

By and large voters sighed deeply and carried on. The admission that the central target had been missed just eighteen months after it was set failed to make any significant impact on the polling figures. By now Britons had had years observing worse economic disasters unfold elsewhere. Each turn of the screw fastened public opinion to the necessity of austerity. Labour's critique that Osborne had choked off a recovery by cutting too far, too fast had its supporters among economists but failed to resonate. Europe's crisis of confidence seemed, to most, a far more relevant factor.

At the turn of the year Cameron decided the risk to his own brand of appearing weak outweighed the risk to his party's NHS trust ratings and opted to push ahead with the health bill. It was heavy-going, not least because Cameron and Lansley shied away from selling the bill's central purpose: to devolve responsibility for rationing healthcare away from the government and towards GPs. Further, the legislation's other central measure, to introduce more competition in the NHS, was diluted even before what appeared certain to be a long and difficult parliamentary passage. No-one thought that the arguments would not stop with Royal Assent.

The risks of allowing Labour to run a 'save the NHS' campaign at the next general election were plain. But Cameron, for whom the reform was almost an afterthought, had allowed it to become a test of his leadership. The 'heir to Blair' was learning each prime minister makes his own mistakes.

BUMPS AND SCRAPES
Coalition and internal party tensions
2010–2012

'Being leader of the Liberal Democrats [is] a tremendous test of your self-confidence,' says Lord Ashdown. Ashdown, who was courted by Tony Blair before the 1997 general election and then dumped after the Labour landslide made talk of coalition otiose, should know.

Clegg, at least, had delivered what no Liberal leader since the 1920s had done and got his party into power. Like the well-bred host he is, Cameron did all he could to make the new arrival feel at home on the estate which he himself knew well, having returned after a regrettably long enforced absence. For weeks the newspapers carried examples of how well Cameron and Clegg were getting on, stories of late-night texting and games of tennis. In March, as Cameron and Clegg left a joint appearance in Nottingham, the Lib Dem leader, courtesy of a forgotten radio mic, was heard to say: 'If we keep doing this we won't have anything to bloody disagree on in the bloody TV debates.'

The government, it was said, was being run by Cameron and Osborne on one side and Clegg and Laws on the other. This central foursome, which later became nicknamed 'the quad', collapsed into a triangle on 29 May when the *Telegraph*, dusting down its expenses file, proved that Laws claimed rent on his lover's property. Laws, who had kept his homosexuality a secret, was devastated and resigned. Danny Alexander was elevated from Scottish Secretary to Chief Secretary of the Treasury, a giddying promotion.

Clegg had sounded a cautionary note in euphoric melody of the rose garden, predicting 'bumps and scrapes along the way'. But it's doubtful he foresaw then how personally abrasive the new set-up would prove.

It wasn't long before Clegg was being lampooned by *The Times'* cartoonist Peter Brookes as 'Cleggers', Cameron's hapless school fag. Through the summer and into the autumn after the election it did indeed seem that Clegg was doing most of Cameron's dirty work in keeping the coalition together.

He had accepted the need for Osborne's deficit reduction plan on face value and part of the bill was a series of broken manifesto promises. The two most damaging were support for an increase in VAT to 20 per cent and a huge increase in tuition fees, both of which he had specifically campaigned against during the election.

The latter in particular caused deep anger among the Lib Dem base, concentrated as it is in university constituencies. It may have been the Tories' HQ which was attacked in a student riot but it was the Lib Dems that were taking the greatest damage.

Clegg took every opportunity to remind an increasingly fractious party of the prize that he had won in a referendum on voting reform, fixed for the following May to coincide with local council elections and those for the Scottish and Welsh legislatures. Cameron, anxious not to make Clegg's position any more difficult, had always told the Lib Dem leader privately that he would take no part in the 'No' campaign (a prediction rather than a promise, as it was later described). There were even reports that some Tory figures, identified as Letwin and Hilton, had been heard to voice support for a move to the Alternative Vote system in which candidates are ranked and which is supposed to ensure that the winner has attracted support from at least 50 per cent of an electorate.

Cameron had his own party management issues. He had tried and failed to neuter the 1922 Committee just a week after becoming Prime Minister. Having evaded becoming a prisoner of the right, Cameron announced that ministers as well as backbenchers should be entitled to vote. The change – put to a (covertly whipped) vote – was a transparent attempt to fix the election for its new chairman. New backbenchers, already pressured to accept the coalition agreement and its unpalatable commitment to a referendum on voting reform, were even canvassed on whether they'd vote for Desmond Swayne, Cameron's Parliamentary Private Secretary, as the man to represent their interests.

Although Cameron got his rule change through on 20 May the victory proved to be pyrrhic. Such was the backlash, Cameron had to back down and abandon the attempt. Among those furious was Osborne, who, had he been consulted, would have pointed out how counter-productive it was to martyr Graham Brady and provide the right with an opportunity to rally around.

Another consequence was that it alienated some of the vast inflow of new Tory MPs who had arrived quite willing to be loyal. Charles Moore wrote that Cameron had thrown 'good faith and good manners to the winds'. A senior Tory agreed: 'It was totally unnecessary because the bulk of [backbenchers] were the one hundred and forty-six new members, that's half the parliamentary party. They're all for modernising, pro-David Cameron, or at least the vast majority, they're natural allies.' 'We didn't need to have all that agitation at the beginning.'

Emboldened by Cameron's retreat on the 1922, right-wing MPs, with vocal support from the Conservative press, began a loud complaint about the watering down of tax breaks promised in the Tory manifesto but ditched in coalition. In July, David Davis, a lone wolf patrolling the borders of the right, mocked Cameron and Clegg's partnership as the 'Brokeback Coalition', a reference to the film *Brokeback Mountain* about a couple of ill-fated gay cowboys.

Simon Heffer, admittedly never a fan, acidly but accurately voiced the privately expressed criticism of many MPs thus: 'How sad do we think Dave is at being made to ditch the remotely Conservative parts of his election manifesto in order to stay in his loveless marriage with the Liberal Democrats? He appears to be bearing the blow of ditching the reform of badly-drafted human rights legislation, having to maintain inheritance tax, forcing swingeing rises in capital gains tax and abandoning the party's pledge to support married families surprisingly well.'

On occasion Cameron forgot that he was supposed to regret having had to ditch Conservative policies – although often Tories, when asked, were hard pressed to recall which ones they had ditched – describing the coalition agreement, for example, as 'more radical and comprehensive than our individual manifestos'. Or indeed that he was a Conservative at all. 'I think we know in 1997 the country needed change,' said the Tories' former parliamentary candidate for Stafford (1997).

Cameron had always found it impossible to counter the claim that his project was run by a small clique in Opposition, largely because it was true. As Rachel Sylvester wrote: 'The political and social lives of the Notting Hill Tories are more closely entwined than any other Westminster set I can think of, either current or historical. They eat at each other's houses, are godparents to each other's children, share school runs, co-edit church magazines, holiday together – all between discussing the next stage in the politics of the post-bureaucratic age. This isn't The West Wing, it's an episode of Friends.'

'Tory MPs who do not have the gold swipe card that accesses the inner circle – which is nearly all of them – grumble about his remoteness and arrogance. That is echoed by discontent among Tory activists in the country,' wrote Andrew Rawnsley at around the same time. In government that 'gold swipe card' became even more elusive.

As the referendum approached, Cameron's dilemma sharpened. Should he stay above the fray, as he had said he would do, for the sake of the unity of the coalition?

But the drumbeat from the right for Cameron to prove that he was prepared to put his party's long-term interests ahead of his own grasp on power grew louder through the autumn.

Unloved by the leadership and underfunded, the 'No' campaign looked outgunned. Faced with another failure at the polls Cameron first asked his friend Feldman to rattle the tin in the City and then stepped in himself.

'He hoped that the "No" campaign would be clearly winning and that he could achieve [a rejection of AV] without having to test the relation with the Lib Dems, but when it became clear that the polls were saying it was neck and neck he said, "Right we are going for this and we are not going to take our foot off the gas", recalls an ally.

Clegg had an altogether different problem. He desperately wanted to put himself at the head of the 'Yes' campaign. As the champion of 'new politics' he could reassure his own party and gain some much-needed definition against his older political 'sibling'. The problem was Clegg, with his record of compromise, was not an attractive advertisement for the cause of a polling system that made coalitions much more likely.

A leaflet for the 'No' campaign put it thus: 'Nick Clegg is unpopular because he broke his promises: job cuts, VAT increase, tuition fees, public spending cuts. That's why he's pushing for AV to save his party.'

Vince Cable was outraged: 'He [Cameron] may not directly control what his supporters are up to. But he must make it clear that he doesn't condone and will endeavour to stop personal attacks on his deputy for loyally supporting coalition policy. To stand by and let this happen is dangerous and puts considerable strain on the coalition.'

Huhne, too, was vociferous about Tory 'dirty tactics' both at the time and afterwards. Cameron did in fact break an understanding that the Prime Minister wouldn't himself deploy the so-called 'broken promises' line of attack. 'The more people see a clear link between pledges in a manifesto and the action taken in government, the greater the sense of accountability,' he said in a speech in late April, adding that AV 'would damage that chain of accountability because it makes coalitions much, much more likely'.

Cameron's entry into the fray helped seal a decisive rejection on 5 May. On a turnout of 41 per cent, 32.1 per cent had opted for change while 67.9 per cent had voted to stay with the current system. More surprising was a slew of Conservative gains in the local elections. Despite the cuts, the Tories had held onto their share of the vote and actually increased the number of Conservative councillors. The Lib Dems, on the other hand, lost 748 councillors and the control of nine local authorities.

Defeat left a bitter taste. There were other signs of real tension between the two men aside from electoral reform. When Clegg, seeking to make social mobility a personal theme, attacked the awarding of internships to the well-connected, Cameron replied that he was 'very relaxed' about giving stints of work experience to the offspring of friends. The two men were overheard bickering about the health reforms – which the Lib Dems were now openly opposing – as they waited for Barack Obama to address MPs in Westminster Hall.

Despite the pressures it placed on the coalition, there was only a little remorse in Number 10 in the immediate aftermath. 'Looking back on it we could have eased up a bit,' says a Cameron ally of the AV campaign around a month afterwards. 'But there are a couple of weeks where the most important thing is to win.'

For all the Lib Dem complaints about the ruthlessness of the 'No' campaign, there was in fact a measure of relief in Clegg's office at the margin of the defeat, according to the same ally. 'The Lib Dems were very clear beforehand that if they were going to lose they'd much rather lose big than small. If they'd lost narrowly it would have put much more pressure on Clegg – they [would have] lost because of Clegg.'

The calculation that the Lib Dems, whose poll ratings barely scraped into double figures for most of 2011, could not afford to 'flounce out' proved correct. As the year ended Cameron was braced between a surly junior partner on his left and increasingly rebellious backbenchers on his right. That he did not seem overly concerned might be explained by this analysis offered by a senior ally. 'In a single-party government there is internal division always happening. That hasn't happened because it's sort of institutionalised. We know what the internal division is – there's the Liberal Democrat party and there's the Conservative Party.' Disagreements are about policy not personality, he claimed. 'It's greatly reduced the sort of factional tension that you get within the Conservative Party in a single-party government.'

Implicit in this analysis, however, is that the two 'factions' of the government would come under increasing pressure to define themselves in opposition to one another. In balancing the coalition Cameron was by 2012 finding himself increasingly pushed to the right in both the domestic and foreign spheres.

Cameron's allies were alarmed at the drift. In pacifying the right of the Conservative parliamentary party he was failing, almost without knowing it, to cultivate and strengthen a loyalist centrist base, they feared. 'Dave is suffering from headmaster/naughty boy syndrome where the only people he sees are the malcontents,' complained one.

For their part the Liberal Democrats positioned themselves increasingly as a constraining, tempering force, notably over Lansley's health bill.

SUB-CONTRACTORS
George Osborne and Steve Hilton:
the battle for Cameron's soul

The single biggest factor ensuring the stability of the early Cameron government was George Osborne. The pair may have misunderstood or misapplied other lessons from Blair but their disciplined determination to avoid a rupture at the top of government was handsomely repaid.

Conditioned to believe that tension, creative or otherwise, between Number 10 and the Treasury had the status of constitutional convention, the civil servants serving the First and Second Lords of the Treasury initially struggled to adapt to the new model.

It was not uncommon for the Chancellor to chair the Number 10 morning meeting – something quite unthinkable under Labour, or indeed previous Conservative, administrations. 'There's no modern precedent for it,' said a senior Downing Street figure.

Not only were Prime Minister and Chancellor discreet about their disagreements, but Osborne began to act as Cameron's de facto political secretary. After Cameron's bungled attempt to fix elections to the '1922' he once again handed party management largely to his ally.

A friend says Cameron, when faced with a big political call, will almost invariably consult Osborne before making his decision. 'David defers to George's political judgement.'

Another close friend of both men describes the difference of their approach in the following way: 'George [Osborne] is more of the MI5-style, [like] Smiley, a reader of human character. Whereas Dave is more school captain, "You're on my side, good man [to have] in a rough spot".

'Once [Cameron's] made a friendship, unless they're very naughty, he keeps them, but in a slightly school way. There are some people from relatively early days he just thought they are dreamers or nerds or nutters or bores or bullies or bad hats.

'George has probably one less millilitre of the milk of human kindness in his veins.'

The metaphor of Cameron as team captain has even been extended to promote Osborne as team manager.

Such very high levels of trust required Osborne to sublimate his own agenda and political ambition – at least for now. It helps, concedes a senior figure, that the Prime Minister has accepted Osborne's economic analysis and prescription in full.

'It's impossible to exaggerate the extent to which George loves being Chancellor of the Exchequer,' says a friend. 'He genuinely cares about the Cameron premiership. David gets to be Prime Minister and he gets to be on the world stage.'

What rivalry there is appears to be almost self-mocking. A close observer, for example, has heard the pair indulge in 'one-upmanship' over which of them has travelled in Marine One and Airforce One, the US presidential aircraft. But while Osborne may give a convincing impression he does not regret turning down Howard's offer at a tilt at the leadership, he is careful not to say he does not, in time, want the top job himself. By 2012 it was becoming possible to discern both an Osborne agenda and a Cabinet faction which included Philip Hammond and Justine Greening. Although Cameron's·closest allies admitted to some wariness about Osborne's power the government's central compact was holding.

Cameron admires Osborne's grasp of short-term political advantage. Osborne has a Mandelsonian eye for securing petty victories, for positioning himself and his party in the best position for winning public approval. But to some he can appear too tactical by half, too interested in point scoring at the expense of the bigger, longer-term picture and guiding principles of Tory philosophy. When Osborne does look at the wider picture, it is with electoral success as his lodestar.

Cameron might have delegated party management and even some day-to-day running of Number 10 to Osborne, but Steve Hilton had the contract for the Prime Minister's conscience. He was awarded it the weekend after Cameron became Prime Minister. 'David said to him that he wanted Steve to make sure that he actually got done some of the big changes they'd always wanted to make,' reveals an ally.

So where Osborne is the man who wants to make sure the Tories are re-elected, Hilton is the one who wants to make sure they have left their mark if they are not. He should be 'Mr Further and Faster', as Cameron put it. So as well as being the licensed blue-sky thinker, he is also the progress-chaser, the man whose job it is to be disappointed by failure to make the country a more radically capitalist and democratically accountable one.

It was unsurprising that Cameron wanted Hilton close: they have had a twenty-year dialogue about Conservatism. Hilton is the man who, in 2001, in a contribution to a collection of essays entitled *The Blue Tomorrow* and edited by Ed Vaizey, Nicholas Boles and Michael Gove, spelled out how the Tories could harness the power of capitalism, especially in the use of brands, to produce social goods. 'Here's an exciting new agenda for a new Conservative leader,' he wrote. Recalling the early days of Cameron's leadership one insider said, 'Steve would write a speech, a draft would be circulated the night before – if you were lucky – and you would try and feed in your views, but it was very much David and Steve.'

Hilton had briefly left Britain in 2008 to accompany his partner Rachel Whetstone as he began a new job with Google in California. But Cameron had persuaded him to stay employed (on a salary reported to be £180,000).

In Opposition, Hilton had been an infuriating colleague: now it was the civil servants' turn to experience the 'shaven-headed guru'. Hilton's modus operandi is deliberately non-consensual. 'Steve operates in such a guerilla fashion', a complaint voiced by a senior Number 10 official in the summer of 2011, was typical. Characteristically, Hilton would swoop on a policy that caught his eye and demand changes. His selection of targets mystified officials. 'He doesn't engage with the process until the very last minute and then he unpicks things.'

Unsurprisingly this led to friction. 'The officials can't stand Steve, absolutely can't stand him,' said one Cameron ally. Relations with officials in the Number 10 policy unit became so bad that he had to move office in the autumn of 2011.

There were other signs that Cameron's Number 10 was not functioning as smoothly as it should. Sir Gus O'Donnell, despite having played such a key role in brokering the coalition deal, was edged out, replaced as Cabinet Secretary by Jeremy Heywood.

It had been notable that Sir Jeremy (the knighthood arrived in January 2012) had been on first-name terms with Cameron from the moment he arrived in Number 10. The pair had formed a bond working under Lamont and had tracked each other's progress up the ladder subsequently. Having been Brown's Chief of Staff the civil servant might be expected to feel vulnerable: in fact he quickly showed a prodigious ability to anticipate and service the needs of his new master.

But since Ed Llewellyn, Cameron's low-profile but greatly trusted right hand man, does not fulfil all the usual functions of a chief of staff, Heywood had no direct political opposite number. As a result he found himself facing sometimes contradictory agendas. Smoothing the edges and filling the gaps, the only civil servant who called the Prime Minister 'Dave', steadily grew more powerful.

Occasionally Osborne and Hilton would clash but on the whole the Chancellor was not troubled by an agenda he viewed as eccentric and romantic but essentially irrelevant to the over-riding imperatives of cutting the deficit and winning an overall majority in 2015. When the pair do argue, it is in a context of mutual admiration. There is a trust between them which ensures that disagreements don't become personal. By general agreement, this was not the case, for example, between Hilton and Andy Coulson.

Nevertheless, by the summer of 2011 it seemed increasingly likely that Cameron's 'guru' might desert him, not least because there were signs that Cameron was finding the demands of his conscience wearisome. 'David's less indulgent of him than he used to be, and listens more and is more balanced in terms of who he listens to.'

Part of Cameron's frustration was the continuing failure of the Big Society agenda to take off. After a couple of further relaunches, one immediately after the election and another in early 2011, Cameron all but gave up trying to explain what was supposed to be the over-arching theme of his premiership.

Defensive, Hilton has argued that the phrase Big Society was never supposed to be campaign slogan, still less the definition of the essence of Cameronism.

It was one half of a soundbite 'Big society, not big government', itself a distillation of the saying supposedly coined by Samantha Cameron, 'There is such a thing as society, it's just not the same thing as the state.' But when the phrase caught on in the media as a shorthand for Cameron's agenda there were initially no objections. If over time it was reduced to a bromide on the value of volunteering, whose fault was that?

Lord Tebbit described it as 'a buzzword, a logo looking for a product'. Even Cameron's close colleagues seemed to shrug implicitly when it was raised. Andy Coulson, never a fan, talked Cameron out of making two big speeches on the Big Society in late 2010, but Cameron referred to it at some length in his 2010 party conference speech. William Hague was asked on television why his leader kept returning to this unpromising theme. 'Because he believes in it,' said the normally ultra-loyal Hague, tellingly forgetting to express the faintest endorsement of it himself.

Presentation apart, there was a growing sense that Cameron needed to find a different 'positive vision' if he were to win an absolute majority at the next election.

Even if Cameron is seen as having successfully dealt with the deficit, voters may not reward him and could well punish what they see as a failure to deal with the country's other problems, strategists feared.

One defined the problem with 'Steve's vision' thus: 'What it feels like for an ordinary person is that they are being asked to put more in. It feels onerous to have to step in and give more time and go to meetings and run things and fill in the gaps of the things you're cutting,' said one.

Cameron is in a sense lucky with his economic inheritance since it gave him ready-made definition. 'If the Fates hadn't handed him that hand, and he didn't have the deficit, what would he be doing instead? I don't think people have got any idea, that's a problem for the longer term.

'The danger is that at the next election it will still be "time for a change".'

As the government approached its half-way mark Hilton remained the player in the team 'who believes in things', as one Tory puts it, and one who wants to make bold, radical changes. Partly as a consequence he was more frustrated by bureaucratic inertia than most of his colleagues. He more than most found the demands of coalition government irksome, particularly since the Liberal Democrats lost the AV referendum and became, Hilton told one friend, 'much more bloody-minded'.

Hilton's friends began openly wondering whether Cameron shared his passion. Having achieved his goal of being Prime Minister, he can appear suspiciously at ease managing the day-to-day demands of power. People still wondered if he had a sense of vision. What would his new Jerusalem look like? Peasmore, suggest some who accuse him of a lack of imagination. As Norman Tebbit puts it, 'David was more concerned about *being* Prime Minister than what he was going to *do* as Prime Minister.'

At the end of 2011, a friend of Hilton said: 'He's having a miserable time. He can't believe what power has done to them all, including Dave. He thinks Dave has just become focused on power. He's not the person he thought he was. I don't think he's sure who Dave is any more.'

In late February 2012 Hilton announced that he was taking a year-long sabbatical to teach at Stanford University, California, a move that would enable him and his wife to spend more time together. Number 10 put the best gloss they could on what looked to others like a desertion.

Cameron was said to be confident that he could, again, lure back (if only for the run-up to the election) the man who spotted and helped realise his potential, who defined his brand and was a proof against his own tendency to complacent managerialism.

A few days after the news broke that Hilton was walking out on Number 10 (albeit with a promise to return) Cameron delivered a speech to the Tories' spring conference.

Cameron chose to present himself as a brave radical resisting the demands of those who wanted him to be 'safe hand on the tiller'.

'I didn't come into politics to play it safe,' he claimed, adding, 'We've got to be tough and bold.'

It was difficult not to hear in his words faint echoes of rebuke, as well as self reassurance. For the next 12 months at least Cameron would have to be his own conscience.

Frustrated and impatient, Hilton had continued to be indulged by Cameron, but when cold calculation was called for, it was Osborne to whom Cameron would listen. This meant that some of Cameron's early, more idealistic enthusiasms took a back seat. The appointment of the Liberal Democrats' Chris Huhne to the Department of Energy lent credibility to Cameron's expressed concerns about global warming. Those who had doubted Cameron's green credentials and who had seen the 'hug a huskie' photo opportunity of 2006 as simply a branding exercise had to admit that Huhne was a formidable advocate of the green agenda, and that particular cabinet brief suited him – and Cameron – perfectly.

As ever, though, Cameron had a balancing act to perform. His wife and his Lib Dem partners were keen to tick the green boxes, but this was a hard sell in a time of economic austerity. In May 2010 Cameron had pledged to head 'the greenest government ever', and while Huhne was locking horns with George Osborne, among others, across the cabinet table, the PM could not be accused of selling out. But towards the end of 2011, notwithstanding some notable achievements, that case became harder to make. For one thing, Cameron himself had barely mentioned the environment in any speech. Osborne, always mindful of his audience's likely reaction, told the Conservative conference 'we're not going to save the planet by putting our country out of business … so let's resolve that we're going to cut our carbon emissions no slower but also no faster than our fellow countries in Europe.' It was confidently asserted by greener elements in the government that Osborne had gone off-piste with this flagrant tweaking of the Lib Dems' tail, and that Cameron was furious with his Chancellor for disturbing a delicate balance. In fact Cameron's major concern was that the Osborne intervention undermined delicate negotiations with foreign energy companies which, that very month, were seeking reassurance about Britain's long-term commitment to the green cause.

Whatever the minutiae, the Conservative forces aligned against, for example, substantial public investment in green energy, are formidable. Cameron's green credentials were further undermined when Steve Hilton, who had voted Green in the past and was always regarded as being personally committed to reducing carbon emissions, let it be known that he was unconvinced by the science that global warming is man-made.

Those who suspected the green commitment was a sham could not have asked for clearer evidence. 'I think Samantha is the greenest person in that household,' remarked one Lib Dem with understated irritation. The green cause received a further setback in February 2012 when Huhne was forced to resign his cabinet seat after being charged with perverting the course of justice following an alleged motoring offence nine years earlier. Those Tories who saw no votes (or sense) in carbon reduction struggled to conceal their glee. It remained to be seen whether Ed Davey, his Lib Dem replacement, was quite large enough for the role as Cameron's green fig leaf.

FLASHMAN
The trappings of office

After months of range-finding, Ed Miliband began to zero in on perceived weaknesses in Cameron's style: inattention to detail, laziness and disdain.

Cameron did sometimes stumble over his facts. He picked a fight with an Oxford college over the number of black students it had admitted but got his numbers wrong. On another occasion he erroneously claimed that the US had been fighting the Second World War in 1940 (he is said to have been advised to avoid dates altogether because of his habit of getting them wrong).

But Miliband's efforts to trip him on questions of detail were largely in vain.

Cameron's fluency and ready wit came at a cost. Telling Angela Eagle, a Labour shadow minister, to 'calm down dear' won laughs in the Commons but brickbats outside. Cameron was told to tone down his 'Flashman' act, a reference to the swashbuckling heroic coward created by George MacDonald Fraser (and loved by the schoolboy Cameron).

There were complaints that Cameron's personal charm was intermittent and selective. Close friends and staff insist he remained even-tempered despite the increased workload. One said he was 'fatalistic' about reverses. While they admit that transport tests his patience, as does pen-clicking and checking phones and BlackBerries, they also insist that a full loss of temper is more often than not followed, five minutes later, by an apology.

A more telling criticism was that Cameron still had a tendency to succumb to the temptation to coast, a failing identified at Eton and by Hilton. In May, James Forsyth, political editor of the *Spectator*, quoted a Tory saying: 'What you have to understand is that the Tory party now only has two modes: panic and complacency.'

A couple of months later Cameron escaped a 'Katrina moment' by the skin of his teeth and only thanks to the RAF. George W. Bush badly erred in failing to visit New Orleans in the aftermath of the hurricane which destroyed the city in 2005. When Britain suffered the worst outbreak of civil unrest for decades in August 2011 it seemed Cameron had made the same mistake. Rioting that had broken out in Tottenham on 6 August, a Saturday night, had by Sunday spread to other areas in London. Cameron, however, saw no reason to cut short a family holiday in Tuscany despite the fact that riots were now spreading to other cities. It was only after desperate calls from Downing Street on Monday – as Britain entered a third night of serious unrest – that Cameron realised he was facing a presentational catastrophe. Unless he got back overnight the country was going to wake up to pictures of looted streets – and their Prime Minister enjoying the sunshine on Baron Luca Sanjust's estate in the heart of Chianti.

By the time he decided to return, however, there were no commercial flights. He was scrambled on to an RAF flight in the early hours. 'It was a very close run thing, he was lucky,' says a friend.

Once in Downing Street, Cameron took command and caught the national mood of anger at rioters. The unrest was even used to vindicate his 'broken society' rhetoric: here was proof of the moral decay that had bred in an underclass of untrained, uneducated youth led by Labour to believe the world owed them not a living but a free pair of trainers.

His speech to a recalled parliament was classic Cameron:

This is not about poverty, it's about culture. A culture that glorifies violence, shows disrespect to authority, and says everything about rights but nothing about responsibilities. In too many cases, the parents of these children – if they are still around – don't care where their children are or who they are with, let alone what they are doing. The potential consequences of neglect and immorality on this scale have been clear for too long, without enough action being taken.

Within forty-eight hours he had averted a potential Katrina moment and turned terrible social disorder to his advantage. Yet in catching the wind of public opinion, he also managed to alienate several senior police officers. They resented his criticism of their handling of the riots, and particularly suggestions that it was only after government pressure that police numbers on the streets had been increased. One was quoted as saying: 'David Cameron blamed the police for not having a crystal ball and not anticipating the most serious set of circumstances ever seen. The confidence of the police leadership in the government is at an all-time low. Cameron dumps on the police when it suits him, to deflect blame from himself.' Within days he was backtracking with emollient remarks about police bravery, although the price for saying what he thought the public wanted to hear came at a price in police support which may yet not be fully paid.

The riots episode would not have been complete without an unhelpful intervention from his old sparring partner Boris Johnson, by then preparing to stand for a second term as Mayor of London. Boris had chipped in by denouncing the government's plans to cut police funding, in defiance of David Cameron's assertion that police bosses had said their resources were sufficient. While this could be written off as a populist tokenistically asserting political independence, he invariably manages to cause a rolling of eyes in Downing Street and provoke a wave of 'naughty old Boris' media coverage.

Johnson continued to back plans for a new airport in the Thames estuary, insolently recruiting Steve Hilton as an ally in the campaign and forcing Cameron to take the issue seriously. Boris was also notably slow to endorse Cameron's premiership during the revelations about phone hacking, and casually accused Cameron of being lily-livered over reform of trade union law, claiming that the Prime Minister had made a private pledge to him to make strikes on the London Underground harder to organise. By accusing Cameron of 'Kosovo-style social cleansing' of London – by capping housing benefit – and proudly playing on Cameron's hesitation about wearing a morning suit to the royal wedding, or adding to public pressure about the size of the bonus for the boss of publicly owned Royal Bank of Scotland, Stephen Hester (just when Cameron was claiming credit for having halved it), Johnson was continuing to conform to a pattern set years before. Everybody knows the game, yet Boris can't help playing it and Cameron can't help being riled by it. Yet when accused of wanting to be Prime Minister, Johnson insisted that that was about as likely to happen as him as being 'decapitated by an asteroid which bore an uncanny resemblance to the Mona Lisa'. As a denial, for colour and credibility it stands comparison with his finest.

The reaction to the riots and to Cameron's rhetoric affirmed the right's belief that Britain was rediscovering its Conservative impulses in the teeth of austerity.

But it confirmed a clear pattern emerging in his premiership: the flip-side of Cameron's ability to seize a propitious moment, or turn disaster into triumph, is that he does not himself generate his own urgency. Even a friend remarked that 'you can hear the ticking of the clocks in Downing Street', so smoothly does the Cameron operation run whatever the chaos outside. A columnist dubbed him the 'essay crisis Prime Minister'.

Sir Peter Tapsell, the Father of the House, drew blood with his observation that he had never known a Prime Minister so good at getting out of scrapes – or so good at getting into them. The Flashman jibe was also another iteration of the 'toff' caricature. David Cameron's initial refusal to wear tails to the wedding of Prince William and Catherine Middleton in the spring of 2011 was taken by most commentators as an example of how contorted he had become about his own background.

For all Cameron's pretended insouciance about his upbringing he took great care, especially before the election, to avoid needlessly reminding voters of it. The narrowness of his political and social circles, undeniably cliquish, and the nature of his leadership made it all the more important to avoid the settings and costumes of his class.

But while there was undoubtedly a presentational calculation in his reluctance to dig out his morning suit for a public outing, the incident also supports a theory held by some of his friends which is intriguing if only because it is so contrary to the settled view.

This holds that, far from being a secret admirer of the upper class, Cameron nurses a strong dislike bordering on contempt for the aristocracy. The evidence, slim and wholly anecdotal, starts with his schooling where he was surrounded by the titled but remained plain master.

He married into the aristocracy and, like all those who marry up, is likely to have suffered the occasional stinging reminder of the gap in social standing. An echo might be heard in his complaint that when his in-laws were first shown around Chequers, they commented on the disappointing size of its grounds.

Another titled friend recalls Cameron, in a moment of frustration, letting loose a salvo at the extent of his land ownership. And then there is the claim that he agreed with the view, advanced by the father of another friend, that Prince William gives insufficient return for a life of idle privilege.

Of course Cameron is, on any account, a member of the English Establishment and his instinct is to defend it from outside attack, as in

1 – a simple matter of picking up
f which is connected to Downing
ver for game of snooker.

lasé about Chequers. He would
or pictures with him, explaining
g-lived and they might not get
n endorsed by daughter Nancy,
armingly: 'Daddy says we're to
ng.' Certainly he shows no sign
when in residence, listening
g up the karaoke machine, a
rst Christmas after he moved
of staff, hearing the Prime
known ballad, was heard to
he day job'.)

read some prime ministerial
o Chequers, published in July
y to friends old and new, but

among the first visit to nch, have
had finally reach e sight
bound an 'Cameron an was
e room that use of a
it was up a n, which he
his disability –5) victory over
n seeing the nine was sufficient
ampion Boris Becker,
rmans have been invited
an hour: we both had a

use one weekend early in his

premiership Cameron called a friend
any of the sets in the mansion, each o
Street's switchboard – to invite him

Visitors say Cameron is far from
encourage visiting children to pose f
that his tenure there may not be lon
another opportunity. It's an assertion
who has a tendency to tell guests dis
enjoy it here as we won't be here for lo
of suppressing his appetite for life
unaffectedly to pop music and firin
Christmas present from friends the f
into Downing Street. (One member
Minister unleash himself on a well-
whisper 'Let's hope he doesn't give up t

Ever the host, he was anxious to sp
beneficence. The list of those he invited
2011, says a good deal about his loyalt
also invites scrutiny of his judgement.

Naturally enough, his parents were
Chequers in the months after Cameron
10. Ian Cameron was by now wheelchair
of one eye.

After wheeling him around the gar
wanted to show off one of the house's rare
features Oliver Cromwell's sword. The t
flight of stairs. Ian Cameron, who
unnecessary allowance, wasn't going
full run of his second son's new esta

Telling the story later, Camero
the stairs, it was bit like going up
and was pushed and finally we

Asked by Chequers' waiting staff what he would like to drink, Ian Cameron ordered an old favourite – and enjoyed it to the full. 'That gin and tonic must have offered him one of the proudest moments of his life,' said a close friend of the family.

Several weeks later, on 8 September 2010, Cameron was just turning his thoughts to that day's dominant event, his weekly appearance in the Commons for Prime Minister's Questions. It was 6.00 a.m.

A call from his mother put a juddering stop to daily politics. She told him that his father had been taken seriously ill in the night and that the doctors attending him thought his family should be called immediately to his bedside.

The pair had been holidaying with friends in the South of France at a hotel outside Toulon. It had been a good break but at 2.45 that morning Ian Cameron had what appeared to be a stroke. Mary Cameron called John Pender, a peer and friend Ian had known from school, from his room and he held his hand while they waited for an ambulance.

When it arrived the paramedics at first sought to prevent Mary from travelling in the ambulance with her husband, quoting French ambulance protocol. The former chairman of the Newbury magistrates' bench travelled in the ambulance.

Now, as she sat in Toulon's Font-Pré hospital, she wanted her sons and daughters at her side. Together they would say goodbye to this remarkable man. The logistics were against them: there was a commercial flight to Nice leaving from City Airport at 9.30 a.m. but the airport was some way from the hospital.

The redoubtable Liz Sugg got cracking. First the flight was delayed just long enough for Alex, Clare and David Cameron to get on board (although Number 10 denied that it was deliberately held). More importantly, the Elysée Palace got involved. Nicolas Sarkozy, with characteristic energy, had ordered that the Camerons be provided a military helicopter to fly them directly from Nice airport to the hospital's helipad in Nice.

That gesture allowed the Camerons to be at their father's bedside in the final moments. They arrived shortly before their father passed away. A family friend confirmed later that, without the French president's personal intervention, the Prime Minister would not have made it before his father died.

Sarkozy gave the family the presidential retreat of Fort Brégançon, surrounded on three sides by the sea, to grieve in private for the rest of the day and that night. The siblings composed a statement put out through Number 10:

> Our dad was an amazing man, a real life-enhancer. He never let the disability he was born with or the complications in later life get in the way of his incredible sense of fun and enjoyment. He touched a lot of lives in lots of different ways and was a brilliant husband and father. You could never be down for long when he was around. We will miss him terribly, but have a bank of memories that can never be exhausted.

To friends Cameron, perhaps defying the English stereotype, expressed his feelings about his father's passing with minimal sentimentality and with a full regard for how unhappy his father would have been to be further incapacitated.

'David was deeply anxious about the general deterioration of his health,' says an intimate, 'so he had mixed feelings of loss and relief that his dad had not had a slow and gradual deterioration.'

A colleague confirms the family was worried about Ian, in the past the most active of men, being increasingly prone to infections and needing long-term care, a subject that had already been broached. 'He died on holiday,' said a close colleague, 'after he'd seen his son become prime minister, and I think Mary Cameron had come to be at peace with the idea. There was more the celebration of a life lived than a sadness that a life had come to an end, and a faint sense of relief that he had been spared many years of care and pain.'

Recounting how father and son had inched up the stairs in Chequers that summer, Cameron said: 'We sat and had a drink together and a chat. He was very proud of what I was doing. He was always very worried about all the responsibility I was taking on. I didn't know it was "goodbye". His last bit of advice to me was, "Do the right thing". That was always his advice.'

'My last memories of him are very happy.'

In October 2010, Cameron marked an unexceptionably happy occasion, celebrating his forty-fourth birthday. This was the first time for months that he had truly let his hair down with old friends, many of whom he had not seen since long before the election. Among Cameron's friends, the guests were identifiably 'old school', many literally so, and some from more than one old school, and included David Granger, Christopher Lockwood, James Ferguson, Robert Hardman and Harry Eastwood (from Bullingdon days). The evening received no publicity and had one object alone: for Cameron and his friends to enjoy themselves. There was, with only one exception, no obvious ulterior motive. One of the very few politicians in attendance was Michael Gove, who made a droll speech which included less than flattering references to Chequers's bleached panelling ('We'd all like to thank the Prime Minister for inviting us to the Aylesbury Ramada Jarvis'). The other guests were almost entirely friends from Heatherdown, Eton or Oxford. This was Cameron making a point of not forgetting his mates, and they were not disappointed. The drink flowed, the evening beginning with gin slings, followed by fine wine at dinner and Moscow Mules to follow – until 3.00 a.m., when the party broke up. Cameron was in no mood to take prisoners, and nor were his friends.

But this understandable catharsis after a stressful year of ups and downs was not wholly hedonistic. The one concession to political advancement was his decision to invite Rebekah Brooks, chief executive of News International and the chief architect of Rupert Murdoch's conversion to Cameronism. (As it happened, Cameron was and is genuinely fond of Brooks, but he was to claim later, rather lamely, that Charlie Brooks, her husband, was a very old friend of his: in fact, Brooks is three years older than Cameron and was a friend of his brother Alex, an association which, alone, would not have been sufficient to win him an invitation.)

While some of Cameron's friends were bemused to see the sociable redhead at the party, she was evidently no less bemused by some of them. One, the affable Giles Andreae, whose formerly flowing red hair is now shorter and more dirty-brown in hue, sought to make conversation with her. Unfortunately the evening's consumption had taken its toll on him and he delivered a conversational *coup de grâce* even before they had started, when, seeking gamely to find common ground late in a long evening, he asked her: 'Isn't it awful being a red-headed twat?'

One or two of Cameron's friends were struck by Brooks's presence that night. He didn't have to ask her, did he – although it has been mooted that he didn't particularly want to invite her but felt obliged – but this convenient friendship had to be fed and watered. It was the job of both of them to mix with powerful people, and it might seem churlish not to ask her. Besides, he found her good company, and surely no harm was done.

'ON MY WATCH'
The phone-hacking scandal

Until 4 July 2011 Cameron had displayed, in public at least, the same heroic incuriosity about the extent of phone hacking as he had over Ashcroft's tax status. In hiring Andy Coulson as his media supremo more than four years earlier, he decided that the benefits outweighed the risks. He had affirmed that calculation the previous year, bringing Coulson into the heart of government against the advice of a number of senior Fleet Street figures.

Even when Coulson was forced to resign, his closest and most senior allies believed it had been correct to hire him. 'I think Andy Coulson was a brilliant hire,' said one in June 2011, adding that he had done a 'brilliant job'. But when weeks later it was revealed that the phone of Milly Dowler, a missing thirteen-year-old schoolgirl, later found to have been murdered, had been hacked, all hell broke loose.

How could Cameron have hired Coulson, a former editor of the *News of the World*? What research had been done into the circumstances of his resignation in the wake of the conviction of his royal reporter, Clive Goodman, for hacking?

Just how close was Cameron to Rebekah Brooks, who had been editor of the *News of the World* at the time of the Dowler case, and was now the chief executive of the paper's parent, News International?

Was there not at least the suspicion of a confluence of interest between the Conservatives, backed by News International titles before the election and since, and Rupert Murdoch, the papers' ultimate owner, on the brink of securing government approval to increase his media empire in the UK?

Two years previously, Cameron had managed to turn the public's anger over MPs' expenses to his advantage. As disgust over hacking grew he tried hard to repeat the trick.

Apologising that the scandal had broken on 'his watch', thereby reminding the world that Labour had also assiduously courted Rupert Murdoch, he gave the impression of accepting responsibility. Establishing a judge-led commission into press ethics, meanwhile, shifted the focus away from his own embarrassment over the scandal.

Andy Coulson had had no choice but to leave his job at the *News of the World* in 2007. His resignation was presented as the honourable taking of responsibility, but as editor he had little choice. He didn't want to go, and, as a hands-on exponent of a style of editing of which he felt his superiors knew and approved, he felt resentful at falling on his sword. The other person on staff to pay the price, Clive Goodman, who went to prison, had been presented as a 'rogue operator'. Goodman disputed this, writing in a confidential legal letter in early 2007 that some of the senior executives knew of the scale of phone hacking, and worse practices on the paper.

Being the only senior figure in the hierarchy to walk the plank, Coulson was paying heavily, and was far from happy. It is fair to assume his future weighed heavily on the minds of some of his former associates at News International. In plain terms, Coulson needed looking after. A return to the stable was not ruled out. People close to Coulson say that Murdoch himself phoned to tell him he had 'done the right thing' by resigning.

While News International worried about what to do with a disgruntled former editor, Cameron continued to fret over his relations with Murdoch. Cameron's 'arm's length' experiment had been abandoned but the prospect of a full embrace from the media tycoon was remote. Murdoch continued to regard the leader as inexperienced and lightweight. In an interview in the *New Yorker* at the end of 2006, Murdoch had shown what a mountain Cameron had to climb. 'Look, he's charming,' said Murdoch, 'he's very bright, and he behaves as if he doesn't believe in anything other than trying to construct what he believes will be the right public image. He's a PR guy.'

It was a view not shared by Rebekah Wade (her maiden name), nor James, his youngest son, then head of BSkyB and about to take over operational control of the British newspaper titles. To Wade, at least, a shared solution to their problems seemed to be at hand, available to start work immediately in fact.

Cameron was looking for a new press chief and, according to Simon Walters of the *Mail on Sunday*, Rebekah Wade, with George Osborne's support, proposed Coulson. Osborne had had extensive dealings with Coulson, not least over a picture of him at the age of twenty-two, seated at a table alongside a prostitute and with a suggestive white powder in front of him, that the *News of the World* had published. It has since been said that Coulson gave Osborne a comparatively easy ride over that story, which appeared in other papers, prompting unsubstantiated suggestions that in some way Osborne 'owed' Coulson, but Osborne denied having any sort of relationship with the woman or that the powder was cocaine.

Osborne has claimed it was his idea to hire Coulson but, if it was, it was one Wade seems to have inspired and one that had the enthusiastic support of William Hague, a *News of the World* columnist. 'Cameron was told [his new media boss] should be someone acceptable to News International,' someone involved in Coulson's recruitment told Walters. 'The company was also desperate to find something for Andy after he took the rap when the phone hacking first became a scandal. The approach was along the lines of "If you find something for Andy, we will return the favour." ... "George is fixated with following how Tony Blair did everything but the decisive factor was Rebekah."' A few months earlier Cameron had been trying to keep his distance from newspaper barons in general and News International, in particular now, when he hit choppy waters, he was, it seems, having his head of media chosen for him.

When Brooks was challenged about her alleged initiative of hiring Coulson by the Commons Media Select Committee, she denied it. Intriguingly, when David Cameron was questioned about it in the House of Commons, he did not deny it but instead referred the questioner to Ms Brooks's denial.

The about-turn was exercised with apparent confidence, but there was, initially at least, a degree of wariness on Cameron's side. After all, she had been so close to both Labour's recent prime ministers and was now looking to complete the hat-trick with a member of a different party. As Cameron prepared to be charmed, Ed Llewellyn was heard to remark warily: 'Your turn next, Dave. Wear kid gloves.'

In fact Cameron had misgivings about appointing Coulson. It wasn't the circumstances of his resignation from the *News of the World* that worried him as much as a wariness of journalists as a breed. He had seen how Amanda Platell, another former editor turned press secretary when working for William Hague, had gone home at night during the election campaign to record a video diary, later seen on national television. Cameron wanted a clause inserted in Coulson's contract guaranteeing that he would not write a memoir, but Coulson refused.

Tellingly, Osborne, tasked with brokering the hire, didn't feel they could insist and backed down. There was a cursory check into whether there were any outstanding court cases or industrial tribunals which might throw up further details. A background check by a commercial company, believed to be Control Risk Services (but never confirmed), was conducted. 'We wanted to be sure there were no outstanding legal cases,' said one of those involved.

In March Coulson met Steve Hilton to discuss how the pair's roles might dovetail. Once Hilton, who had been pushing the claims of

Guto Harri, had professed himself happy, the deal was as good as done.

The job was announced at the end of May. 'Andy is a hugely experienced journalist,' gushed Cameron in the press release. Those who raised the issue of the Goodman case were referred back to the News International statement at the time of his resignation. On 26 January 2007, Coulson said: 'I have decided that the time has come for me to take ultimate responsibility for the events around the Clive Goodman case. As I've said before, his actions were entirely wrong and I deeply regret that they happened on my watch. I also feel strongly that when the *News of the World* calls those in public life to account on behalf of its readers, it must have its own house in order. It has been a privilege to lead such a talented and dedicated team and I've no doubt the successes of the last four years will continue.'

It was doubtless heartfelt, but it shed no light on an obstinate question, namely whether he had known about the hacking. Coulson said nothing else on the record about the matter at the time of his appointment. George Osborne addressed the shadow cabinet, telling members there was nothing to worry about. 'It was fairly cursory, as I remember,' says one cabinet minister.

The new media chief lost little time in getting close to the boss. Coulson, on a salary reported to be £475,000, picked up the remainder of the contract on the cottage formerly occupied by his boss Rebekah Brooks on the Blenheim estate. Coulson had joined the Chipping Norton set.

A constellation of decidedly urban television celebrities and socialites within a ten-mile radius of the Oxfordshire town had, in Cameron, a lustrous centre. Television presenter Jeremy Clarkson, Pret A Manger boss Julian Metcalfe, Henrietta Conrad, Amanda Staveley, Blur bassist Alex James, Lord and Lady Bamford, of JCB and Daylesford organic food fame (and a frequent provider of air transport to the Tory leadership), Charlie Dunstone, of Carphone

Warehouse fame, and heiresses Rosie Pearson and Emily Oppenheimer were all likely to bump into Cameron at local barbecues, point-to-points or the local swimming pool. Neighbours of Coulson on the magnificent Blenheim estate included PR man Chris Thykier and his wife Claudia Winkleman and Simon Kelner, then editor-in-chief of the *Independent*.

And there were plenty of after-dark occasions, too, for which the adults seemed able to summon reserves of energy. One local recalls a party a year or so before the election attended by the main dramatis personae – including the Camerons – which continued till dawn.

Until Cameron's political fortunes began to shine brightly in the second half of 2007 the set's most starry couple were Matthew and Elisabeth (daughter of Rupert Murdoch) Freud, who lived in a house called China Corner and later bought the magnificent Priory in Burford, one of the Cotswolds' loveliest villages.

At Liz Murdoch's birthday party in 2008, said one breathless local, '*everybody* was famous'. At Burford Priory Cameron might meet figures like Tony Blair and Peter Mandelson and the illustrious from show business, the City and the arts. Such encounters would have felt like vindication: to win elections, like Blair, it paid to be on good terms with the British media's first family.

Having helped organise it, Wade wasn't going to be left out of the party. She had in fact moved away from the area after splitting up with her former husband Ross Kemp. But in June 2009, at a ceremony attended by Tony Blair, Gordon Brown and David Cameron, she married Charlie Brooks, a raffish Etonian racehorse trainer, whose family had lived near Chipping Norton for generations. The pair, having been introduced by the Bamfords, established themselves in Sarsden, a handy four miles from Dean. One old friend of Rebekah Brooks said uncharitably: 'I'm not saying she married Charlie to be close to Cameron, but goodness me it was a piece of good fortune that Cameron was so close.' In fact this is unfair. Friends speak of what respite the uncomplicated Charlie provides from her gruelling career, and her willingness to adapt to the rural life (this pretty part of Oxfordshire has been called 'countryside for people who don't like the countryside') extended to borrowing a retired horse from the Metropolitan Police to keep on their land. Nevertheless the proximity seemed to suit both sides. One longstanding Chadlington resident said: 'We all thought she had moved in because Cameron was nearby, but then we thought Cameron wouldn't be so stupid as to allow her to get so close to him. I'm not sure if we were wrong.'

This was an intimate circle in which David and Samantha Cameron could unwind at weekends, bonded by shared experiences and untroubled by media intrusion, notwithstanding – indeed very probably because of – the amount of media firepower in the vicinity.

The concentration of success, wealth and power around north Oxfordshire has given rise to a degree of exclusive hedonism which some have claimed goes beyond the strictly legal. A fair proportion of the set have drug histories.

Matthew Freud was caught at Westminster School with cocaine. Josh Astor, a relation and friend of Samantha Cameron, was expelled from Eton for drug use. Closest to Cameron's own off-duty life, one of his frequent tennis partners, the Hon. Henry Allsopp, son of Lord Hindlip, was caught attempting to enter Bermuda with half an ounce of cannabis hidden in a condom (which he was wearing at the time), and others, unnamed above, in that circle are known to the authors to have used Class A drugs. The flip soubriquet 'Tooting Norton' has at least some basis in the past of some of the area's inhabitants.

One good friend of Cameron, for instance, attended the exclusive, invitation-only Kimberley Music Festival outside Norwich, on the Kimberley estate, one weekend in late July 2011. Someone in a position to know reported that Cameron's friend enjoyed the heady event to the utmost, sleeping little during the first two nights before catching up on rest on the Sunday night and returning to a particularly demanding Monday back at work.

This was not a set which would be selling stories about one another to the press, short of some major breach of faith, which is why their world is more speculated about than known about.

If the appointment of Coulson appeared to align the interests of the Conservatives and News International, it also aligned mutual enemies. Cameron was about to find that Murdoch brought new foes as well as friends. And it was Coulson's past, which had brought them together, that was a vulnerable flank.

For all his outward lack of concern – he would constantly fall back on a refrain about how few letters he received on the subject – David Cameron was becoming worried about the phone-hacking story. With the next election still a couple of years away, according to a friend of Cameron, the leader asked Coulson outright if he had known anything about the phone hacking, to which he replied 'categorically not'. In a private context, he also asked people with extensive dealings in newspaper regulation, who he had good reason to believe would be familiar with the workings of the grubbier end of Fleet Street. In good faith, it is fair to assume, they too reassured him that he had little to worry about.

When in August 2008 Cameron and his family were invited to visit Rupert Murdoch's yacht *Rosehearty*, the flights to Santorini were paid for by Matthew Freud (which concerned some of Cameron's advisers more than it did him). For Freud, this was the ultimate piece of political match-making.

This was jet-setting of the old school. But in a private one-on-one Cameron asked Murdoch directly about the continued rumblings about his press chief. Murdoch replied that, as far as he was concerned, the police knew everything. There was no new evidence of wrongdoing. He blamed his political enemies in the British media for stirring up trouble.

The trouble was, the 'stirring' didn't stop. The House of Commons Select Committee for Culture, Media and Sport spent a considerable amount of time investigating media standards, forcing a variety of News International executives, and, in July 2009, a well-prepared and apparently confident Andy Coulson, to appear before it and explain how they had no recollection of anything other than a vigorous and pure-hearted defence of the British public interest. The committee later concluded that it was 'inconceivable' that none of the *News of the World* employees past and present had known about the phone hacking and accused senior executives of suffering from 'collective amnesia'.

Cameron was to seek assurances from Murdoch again before the 2010 election, and Murdoch's answer was the same. In that case, said Cameron, he would stand by Andy and make sure the 'witch hunt' was unsuccessful. The Murdoch reassurance chimed with Cameron, whose cast of mind inclined him to believe that if the police had found nothing, there must be nothing there. But a slight switch to how Cameron responded to questions about Coulson was introduced. As a close colleague says, 'when there's a bit of doubt, the position shifts, the language changes', and so it did on this occasion. Previously, on the rare occasions he had been asked, he would offer a vague suggestion that he was led to believe Coulson knew nothing about the phone hacking. But now, on 10 July 2009, the words 'I believe in giving people a second chance' received their first airing.

Gordon Brown miscalculated that his genuinely warm personal relationship with Murdoch was a guarantee of the political support of his papers. When the Dowler story broke, the former Prime Minister reacted with the passion of the scorned, he laid out what he called the 'brutal ... simplicity' of News International's agenda. Its aim, he said, 'was to cut the BBC licence fee, to force BBC Online to charge for its content, for the BBC to sell off its commercial activities, to open up more national sporting events to bids from BSkyB and move them away from the BBC, to open up the cable and satellite infrastructure market, and to reduce the power of their regulator, Ofcom'.

Drawing on this checklist, Brown talked of the 'strange coincidence' of how News International and the Tory Opposition came to share almost exactly the same media policy 'often expressed in almost exactly the same words'.

Certainly, by 2009, the Tories began to show a new antipathy to the BBC, floating the freezing of the licence fee and urging the corporation to 'do more with less'. This chimed handily with James Murdoch's 2009 McTaggart Lecture at the Edinburgh TV Festival. The Tories and the Murdochs shared a striking identity of interests. With the Tories looking good in the polls, what more could the media empire ask for? Just a few weeks later, at the most damaging of moments for Labour (i.e. during its conference), the *Sun* announced it was to support the Conservatives in the next election. The timing was unprecedented: normally newspapers allow at least for the pretence that they have weighed each party in the balance during an election campaign before delivering their verdict. The value of endorsements has always been disputed with cynics claiming that newspapers do little more than cheer a winning horse over the line. With more than six months to go before polling this was a different, potentially more valuable vote of support. (Whether the *Sun*'s support did, in fact, do any good, of course, is a different matter: Conservative polling leads never recovered from the high they enjoyed just before the endorsement.)

Although Cameron had satisfied himself that Rupert Murdoch, Andy Coulson and (presumably) his friend Rebekah Brooks were all telling him the truth when they said the phone-hacking story was a dead duck, others were concerned.

In early 2010, Steve Hilton was informed that Coulson, as editor of the *News of the World*, had employed a private detective called Jonathan Rees, then facing charges for conspiracy to murder (later acquitted), and previously jailed for conspiracy to plant cocaine on an innocent woman. Hilton says he mentioned this to Ed Llewellyn, which he says he cannot remember. In any event word never reached Cameron. Conceivably Llewellyn felt he had been round this course with Cameron before – and that unless he was presented with cast-iron evidence of wrongdoing by Coulson, he wanted to hear no more about the matter. One unnamed Cameron aide was quoted at the time as saying: 'Ed simply decided not to mention anything for fear of creating unpleasantness and disturbing the equilibrium of the team. Also, David Cameron never likes being given bad news.' Candid friends of Cameron say his lack of a muscular, no-nonsense chief of staff willing to make the leader confront uncomfortable truths was felt most acutely over this issue.

Representations were also believed to have been made by senior courtiers at Buckingham Palace, which had always been unhappy at Coulson working by Cameron's side in opposition, but hitherto had been pacified by Coulson's intention to find another job after the election, according to an unimpeachable royal source. The Palace insists the Queen herself did not initiate an attempt to influence Downing Street staffing, but acknowledges the possibility that Cameron's circle was sent a message informally about the feelings of the Royal Household about the prospect of the former *News of the World* editor in Downing Street. Representations were also made to Cameron's office, at least, by Nick Clegg, Lord Ashdown, Zac Goldsmith, Sir Max Hastings, *Daily Mail* editor-in-chief Paul Dacre and others. And a more surprising voice spoke to him to question whether Coulson should follow his master into Downing Street, that of Coulson himself, who worried that he was becoming an embarrassment to Cameron. Cameron waved his concerns away – he needed him, he was coming to Downing Street. It was a terrible mistake for both of them.

Had Coulson left at the election the interest in hacking might have largely died away. His presence at the heart of Britain's government, however, redoubled determination to expose the truth.

On 1 September 2010 the *New York Times* published a lengthy and detailed account of the extent of phone hacking at News International, and included an explicit claim that Coulson had known about the hacking. Cameron was lobbied yet again by those who felt he was being overgenerous to Coulson. Cameron told a friend at the time: 'I can't go round sacking people on hearsay. There's no evidence against Andy.'

'I have heard Cameron describe [Coulson] as a genius ... There is a high level of confidence among the Camerons that there is nothing much here that would stand up in court, or indeed to reasonably well-informed scrutiny,' wrote Matthew d'Ancona in the *Sunday Telegraph*. This may still turn out to be correct, or it may well turn out to be astonishing naïvety. Cameron admitted enough to say, to a close friend at the time, 'if it does turn out he's been lying to me, he'll be out of here tomorrow'.

But while Cameron toughed it out, there had been a change of attitude inside News International. Emails emerged that, it was reported, showed much wider knowledge of unlawful activity than had been previously admitted. At around this time, with Murdoch furious at not having been told the full extent of what had been going on, it was made known to Cameron that he should no longer feel obliged to protect Coulson. In fact, Coulson had been telling an unheeding Cameron for some months that he felt he should stand down. It was clear the 'rogue reporter' defence was in shreds, and on 21 January he resigned as director of communications, deploying the classic departing line that the controversy was preventing him from doing his job properly.

The flurry of activity in January significantly widened the net of those with questions to answer about the whole affair, but relations between the Tories and News International remained essentially trusting. George Osborne celebrated his fortieth birthday with a lavish party. William Hague made an affectionately double-edged speech which enumerated Osborne's four mottoes for political success, ending with: 'Number Four, remember Number One.' Among the presentations was a framed mocked-up *Sun* front page, arranged by his friend Rebekah Brooks, which he later hung proudly in his office, bearing the date of Osborne's birth and the headline 'Ozzy Was Born'.

By the late spring of 2011 Brooks was beginning to hope that she'd weathered the storm. In a stroke of luck for the company one of its few Cabinet enemies was caught in a sting.

As Business Secretary, Vince Cable had to rule on whether News International should be allowed to increase its stake in BSkyB, a contravention, according to critics, of media ownership laws. Cable, tricked by two undercover reporters posing as constituents, boasted that he had 'declared war on Rupert Murdoch', which was to preclude him from being the detached arbitrator in charge of the nation's media.

He kept his job, but the BSkyB decision was taken out of his hands in favour of Culture Secretary, Jeremy Hunt, someone more likely to be less personally antagonistic to the bid.

Cameron showed no signs of distancing himself from the group. In May 2011, the *Sun* asked for Cameron's support for its campaign to have the search reopened for Madeleine McCann. One furious senior police officer called it 'a complete waste' and 'obvious crowd-pleasing', while others worried about police independence.

'There was definitely a feeling that Rebekah felt the PM owed them,' said someone who was intimately involved. 'The fact that Rupert had given his backing in the election was not something to be forgotten quickly. In Wapping they regarded that as very, very important.'

Then the Dowler story broke. The voicemails of a thirteen-year-old kidnap victim were intercepted and, or so it was reported at the time, deleted by people working for News International. The nation was outraged. In the following fortnight detectives revealed they had identified four thousand potential victims of phone hacking, two of the nation's top police officers resigned, the *News of the World* closed,

Andy Coulson was arrested, Les Hinton, News International's Executive Chairman from 1995 to 2007 and then chief executive at Dow Jones, resigned, Rebekah Brooks was arrested and later resigned, a former executive at *News of the World* and arrestee, Neil Wallis (a former recipient of Cameron's Christmas cards), turned out to have been giving advice to Andy Coulson while the latter was working for Cameron, Coulson's Downing Street vetting, it was reported, had been carried out by a private investigator who had worked extensively for News International, and News Corp withdrew its bid for BSkyB a matter of days before its anticipated successful completion.

Until then, for most people David Cameron had been on the periphery of a long-running media story. Hindsight had a field day. Why on earth did he employ Andy Coulson, wondered a lot of people to whom the question had apparently not mattered before? Why had he spent quite so much time in the company of News International's senior management? He told parliament that he was setting out 'every single meeting since the last election' with News Corporation, both in News International and its New York-based parent company people, pointing out that this was more than Tony Blair and Gordon Brown had done. The figures he revealed showed he had met senior executives from News International more times than all other media groups combined. But even with that admission the public perception was one of evasiveness. The first time the list was published it omitted Rebekah Brooks's presence at his birthday party at Chequers. The corrected version omitted their pre-arranged meeting (when they texted one another to make sure they weren't seen together) at a local point-to-point, at Heythrop, and then yet another meeting at the Chipping Norton Fair was omitted. He omitted to mention, too, that Les Hinton of News Corp had attended one of the 'social' Christmas events that had prompted the publication of the list. The games of tennis the pair played continued to go unmentioned, as did the frequency with which they would pop round to one another's houses for meals. ('They do see an *awful lot* of Rebekah,' remarked one friend.) The wider public might have liked to know, too, of the text message that Charlie Brooks told friends Cameron sent to Brooks at the beginning of the week in which she resigned, telling her to keep her head up and she'd get through her difficulties. Such contact came to an abrupt halt soon afterwards, with Brooks not wanting to embarrass Cameron and he wanting to be able to say, hand on heart, that they had not been in touch. But it was claimed that Cameron did send an emissary to Brooks to mitigate his sudden coldness towards her. The gist of the message was 'Sorry I couldn't have been as loyal to you as you have been to me, but Ed Miliband had me on the run.' The pair have continued to avoid one another for understandable reasons. The Chipping Norton set's golden age, such as it was, was over.

It may have served its purpose in amusing its main dramatis personae, but it was still to provide plenty of entertainment for the wider public. On Tuesday 28 February 2012, news broke that Rebekah Brooks had borrowed Raisa, a retired horse, from the Metropolitan Police. In the context of the ongoing hearings into links between the police and the media, this was interesting enough. But a journalist at the *Telegraph* asked Downing Street if David Cameron had ever ridden Raisa. Not for the first time, Cameron's spokesman sought to treat a legitimate question as too trivial to merit a response. Another two days of jousting over 'horsegate' (or perhaps 'fivebargate') followed. On Thursday, Cameron was forced to give a hastily arranged television interview in which he sought to parry the issue. 'It's a matter of record that I have ridden horses with Rebekah Brooks's husband in my constituency. Since becoming PM I may have got on a horse once, but not that one.'

The lawyerly construction was moot on the question of whether Cameron had ridden Raisa before the election and the following morning he came clean. He had indeed ridden Raisa and he had known that she had been loaned by the Met.

'If a confusing picture has emerged over the last few days, I am very sorry about that,' Cameron said, head bowed, when questions over the issue pursued him across the Channel to an EU summit. With the truth out Cameron's friend Jeremy Clarkson tried to close the stable door.

He announced – also on the Friday – that he could 'categorically state that he [Cameron] never rode that horse. I do live there. It's all rubbish.' And on the Sunday, adding further to the sense that there was something to hide, the *Mail on Sunday* alleged that a year earlier it had asked if Charlie Brooks and Cameron had ever been riding together, which Downing Street had denied at the time.

MPs had been demanding to know whether Cameron and James Murdoch or Rebekah Brooks ever discussed, say, the BSkyB deal during any of their encounters. Given that an enormous amount of money was riding on the deal, it would be astonishing if News International didn't at least have it on their minds. Two days after the removal of Vince Cable from his role deciding on the BskyB bid, James Murdoch told the Leveson inquiry that he had had an insubstantial 'tiny side conversation' on the periphery of a dinner party at Rebekah Brooks's home on 23rd December 2010. Evidently more to the point was a conversation on another occasion when the News Corp man had with Lib Dem minister Chris Huhne when he sought to persuade him that the News Corp bid for BSkyB shouldn't be referred to the competition commission. And it was not until five months later, during a moment of maximum press distraction, that details of a meeting that Rupert Murdoch had had with Cameron a month after the BSkyB bid was launched were published. During the Leveson inquiry, this meeting was removed from the record, curiously due to lack of evidence.

Yet Cameron is by disposition almost painfully scrupulous in matters of political probity. He told the House of Commons that he 'completely took myself out of any decision making about this bid' (an assertion vigorously endorsed by those who work for him), and that he never had a conversation that was 'inappropriate'.

Without complete knowledge of his conversations with all the key players it is, of course, impossible to disprove this self-acquittal. But what could be said with certainty is that it *looked* inappropriate for the Prime Minister to be partying so assiduously with media barons whose future he was in a position to influence.

Cameron is not the first to treat the demands of high office on his social life casually. A friend says 'he is naturally a social guy. He enjoys getting on with people. He doesn't see the need to take a moral position on every aspect of someone's life in order to get on with them.' In the public – particularly the foreign – sphere, it's an attitude that prime ministers find they need. They can't afford to be too choosey about who they do deals with. In the private sphere, given the risk of public exposure, it's an attitude they can't afford.

As of spring 2012, no evidence had come to light that Andy Coulson was guilty of anything. 'I have an old-fashioned view about innocent until proved guilty,' opined Cameron, characteristically without gerunds.

In June 2007, in 'You ask the questions ...' Cameron was asked by a reader of the *Independent* newspaper, 'How can you have as your director of communications a man who resigned for tapping into the Royal Family's telephones? Is this the sort of new image you want for the Conservative Party?' Cameron's answer did not say 'Andy tells me he knew of nothing unlawful and that's good enough for me', or anything so direct. Instead he opted for a more ambiguous form of words, saying: 'I am satisfied that Andy Coulson was not aware that a journalist at the *News of the World* was engaged in this practice.' David Cameron told the Commons six times in July 2011, he had received assurances from Coulson that he knew nothing incriminating. And yet even as he professed loyalty he edged away. 'With 20:20 hindsight and all that has followed, I would not have offered him the job, and I expect he would not have taken it. But you do not make decisions in hindsight; you make them in the present. You live and you learn, and believe you me, I have learned.'

He told questioners that he had no evidence against Coulson, but added:

> If it turns out he knew about that hacking, he will have lied to a Select Committee, he will have lied to the police, he will have lied to a court of law and he will have lied to me. I made the decision to employ him in good faith, because of the assurances he gave to me … [if he knew about the hacking] that will be a matter of huge regret and a matter for great apology, and it will be … a disgrace that he worked in government …

Cameron choosing to seek refuge in hindsight is disingenuous and vacuous. Of course few politicians, given the power of hindsight, would advocate repeating a disastrous course of action. Cynics paraphrased his attitude as 'I thought I'd get away with it', and a source extremely close to Cameron agreed that he had taken a gamble. 'We took it at face value that the whole hacking thing had blown over,' he says. 'David took a calculated risk that it wouldn't go any further, and I think his main concerns at the time were generic ones about having journalists in that role.' Cameron also insisted that nobody had complained about Coulson's behaviour while he was working for him. Certainly he had many admirers in Downing Street, although his reluctance to engage directly with more than a small handful of lobby journalists limited his sphere of influence. Unlike Alastair Campbell, rightly or wrongly he failed to develop a loyal cadre of reporters willing to communicate the government's message. But given that his chief function seemed to be as a bridge to Wapping, maybe he felt this unnecessary.

Oliver Letwin was candid: 'The realpolitik is that you have to get on with people who run newspapers,' he said. 'Labour did the same. If you are on the same side as her, you have to see her every week. This was how it worked. It was what was demanded if you wanted them on your side. All of us should have said we'll have nothing to do with them and we'll only meet them when we absolutely have to. But the problem with that is if the other guy is doing it … it's an arms race. I don't think this was a love affair based on a misjudgement. I think it was a carefully calculated view of what you had to do in order to carry the people onto our side. That game is over, thank God.'

Although in the Commons and on no fewer than eight occasions Cameron claimed personal responsibility for Coulson's appointment, in private he blamed Osborne. It was whispered that the Chancellor assumed that William Hague, who had written a weekly column for Coulson's *News of the World* and who got on well with him, had checked up on Coulson's suitability, according to one source. In fact, Hague, though an enthusiast for Coulson's hiring, had done no such thing, nor been asked to.

In truth, once the idea had been sown, Osborne had been the Tories' main driver of the appointment. As a Tory strategist put it, 'Osborne was actually quite overawed about how close he [Osborne] was to the Murdochs. He would boast to colleagues that he had been invited to Elisabeth Murdoch's party and that he had had dinner with James. He sold Coulson hard. He unashamedly talked of making a study of Blair's success and copying everything Blair had done, including building relations with Murdoch.'

Someone close to the affair puts it like this: 'David Cameron is one of those leaders who allows people to do their jobs, and he doesn't want to be bothered with matters that he doesn't need to know about. He assumes George will do a job thoroughly and George was one of those keenest on signing up Coulson. It's a mark of Cameron's relationship with George, though, that he went out of his way to protect him in the whole affair. He knows that the public perception of George's judgement is central to the government's success in overcoming the country's economic difficulties.' In shouldering the blame, he also subverted the belief that Rebekah Brooks had had a hand in the appointment.

One associate of Cameron puts it brutally. 'To my knowledge, he never asked Coulson. George wanted Coulson so badly and David agreed to it after just the briefest of meetings with Coulson. When David says he was given assurances, I think he means given assurances by others, including George Osborne and Rebekah Wade. David didn't want to have an uncomfortable meeting with Andy.'

Downing Street insists that Cameron was indeed told by Coulson that he knew nothing of phone hacking, and in explaining his previous assertions, he can fall back, a little feebly perhaps, on the written declaration that all Tory party employees have to sign, that they are not guilty of anything that would embarrass the party. In the absence of a verbatim account, it is at least possible that Cameron's assertion – that Coulson told him he didn't know about the phone hacking – relies on a stretched, almost regal definition of the word 'me'.

Asked if Cameron wasn't guilty of naïvety, at the very least, one News International source who knows them both well said charitably: 'Yes, but she really moved in on him.' In any event, he had gone along too easily in sharing Osborne's enthusiasm. The climax, at the end of the parliamentary session, was the setting up of the Leveson Inquiry into journalistic practices, press supervision and the relationship between politicians and the media. It was to be hugely wide-reaching and have considerable powers to call for witnesses and documents. Government sources made it clear that its recommendations would likely be made law. This was a Cameronian broad brush, presented as bringing in a new era of probity.

But several figures felt the exercise was a smokescreen. One senior public servant was scandalised at the decision to allow the Leveson Inquiry to proceed while the criminal investigation was still going on. 'There was absolutely no need for it to run concurrently,' said the source. 'It was nothing to do with justice. It was like Blair, he just wanted to be seen to do something, anything.'

Setting aside the rights and wrongs of phone hacking, it didn't require a High Court judge to establish that Cameron had sought to curry favour with Rupert Murdoch. Cameron's unstated but implicit defence that Labour had done it too (with its echoes of the phone hacker's claim that 'everyone else was doing it') is particularly inglorious in a Prime Minister who says he wants to clean up politics. As Max Hastings wrote in the *Financial Times*, Cameron had 'committed himself to review relations between ministers and the press because it suits his political convenience to pretend that the scandal reveals a systemic problem. In truth, all that has been lacking is personal judgment in Downing Street.'

So the Coulson appointment affronted most people's idea of probity in public life, even if only in hindsight. It has caused more embarrassment and distraction than any single decision Cameron has made. And Cameron's 'believe you me, I have learnt' to the House of Commons seemed heartfelt indeed. What is harder to know is whether, given the chance to undo that decision, a Machiavelli would stand by it and risk not reaching Downing Street. After all, he would say, Cameron's level of perceived competence remained high, Coulson helped get the Murdoch papers on board, keep the right at bay and secure the keys of No. 10 for David Cameron. Wasn't that exactly what it was meant to do? If Cameron ever confronts himself with that question, presumably a sense of honour and squeamishness would tell him to regret the decision. Everything else would tell him to be thankful it's a hypothetical question.

Given the difficulties that the Brooks/Coulson pair have brought on Cameron, it would be surprising if he didn't feel both ashamed, at what his ambition made him do, and angry. He has been at pains to reveal no anger even to those quite close to him, yet those who know him best say it is there. It is unlikely to be ventilated, though, partly out of a sense of decorum, but also because a slanging match would bring political dangers of its own. 'He is angry, but he knows he needs to go gently on this,' says a close associate. 'If he tries to cut them off, they'll turn on him and leak against him, not least about the process of Coulson's appointment, who knew what and how they failed to ask the right questions. He can't just decontaminate that lot as he decontaminated the party.'

And among his political colleagues his movement is highly restricted. He is unable to blame George Osborne, since Osborne's perceived competence is central to his own chances of re-election. The state of relationship between the two, moreover, determines the health of his government. Scrutiny of this issue, and specifically what questions Osborne and Cameron asked Andy Coulson before they hired him, seem likely to test the strength of that relationship. In any case, whoever else might be to blame it is clear that Cameron's office, in its alacrity to get in with Murdoch, may have failed to exercise due diligence.

'GOLDEN HOUR'
Cameron and Libya

In Opposition Cameron had sought to be a dutiful student of foreign affairs while relying heavily on his chief-of-staff Ed Llewellyn to plug the gaps in his knowledge. 'David said to his aides, "Look, this is an area where I need help",' remembers an ally.

His caution was understandable: he had a track record of asking the right questions but drawing the wrong conclusions. He had been rightly sceptical over the case for an invasion of Iraq but, swayed, as he himself confessed, by Tony Blair's passion and eloquence became a zealous convert to the cause.

On Afghanistan, too, although he sought the advice of friends who knew the country well he chose to ignore their advice to oppose further troop deployments and distance himself from a military strategy doomed to fail.

Sometimes he had been rash, as when he supported Georgia's application to join NATO, a highly inflammatory step that could have provoked full-scale war with Russia.

As with his 'liberal conservatism' speech in Berlin, he gave the impression that he had not a fixed position on how Britain should engage with the rest of the world but a slide-rule from neo-Conservative interventionism, as preached by his friends Gove and Osborne, to pragmatic isolation typified by that shown by Douglas Hurd as Foreign Secretary during the Balkans conflicts.

In his first major speech on foreign policy he said that 'democracy cannot be dropped from the air from an unmanned drone'. And yet one of Cameron's better-kept secrets is that among his favourite prime ministers is Lord Palmerston, famous for sending British gunboats abroad to secure the nation's interests.

Cameron did, however, think deeply about the structural deficiencies exposed by Britain's foreign policy shortcomings. He watched Blair's so-called 'sofa government' picked apart by official inquiries and then how Brown was thwarted by a Foreign Office and Ministry of Defence pursuing contradictory agendas.

The result of this analysis was the formation of the National Security Council, a body of the most relevant senior politicians and intelligence and military officers to coordinate and direct policy. One of its first tasks had been what to do with Britain's engagement in Afghanistan. Initially against setting 'artificial' deadlines for withdrawal, in Opposition the Tory leader's main focus was to reassure the military and voters that he would be a competent war leader. Frequent visits to the conflict were intended to show solidarity with and support for Britain's mission in Afghanistan.

Behind the public support there was growing private fear over an unending, unwinnable war that Cameron might inherit, however.

Osborne is said to have been pressing for a policy which would ensure that the conflict was 'receding' by the time of an election in 2015. Aware of military opposition, Cameron chose his words carefully through the 2010 election, 'hoping' only that troops would come home some time in the next parliament.

As the White House began also to inch towards the setting of a political timetable for withdrawal so, too, Cameron added substance to his policy.

On 1 June, less than two months after entering Downing Street, he held what was dubbed a 'seminar' on Afghanistan to which he invited sceptics like Rory Stewart, the new Tory MP for Penrith and an expert on the country, as well as the usual military and intelligence chiefs. To this gathering he made clear that there was to be no dramatic change of course – Britain would still support the NATO-led mission, and by extension, the Americans. But it was obvious from the need to express that support that a shift was underway.

Within a month Cameron had committed Britain to withdrawing all combat troops from 2015 and, for good measure, announced an immediate drawdown of five hundred troops. He had by then experienced what he has said is the worst part of being Prime Minister. 'The thing I dread most is news of casualties from Afghanistan, because that's the greatest responsibility,' he said in November 2011.

'He gets the Afghan thing absolutely,' says one authority he consulted. 'We're in coalition with the Americans, who call the shots. The US military are saying we can always win this and of course we never can. As long as things stay like that, the policy is insane.'

Cameron also signed off a new, more mercantile approach, directed more effort at emerging economies and what he hoped would be a more creative projection of soft power.

In February 2010 he had promised to fly the flag for Britain and to fill planes with businessmen (not journalists) to tour the world looking for new trade. On becoming Prime Minister he gave the new policy its first run out with a trip to India, via Turkey, in July. His chartered plane was indeed full of businessmen, as well as six other Cabinet ministers (and a few journalists). The trip – which was supposed to kick-start 'an enhanced partnership' with one of the world's fastest growing markets – proved an eye-opener for the Foreign Office.

Cameron's instincts about diplomats had never been overly favourable. 'They are very good at giving you twenty reasons for telling you why you can't do something,' he grumbled a year before the election. On being shown a copy of the speech he planned to deliver in Ankara on his way to India, 'they' raised objections. Cameron pressed on regardless in comparing the Gaza strip to a 'prison camp'.

The Israeli protests were still reverberating when Britain's new Prime Minister touched down in Bangalore. But he was not finished. In an answer to a question on Pakistan, always a sensitive subject in India, he referred to private discussions he had had with the US President Barack Obama and warned Pakistan not to 'look both ways' on terror. He later made clear that he was indeed accusing elements of the Pakistani state of conniving in the export of terror.

Islamabad promptly cancelled a planned summit on security in London. (The price of restoring good relations was a weekend with Pakistan's president Asif Ali Zardari in Chequers later that summer.) The next day, as Cameron hit Kapil Dev's long-hopped tennis ball for six in a publicity stunt in Delhi, a deadpan William Hague described him as a 'natural diplomat'.

Six months later, on another trade mission, this time to the Middle East and Gulf, Cameron's mercantile foreign policy hit a more severe embarrassment.

In a hastily arranged addition to the original trip, Cameron first visited Cairo where protestors had overthrown the regime of Hosni Mubarak. But after preaching the sanctity of the ballot box, the Prime Minister next headed for the Gulf, where, in the company of some of Britain's biggest defence firms, he promoted arms sales to a number of unelected governments. 'I simply don't understand how you can't understand that democracies have a right to defend themselves,' he snapped at one point, glossing over the lack of an elected government in Kuwait by insisting it had a 'level of democracy'. But if Cameron's initial response to the Arab Spring was less than convincing, his allies would contend that he more than made up for it in the months that followed.

During the years of the youthful Cameron's political development, Colonel Muammar Gaddafi had been the West's most hated pariah. The murder of PC Yvonne Fletcher by a bullet fired from the Libyan Embassy in London in 1984 was followed two years later by the bombing of Tripoli by US planes flying from UK bases. He had been at the Conservative Research Department when Pan Am 103 exploded over the Scottish town of Lockerbie on the night of 21 December 1988. And he had been at the Home Office, at Michael Howard's side, as the then Home Secretary sought the extradition of Abdelbaset al-Megrahi from Libya.

When, in 1999, al-Megrahi was finally handed over, it cleared the way for a gradual rehabilitation concluding in 2004 with a deal, blessed by Blair in Gaddafi's tent, to end the country's nuclear weapons programme. Cameron opposed the release of al-Megrahi in 2009 but otherwise seemed to share a view prevalent in the British Establishment that the Libyan threat had been satisfactorily contained. That was a view that took no account of domestic resentment at the dictator's excesses, a fury which risings elsewhere in the Maghreb sparked to life, however.

Even as Cameron flew home from the Gulf opposition militias took control of Misrata. The action had been sparked by the arrest a week earlier of a human rights activist in Benghazi. A UN Security Council resolution condemning the subsequent repression of the uprising was diplomatic boiler-plate. But as evidence of Gaddafi's brutal repression mounted so calls grew for a response that went beyond what Dr David Owen, a former Foreign Secretary, dismissed as 'the usual diplomatic caution and waffle'.

The deliberate targeting by roof-top government snipers of women and children forced from their houses, food and medicine withheld, the use of tanks against civilians: a grim checklist of war crimes was filling up fast.

Only intervention would stop the killing, warned Owen. If not a lone voice, the greater chorus was on the contrary side. The opposition of Russia and China among the permanent five of the UN Security Council, the reluctance of US President Barack Obama, and over all the spectre of Iraq, meant the prospect of military action in support of the rebels was at first very remote.

The French president, Nicolas Sarkozy, became the first Western leader to take up the cause when he called for the West to impose a no-fly zone over Libya. On 28 February Cameron followed suit, asking the Ministry of Defence to prepare plans for a Libyan engagement, to the surprise and alarm of Washington. US Defense Secretary Robert Gates, a survivor from George Bush's White House, growled that it amounted to 'loose talk'. It was the first time Cameron and Obama were publicly at odds. Personal relations had been superficially friendly if not warm on previous meetings although Cameron privately admitted he was fazed by Obama's lack of small talk. (On his first visit to the Cameron Number 10, Obama stretched out his hand to the new British Prime Minister on the steps of Downing Street and introduced himself thus: 'I've been looking at your poll ratings, David. Things are looking very good for you but not so good for the Liberals.')

Now he was supporting the French in a call for a military engagement in a Muslim country in defiance of Washington. 'He probably hadn't realised how far he was flying on his own,' concedes an ally.

One day in early March, Cameron was asked by an old and trusted colleague to make the case for a Libyan engagement in the simplest possible terms. 'Because thousands of people will die who don't need to die,' he replied. 'I just think it's the right thing to do.'

Key to Cameron's decision was Llewellyn. The beetling *consigliere* is sometimes criticised for caution and inaction. But as former adviser to Lord Ashdown when he was UN envoy in Bosnia, Llewellyn had seen the terrible cost of failing to seize the moment. In *Swords and Ploughshares*, his account of his time in the Balkans, Ashdown writes of a 'golden hour', a period, which may never be repeated, when effective action is possible. Even his enemies would concede Cameron has the ability to seize a moment. Other close allies like Gove saw not just the chance to realign Britain's interests with those of the Arab world but a chance to cleanse interventionism from the taint of Iraq.

In an authorised account of the Libyan action given to Patrick Wintour and Nicolas Watt of the *Guardian*, a Whitehall source says Cameron was haunted by Douglas Hurd's failure to arm the Bosnian Muslims during the Balkan conflict which led, indirectly, to massacres such as the one committed at Srebrenica in July 2005. 'There was a very strong feeling at the top of this government that Benghazi could very easily become the Srebrenica of our watch. The generation that had lived through Bosnia is not going to be the pull up the drawbridge generation.'

Once Cameron chose to engage Britain wholly in a Libyan intervention the machinery he had set up swung into action – at least in Whitehall. A National Security Council (Libya) was set up with meetings, sometimes three a day, in Cabinet Office Briefing Room (A), a workaday facility whose acronym nevertheless always excites the media.

Outside Whitehall, things were a little less responsive. Hanging over the discussions of military options was the question of what materiel was available. A so-called strategic defence review conducted just months before had reduced Britain's ability to mount just the sort of mission now under consideration. Nevertheless the military advice was that – using Italian airfields – British jets could wage an air campaign against the Gaddafi regime so long as there was sufficient legal and political backing.

The news on the diplomatic front seemed dispiriting over the weekend of 11 March, when first the EU summit failed to reach agreement, and then the G8 couldn't agree on the wisdom of a no-fly zone. But while newspapers reported defeat for Cameron, in fact there had been a breakthrough. The Arab League, not a group which easily found consensus, found that it could agree at least on its dislike of Gaddafi. It was to be a vital building block. The following day, in New York, Britain's ambassador to the UN, Sir Mark Lyall Grant, set about the task of accumulating the necessary votes at the UN to give authorisation of a no-fly zone. It took just one of the fifteen members of the Security Council to veto the proposal for it to be lost. Not only were Russia and China obvious threats, the council included rotating members, one of which was Lebanon. On Sunday 13 March, Lyall Grant, together with French diplomats, met representatives from Beirut. Given the Arab League's stated support, could Lebanon consider abstaining? During the meeting, he took a call from Susan Rice, the US's ambassador to the UN, who was surprised to discover the nature of the discussion she had interrupted. Clearly Britain and France were prepared to do their own diplomatic heavy lifting on Libya.

That night, Lyall Grant sent a cable to Downing Street saying that if the US could be signed up, he thought there was a chance of success. A conversation between Cameron and Obama about possibly imposing a no-fly zone had been inconclusive, beyond Cameron being confident that Obama would not be leading the public calls for one. The Americans – vital to the exercise – were torn. Vice-President Joe Biden and Hillary Clinton, the Secretary of State, perhaps sharing her husband's sense of guilt at the West's failures over Srebrenica and Rwanda in the 1990s, took a markedly different position from Gates. In the end Mrs Clinton prevailed, but, at Gates's suggestion, the US indicated support for a tougher resolution, making it clear that attacks on tanks and ships would be permitted, as would the vigorous defence of civilians.

Although this was a more muscular mandate it made the diplomatic task of achieving it harder to achieve (which may have been the intention).

By the time New York was awake the following morning, Lyall Grant had received further instructions and encouragement from Cameron. The traffic of memos between the two men grew more and more hopeful as the days passed.

The greatest obstacle to the draft resolution, tabled that Monday, seemed likely to come from Russia, which had its own plan, calling for a ceasefire. But once it became apparent – with a bit of British help – that that plan had insufficient support, and with Gaddafi showing no sign of easing up and the Arab League having endorsed action, the Russians agreed not to oppose the British/French plan. This was a major breakthrough as China, normally a foot-dragger in tandem with Russia, was generally disinclined to veto on her own and would follow suit.

Meanwhile, Cameron was anxious to lend his weight to the diplomatic effort. He telephoned the Crown Prince of Abu Dhabi, the King of Jordan, the King of Saudi Arabia and the Qatari prime minister seeking to bolster support among Libya's neighbours.

But Lyall Grant needed to secure nine positive votes in addition to Britain's. It was 'touch and go' as to whether they would get them, said one senior official. So, when Cameron phoned New York on the Wednesday asking if there was anything he could do to help, Lyall Grant accepted. Please could he call three leaders of Security Council nations, Jacob Zuma of South Africa, Germany's Angela Merkel and Goodluck Jonathan, president of Nigeria, to ask for their support? Germany, like Brazil, concerned at the US's beefing up of the resolution, opted to abstain, but Nigeria and South Africa, once a trusted go-between for the Gaddafi regime, said yes. On Thursday night, as Gaddafi's tanks closed in on Benghazi, the UN passed resolution 1973 by ten votes, with five abstentions.

Cameron called Clegg to tell him the news, and share their surprise that the deal had been done. The Prime Minister celebrated with his staff in London with pizza and Coke. The next day he woke particularly early – thanks to his daughter Florence – to learn the tanks were closing in on Benghazi, to which the coalition forces responded by dusk the next day. On the afternoon of Saturday 19 March, a French Rafale fighter jet destroyed a Libyan military vehicle near the town. Some hours later, after nightfall, a hundred Tomahawk missiles, launched from a British Trafalgar-class submarine and two warships in the Mediterranean, had landed along the Libyan coastline, seeking to undermine Gaddafi's military communication network. Although the Libyan regime hit back with surface-to-air missiles they were elderly and mostly ineffective.

A humanitarian catastrophe had been averted. It has been suggested that Cameron was so determined to avoid a massacre at Benghazi that he was prepared to act without a UN mandate. Friends of Nick Clegg say the possibility was never discussed and that the Lib Dem leader would have refused to condone a British and French airstrike without full legal backing.

Even within the UN framework, Cameron's Libyan policy was taxing the coalition, his own party and, otherwise fulsome, supporters in the media.

Clegg and Gove had had a memorably lively exchange at Cabinet and Ken Clarke had made it clear he thought partition of Libya was inevitable. Liam Fox's silence spoke volumes about his own doubts. The Secret Intelligence Service (MI6), meanwhile, made its opposition felt.

Military historian Sir Max Hastings, setting aside family friendship, said the rebels could not prevail without Allied boots on the ground. Cameron, he said, had exposed his inexperience. 'For a British prime minister presiding over draconian cuts in his own armed force to posture ahead of the US in favour of military action invited the ridicule that it received, not least in Washington ... Grown-up governments do not indulge in emotional lunges, committing warplanes as if sending a donation to Oxfam. They make cool calculations about self-interest.'

Cameron, who had a live feed of unfolding Gaddafi atrocities, became more not less determined. 'We were getting reports hour to hour in real time from Libya about the violence going on there,' says someone in Cameron's team, adding that the intelligence wholly vindicated the policy. 'It was quite clear it was the right thing to do. It had been Cameron who suggested a no-fly zone, and he was ridiculed for it.'

There was little time for self-satisfaction given a row with France over whether the mission should be under NATO control (won, in the end by Cameron) and on-going tension with the US. Public disagreements over whether Gaddafi was a legitimate target and a bungled British-led mission to Benghazi added to the impression of an inexpert grip.

Cameron, however, remained confident of the support of his key allies, Osborne, Hague and Gove, as well as Andrew Mitchell, at the Department for International Development. Throughout, Cameron was the most hawkish voice around the table on Libya but allowed himself to be guided by Llewellyn. One account of National Security Council meetings suggests that Cameron would ask his chief-of-staff what he could do to be helpful. When Cameron suggested bombing Libyan oil fields to cut off Gaddafi's energy supply it was Llewellyn who applied the fire hose.

Among the officials running the policy he had another Old Etonian friend, besides Llewellyn, to turn to. Hugh Powell, son of Margaret Thatcher's foreign policy adviser, Charles Powell, had been a contemporary at school and Oxford. As a young man in politics and then the City, Cameron had kept up with Hugh, who went into the Foreign Office, and his wife Catherine Powell, now a senior executive at Disney, sharing secrets around their dinner table.

Once he became PM, Cameron had asked for Powell to head the NSC secretariat and came to rely on and value his advice. 'The Prime Minister has confidence in Hugh Powell. He felt this was someone who absolutely got it and who was imaginative and was thinking all the time, within the boundary of the UN mandate, about how to shove things forward.'

The need to 'shove things forward' became acute as spring turned to summer and the Gaddafi regime failed to crumble. It looked as if Hastings and Clarke had been right – without ground support a stalemate and partition looked the best that could be hoped for. Cameron became concerned enough in July to sanction the preparation of an admission of stalemate in his autumn conference speech. But, just as humiliation loomed, a switch in resources to the rebels in the west of Libya brought a breakthrough.

The fall of Tripoli in late August was followed two months later by the brutal death of Gaddafi. Cameron's welcome of his demise was all the more statesmanlike for being understated. 'People in Libya today have an even greater chance, after this news, of building themselves a strong and democratic future. I'm proud of the role that Britain has played in helping them to bring that about and I pay tribute to the bravery of the Libyans who have helped to liberate their country.'

Cameron is said to have 'got lucky' over Libya, a gut call proved right. But the enthusiasm with which he set about the task does not prove that he simply succumbed to a gut feeling or, as Hastings puts it, indulged in an 'emotional lunge'.

It is true that the defence cuts had left Britain needing to rely on others rather more than was admitted. Professor Michael Clarke, Britain's most respected military expert, described Cameron as an 'accidental' hero. 'The fact is the operation was successfully conducted without a British aircraft carrier being available. But it is equally a fact that the operation involved four major ships capable of launching aircraft – the French and Italian carriers, the US assault ship and Britain's HMS *Ocean* acting as a helicopter carrier.' The engagement had put British forces elsewhere under 'considerable strain'. Palmerstone's admirer had had to rely on other nations' gunboats.

Cameron benefited, too, from French political as well as military cover. Would Cameron have been as firm about the need for a no-fly zone had not Nicolas Sarkozy also been calling for it?

Oliver Letwin rejects the suggestion that Cameron was lucky or opportunist over Libya. The response 'was the product of five years' thinking'.

Pauline [Neville-Jones] and Ed [Llewellyn] and I started thinking about how you end ludicrous situations where your presence in some of the states in question is part of the problem. We were trying to work on a framework of liberal conservative intervention. David was very intimately involved in that and very much chose what he wanted out of a menu of things with which he was presented.

But we wanted to intervene to promote democratic ideals but do it in places where it would work and not become part of the problem. We talked it through at great length with the experts, the ambassadors, the military and so on, and of course Af-Pak [the Afghanisan conflict in which Pakistan is a key component] was happening in real time for us. It became clearer and clearer that the political, diplomatic work that should have been done years ago, bringing aid into the equation, had not been properly considered. We had a pretty fully developed sense of where it was practical and could do it and make it work. By the time we got to Libya, it wasn't just that you had the present reality before our eyes of 100,000 people in Benghazi who were about to be slaughtered, it was also that we had a fully developed view of what you could and couldn't do to help democracy in such a place. First is, you shouldn't invade. Second, you had to get local and international backing and, third, you had to have the firepower that would give us a very strong chance of success. None of those conditions have been met in Syria, for example. The final moment was a lonely moment of decision making for David, but William [Hague] thought we had a good chance of success and the building blocks were already there.

'When people said it was "stalemate",' says a very close adviser, 'he was very good at pushing people on the NSC and getting them up to the mark to come up with solutions. It was real leadership.'

Oliver Letwin says that having to make such decisions changed Cameron from someone whose prime concern was to get elected. 'Once in government, and once we started having serious sessions of the National Security Council and were dealing with Afghanistan,' he says,

> increasingly I have an impression that his sense of himself is of someone having a quite direct responsibility for the UK and its citizens. There has been a considerable slide from party leader to statesman. While George is driving for the books to add up and make the budget work, David is very concerned with the military. I don't think he'd thought of that much before. There has been a considerable shift. He now has to spend a lot of his time with other people round the world and have quite a relationship with them. There's a distance between him and us because he carries that burden and we don't. He gives a sense of being in a different place, as it were.

Adam Holloway, an independent-minded Tory MP with a questing interest in military matters, was initially unconvinced about the wisdom of what was planned. But he visited Libya about a month after the no-fly zone was introduced and changed his mind. 'At the edge of Benghazi, where the fields start,' he remembered, 'there were literally dozens of armoured vehicles burned out. There could be no stronger image of just how timely the intervention had been. There is no doubt that without our intervention the people there would have fought with kitchen spatulas and whatever they had. Many thousands would have been killed. It was bloody brave of Cameron, it really was, given the disasters we have had across the Muslim world.'

Holloway tells the story of how he went to see an Islamist commander, a veteran of Iraq and Afganistan. 'He said, "This is the first time the West has stood with the ordinary people, and we won't forget this". To me, since 9/11, when we should have been separating mass populations from the extremists but have in fact increased the number of extremists and made them more attractive to the mass of the population, this was real progress. Cameron has understood that central point.'

'ONE OF US'
Cameron and Europe 2010–2012

On the face of it David Cameron's credentials as a Eurosceptic looked solid. He had been at Norman Lamont's side when Britain endured her humiliating exit from its one attempt at monetary union and had gone on to work for Michael Howard, one of Major's 'bastards'.

In 1997 he had himself rebelled, defying the then Prime Minister and signing a pledge that he would never, in any circumstances, support Britain joining the euro. But at the next election, as William Hague warned that Britain had only days to save the pound in 2001, he publicly criticised an approach that risked ignoring voters' more pressing concerns, like having a decent local hospital or school.

He accepted early the insight that, however much they might share Eurosceptics' views, ordinary Britons did not care for their passion.

He was forced into giving a commitment to take the Conservatives out of the centre-right grouping in Strasbourg, the avowedly federalist European People's Party (EPP), during the 2005 leadership campaign and took his time in honouring that pledge.

Further, a 'cast-iron guarantee' he gave to hold a referendum on the Lisbon Treaty proved irredeemable once the surrender of further powers to Brussels had actually taken place.

Anticipating heading a minority government, Cameron foresaw how easily the party could split again over Europe. Not as in the past between those federalists and sceptics – only Ken Clarke remained of the former view – but between those whose opposition to the EU was fundamental and the pragmatic sceptics who thought other issues took priority.

Denying a clique of ultras on the right, effective control over Britain's European policy was one of the greater attractions of coalition.

Conservative manifesto commitments to repatriate powers from the European Union were among the first to be sacrificed in the negotiations, although, for form's sake, they received a mention in the agreement.

Before the election senior Conservatives close to the leader admitted privately they were relieved that the Lisbon Treaty had been ratified. The decade-long wrangle over the proper institutional structure for an expanded EU had, at last, been put to bed.

Cameron, if he was going to cut public spending in the way he thought he had to, had enough on his plate with the unions. He didn't want a row with Europe.

Initially, even the tumultuous events within the eurozone were helpful, bolstering the case for deficit reduction. Indeed, the coalition had been forged in the heat of its first crises. Clegg has justified agreeing to spending cuts with reference to the plight of Greece, Portugal and Spain at the time.

In the first months of the new government the presence of Clegg, who if nothing else is surely a 'good European', was a relief as much to Cameron as to Britain's EU partners. Britain's relations with the EU were, to everyone's pleasant surprise, generally positive. The eurozone crisis, however, revealed structural flaws, not just in the currency's credibility but in the UK's heavily caveated relationship with the 'ever closer union' of her European neighbours.

Eighteen months of failed bail-outs and other palliative measures had made it clear that the euro's only hope of survival lay in a fundamental overhaul of a discredited system. But changing the rules was supposed to require the agreement of all twenty-seven members, even those who were not in the single currency. Institutional EU reform, the bugbear of all previous British governments since 1974, was back.

For the ultras the eurozone crisis was a final, glorious vindication: Britain had been right to stay out of the currency. Emboldened, they demanded a referendum on the country's continued membership. In the Cabinet, Iain Duncan Smith, Owen Paterson and Liam Fox represented backbenchers pressing for Cameron to force the UK's advantage. It had been to block Fox that Cameron had had to make the pledge on the EPP. As Defence Secretary he had displayed flashes of menace, notably in the fight to limit cuts on military spending, but at the moment a resurgent right was looking for a leader Fox was forced to quit.

Just as David Davis self-imploded so Fox, another former rival, fell victim to his own lack of judgement. On 14 October 2011 he was forced to admit that he had broken the ministerial code in allowing Adam Werritty, an unofficial aide, to accompany him on government business.

Cameron played Fox's departure well, appearing supportive while allowing the pressure to build, but he blundered badly a week later. In an echo of the 1922 debacle he dignified the posturing of a handful of ultra backbenchers who had a symbolic vote calling for a referendum on Britain's membership. Instead of allowing the 'usual suspects' to blow off steam in an empty Chamber, Cameron turned it into a test of authority, unleashing a full-scale whipping operation. The test results were not good: Downing Street was shocked when eighty-one MPs defied the whip and voted for an in-out referendum.

The rebellion did at least give Cameron some ammunition in his negotiations with Sarkozy and Merkel over the proposed euro reforms. It was a timely reminder of the political pressures on a British PM ahead of deals in Brussels: if they wanted Britain's help in introducing credible enforcement powers to shore up the euro, France and Germany would have to give a little in return. In particular they would have to ensure that the City of London was not adversely affected by the new regulations.

Sarkozy was in no mood to listen. The camaraderie of the Libyan engagement had faded as Britain joined the rest of the world urging the eurozone countries to do more at summit after summit. Long-standing resentment of Britain's lucrative financial sector – responsible, in many continental eyes, for blowing up the credit bubble in the first place – flared. Why should the City be spared the consequences of its recklessness?

At a Brussels meeting days after the Commons rebellion Sarkozy snapped. 'You don't like the euro so why do you want to be in our meetings?' he demanded of Cameron, adding that he had 'enough' of unsolicited British advice.

Both Osborne and Hague had stirred the pot. The Foreign Secretary described the euro as a 'burning building with no exits' while the Chancellor had infuriated Paris by suggesting that France could yet be engulfed by a sovereign debt crisis.

The stage was set for Cameron to give a definitive answer to those who questioned what he would do when his professed scepticism was tested. It came in the early hours of Friday 8 December when the British Prime Minister refused to go along with the blueprint.

Before the summit, Downing Street decided on a strategy of high secrecy, fearing that any leaks about its inferred negotiating position would inflame both the ultras, who were seeking the faintest pretext to demand a referendum on continued EU membership, and the French, whose president's admiration for Cameron was declining visibly and who suspected Britain of wanting to overprotect its bankers.

The secrecy strategy would have been risky at the best of times, but the context made it doubly so, and in a way that its architect – seemingly George Osborne – seems not to have appreciated. In not telegraphing its intentions Britain may have encouraged France and

Germany to pursue their own secret agenda. A couple of days earlier, in Marseilles, a meeting had been held of the EPP at which Sarkozy persuaded Merkel it might become necessary to call Britain's bluff and reform the euro outside the formal twenty-seven-nation structure. The fall-back position agreed at Marseilles was hardened up at a pre-summit dinner in Brussels. The rules had been changed before the game.

The circumstances for Cameron were not propitious when he presented a list of non-negotiable safeguards for Britain's financial sector, effectively his price for allowing a full EU treaty change. Merkel described the demands as 'terrible for us'. Other nations fell behind the Franco-German position that reform could not be delayed by the special pleading of a nation not even in the currency zone. If Britain would not allow reform within the EU a separate structure would have to be created.

The version fed to the weekend newspapers presented a resolute leader accepting a fate he foresaw. Addressing Llewellyn and Sir Jon Cunliffe, Britain's senior EU diplomat, as he left the negotiations at 3.30 a.m. Cameron was reported to have said: 'We cannot sign up to this. They just won't give in. We always knew it might come to this. So be it.'

Cameron's stand proved to be popular with the voters, at least in the short term. But was this a case, as some have argued of Libya, where Cameron ended up the 'accidental hero'?

Federalist critics say, on the contrary, Cameron arrived in Brussels determined to scupper any new EU treaty which would have brought with it strong pressure for a referendum. Charles Grant, director of the integrationist Centre for European Reform, is among those who believe so. 'Britain didn't want a deal,' he said. 'It pretended it wanted one, but it didn't. If Cameron got some kind of safeguard for the City adopted by the 27 he would then have to sign up to a new treaty. That would then have to go through the British Parliament, which would split the Conservative Party. So Cameron bid for something he knew was impossible, a complete opt-out of financial regulation which nobody was ever going to agree to.'

Angela Merkel has said she didn't believe 'Cameron was ever with us at the table' while a French diplomat compared him to 'a man who wants to go to a wife-swapping party without taking his own wife'.

One Scandinavian official was quoted as saying that twenty-four hours earlier he believed the British were intent on resolving the issue. 'When we saw their list, our experts said: "They're not serious. It's just too much."'

An alternative explanation, however, is that Cameron – who had little objection to the eurozone nations observing tighter fiscal regulations per se – was forced into opting out as a consequence of his determination to keep the negotiating strategy secret. That failure to telegraph intentions and Osborne's rash attack on the state of the French economy forced Merkel into Sarkozy's camp and set the conditions whereby Cameron had no choice but to carry out his threat.

But the most pertinent question for the diplomatic post-mortem was: what did the supposed 'veto' achieve? After all, it didn't prevent a new agreement, it just ensured that the deal will be concluded outside the formal architecture of the EU, for Cameron had insisted that European institutions should not be used in the enforcement of the new fiscal pact.

It put Cameron in a lonely place – even most of the other non-euro members of the EU agreed to work together. This wasn't just two-speed Europe, it was a three-speed Europe and Britain, quipped one commentator, was on the hard shoulder.

Clegg, who had worked feverishly for an accommodation and believed one was possible, was furious. He made his displeasure clear by staying away from the Commons when Cameron delivered a statement on the summit the following Monday.

The same electoral mathematics that had kept the Lib Dems from walking out after the AV defeat kept the coalition together but the gulf between the parties had never appeared wider. One of the peculiarities of the coalition's dynamics is that it allows, even at times requires, Cameron to curry favour with his right.

By chance, he returned from that fateful Brussels summit to a dinner that had been arranged for Tory backbenchers at Chequers that evening. He was given a hero's welcome. In high spirits they toasted him as having done what Margaret Thatcher would have done. It seemed that he was, after all, 'one of us'.

But their delight was misplaced. Just a couple of months later, their tune had changed again. Back in Brussels at the end of January, Cameron went along with the 'fiscal compact' between twenty-five EU states, dropping his veto of the use of EU institutions, though reserving Britain's right to take legal action to protect UK independence. Cameron's previous intransigence, lauded by some as reflecting his Eurosceptic soul, now looked more than ever like the result of a bungled, too-clever-by-half diplomatic manoeuvre.

He continued to insist that this was not a climbdown, and Lib Dems applauded his 'pragmatism' in – in all likelihood – succumbing to their pressure. His supporters said Britain, having taken a stand, was not giving way on anything substantial. But others said he had conceded a key principle over unanimity of use of EU bodies. Daniel Hannan wrote two days later: 'We have set the precedent that, if some integrationist states want to go further but fail to gain the approval of all 27 EU members, they need only sign an intergovernmental accord among themselves and carry on using EU institutions. This, in effect, means there can never be any more vetoes – ever.' In short, he argued, Britain was even worse off than before the first Brussels summit.

The enigma of Cameron's true position on Europe remains, as it must if he is to keep both his own right and his coalition partners believing that, at heart, he shares their views.

EPILOGUE

In his last heart-to-heart with his son, Ian Cameron told Britain's new prime minister always 'to do the right thing'.

That David Cameron would be able to divine what that was at any time and in any circumstance was not in question. Certainty of his own decency is not the least of a rich inheritance.

A stable, loving family led by an inspirational father, an enviable education and successful political career have bred self-belief in the bone. He is, as Charles Moore among others has pointed out, 'a modern example of a very old British type', the all-rounder. Cameron has the virtues of conservatism: moderation, respect for tradition and equanimity. He professes a deep suspicion of ideology and is unabashed about his pragmatism.

But his 'type' has its besetting vices, identified by Moore as 'a lack of originality ... the temptation of complacency'. Moore also identifies 'an absence of passion', which may be unfair. Critics see this purported lack of fire in the belly as reflecting a lack of principle or conviction. He is, though, prone to passionate 'enthusiasms', of which the unseating of Muammar Gaddafi was an example.

His politics tend to the second-hand or the downright expedient. The 'heir to Blair' became the fiscally conservative son of Thatcherism when a global downturn that he failed to spot required an about-turn.

The failure of his one attempt to craft a distinctive message, 'The

Big Society' – a national exhortation to 'do the right thing' – helped cost the Conservatives an outright win.

His lack of originality might have mattered more were it not for the other part of his inheritance: the political landscape he was given in May 2010. A collapsing global economic order and the first hung parliament since 1922 handed Cameron both an all-defining mission and a novel form of government. His old-fashioned charm and received, middle-of-the-road tastes turned out to be a comfortable fit for the straitened times.

But Cameron has made at least some of his own luck. Although in many respects a cautious man, he has the ability to seize a moment. Not only can he seize a moment, but he can turn it explicitly to his advantage. Many of the most egregious offenders in the MPs' expenses scandal were Conservatives: David Cameron emerged from it with his reputation enhanced.

He failed to land a knock-out electoral blow on a tired and discredited thirteen-year-old Labour regime: he formed a coalition government, winning power and defeating his internal enemies. He continued with a holiday despite the worst civil disorder in decades: but turned the nation's anger on the rioters and their apologists on his return.

Andrew Gailey, his former teacher, saw in Cameron the rare gift of not dwelling on past setbacks: 'There is a mindset which is crucial to all winners which is the ability to think of what is to come, not what has just passed, to be able to move on.'

Michael Portillo attributes Cameron's success to the completeness of his skills and his equanimity: 'It is the all-round nature of David Cameron that marks him out. He has entirely the right aura to be a top-flight politician … When he is under great personal pressure, he remains calm, which I think is an exceptional gift. Not only does he remain calm, but because he remains calm he appears relaxed and friendly.'

Michael Gove finds Cameron's ability to switch off from politics remarkable.

The well-drilled and oiled order of his office in Number 10 led one close friend to remark, not altogether admiringly, that 'you can hear the clocks ticking in Downing Street'.

He has an acute sense of hierarchy informed by a conformist, institutional rise to power by way of Eton, Oxford, Conservative Research Department, Treasury, Home Office, the City and the House of Commons. As Nicholas Boles says, he 'worked his way up on the inside floor by floor'.

An inflexible belief in loyalty owed to office and seniority helps explain why he is a poor manager of his party. His personal loyalty is admirable and presumption of others' goodwill endearing and yet his innermost political circle is dominated by those whom he has known for more than half his life.

Cameron is wise to share his belief that he 'was born to do this job' only among these trusted friends – not all of whom were always so sure.

George Osborne, a much better reader (and manipulator) of human nature, confessed to a friend that he had been surprised first at Cameron's ability to rise to the challenge of Tory leadership and then, again, at his mastering the role as prime minister.

But then another part of his legacy is a resilience informed by his father's refusal to make allowances for his disability, and further tempered by the birth and death of his own son, Ivan. Michael Green, his boss at Carlton and a famously challenging employer, has warned he can be ruthless. 'I thought, here's this decent English gentleman, well-spoken and well-educated, a man that played cricket. Actually he was as tough as they come.'

His period as a communications executive for the TV company brought him the most critical notices of his career. He has been accused by those he dealt with of being, at the least, selective with the truth. His failure to investigate Lord Ashcroft's tax status or the true extent of phone hacking add to worries that he is too willing to allow sleeping dogs to lie.

Gordon Brown thought the most telling attack on Cameron was to compare him to a slick salesman, concealing the unappealing nature of his product with an expensive rebrand. But Brown was describing how many see all modern politicians – including himself.

In any case Cameron has always been unapologetic about his pragmatism. In delivering the Keith Joseph Memorial Lecture in March 2005 he explicitly rejected 'ideological' politics in favour of 'practical conservatism'.

The Libyan action helped Cameron overcome doubts over his ability to handle foreign policy crises even if it does not provide a guide to future responses. How the doctrine of 'liberal conservatism' applies to Syria or to Iran or some other troubled nation will only reveal itself when Cameron himself chooses where to place his thumb on the balance.

For the essence of Cameron politics is Cameron himself. His vision of Britain is one based on his constituency and the home in which he was raised. It is born of affection, and a sense of obligation.

This is a disappointment to ideologues. Cameron's first boss in politics, Robin Harris, former director of the Conservative Research Department, has been the most forthright in his condemnation: 'I don't think that in any shape or form he could be described as a Conservative in philosophical terms. He has no principled sense of direction; his only sense of direction is upwards.'

It is true that Cameron has still so far failed to provide a convincing answer to the question of why he pursues power. As leader of the Opposition, he said that he felt under a patriotic obligation to serve his country through the application of Conservative values to its governance.

Attempts to draw out a deeper explanation of motive were discouraged, then as now. His sense of duty, like his conservatism, and belief in his own decency flow from a source seemingly largely unexamined by him.

If this is a failure it appeared to be one voters were increasingly less willing to forgive. His personal approval ratings suffered a steep slide as he headed towards the mid-term. David Cameron, is still trusted by many to 'do the right thing' even if he cannot in advance tell them what it might be. But if he wants to win an outright majority, or even a second term of coalition, he must provide a more reassuring guide than pragmatism informed by decency.

NOTES

PEASEMORE

1 The cheering delegates: Kennedy declared, 'Let the word go forth from this time and place, to friend and foe alike, that the torch has been passed to a new generation of Americans.' JFK inaugural address, 20 January 1961.

2 Cameron's was a world: Beak is Eton slang for teacher, while boys' maids tidy Etonians' rooms.

2 He likes to say he is an optimist: *The Times*, 2 December 2006.

2 At the age of twenty-six, Donald: Curiously, Enid's father Arthur had also worked at Panmure Gordon, from its formation in 1877. He died when his daughter was just two; and at the time of Donald and Enid's engagement, they had no idea that both their fathers had worked for the firm.

3 To this day he feels: Private information.

4 'You can imagine what': Interview with Marielen Schlumberger. After Donald Cameron's death in 1958, his widow remarried and became Marielen Schlumberger, the wife of an Austrian diplomat. Enid Cameron eventually remarried and settled near Sunningdale.

4 Cooper used to claim: Philip Ziegler, *Diana Cooper* (London: Hamish Hamilton, 1981, p. 34)

4 David Cameron has expressed relief: Duff Cooper's son, the historian John Julius (Lord) Norwich, is Ian Cameron's cousin, as was the publisher Rupert Hart-Davis.

4 A lifelong friend: Interview with Ben Glazebrook.

6 The patrician spirit: John Trigg, *The Mounts of Wasing, 1653–1993* (Woolhampton: John Trigg, 2002), p. 99.

8 'The Mounts are very old fashioned': Interview with Ferdinand Mount. David Cameron's wonderfully politically incorrect (he says the working classes prefer to be led by an aristocrat) but modestly heroic uncle, Sir William Dugdale, husband of Mary Mount's sister Cylla, gives an extensive taste of this old-fashioned world view in his memoir *Settling the Bill* (Endeavour, London, 2011).

8 The journalist William Rees-Mogg: *The Times*, 24 October 2005.

10 'Gwen pretty much brought': Private information.

11 'argumentative and interesting, holding court': Private information.

14 'Whingeing wasn't on the menu': Private information.

14 'thought things would turn out OK': *Guardian*, 26 November 2011.

15 '[David's] parents were fantastic': *Daily Telegraph*, 3 December 2005.

15 There may be, she says: Cameron himself, perhaps revealingly, says he was profoundly unconscious of his father's condition. Interview with Charles Moore, *Daily Telegraph*, 27 September 2008.

15 'He is my role model': Caroline Graham, *Mail on Sunday*, 23 October 2005.

HEATHERDOWN

17 'an unbearably young age for them to start': Richard Pendlebury, *Daily Mail*, 15 May 2010.

18 'rather tubby' as a boy: *Daily Telegraph*, 3 December 2005.

19 More often, though, the royal presence: One former boy remembers that 'the detectives used to run around like bluebottles whenever someone escaped from the loonybin next door'.

20 Nor was Edwards squeamish: Prince Andrew is said to have vowed not to send his children to a 'beating' school, after what he underwent at Heatherdown, and there have been claims that Prince Edward would be terrified of returning to the place at the end of school holidays.

22 'which lay in between the two': *Ibid.*

22 as David was to admit subsequently: He told an interviewer Alex was always better at sport than him and 'a brilliant actor. He was in every school play – he's a really, really good actor', Ginny Dougary, *The Times Magazine*, 16 May 2009.

22 'ambition was already much in evidence': Emily Andrews, *Daily Mail*, 10 May 2010.

23 Years later, answering claims: *Sun*, 26 October 2005.

ETON

20 'I don't know. You can try': *The Times*, 2 October 2004.

27 Cameron himself has said: David Cameron and Dylan Jones, *Cameron on Cameron: Conversations with Dylan Jones* (London: Fourth Estate, 2008), p. 37.

29 'What's your name?': Private information.

35 '"you're not going to make much of your life"': Jane Fryer, *Daily Mail,* 10 April 2010.

35 Cameron, as he says himself: BBC Radio 4, *Desert Island Discs*, 28 May 2006.

40 'We were convinced': *Daily Telegraph*, 3 December 2005, source unknown to the authors.

41 'Lots of it I disagree with': *Observer*, 18 December 2005.

43 'He instantly put me': Ferdinand Mount, *Cold Cream* (London: Bloomsbury, 2008), p. 342.

43 In an early newspaper profile: *Sunday Times*, 9 October 2005, source unknown to the authors.

44 People tend to assume: Nick Fraser has written that 'the best thing in Eton, in life indeed, is to have been elected a member of Pop – near-grown boys pine for the honour, and those who narrowly miss Pop are said never to recover, going through life as if they were second best.' Nick Fraser, *The Importance of Being Eton* (London: Short Books), p. 99.

45 'Cameron was very mature': *Ibid.*, source unknown to the authors.

46 'But I don't feel I have a direct line [to God]': *Evening Standard*, 6 November 2009.

OXFORD

54 Toby Young, a satirist: Toby Young, 'Class', in Rachel Johnson (ed.), *The Oxford Myth* (London: Weidenfeld & Nicolson, 1998), p. 14.

62 'by joining the Bullingdon': Private information.

62 It is a view endorsed by an unnamed former Eton master: 'He didn't get into Pop because he so wanted to get in ... I think that's why he was so keen to get into the Bullingdon': Harry Mount, *ES* magazine, 30 April 2010.

64 'I didn't go skiing': Interview with Francesca Ferguson.

67 singing Chrissie Hynde and UB40's 'I Got You Babe': *GQ*, Matthew d'Ancona interview, May 2010.

SMITH SQUARE

73 David Cameron's political career: *Spectator*, 23 February 2006.

74 The story first surfaced publicly: Robin Harris has been quoted as saying that Cameron was originally turned away. 'He applied to the research department, but there were no spaces. Then we received a call from a royal equerry wanting to know why he had not been hired.' *Express*, 12 May 2006.

75 But Cameron, despite: Cameron has not denied calling on his social network to help him secure his first job but, asked about

the incident in May 2006, cleverly suggested it was not as if the Tories made a bad appointment. 'I had a godmother whose husband worked there [at Conservative Central Office], who knew Robin or something. Anyway, I hope he doesn't regret employing me.' *Daily Express*, 12 May 2006.

75 'nursery of Tory talent': Michael Gove, *Michael Portillo: The Future of the Right* (London: Fourth Estate, 1995), p. 62.

79 'Were it not for what': Private information.

81 'we're taking so they can't do that': Interview with Michael Keegan 21 June 2011.

85 to identify sympathetic MPs: *Independent*, 26 October 1994.

87 'had a certain golden-boy aura': Interview with Rupert Morris.

88 and Red Wedge: Charles Moore, *Spectator*, 2 November 2009. He says the name might have been Norse: he couldn't hear well.

91 His defiance of orthodoxy: Private information.

91 Cameron has said that: BBC Radio 4, *Desert Island Discs*, 28 May 2006.

91 'I was the Trade researcher': *Daily Telegraph*, 30 September 2004.

91 'It's an old tune but a good one': *Ibid.*

92 'he presented himself as on-message': Interview with Michael Keegan, 21 June 2011.

95 Major scored a hit: *Hansard*, 27 June 1991, col. 1134.

96 'There is increased speculation': *The Times*, 14 August 1991.

GAYFERE STREET

98 Cameron has described his role: *The Times*, 2 October 2004.

100 Hilton's team illustrated: Not everyone got the point, however. When Lamont was taken through the proposed tax campaign complete with mock-ups of the bombshell posters, he is said to have remarked, 'Okay, I understand all that – but I don't understand why you've painted it on the side of a fish.'

104 'I vividly remember being pinned': David Cameron, *Guardian Unlimited*, 25 January 2002.

105 Major had once lost his temper: Private information.

11 DOWNING STREET

112 Also at the lunch: Portillo's relationship with Sharratt and Kerr McGee was to surface as a minor scandal in 2001 when as shadow Chancellor he was accused of failing to declare the firm's support.

117 After some desultory work: The document is interesting principally because it includes a line that Cameron later deployed in the 2006 leadership election. 'An advertising executive advising the Conservatives on how to respond to Labour's attempts to copy our policies might have recommended following the "Coca Cola" strategy. The company sells its product as "the real thing"' (Michael Portillo, *The Economics of John Smith*, London: CPC, July 1992). 'David Davis has moved in [a modernising] direction but I would say buy "Coca Cola", if you like Coke get the real thing' (David Cameron, 2 October 2005).

118 For all his deep misgivings: Norman Lamont, *In Office* (London: Little, Brown, 1999), p. 226.

121 'I felt like a TV surgeon': *Ibid.*, p. 249.

121 Major for his part suggests: John Major, *The Autobiography* (London: HarperCollins, 1999), p. 332.

122 'That's the good news': The story appears to be an embellishment. In fact Lamont had heard about the wheeze before it was published when, over a lunch, the tabloid's deputy editor showed him a proof. 'I was pretty pissed off,' he recalls.

123 'becoming a cult figure': Bill Robinson's diary.

127 So when the *Sun*'s much admired: Kavanagh cannot remember dealing with Cameron. Other political journalists of that era

remember him as a 'bad lunch' – too discreet or cautious to justify the expense and time needed to entertain him.

128 'I'd find an issue': Lamont, *In Office*, p. 290.

129 While Major praised his Chancellor's. *Ibid.*, p. 366.

TUSCANY

131 'If that's Norman Lamont': Private information.

132 'Nothing. Why?': Private information.

133 'it gives us more hold': Anne Sebba, *Enid Bagnold: A Life* (London: Weidenfeld & Nicolson, 1986), p. 164.

133 Diana Cooper, a friend: *Ibid.*, p. 165.

134 'She was considered an unlikely person': *Evening Standard*, 14 December 2005.

135 'It's so *common* to mind': Interview with Anne Sebba.

135 Within a decade or so: Interview with Sir Reggie Sheffield.

135 'I think we both knew instantly': *Daily Mail*, 1 May 1993.

136 'wasn't the kind of mum': *Evening Standard*, 15 July 2005.

137 'bikers mixed with drug dealers': *Mail on Sunday*, 16 October 2005.

138 'She belonged to a crowd': *Express*, 10 December 2005, source unknown to the authors.

140 'It was a prostitute': *Mail on Sunday*, 16 October 2005.

141 'When we started going out seriously': *Ibid.*

142 'You can see Annabel in Samantha': *Evening Standard*, 14 December 2005.

QUEEN ANNE'S GATE

148 'If youth is oppositional': *The Times*, 17 July 1993. The piece also includes this gem from a youthful David Miliband: 'The old answers are inadequate, and our generation has the chance to play with new ideas. Those sticking to the left have to believe in something. I think you have to believe that your friends will get it together again.'

152 Another acquaintance of the time: Private information.

152 Anne McElvoy, who is now married: *Evening Standard*, 24 August 2005.

153 Howard's biographer quotes: Michael Crick, *In Search of Michael Howard* (London: Simon & Schuster, 2005), p. 267.

153 And at around this time: Interview with Richard Ritchie.

154 'One of his special advisers': Derek Lewis, *Hidden Agendas* (London: Hamish Hamilton, 1997), p. 117. It is believed that the Howards' decision not to sue was because Lewis's account was corroborated by a senior civil servant who is still serving.

158 'I remember going for a drink': The pub was the Two Chairmen in Westminster.

158 'When at the Home Office': *Guardian Unlimited*, 21 June 2001.

ST GEORGE STREET

162 'She couldn't really get her head': Private information.

163 'we watched a video of *Mean Streets*': Jane Moore, *Sun*, 3 October 2009.

164 'He said the job was off': Cameron and Jones, *Cameron on Cameron*, p. 72.

165 'I learned a lot from Michael Green': *Evening Standard*, 18 July 2005.

166 She resigned just over: Raymond Snoddy, *Greenfinger: The Rise of Michael Green and Carlton Communications* (London: Faber & Faber, 1996), p. 281.

168 'It is incredible': Quoted in James Robinson and David Teather, *Guardian*, 20 February 2010.

168 In a phrase that may come back: 'City Diary', *Daily Telegraph*, 18 October 2005.

170 He has seen *Where Eagles Dare*: Cameron and Jones, *Cameron on Cameron*, p. 236. Cameron told an interviewer with 'no hint of shame, that he doesn't really read novels'. *Observer Woman* magazine, February 2007.

170 (though, reluctant to amplify the comparison, doesn't advertise the fact): Private information.

170 *Nashville Skyline* and *Blood on the Tracks*: Matthew d'Ancona, May 2010, about his *GQ* interview.

171 One friend has sighed: His favourite record was 'Tangled Up in Blue' by Bob Dylan; other selections included tracks by the Smiths, R.E.M., Pink Floyd and Radiohead. There was one selection, Mendelssohn's 'On Wings of Song', that could be termed classical. His choice of Benny Hill's ditty 'Ernie' excited most comment at the time of his appearance on the show (BBC Radio 4, *Desert Island Discs*, 28 May 2006).

175 'hung him from the polenta machine in the kitchen': Quoted in James Robinson and David Teather, *Guardian*, 20 February 2010.

175 'there are few industries': *The Times*, 8 May 1998.

176 'I am not sure we are ready': *Guardian Unlimited*, 18 July 2001. Patten queries Cameron's recollection: 'I don't recall saying that. I have a slightly higher opinion of Michael.'

177 One of those who worked: Gove, *Michael Portillo: The Future of the Right*, p. 328.

178 Another says Cameron 'thinks class doesn't matter': Private information.

178 he did call Major a 'loser': Private information.

179 'I was itching to get my hands': *Evening Standard*, 15 July 2005.

185 The scene of pathos: *Guardian Unlimited*, 20 September 2002.

KNIGHTSBRIDGE

191 'We were putting gold-stamped initials': *Evening Standard*, 15 July 2005.

196 'I've spent some interesting times': *Guardian Unlimited*, 9 December 2002.

197 'Who is Jeff Randall?': Private information.

197 'he apologised for being such a wanker': *Ibid*.

200 'aggressive, sharp-tongued, often condescending': *Evening Standard*, 11 May 2006.

200 'His PR needs were many and varied': *New Statesman*, 12 December 2005.

WITNEY

207 Cameron hadn't ridden a bicycle: *Guardian Unlimited*, 4 May 2001.

208 In between such notes from the stump: The campaign was run by two of Cameron's colleagues from 1992, Andrew Lansley and Tim Collins. Both were heavily blamed for the tactical switch away from public services.

210 His mother's observation: *Guardian Unlimited*, 18 July 2001.

211 'I have not faced personal adversity': *The Times*, 23 July 2005.

212 While he shared: 'Modernisers can hold their heads in their hands and drone on about how impossible it all is, or they can put their shoulders to the wheel and try to give the rusting machine a push in the right direction' (*Guardian Unlimited*, 15 May 2003).

213 'On the drugs issue I am': *Guardian Unlimited*, 2 August 2001.

220 As a member of the Home Affairs: At one such event he claims that Alastair Campbell had to ask him the identity of a Labour MP, a fellow committee member, the late Rachel Squire.

221 'I am an instinctive hawk': *Guardian Unlimited*, 15 August 2002.

221 'Everyone knows that Saddam': *Oxford Journal*, 12 February 2003.

222 'the "British interests first" brigade': *Guardian Unlimited*, 18 February 2003.

223 'grudgingly, unhappily, unenthusiastically': *Guardian Unlimited*, 17 March 2003.

223 'Blair himself has been masterful': *Guardian Unlimited*, 1 April 2003.

223 'A long, unpopular war': *Ibid.*

224 He himself once recalled: *Guardian Unlimited*, 9 January 2003.

226 Cameron's putative boss: After Cameron's election as leader Forth was invited to toast the 'end of Blairism' by Davis at a meal for his defeated leadership team. He rejoined: 'Especially in the Conservative Party!' before draining his glass.

IVAN

232 With ominous purposefulness: Private information.

233 'like a freight train': *Guardian*, 29 September 2005.

233 'You are depressed': *Ibid*.

233 'There was a moment': BBC Radio 4, *Desert Island Discs*, 28 May 2006.

234 'Having a severely disabled son': *Observer*, 15 May 2005.

236 'The really difficult thing': *The Times*, 2 October 2004.

237 'those families that do the most': *Oxford Journal*, 29 October 2003.

238 '[Ivan's] epilepsy [is] so powerful': *Daily Telegraph*, 22 May 2004.

239 'racked with doubt and scepticism': Cameron and Jones, *Cameron on Cameron*, p.180

240 'but I go to church': PA interview, 15 November 2009.

240 'A merciful God?': *The Times*, 2 December 2006.

244 'I can't help [thinking]': *Ibid*.

247 'from the aired version of the interview': *When a Mother's Love Is Not Enough*, BBC1, 10 November 2009. Monckton's assurance didn't stop one of Cameron's more heavy-handed colleagues coming on the line an hour later faithlessly demanding control of the relevant exchange.

FINSTOCK ROAD

253 'I'm one of the self-confessed anoraks': *Guardian Unlimited*, 8 January 2004.

256 Finally in an interview: *Sunday Times*, 18 July 2004.

256 'There are those who say': *Oxford Journal*, 21 July 2004.

260 'I had a dinner party for him to meet Charles Moore': In fact, as we have seen, Cameron and Moore had already met three years previously.

263 In the best of these: *Guardian*, 28 July 2004.

265 Willetts carried the blame: It would be strange if this blow to Willetts's ego did not inform his decision to back David Davis rather than Cameron in the leadership election.

266 Cameron was already a party: Private information.

267 'The biggest problems today are cynicism': *Oxford Journal*, 22 September 2004.

268 It was a debut he described: *Parish Pump*, 12 October 2004.

268 'Things have changed': *Independent*, 6 October 2004.

268 'There is already deep upset': *Daily Telegraph*, 27 November 2004.

269 In tribute to his tribe: In the event the 2005 manifesto began, 'I believe that Britain could be doing so much better.'

271 'We've got to implement': *Daily Telegraph*, 25 April 2005. According to one senior staffer Cameron was 'totally open' about being the source of the story.

BLACKPOOL

277 He told senior aides: Private information.

277 By contrast – despite inaccurate reporting: Osborne's only concern was being made to unveil with Liam Fox a poster calling Blair a liar over Iraq. The irony that the two were the only senior Tories who did not believe that claim did not pass unnoticed at the time.

278 'You wake up in different moods': Channel 4, *Richard and Judy*, 24 November 2005.

279 'I remember walking around talking to Sam': *The Times*, 2 December 2006.

279 Samantha understood – and shared – his professional drive: Paddy Byng, a contemporary of David Cameron at Heatherdown and Eton, and now CEO of Smythsons, says he was 'flabbergasted' to discover how much Samantha Cameron did at the firm when he joined. 'In a company like this you normally have a design department, which thinks about colours, materials and so on, and you have a product development department, which liaises with the manufacturers, negotiates the prices, ensures the product is made to the correct specification, is responsible for quality control and so on and comes back to the designers and checks if it is what is wanted. But here product development didn't exist, she had to do it all. She did an amazing job. She is still in charge of it all, but she has more help now, which gives her more time to design new product. She takes her work very seriously, is hugely conscientious and works her socks off.'

279 'In politics, there is a mixture'. *The Times*, 2 October 2004

279 Osborne himself admits: *The Times*, 23 July 2005.

280 'There has been some media speculation': *Daily Telegraph*, 20 May 2005.

281 'In the sort of politics I believe in': *Observer*, 15 May 2005.

282 'It may well be the case': *Evening Standard*, 24 May 2005.

284 'Someone recently gave me': *The Times*, 18 May 2005.

287 By the end of the month: *The Times*, 13 September 2005.

287 When a profile-writer sneaked a look: *Guardian*, 29 September 2005.

292 'lots of little chimes and bells': *The Times*, 30 September 2005.

298 A dinner with News International editors: Clarke declined this humiliation.

298 'D-Day, A Dismal Day for Davis': *Daily Telegraph*, 6 October 2005.

299 'I did all sorts of things': BBC1, *Sunday AM*, 9 October 2005.

299 'I'm allowed to have had a private life': Cameron was criticised for giving this answer by fellow panellist Mark Oaten, then the Liberal Democrats' Home Affairs spokesman. In the light of subsequent revelations about his own private life, Mr Oaten might have been wiser to have rallied to his defence.

304 'We had his arms, you had his legs': Private information.

305 where he insisted the interview be recorded: Cameron's office rejected one suggested venue, a smart hotel, on the grounds that it looked 'too baronial'. Private information.

305 'I rang the BBC': *The Times*, 22 November 2005.

NORMAN SHAW SOUTH

308 William Hague, a fund of: *Sunday Times*, 22 April 2007.

310 Cameron, who hates sweet tea: *Observer*,11 February 2007.

314 'Crime, drugs, underage sex': David Cameron, 10 July 2006, at the Centre for Social Justice.

314 'I'm not sure what my leader': *Daily Telegraph*, 11 July 2006.

314 'No, no, no! You can't say that': *Daily Mail*, 29 September 2007.

315 'When your family relies': David Cameron speech to Conservative Conference, 4 October 2006.

324 which effectively killed it: A comparable tale did surface two years later, but was handled very differently, with Cameron prolonging the story, according to some, by apologising.

330 'I thought it the right thing to do': Cameron and Jones, *Cameron on Cameron*, p. 112.

331 'fascinated by the phenomenon of David Cameron': Despite this fascination Blair has been careful to keep his distance since leaving office. He has met Cameron only once, in the spring of 2008 when he briefed him in the course of his work as Middle East envoy of the so-called Quartet.

332 'We're quite happy Blair's going': *Sunday Times*, 22 April 2007.

332 'That strange man in Downing Street': *The Times*, 28 January 2008.

333 'slick communication skills': *Sunday Times*, 22 July 2007.

339 His announcement that a Tory government: Osborne's allies say he had the idea of funding the IHT cut by introducing a tax on wealthy foreigners – so-called non-domiciles – as he lay on a hammock during his summer holiday. Labour, who were plotting to make just the same move that autumn, claim their idea was leaked to him by a Treasury mole.

340 'incredibly nervous': Cameron and Jones, *Cameron on Cameron*, p. 212.

341 Coulson also told Cameron: The survey is now regarded in CCHQ as a rogue poll.

MILLBANK

343 'most violent earthquake': Peter Kellner, *Daily Telegraph*, 9 October 2007.

346 Cameron was comparatively strait-laced: It is possible that Boris's undergraduate behaviour was also comparatively mild, and that he enjoyed the persona of 'the wild man' rather more than he lived up to it – see *Just Boris*, Sonia Purnell.

350 'If you believe the politicians': *Daily Telegraph*, 19 August 2008.

350 'I sometimes think there are people': Cameron and Jones, *Cameron on Cameron*, p. 70.

354 'I believe that in the last five years': David Cameron speech, 11 September 2006.

355 'a humanitarian interventionist': Cameron and Jones, *Cameron on Cameron*, p. 263.

356 'We don't have to say': *Ibid.*, p. 258.

359 'I'm going to be as radical': *Ibid.*, p. 315.

364 would not be regarded as profligate: Charlie Brooks, *GQ*, May 2010.

369 '"doing his head in", which is an un-George thing to say': A. Cooper.

FALLING SHORT

374 'on Gordon Brown's neck as he always put it,' recalls one insider: Private information.

375 'took their foot off Gordon Brown's throat,' says a close observer: Private information.

377 he had not found the 'navel gazing' useful: *The British General Election*, Dennis Kavanagh and Philip Cowley.

381 'Well, I'm voting for Nick Clegg': *Ibid.*

70 WHITEHALL

390 'he could have failed': *Sunday Times*, 16 May 2010.

392 'furious about the way the campaign was handled': *Sunday Times*, 16 May 2010.

396 'and he's going to motor': To Nick Robinson, 29 July 2010.

397 'there was a high degree of trust': *Ibid.*

399 'will leave in droves': *Ibid.*

400 authority to deliver on an expansive deal: Private information.

400 'good reason to be certain': To Nick Robinson, 29 July 2010.

'TOO MANY FRONTS'

408 should move more swiftly than he had done in 1997: Ben Brogan, *Daily Telegraph*, 18 May 2010.

409 'They felt they had little to learn,' said one Whitehall figure: Private information.

SUB-CONTRACTORS

425 'Here's an exciting new agenda': Steve Hilton, 'New Businesses', in Ed Vaizey, Nicholas Boles and Michael Gove (eds), *A Blue Tomorrow: New Visions from Modern Conservatives* (London: Politico's, 2001), p. 112.

427 'a buzzword, a logo looking for a product': *Daily Telegraph*, 2 April 2011.

428 'than what he was going to *do* as Prime Minister': *Ibid.*

428 'I don't think he's sure who Dave is any more': Melissa Kite, article on Steve Hilton, *GQ*, December 2011.

FLASHMAN

434 'to deflect blame from himself': *Guardian*, 12 August 2011.

438 'we pushed and finally we got there': Interview, *Daily Telegraph*, 25 September 2010.

441 'That was always his advice': *Guardian*, 26 November 2011.

441 'My last memories of him are very happy': Interview, *Daily Telegraph*, 25 September 2010.

'ON MY WATCH'

445 or that the powder was cocaine: Friends of Osborne say he made an effort to help the woman in question, who had a child by a friend of his, in which case presumably Osborne would have been grateful to Coulson if he showed an understanding attitude.

445 'the decisive factor was Rebekah': Simon Walters, *Mail on Sunday*, 17 July 2011.

446 believed to be Control Risk Services: *Independent on Sunday*, 'Andy Coulson vetted by investigator linked to News International', 7 August 2011.

449 Charlie provides from her gruelling career: Suzanna Andrews, *Vanity Fair* profile, February 2012.

451 before the 2010 election: Private information.

453 'David Cameron never likes being given bad news': Iain Martin, *Daily Mail*, 16 July 2011.

454 most of the UK mainstream media left the story alone: Andrew Marr, in high-profile interviews on the BBC in October 2010 and January 2011, didn't mention phone hacking. Nor was it raised

with Jeremy Hunt, the minister responsible, in an interview for the *Observer* in December 2010.

455 and 'obvious crowd-pleasing': Private information.

457 'Ed Miliband had me on the run': *Daily Mail*, 4 February 2012. Downing Street denied the story on the day it appeared, but Kelvin MacKenzie, who wrote it in his column, has since told the authors that he is '100 per cent sure' the story is true, and that his source is 'unimprovable'. Cameron had told the Commons on 8 July that, had it been his call, he would have accepted Brooks's resignation.

458 shouldn't be referred to the competition commission: Roger Cohen, *New York Times*, 29 July 2011.

459 'at the *News of the World* was engaged in this practice': 'You ask the questions ...' *Independent*, 11 June 2007.

461 'That game is over, thank God': Interview with the authors.

461 'including building relations with Murdoch': Quoted by Andrew Gilligan, and attributed to a senior strategist who was not Eustice, who had been quoted elsewhere in the article, *The Age*, 20 July 2011.

462 'he just wanted to be seen to do something, anything': Private information.

463 'all that has been lacking is personal judgment in Downing Street': *Financial Times*, 23 July 2011.

'GOLDEN HOUR'

467 he said in November 2011: *Guardian*, 26 November 2011.

468 it had a 'level of democracy': *Financial Times*, 25 February 2011.

471 'is not going to be the pull up the drawbridge generation': *Guardian*, 2 October 2011.

474 he was prepared to act without a UN mandate: Matthew d'Ancona, *Sunday Telegraph*, 20 March 2011.

474 'They make cool calculations about self-interest': *Financial Times*, 18 March 2011.

475 'about how to shove things forward': *Guardian* 2 October 2011.

476 under 'considerable strain': RUSI report, 23 September 2011.

'ONE OF US'

483 'We always knew it might come to this. So be it': *Mail on Sunday*, 11 December 2011.

484 'which nobody was ever going to agree to': *Daily Telegraph*, 10 December 2011.

484 'They're not serious. It's just too much': Alex Barker and George Parker, *Financial Times*, 17 December 2011.

484 delivered a statement on the summit the following Monday: He later opted not to deny that Cameron had promised to call him if the talks hit a real stalemate. BBC *Today* programme, interview with Clegg, 5 January 2012.

485 'This, in effect, means there can never be any more vetoes – ever': Daniel Hannan, *Guardian*, 1 February 2012.

ACKNOWLEDGEMENTS

This book owes a great deal to a great many people. The initial spark came from Heather Holden-Brown, who, in December 2005, beat her literary agent peers to the realisation that demand for a David Cameron biography would grow. Her choice of one unpublished author was bold; her acceptance of another on the project brave. Her belief did a great deal to secure a publishing deal.

This book is unauthorised. Our intention throughout has been to write a fair-minded, thorough, independent account of David Cameron's life. Cameron's office, wary at first, became less so over the course of the first edition's year in preparation. We are grateful to it for clarifying issues of simple fact. In one area only, that of Ivan, David and Samantha Cameron's eldest son who so sadly died in February 2009, did co-operation extend beyond this facility. Due to the sensitivities of his condition, we agreed that that chapter should be checked for accuracy by an intermediary, Ian Birrell, then Deputy Editor of the The Independent. We also owe Ian an enormous debt for his help in clarifying aspects of the care and treatment of children with severe epilepsy.

Well over 300 people gave interviews or otherwise provided information for the research on this book. Around a third wished to remain anonymous. Our thanks to the nameless are no less sincere for remaining a matter between them and us.

To single out a few for special thanks does not belittle the contribution of many others, and it would be a mistake not to mention the following: Bill Robinson, for his recollections and for letting us see and quote from his Treasury diary; James Fergusson, Dom Loehnis and Steve Hilton, for much of their time and their insights; Margaret Crick, for her tireless and pinpoint digging; John Rentoul, for lending his expert eye and offering flawless advice on the text; and Tristan Davies and John Mullin, for their encouragement.

In a large variety of ways, we are also grateful to the following: Eric Anderson, John Anderson, Hugh Anderson, Giles Andreae, Bob Baird, Greg Barker, Alexander Bathurst, Matthew Bell, Tony Bell, Gabrielle Bertin, Chris Blackhurst, Vernon Bogdanor, Nicholas Boles, John Booth, Brian Brady, Jeff Branch, Angie Bray, Ruth Burnett, Paddy Byng, John Clark, Michael Cockerell, Alistair Cooke, Andrew Cooper, Sam Coutes, Essie Cousins, Michael Crick, Richard Crossley, Fred de Falbe, Peter de Savary, Rupert Dilnott-Cooper, Mark Dineley, Mark Dunhill, Ruth Elkins, George Eustice, Andrew Feldman, Francesca Ferguson, Adam Fergusson, Daniel Finklestein, John Foster, Nick Foulkes, Maurice Fraser, Andrew Gailey, Joss Garman, Helen Georghiou, Andrew Gimson, Ben Glazebrook, Tom Goff, Emily Gosden, Miles Goslett, Michael Gove, Peter Gummer, Caroline Graham, Michael Gray, Michael Green, Caragh Hanning, Dan Hannan, Max Hastings, Penny Hatfield, Robin Harris, David Hellier, Michael Howard, Oliver James, Nicola Jeal, Heidi Johansen-Berg, Henry Keswick, David Kidney, Michael Kidson, Ian King, Soraya Kishwari, Norman Lamont, Andrew Lansley, Derek Lewis, Rhidian Llewellyn, Sir Peter Lloyd, Joy Lo Dico, Laura Longrigg, Tom Lyttelton, Ed Marriott, Georgia Mason, Ashton May, Anne McElvoy, Brian McGrath, Michael Meredith, Jane Merrick, Charles Moore, Cole Moreton, Ferdinand Mount, Rupert Morris, Caroline Muir, Matthew Norman, Peter Oborne, Jon Oliver, Jonathan Owen, Simon Parry, Chris Patten, Jane Peyton, Mark Philp, Michael Portillo, James Pryor, Sonia Purnell, Jeff Randall, Steve Rathbone, Susan Rathbone, Alex Renton, Joy Richardson, Peter Riddell, Richard Ritchie, Andrew

Robathon, Andrew Roberts, Lesley, John and Stephanie Robertshaw, Patrick Rock, Tom Rodwell, Matthew Rushworth, Giles St Aubyn, Maurice Saatchi, Sarah Sands, Marcus Scriven, Anne Sebba, Tess Simpson, Ray Snoddy, Rupert Stephenson, Hugo Swire, Jackie Tarrant-Barton, Marielen Schlumberger, Reggie Sheffield, Emily Sheffield, Sion Simon, Peter Sinclair, Kerry Smith, Anne Trenemen, John Trigg, Andrew Tyrie, Lizza Ollard, Simon Parry, Karl Plunkett, Rose Prince, Steve Richards, Sebastian Shakespeare, Miranda Villiers, John Wakeham, Tim Walker, Joyce Walters, Marcus Warren, Philip Webster, Sheridan Westlake, Anne Widdecombe, Daniel Wiggin, Robin and Ginny Wolstencroft, James Wood, Marie Woolf and Tim Young.

At 4th Estate and Harper Perennial, Louise Haines, Georgia Mason and Robin Harvie provided expert guidance and hand-holding, particularly at some of the book's trickier stages, and the copy-editing of Peter James was outstanding.

But the greatest thanks of all, by some distance, is owed to our wives. Both authors have two young children, and for various stages in the last six years we have been pretty much absentee fathers and husbands. Our debt to them is immeasurable.

INDEX